Social Marketing
Promoting the Causes of Public and Nonprofit Agencies

SEYMOUR H. FINE

Rutgers—The State University of New Jersey

ALLYN AND BACON

Boston ■ London ■ Sydney ■ Toronto

Series Editor: Henry Reece
Series Editorial Assistant: Katherine Grubbs
Production Administrator: Annette Joseph
Production Coordinator: Holly Crawford
Editorial-Production Service: Laura Cleveland/WordCrafters
    Editorial Services, Inc.
Copyeditor: Venka V. Macintyre
Cover Administrator: Linda K. Dickinson
Cover Designer: Susan Slovinsky
Manufacturing Buyer: Tamara McCracken

Library of Congress Cataloging-in-Publication Data

Fine, Seymour H.
    Social marketing : promoting the causes of public and nonprofit
agencies / Seymour H. Fine.
        p.   cm.
    Bibliography: p.
    Includes index.
    ISBN 0-205-12084-9
    1. Social marketing.   2. Corporations, Nonprofit—Marketing.
3. Advertising, Public service.   I. Title.
HF5415.122.F56   1990
658.8—dc20   89-6977
                                                             CIP

Printed in the United States of America

10 9 8 7 6 5 4 3 2 1   94 93 92 91 90 89

Contents

Preface

The American economy is said to contain three sectors. The first is the commercial sector, which is made up of profit-making companies. The second is the public sector, wherein are found government agencies at every level—local, state, and national. The third consists of nonprofit organizations and is sometimes referred to as the third sector, the independent sector, or the voluntary sector. Public and nonprofit organizations (P&NPOs) have been selected as the focus of this book because their institutions share characteristics quite different from those of commercial firms. Together, they make up the *social sector* or the *concept sector.*

In the past few years administrative officers of P&NPOs have become increasingly interested in marketing. Beset with such problems as declining utilization, poor image, funding cutbacks, competition, and the demand for higher standards of service from a better-informed population of consumers, many agencies have turned to the marketing discipline for help. They have come to believe that if commercial marketing methods can successfully move merchandise across the retail counter, those same techniques should be capable of creating a demand for such "social products" as energy conservation, women's rights, and day-care centers. As Wiebe (1952) once observed, we should be able to sell brotherhood like we sell soap.

It turns out that we can and do "spread" brotherhood as well as scores of other concepts, employing methods that are based on marketing philosophy. For examples, one need only look at the accomplishments of the Advertising Council in promoting nonsmoking, crime prevention, and good health, to mention a few items in the council's "product mix." The question is no longer whether social sector institutions should adopt marketing, but how to implement marketing strategy. The goal of this book is to provide social sector executives with some guidelines on how to harness the power of marketing in order to improve service to their constituencies. That particular type of marketing is called social marketing—hence the terms *social product* and *social sector.*

However, the book is not just about marketing. It is also about communication, social change, propaganda, and education. The selling and buying of ideas is education; when I buy an idea, I have learned something. The purpose of this volume is to give the reader an idea of the scope of the concept sector and to show the extent to which marketing can be used in the dissemination of ideas—the principal products of agencies within that sector.

Social marketing is a relatively new but burgeoning concept. At its simplest, it concerns the application of marketing methods to the dissemination of ideas—societally beneficial ideas like cancer research, energy conservation, and carpooling. (To market bad ideas such as tax fraud or arson would not be at all socially acceptable.) The product mix of social marketing depends on the ideas being disseminated, which may range from support for product safety, the various points of view on such controversial issues as gun control, and the promotion of politics and tourism. In the last few years the scope of social marketing has broadened to include services rendered by many public and nonprofit institutions because those services are primarily ideational in nature. Indeed, it is impossible to separate services from ideas when examining P&NPOs. The Planned Parenthood Federation of America is just as concerned with marketing the idea of family planning as with providing birth control information. Social marketing is a tool with which an agency responsible for spreading ideas can enhance its understanding of that function and carry it out in a more systematic and businesslike manner.

The book is addressed to administrators, people involved with publicity, public relations, fund-raising, community affairs, and public awareness, and to all those who are concerned with educating one or more target audiences in the United States and abroad.

A great many papers on social marketing appeared during the 1970s as interest in the new concept gained momentum. The present book indicates the current state of the art. It demonstrates how the principles developed in earlier studies can be applied in actual situations. That theme runs through these pages. Marketing plans prepared for hospitals, transportation departments, and community foundations are as effective as those used in the private sector.

In the early 1970s, the notion that social ideas could be marketed was still in its infancy and was strongly resisted by a good many agency administrators. One reason for this attitude was simply that the concept was new, and like any innovative idea, it was first greeted with some skepticism. In addition, marketing tended to be associated with the forceful selling of unwanted and unneeded goods—this was the "snake oil" syndrome. Another myth was that marketing requires expensive advertising. A significant number of P&NPOs were reluctant to even mention the word in connection with their work. "We are a public agency supported by tax money and it would be unethical to use Madison Avenue concepts to send our message," stated an official of a government department that had purchased T-shirts imprinted with an advertising slogan!

Proponents of social marketing labored strenuously to explain its precepts and to justify its existence as a useful tool. These efforts proved valuable to both sides. The marketing of marketing forced social marketers to crystallize their own thinking, while administrators did indeed learn that the marketing model yielded effective inputs to strategic planning, that consumer orientation was a good philosophy to adopt, and that marketing research was something worthwhile.

After a highly visible beginning in the U.S. economy, social marketing is now emerging as a moving force in other parts of the world as well. This is particularly true in Canada, where several marketing scholars have been researching and publishing on the topic for the past few years. I have made a deliberate effort to cover their work in the present book. In addition, I have included reports of some recent social marketing programs in developing countries. The book will thus have a cross-cultural flavor to it.

Readers should find here an easy-to-follow amalgamation of both theory and application. First principles have been included for those new to the field (see the Introduction and Chapters 7, 9, 10, 12, and 15). Readers will also find contributions by experts on various aspects of social marketing. Whatever the discipline, it is often enlightening to read the works of more than one author, to examine several points of view on a topic. Different scholars are familiar with different bodies of literature. And two researchers might look at the same material through different lenses. Moreover, no one writer could possibly cover in detail the diverse topics discussed in these pages.

The book contains eight chapters of my own and fifteen written by guest authors. The contributed chapters were written expressly for this book; they are not reprints of articles appearing elsewhere. The cases and situations they mention pertain to modest-size social marketing, as well as full-scale projects that large agencies might undertake. The problems differ only in magnitude; no organization is too small or too large to adopt a consumer orientation.

The case studies should be instructive for most organizations. The experience of someone else is always valuable, no matter how unlikely the comparison might seem at first. Although it is true that the local mental health clinic cannot stage a mega-event like the Olympic games described in Chapter 20, the idea of using a mega-event to promote a cause is not too farfetched to be considered. Even if we cannot duplicate a particular action, we can adopt the same breadth of thinking that propelled it into being.

This is the place where an author traditionally expresses gratitude to those who have assisted in the preparation of the book. How to acknowledge those in a long list of people who have influenced my development as a social marketer? I must first thank the contributors to this book, who tolerated my nitpicking; how those debates raged by mail as fine points were patiently ironed out! I knew they had the book's interests at heart when they volunteered to proofread each others' papers. I must also thank my students for letting me use them as sounding boards for my ideas. It is an oft-repeated truism that one learns best who teaches. I would also like to thank the following individuals, who reviewed the manuscript in its preliminary stage: Russell Belk, University of Utah; Linda A. Felicetti, Clarion University of Pennsylvania; Michael F. Smith, Temple University; Teresa Swartz, Arizona State University; and Josh Wiener, Oklahoma State University. I cannot find the words to tell the members of my family how much I have appreciated their love and support. They read portions of the manuscript and came up with many constructive comments. In particular, my wife Adell has imprinted her wisdom on so many of these pages. Because we celebrated our fortieth anniversary during the preparation, it is with deepest affection that I dedicate this book to her.

S.H.F.

About the Author

Seymour H. Fine is principal of Fine Marketing Associates, consultants on marketing research and strategic planning. His clients include private sector firms, nonprofit institutions, governments, and the United Nations. He is a marketing professor at Rutgers University and, as this book went to press, was teaching the course Services and Nonbusiness Marketing at New York University's Graduate School of Business.

Fine started his career in 1950 as founder and president of a wholesale firm dealing in decorative accessories for the home. He retired in 1975 at the age of 50 and for the next two years was a full-time student at Columbia's Graduate School of Business where he received a Ph.D. in marketing research and analysis.

Dr. Fine has published more than two dozen articles on both commercial and social marketing topics. His 1981 book, *The Marketing of Ideas and Social Issues*, was the first to be written on the subject of a marketing approach to the dissemination of concepts by public and nonprofit agencies. He is also co-author of a book on customer service. Fine is a member of the American Marketing Association, the Association for Consumer Research, and the American Academy of Advertising. He lives in Glen Rock, New Jersey, with his wife Adell, a marriage and family counselor.

About the Contributors

Gary J. Bamossy is universitaire hoofddocent (associate professor) of marketing in the faculty of Economics at the Vrije Universiteit, Amsterdam, the Netherlands. He has a Ph.D. in marketing management from the University of Utah (1983). His research interests are marketing for public and nonprofit organizations, and his publications appear in such research annuals and journals as *Advances in Nonprofit Marketing* (JAI Press), *Journal of Cultural Economics*, and various proceedings of the Association for Consumer Research. In addition to his faculty appointment, Dr. Bamossy is active as an occasional consultant to service organizations in both the public and private sectors of the economy.

Marvin Berkowitz is a marketing consultant in New York City. He holds a doctorate from Columbia University. His interest in social marketing is a natural outgrowth of his many years as a social activist, and he has been active in self-help groups since a teenager. He was vice-president of the Westport Unitarian Singles Group during the period of time when the research was conducted for his chapter. Dr. Berkowitz has had varied work experience in university teaching, government, nonprofit health organizations, and the private sector. Currently, his consulting focuses on health and social services.

Paul N. Bloom is professor of marketing at the University of North Carolina at Chapel Hill. He has written several articles on the subject of social marketing, including "Problems and Challenges in Social Marketing" (*Journal of Marketing*, Spring 1981, with William D. Novelli). Professor Bloom serves as the editor of the JAI Press series *Advances in Marketing and Public Policy* and has written extensively in the areas of public policy toward marketing, services marketing, and knowledge development in marketing. He holds a Ph.D. from Northwestern University (1974) and formerly served as the visiting research professor at the Marketing Science Institute (1980–81).

Clarke L. Caywood is a visiting assistant professor at the Graduate School of Business of the University of Wisconsin–Madison. Clarke's research interests include political advertising and marketing, competitive analysis, issues management, and manufacturing technologies adoption. Clarke managed the successful campaign of the current Republican lieutenant governor of Wisconsin in 1986 and has worked on the staffs of a Wisconsin governor and attorney general. He holds two degrees from the University of Wisconsin–Madison including a Ph.D. granted in 1985 and a graduate degree from the Lyndon B. Johnson School of Public Affairs at the University of Texas–Austin.

John L. Crompton is professor of Recreation and Parks at Texas A&M University. He received his M.S. in recreation and park administration from the University of Illinois, an M.S. in business administration from Loughborough University of Technology, and his Ph.D. in recreation resources development from Texas A&M University. A former managing director of Loughborough Recreation Planning Consultants, Dr. Crompton has conducted numerous workshops on marketing and/or financing public services. Coauthor of *Financing, Managing and Marketing Recreation and Park Resources* (William C. Brown, 1980) and *Marketing Government and Social Services* (John Wiley & Sons, 1986), he is also the author of over 150 articles and monographs that have appeared in the recreation and marketing literature.

Since 1980, **Gerson da Cunha** has been with the United Nations Children's Fund (UNICEF), five years in Brazil and two at the headquarters in New York, always in the area of Program Communications and Information. Before that, he spent twenty-seven years in advertising and marketing with Unilever and Lintas, working in India, London, and New York. He took an honours degree in chemistry at the University of Bombay and for five years was a journalist with the Press Trust of India-Reuters, before entering the field of advertising and marketing. During the period 1968–1975, he served in an honorary capacity with the government of India as adviser in communications on subjects ranging from tourism to family planning.

John R. Deats is director of public affairs at NYU Medical Center in Manhattan. His responsibilities include traditional public affairs activities as well as marketing. A graduate of Louisiana State University, Mr. Deats received a master of arts in journalism from the University of Missouri. Before joining NYU in 1981, he was with the public relations agency, Carl Byoir and Associates. Before that, he was a member of the Foote, Cone &

Belding advertising agency in New York City and was employed by Sears, Roebuck and Company. Mr. Deats resides in Irvington, New York, with his wife Gail and children Michele and John.

Douglas Gould is vice-president for communications for Planned Parenthood Federation of America. Before joining the national headquarters staff, Mr. Gould served for two and a half years as executive director of Planned Parenthood of southeast Iowa, and then, from 1978 to 1985 as associate executive director of Planned Parenthood of New York City. In the latter post, he successfully managed a legislative effort to preserve legal, publicly funded abortion in New York State. He developed and produced a series of award-winning advertising campaigns and published a broad range of materials for lawmakers, citizen lobbyists, and the media. A graduate of Iowa Wesleyan College, Mr. Gould is a member of the American Public Health Association and the Academy of Political Science. He lives in New York with his wife and two children.

Mary L. Joyce is associate professor of marketing, San Francisco State University. Her areas of specialization include health care marketing and nonprofit marketing. She has examined behavioral determinants of blood donor behavior and preventive health behavior under the sponsorship of the University of San Francisco's Nonprofit Institute and the Ephraim McDowell Cancer Network in Lexington, Kentucky. Dr. Joyce's works have been published in the *Journal of Health Care Marketing, Journal of Psychology,* and *Journal of Marketing Education.* She has presented numerous papers at conferences sponsored by the American Association for Advances in Health Care Research, the American Marketing Association, the American Association of Blood Banks, the American Red Cross, and the Southern Marketing Association.

Gene R. Laczniak, professor and chairman of the Marketing Department, Marquette University, earned his Ph.D. from the University of Wisconsin–Madison. He has also taught at the University of Wisconsin and John Austin University in Australia. Dr. Laczniak has published many articles and papers in the *Journal of Marketing, Journal of Retailing, Journal of Consumer Affairs,* and *Journalism Quarterly.* Laczniak is coauthor of the textbook *Marketing in an Age of Change* (John Wiley & Sons, 1981). He is also coeditor of and contributor to the book *Marketing Ethics* (Lexington Books, 1985). Dr. Laczniak was a marketing research specialist for the U.S. Treasury Department and a member of the NASA Biomedical Applications Team. He is also a past president of the Midwest Marketing Association.

Charles W. Lamb, Jr., is the M. J. Neeley Professor of Marketing at the M. J. Neeley School of Business, Texas Christian University. He received the baccalaureate, masters, and doctorate degrees from Miami University, Wright State University, and Kent State University, respectively. His primary teaching, research, service, and consulting interests are in the areas of marketing management and strategy and marketing for nonprofit organizations. Dr. Lamb has contributed over fifty articles to academic and professional journals on these and related topics. He has coauthored *Marketing Cases*, 2nd edition (Houghton Mifflin Co., 1985), *Strategic Marketing Cases and Applications*, 2nd edition (Richard D. Irwin, 1986), *Marketing Government and Social Services* (John Wiley & Sons, 1986), and *Strategic Marketing for Nonprofit Organizations: Cases and Readings*, 3rd edition (Prentice-Hall, 1987).

Michael P. Mokwa is an associate professor and doctoral studies coordinator in the Department of Marketing at Arizona State University (ASU). He also serves as director of the Services Marketing Institute at ASU. His primary teaching and research interests focus on strategic marketing management, particularly in service and nonprofit organizations. He is the contributing editor of two texts, *Marketing the Arts* (Praeger, 1980) and *Government Marketing, Theory and Practice* (Praeger, 1981). His research has been published in the *Journal of Marketing*, *Journal of Business Strategy*, *Health Care Management Review*, *Journal of Health Care Marketing*, and elsewhere. He earned the M.B.A. and Ph.D. at the University of Houston, University Park, and formerly served on the faculty of the University of Wisconsin–Madison.

Michael H. Morris is associate professor of marketing, University of Central Florida, Orlando. His Ph.D. in marketing is from Virginia Polytechnic Institute and State University. Active in a number of research areas, Dr. Morris has published articles on price discrimination and the measurement of price elasticity. His research has appeared in *Business Horizons*, the *International Journal of Research in Marketing*, the *Journal of the Academy of Marketing Science*, *Industrial Marketing Management*, the *American Journal of Economics and Sociology*, the *Journal of Business Research*, the *Journal of Business Venturing*, and *Small Group Behavior*. His book, *Industrial and Organizational Marketing*, was recently published by Merrill Publishing Company.

Patrick E. Murphy is associate professor of marketing at the University of Notre Dame. He has written a number of articles and coedited a book on marketing ethics, *Marketing Ethics: Guidelines for Managers*, with Gene

Laczniak (Lexington Books, 1985). Currently, he serves as editor of *Journal of Public Policy & Marketing* and on the editorial boards of several marketing journals. His other research and teaching interests encompass the areas of marketing management, social, nonprofit and services marketing, and public policy issues in marketing. He is a past AMA vice-president of marketing education. He holds a Ph.D. from the University of Houston, an M.B.A. from Bradley University, and a B.B.A. from Notre Dame.

David L. Rados is professor of marketing at the Owen Graduate School of Management at Vanderbilt University, with a special interest in nonprofit marketing. He has a B.S. from MIT, an M.B.A. from the Harvard Business School, and a Ph.D. from the Stanford Business School. He has taught graduate students at Harvard, Columbia, and Vanderbilt and at universities in Australia, Tanzania, and England. Dr. Rados has run successful executive workshops and seminars for over twenty years and has consulted for such companies as Scott Paper, the Columbia University Press, the Girl Scouts of America, AT&T, the New York Port Authority, and Hallmark Cards. He has written two books and many articles on marketing. He is married and has two children.

J. R. Brent Ritchie is professor and associate dean in the Faculty of Management, the University of Calgary. He also served as the volunteer Chairman of Research for the XVth Olympic Winter Games hosted by the City of Calgary in February 1988. Dr. Ritchie has previously held positions at l'Institute pour l'Etude des Methodes de Direction de l'Entreprise (IMEDE) in Lausanne, Switzerland, and Université Laval, Quebec, Canada. Dr. Ritchie is a recognized leader in both the scholarly and applied dimensions of tourism. He has authored over fifty academic papers in the field and recently published the *Handbook of Travel, Tourism and Hospitality Research*. He currently serves as associate editor of the *Journal of Travel Research* and is a past president of the International Travel and Tourism Research Association and the Administrative Sciences Association in Canada. Dr. Ritchie is a past president of the Tourism Industry Association of Alberta and currently serves as chairman of the Calgary Tourist and Convention Bureau.

Stanley J. Shapiro is professor of business and acting dean of the College of Business Administration at Simon Fraser University in British Columbia, Canada. Formerly he was professor of marketing and dean, McGill University, Faculty of Management. His B.A. is from Harvard University and he holds the M.B.A. and Ph.D. from the Wharton School of the University of Pennsylvania. Dr. Shapiro has coauthored, edited, or Canadianized fifteen marketing textbooks, compiled two annotated bibliographies, authored or coauthored sixty published articles, and contributed numerous chapters and conference papers. He has consulted over the years with a number of Canadian corporations and with various levels of government. Dr. Shapiro serves on the editorial boards of the *Journal of Marketing* and six other academic journals. He was editor of the *Journal of Macromarketing* from 1983 to 1986.

Jagdish N. Sheth is the Brooker Distinguished Professor of Marketing and Research at the University of Southern California. He is also the founder and director of the Center for Telecommunications Management at USC. Previously, Professor Sheth was on the faculty of the University of Illinois, where he was Stellnar Distinguished Professor of Marketing (15 years), Columbia University (5 years), and MIT (2 years). Dr. Sheth is nationally and internationally known for his scholarly contributions in marketing, consumer behavior, international business, and strategic thinking. Professor Sheth has worked with many industries and companies in the United States, Europe, and Asia, both as a consultant and as a seminar leader. His clients include General Motors, 3M, AT&T, Bell Canada, Whirlpool Corporation, Petrolite, Northern Telecom, and the Bell System. He has taught more than 1,500 seminars in at least twenty countries. His many books and articles are among the most frequently cited publications in marketing. Professor Sheth is one of only three Americans ever honored with the prestigious Viktor Mataja Medal from the Austrian Research Society in Vienna for his contributions to advertising and consumer research.

John H. Thomas is vice-president, communications, of the INDEPENDENT SECTOR. Since the founding of that organization in 1980, he has coordinated the functions of public information, communications, and education. For the previous twelve years, having had experience in both commercial and public television, Mr. Thomas was associated with the Mental Health Association, first in Columbus, Ohio, then with the communications department of that association's national headquarters in Washington. A native of Jackson, Ohio, he is a graduate of Ohio State University and has done graduate work in public relations and instructional television. He lives in Falls Church, Virginia, with his wife Ruth and two sons, John David and Mark Evan.

1

Introduction to Social Marketing

SEYMOUR H. FINE
Rutgers, The State University of New Jersey

On March 1, 1985, *Marketing News*, the official newspaper of the American Marketing Association (AMA), announced a revision in the association's twenty-five-year-old definition of marketing. According to the new definition, "Marketing is the process of planning and executing the conception, pricing, promotion and distribution of ideas, goods and services to create exchanges that satisfy individual and organizational objectives" (AMA 1985, p. 1). This definition differs from the earlier version mainly in the addition of "ideas" to "goods and services," all of which are now considered products. Note, too, that the new term appears at the head of the list, before "goods and services." This change marks a milestone in the evolution of social marketing as it reflects the new emphasis this discipline is placing on the dissemination and exchange of ideas.

As noted in the Preface, this book is the sequel to *The Marketing of Ideas and Social Issues* (Fine 1981), which presented the theory and principles of social marketing. The present work expands on those principles and shows how they can be applied in the concept sector, that is, in public and nonprofit organizations (P&NPOs).

The discussion opens with an overview of social marketing as it might be employed by a university in the conduct of its business. The university provides a convenient example because it can be either a public or a nonprofit institution. In addition, the university administrator is a useful vehicle for explaining the role of social marketing in market planning for college products.

The marketing plan developed in the following pages is based on a "7P's" marketing model, which is an extended form of the widely known "4P's." The so-called turf question is also touched on briefly here, as it gives an idea of where marketing fits in the organizational structure. First, however, a few words on the history of marketing are in order.

1

BACKGROUND

Marketing emerged as a discipline following the industrial revolution, when the supply of goods began to exceed consumer demand. Before then, merchandise was generally made to order. As mass production increased the supply of merchandise, however, there was far more than enough to meet society's basic needs and it became necessary to stimulate demand to take up the excess. Thus, people began to acquire things not only because they needed them, but also because they wanted them. Those wants were created by marketers.

But something else was taking place at the same time. The growing emphasis on material things was accompanied by widespread social change. As factories expanded, cities attracted more people. Forced to live in overcrowded urban areas, people began to develop new psychosocial problems, which gave rise to various human rights movements, new social services, and new social goals. Individuals and organizations concerned about these new "social products" (see Table 1.1) saw that marketing methods could be used to publicize them.

In both the public and nonprofit sectors, social marketing found a fertile seedbed. On one hand, the concern for human rights created pressure for government action. On the other, it led to the establishment of nonprofit institutions, which were seen as a means of meeting social needs being overlooked by public and private enterprises such as the need for schools, hospitals, non–toll roads, bridges, canals, and waterworks. In other words, "the voluntary nonprofit sector emerged to fill a sector gap" (Benson 1985, p. 26).

An early example of a nonprofit institution is the Boston Athenaeum, organized by some of Boston's wealthy citizens in 1807. Its founding statement reads:

> The class of persons enjoying easy circumstances, and possessing surplus wealth, is comparatively numerous. As we are not called upon for large contributions to national purposes, we shall do well to take advantage of the exception, by taxing ourselves for those institutions, which will be attended with lasting and extensive benefit, amidst all changes of our public fortunes and political affairs. (Lipset 1986, p. 11)

Government marketing probably dates back to a statute of 1792 requiring that "openings for mail routes be advertised in one or more newspapers for at least six weeks before contracts could be awarded" (Yarwood and Enis 1982, p. 37). Social marketing became widespread in the public sector following the Depression, when the government began disseminating information about its New Deal programs, such as the

TABLE 1.1 Some Current Social Products

55-mph speed limit	200-mile fishing limits	911 emergency number
Abortion rights	Affirmative action	Alcoholism control
Banking innovation	Birth defects	Blood donations
Blue laws	Cancer research	Capital punishment
Carpooling	Child abuse prevention	Child adoption
Consumer cooperatives	Crime prevention	Direct deposit
Draft registration	Drilling, offshore	Drug abuse control
Drinking age	Drunk driving	Education, continuing
Energy conservation	Equal Rights Amendment	Euthanasia
Fair housing	Family planning	Fashion trend
Fire prevention	Fluoridation	Foreign aid
Forest fire prevention	Foster parenthood	Franchising
Fraternal organizations	Free enterprise	Freedom of the press
Fund-raising	Gay rights	Gun control
Handicapped, employ the	Health maintenance	Health, value of
Hiking, walking	organizations	Legalized gambling
Literacy	Left-handedness	Mainstreaming
Manpower programs	Littering prevention	Marriage
Mass transportation	March of Dimes	Metric system
Military recruiting	Mental health	Motorcycle helmet use
Museums	Minimum wage	Nuclear energy
Nudism	Nature conservation	New York City
Obesity prevention	Nutrition	Outdoor living
Peace	One-dollar coin	Pet responsibility
Physical fitness	Peace Corps	Poetry
Politics	Police, support of	Population control
Prayers in schools	Pollution control	Product safety
Parent-teacher	Prison reform	Reforestation
organizations	Safety	Save the whales
Religion	Seat belt use	Shoplifting
Scouting	Social security	Solar energy
Smokending	Suicide hotline	Trade associations
Subsidies, government	Union label, buy	United Way
UNICEF	Venereal disease hotline	Vegetarianism
Urban planning	Antivivisection	Voter registration
Veteran's rights	Waste recycling	
Wife abuse prevention	Women's rights	

Source: Seymour H. Fine, *Marketing of Ideas and Social Issues.* (New York: Praeger Publishers, 1981), p. 13. Copyright © 1981 by Praeger Publishers. Adapted with permission.

Tennessee Valley Authority, the Federal Housing Administration, Social Security, and Works Progress Administration, which already had its well-known blue eagle logo. Today, the government is one of the largest advertisers in the nation (see Chapter 2).

MERCHANDISING THE UNIVERSITY

At first glance, the idea of marketing a university might remind one of a real estate deal. But the university has far more to sell than buildings, or even its most obvious product, education. Nonetheless, its various offerings—its product mix—can be compared to those of a commercial enterprise.

Like the marketer of any product, one who is marketing a university must consider product design, the potential customers, the price to be paid, the method of conveying product information to the customer, the method of delivery, and the type of information needed about would-be customers and their demands. These are the tools of the marketing approach. They help the university—or any organization for that matter—plan its strategy for solving problems and achieving business goals.

Colleges and universities, spoiled by decades of basking in a seller's market, have been shaken by the recent shift to a buyer's market. Consequently, many education administrators have come to see themselves as professional merchants who must attack their problems from a marketing perspective, where the main emphasis is on the student market. To be sure, the university must "deal with" (this term itself implies that the university is taking on the role of merchant) other groups quite apart from its students—trustees, faculty, staff, contributors, and others. In any case, university marketing is social marketing. What is being sold is the idea that personal development has human value. According to the AMA definition presented earlier, idea marketing is social marketing.

PROPOSED: AN EXPANDED MARKETING MODEL

The marketing of any product, tangible or abstract, benefits from the preparation of a marketing plan, usually one based on the time-honored four P's—*product, price, promotion*, and *place* (distribution). The formula by which the marketer allocates resources to each of the four P's is called the *marketing mix*. Thus, for some total marketing budget, one unversity might invest more in the product (perhaps by rendering higher quality service), and less in the promotion of it (advertising, for example). In theory, the organization that creates for itself the optimum marketing mix should emerge as the most competitive one in the marketplace.

The question is, does the 4P's model provide the marketer with the optimum mix? I suggest that the model needs three more P's: *producer* (marketer or source of the promotion), *purchasers* (those to whom it must appeal), and *probing* (i.e., research). This expanded model provides the broad framework needed to prepare an effective plan and achieve the optimum mix. The 7P's model is used to analyze actual social marketing programs in this chapter and in Chapters 2, 7, 8, 10, 13, 14, and 22.

THE MARKETING PLAN

The first step in devising a marketing plan is to formulate the questions implied by the 7P's:

1. Who is the *producer*, the source of the promotional message?
2. Who are the potential *purchasers* in this particular market and what needs and wants do these people have?
3. What specific *product*(s) can the marketer design to help fill those needs?
4. What *price*(s) must the purchasers sacrifice in order to obtain this product?
5. How can the marketer *promote* (communicate with) the given market?
6. Which parties (institutions) will participate in making the product available at the best *place* and time (best for the purchaser)?
7. What *probing* will be necessary to evaluate the marketer's campaign and to obtain feedback from the purchasing audience?

Goals and Objectives. Planning begins with the identification and statement of the marketer's goals. As Brady (1984, p. 48) has pointed out, however, a distinction must be made between *goals* which are "long term outcomes, usually two years or longer; somewhat generally stated," and *objectives*, which are "short term, one year performance tasks; stated in more specific terms, answering what will happen, by when and with what service or program." This interpretation fits in with the 7P's model, which distinguishes between products (objectives) and the promotional message (goals). However, the two are closely related. For example, if a university's principal goal (message) is to maximize the number of enrollments, then it must develop strategies for increasing student activities (product or objective). Thus, a given goal may imply certain objectives. It is crucial at the outset not only to articulate the organization's goals and objectives, but to rank them in order of importance. No institution can expect to attain all its objectives at once; thus it must first concentrate on the one or two having the highest priority. By listing the objectives, marketers can immediately determine the "optimum product mix"—that is, those offerings the organization should concentrate on in its marketing efforts. The marketing plan is essentially an outline of the 7P's model. Each of the seven elements provides a basis for thought, discussion, and documentation in formulating an effective strategy for meeting one's objectives. Consider how this might apply to a university.

Producer. The main goal of an institution of higher learning is usually to help students achieve their full intellectual and creative potential. To reach this goal, the institution sets objectives having to do with student performance and behavior and it tries to convince the students of the value of these objectives, in the same way that marketers try to convince their customers of the value of a product. Thus, the *producer* or marketer in this case is the university, which most individuals look up to as a trusted and credible source. Were that not so, the producers of a social product might be well-advised to find themselves a spokesperson, as governments often do to promote their programs (see Chapter 22). The point is that "the concept initiator, as the source of the message to be communicated, has a special responsibility in concept marketing. A concept makes more sense to the audience when it is promulgated by a reliable and dependable person or organization" (Fine 1981, p. 56).

Purchasers. This component of the marketing plan is made up of the consumers, also known as the audience, target market, market segment, constituency, customers, and clientele—to use a grammatical term, these are the "direct objects" of promotion. One does not just sell something; one sells it to *people*; would-be purchasers must be identified at an early stage in market planning. The university must appeal to prospective students and their parents, high school guidance counselors, business firms, and many others who "buy" that particular brand of higher education.

Usually, it makes sense to divide a market into smaller segments as it is more effective to address each separately. This process is called market segmentation (see Chapter 11).

Product. According to product management theory, products are designed to satisfy the needs of the markets for which they are intended. The plan should contain a comprehensive list of all "items" in the product mix, some of which are suggested in Table 1.2. The matrix presented there is called a "product market scope."

At one stage of design, one must choose an appropriate name for the product. Marketers have learned from studies in psycholinguistics that what something is called greatly affects a person's response to it. That is what Charles Revson meant when he said that Revlon doesn't sell cosmetics, it sells hope. Similarly, Avis sells transportation, not car rental, and health spas offer "fitness" not "rigorous exercise." It's not the steak but the sizzle. This suggests that one should promote what people want to buy, not what one wants to sell. Should the university, then, sell education or self-improvement? More people want the latter than the former. Thus, the Harvard Executive Training Program is a palatable product that offers a good brand name.

Price. To determine price, the producer must find out what value people place on its products. These values are measured not only in money. What consumers pay in exchange for a product may include time, effort, a change in life-style, or, in the case of higher education, the opportunity cost of delaying employment. These "social prices" must be taken into consideration when planning marketing strategy, particularly in the case of education.

Tuition is only a small part of the total resources students expend, and the university is well-advised to recognize those social prices. For example, waiting in inordinately long queues in antiquated registration procedures is a high social price students must frequently pay for education. A simplified drop–add process reduces this social price for services, and should be promoted as such. One important way to increase patronage is to make the customer feel he or she is getting good value for the product being purchased. That is really what price is all about (see Chapter 9).

Promotion. A vital component of the marketing mix is promotion, which refers to communication. It is a mistake, however, to put this item at the top of the planning list. Before one can shout from the rooftops about the virtues of a product, one must be sure the product is fully designed, as a recent incident will illustrate. An ad in a local newspaper promoted a new continuing education course by a well-known college. The ad had all the requisite parts—an appealing headline, copy, picture, logo, signature, and a good layout. But the product seemed suspect. A telephone inquiry at 9:20 a.m. was met with, "Call after 9:30." Then at 10:15, "Ad? What ad? Call back tomorrow; the office is closed for Washington's birthday."

If the person responsible for that promotion had been an experienced merchant, arrangements would have been made to take phone messages, to return calls, to mail a flyer, and so on. One never promotes a product until it is completely packaged, ready for delivery. In this case, a copy of the ad should have been left with the switchboard together with preliminary information for callers. (For a discussion of advertising for social products, see Chapters 12 and 13.)

The channels used to promote a product include the mass media and such interpersonal channels as publicity, advocacy, lobbying, and educational programs (see Chapter 10). Word-of-mouth channels such as rumor, gossip, gatekeepers, and opinion leaders are exploited less often. The astute social marketer leaves no stone unturned. In fact, several channels are best employed in concert. This is another reason why one does not jump aboard the advertising bandwagon until the entire marketing plan is completed, reviewed, and approved by all appropriate responsible individuals. And the media schedule in the plan should be a masterpiece. It should be refined right down to its reach, frequency, continuity, and pulsing, and given a finite budget (see Chapter 12).

Promotion is one place where it is good to be different, even if only for the sake of being different, because innovation implies creativity. Promotion needs *surprise*. Give any prepared copy this test for good advertising: Can the ad logically be given the word "Surprise" for a headline? If not, the ad should not be placed. If you cannot astonish, you will not draw attention. Slogans provide excellent opportunities to demonstrate creativity, as demonstrated by the child adoption agency that came up with "Take two, They're small," and "To have me all you need is love."

Place. This component of the marketing mix has two different but related interpretations. On one hand, it refers the accessibility of the product to the consumer. Is the product available at a convenient time and place for those who are buying it? Universities are becoming increasingly aware of the importance of location, as indicated by their recent moves to open neighborhood satellite centers and to initiate on-site seminars in industry.

On the other hand, "place" may refer to the producer's place—in this case, the university's place—in the entire system of institutions (the "marketing channel") involved in the marketing process. The channel for conventional products is typically given as producer/wholesaler/retailer/consumer, and thus describes the route taken by the product through these institutions. A number of pertinent questions can be asked about the channel: Who are the intermediaries—the wholesalers—between provider and consumer? What roles and functions do they perform in the marketing scenario? Are they all needed? Is there any duplication of work? And most important, can any function be shifted from one intermediary to another in order to make the entire channel operate more efficiently? A university deciding to offer courses in crisis-intervention training, for example, could enlist the participation of drug- and tobacco-abuse control agencies in the community, or schools offering executive programs might obtain enrollments not only from high schools, but also from business firms. Thus, the recruitment function shifts to others in the channel.

The channel structure also reveals other markets (publics, stakeholders, etc.) that must be catered to. When a list of channel members is completed, the strategist is ready to pair products with members, as shown in Table 1.2. Although all humans share common needs, certain groups have different needs. Thus, each element of the channel may be seen as a market segment consisting of people with needs specific to their group. Trustees, for example, would be interested in the social product called "prestige." Some products listed in Table 1.2 apply to more than one market; the entries are merely suggestive of an important step in the planning process (see Chapter 10 for more details).

Probing. Consumer research is the most powerful and yet the most

TABLE 1.2 A University Product/Market Scope

Market	Product of the University
High school seniors	Educational opportunity
Students	Optimum class size, convenient registration process, counseling service
Graduates	Placement service
Community college grads	Four-year degree
Uneducated, 30- to 50-year-olds	Advancement opportunity
Veterans	Career opportunity
Corporations	Graduates, research, the idea to contribute
Administrators	Leadership
Trustees	Prestige
Faculty	Academic freedom, research assistance
Staff	Pleasant work conditions
Government	Collaborative ventures, educated voters
Students' parents	Pride, security, information
Minorities	Equal opportunity
Foreign students	Cultural exchange
Athletes	Sports programs
Alumni	Sense of belonging
General public	Image
Press	Well-written releases about newsworthy activities
Donors	Publicity, tax deductions

abused item in the marketer's tool kit. All too often, probing is either overdone or underutilized. Universities, like their constituents, have been surveyed and have conducted surveys on others, ad nauseam. Yet, in this era of sophisticated computerized data analysis, it is frustrating to see poor-quality data or old data, that were never analyzed or whose findings were never translated into action. This is like installing plumbing fixtures in a home without turning on the water supply! The explosive nature of higher education has caused it to fall into the hands of inexperienced methodologists all too often. One should conduct research only if there is an important need to do so, and then it should be done carefully and thoroughly. Seasoned marketers are usually good empiricists because they depend on data to learn about their customers.

IMPLEMENTATION: HOW, BY WHOM?

Creating a marketing plan is obviously a significant accomplishment, but it should not be undertaken without some assurance that it will be put into practice. The more thoroughly prepared the plan, the easier it will be to carry out. Once given the seal of approval by top management, the plan's very existence will provide an incentive to implement it, no matter who is charged with the task. However, implementation will be greatly improved if the marketing function has been placed into the hands of a responsible and knowledgeable executive equipped with the resources needed to see it through from inception to conclusion. That person should be in a position to attend top-level meetings of the institution's executives. As in the private sector, university marketing does not exist in a vacuum, and requires the participation of the entire management team. Sometimes the first task of the marketing director is to market marketing to the administrators. Experience has shown that a marketing program cannot succeed without top-level enthusiasm.

THE TURF QUESTION

Another important question to settle is where marketing belongs within an organization. Confusion usually arises over the juxtaposition of the marketing, planning, and public relations functions. The answer is that marketing runs parallel with planning, although the two often overlap because research is conducted in both. But public relations is a part of marketing—an important part of promotion (Mindak and Fine 1981).

All too often, social sector organizations assign the marketing task to a planning or public information officer who is not well versed in marketing. Such an individual needs to obtain some training from a marketing expert, full-time or part-time. The question, however, is whether the training should be given by a marketing generalist or by a specialist in the agency's field (Powills 1986). As McMillan (1981, p. 110) has observed in the context of the hospital,

> Who should lead this marketing effort? . . . The argument in favor of the experienced hospital administrator is that he knows the ropes. He isn't likely to upset the doctors or ruffle the feathers of the trustees. . . . Yet it may be faster for the marketing person to learn about the hospital than for the hospital administrator to learn the subtleties of marketing. The reason is that there is a lot of expertise in the hospital available at all times to help the hospital people avoid the many pitfalls of marketing.

SUMMARY

In the marketing perspective toward higher education, the university focuses on the consumer more than the institution, and on the program more than problems. University administrators and their staffs should add merchandising skills to their fund of knowledge. A business philosophy will not conflict with professionalism. The two are entirely compatible, and synergistic as well. Some of the main principles of marketing can be used to construct a model that will help the university and other P&NPOs devise the appropriate plan for merchandising their product.

The university's marketing plan should begin with a statement of its goals and the product suggested by each goal. The 7P's model provides a framework for constructing the plan. If the plan is prepared meticulously, it will serve as a blueprint or road map of the marketing process by which the university can attain its objectives, with the overall goal presumed to be the adoption of consumer orientation.

NOTE

1. Social causes and movements have, of course, been with us from time immemorial. Consider, for example, the antiwar protests of the women of Troy, the sacrifices of the early Christians, and the democratic reforms of the ancient Greeks.

PART ONE

The Public and Nonprofit Industry

2

The Nature of the Industry

SEYMOUR H. FINE

Rutgers, The State University of New Jersey

Like all businesses, public and nonprofit organizations (P&NPOs) buy, sell, provide, and deliver ideas, services, and goods. They transact with suppliers, middlemen, and customers, and they are counseled by accountants, attorneys, bankers, and insurance specialists. P&NPOs make up a sector in the economy that is no less an industry than the clothing, frozen food, or heavy machine industries.

The search for an appropriate name for that industry, whose agencies disseminate primarily ideas or concepts, led to the coining of "concept sector" (Fine 1983). And because their offerings are variously known as "social products," the expression "social sector" has also come into use. The terms concept sector, social sector, *and* P&NPOs *may all be taken as synonymous; all three are used throughout this book. When we exclude government agencies, nonprofit institutions by themselves are variously said to make up the nonprofit sector, the third sector, the voluntary sector, or the independent sector.*

The social or concept sector can best be described by comparing it with the commercial sector. The particular points of interest are size and scope, some characteristics of sector members, the processes by which they operate, and the issues confronting them.

THE SOCIAL SECTOR

Overlap with Services Sector. The social sector is made up of government agencies and nonprofit organizations that provide individual and community services such as education, health care, protection, and aesthetics, all of which are primarily ideational in nature. That is, these services differ from typical commercial services (such as auto repair, hairdressing, and transportation) in that they consist as much of imparting ideas (concepts, thoughts, notions, impressions, images, and feelings) as providing a physical service. To be sure, there is much overlap between the concept sector and those organizations making up what is called the services sector. But their marketing functions can be differentiated, as is evident from the separate bodies of literature that have arisen around services marketing and idea or social marketing. Furthermore, business schools offer courses in both types of marketing, although social marketing courses often are included in sociology and communication curricula under such titles as diffusion and social communication.

Not only does the services sector overlap with the social sector, but tangibles also enter into social marketing, in products such as condoms to convicts, hypodermic syringes to addicts, food to the homeless, girl scout cookies, second-hand goods bought and sold by the Salvation Army, and so forth.

The Advertising Council. A discussion of the social sector would be incomplete without mention of the work of the Advertising Council, which is at the forefront of the industry's promotional efforts. The council is a private, nonprofit organization that conducts public service campaigns promoting social causes. Under its supervision, private ad agencies contribute creative talent and corporations give financial support for the design of campaigns dealing with such subjects as crime prevention, drunk driving, food stamp information, seat belt use, cooperative education, and "Smokey the Bear."

For decades, this practice was uniquely American. In Europe, for example, social idea dissemination was considered the exclusive province of government, since people did not trust the motives of profit-making firms engaging in social promotion. But that view has changed considerably, and advertising agencies throughout the world have begun to participate in public service programs on a large scale. As Rosenfield (1986, p. 73) observes,

> We're really talking about "social marketing." The idea is to use mass media to educate the public about preventive health measures, and this effort has had impressive results. Some of these successes are detailed in a UNICEF report called "State of the World's Children, 1986." In one of the most remarkable stories, the agency tells how war was stopped (for a few days) in El Salvador so that a public service campaign to encourage vaccination of their children could go forward. Last March, a day had been set aside for thousands of health workers and volunteers to vaccinate children in some 2,000 centers. The campaign was carried out through newspapers, magazines, television and radio announcements. A three-day truce was worked

out between the guerrillas and the Salvadorean government so that plans could be carried out. The challenge worldwide during the next 25 years is to increase this investment in the public good. New advertiser-supported media will create new opportunities to spread public service messages. Some might fear that I am describing the world of "Big Brother," where there will be some form of centralized marketing plan with do-good messages delivered from one place to everybody. Obviously, each nation will continue to develop its own social marketing, its own public service campaigns, predicated on the needs of the people in each country, needs that vary tremendously.

SIZE OF THE CONCEPT SECTOR

The overall size of the P&NPO portion of the U.S. economy can be estimated from figures on total national income. Commercial business accounts for about 80 percent of this total and the concept sector for 20 percent. The latter is divided roughly into 14 percent for government and 6 percent for nonprofit organizations (see Table 2.1).

Much of the other information on the dimensions of the P&NP sector has been fragmentary. For most industries, such statistics as operating revenues, total assets, expenditures, and number of employees are readily obtainable from trade associations or government sources. But those data are hard to find for P&NPOs, although in the northeastern part of the United States *New England Business* compiles statistics annually on the largest governmental and nonprofit institutions in the region. Calling these the "Other Economy," Kozbial (1986, p. 18), points out they constitute "one of the largest elements in the region's economy . . . (and) rank as (its) largest employers."

However, the publication reports considerable difficulty in "discovering" such statistics: "There is no central clearinghouse for information on nonprofits nor any single, comprehensive directory" (Kozbial 1986, p. 24). (Note that *New England Business* includes government agencies in its category of nonprofits. This book, too, recognizes the many parallels between P&NPOs.) Most of the data come directly from the institutions themselves. Consequently researchers often have little choice but to rummage through less-than-complete records. Data on government agencies come from files of the U.S. Census Bureau, comptrollers of state budget offices, and state data banks. In this computerized era, it is surprising that no organization systematically collects and publishes such information.

The Nonprofit Subsector. Nevertheless, a national clearinghouse of information on nonprofits (excluding government agencies) does indeed exist. It is the Independent Sector (IS), which is not only the formal title of the

TABLE 2.1 Some Comparative Statistics on Public, Nonprofit, and Business Sectors of the U.S. Economy

	Percentage of total economy					*Total expenditures*[c] *(billions)*	*Marketing expenditures*[d] *(billions)*
	Number of entitees[a]	*GNP*[b]	*National income*[a]	*Number of employees*[c]	*Wages*[a]		
Social sector	6.5	14.0	20.7	27.9	24.8	1,600	5.2
Public employees	0.4	10.5	14.5	17.6	16.8	1,351	2.7
Paid				16.6	16.0		
Volunteer				1.0	0.8		
Federal	nil	3.4		3.2		786	1.6
State, local	0.4	7.2		14.5		565	1.1
Nonprofit employees	6.1	3.4	6.2	10.3	8.0	239	2.4
Paid				6.0	4.6		
Volunteer				4.4	3.4		
Business	93.5	85.4	79.3	72.1	75.3	4,000	600.0

Note: Totals may not add because of rounding.

Multiple-source data such as these, inevitably vary with respect to reference periods and can only be used to make broad and general comparisons. Estimates for marketing expenditures were made as follows: public agencies, 0.2 percent of total expenditures (after Palmer 1985); nonprofits, 1 percent; business, 15 percent. Business varies from perhaps 3 percent for some commodities to as much as 50 percent for packaged consumer goods. It includes advertising, personal selling, product design, packaging, delivery, display—in other words, the entire gamut of marketing functions. Thus, it is not unreasonable that the total, 600 billion, is almost six times the amount (109 billion) known to be spent on advertising alone in 1987. On more solid ground, 15 percent is what remains after 75 percent of revenues is spent on labor and 10 percent gross profit, according to the standard Cobb–Douglas function. Note, too, that total business expenditure estimates are confounded by transfer payments and receipts.

National income exceeds GNP for the social sector while the opposite is true for business. This occurs because of differences in methods of calculation. In the social sector, GNP is just the cost of labor. National income excludes indirect business taxes, which is not a factor in P&NP accounting. Finally, wages for volunteers are assigned (imputed) values.

[a]Hodgkinson and Weitzman (1986).
[b]*Survey of Current Business* (1988).
[c]*Statistical Abstract of the United States* (1987).
[d]Author's estimates.

organization (see Chapter 3), but one name given to nonprofit agencies as a group. (The British counterpart of IS is the National Council for Voluntary Organisations.) IS has recently begun to gather data on nonprofits in the United States and publishes a biannual compendium, which was the primary source of the data in this section (Hodgkinson and Weitzman 1986).

Of the estimated 1.2 million nonprofit organizations in 1985, the U.S. Department of the Treasury reported approximately 857,000 in its master file of "501 series" (tax-exempt) organizations. Of this group, 366,071 fell into the 501(c)(3) category, which covers those engaging in all types of educational, research, scientific, religious, philanthropic, and other charitable activities. In addition, 130,344 organizations were in the 501(c)(4) category, which consists primarily of civic leagues and social welfare organizations. By law, 501(c)(3) organizations are eligible for tax-deductible contributions from both individuals and corporations. Although 501(c)(4) organizations are not required to file tax returns, contributions to them are not tax-deductible.

Nonprofit organizations (NPOs) have about 7 million paid employees and nearly 5 million volunteers. They appear to be growing larger and in the process are taking on the habits of the corporate sector.

> As these organizations have grown more prosperous, with larger employee bases and greater annual costs, they have had to adopt more sophisticated management styles to avoid becoming victims of their own success. "As associations have grown larger and more complex, they are being run in a more businesslike way with a greater emphasis on finance and marketing," says Elizabeth Allen, president elect of the Northern California Society of Association Executives in San Francisco. "They are less of the 'jolly old boys' club that we've seen in the past. Association members are demanding more sophisticated programs." (Tuft 1986)

Although NPOs can hardly be described as prosperous, they do seem subject to economic swings. One group enjoying success as this is being written is the nonprofit theaters, whose income has been rising faster than operating costs. This change is the result of "newer and more sophisticated methods of fund-raising in response to escalating costs, changing tax laws and uncertain economic climate" (Gerard 1987, p. C15). That is to say, nonprofit companies have been more enterprising than commercial theaters. Thus, as Hummler (1984, p. 262) has reported,

> Authors and their agents, perceiving the economic woes and unwillingness of commercial managements to risk presenting new plays, now turn first to the nonprofit arena, in which competition for new plays of quality has become fierce. Many Broadway producers are never shown new plays by playwrights with proven track records until after they've been produced under nonprofit auspices.

This means that nonprofit organizations are becoming more important in the social sector itself as well as in the economy as a whole. And thanks to the efforts of the Independent Sector, statistics describing activities of the NPOs are now available to researchers and other interested parties.

The Public Subsector. The components of the public subsector are federal, state, and municipal government agencies, which are even more difficult to measure than nonprofit organizations. The federal legislative, judicial, and executive branches contain 25 agencies; another 49 are subsumed under independent establishments and government corporations. All told, the federal government has 128 departments and agencies employing over three million individuals (*Reader's Digest* 1987). (Two agencies, the Central Intelligence Agency and the National Air and Space Administration, are not included, as their employment figures are classified information.) The two largest employers are the Department of Defense, with over 33 percent of all federal employees, and the U.S. Postal Service, which employs about 25 percent.

Total expenditures of the U.S. government amount to some $1,000 billion per year, or 25 percent of the GNP. The two largest-spending agencies—Social Security and Medicare ($268.8 billion) and Defense ($265.8 billion)—account for more than half of that amount (*Reader's Digest* 1987).

PUBLIC AND NONPROFIT AGENCIES COMPARED

The marketing activities of nonprofit and public organizations can be combined into one category since many of their products are similar, particularly in areas of health, education, and welfare such as mental health, substance control, fire and crime prevention, family planning, nature conservation, and civil rights. Nevertheless, a few differences between these two subsectors warrant mention. Of course, the public sector receives virtually all its financial support from public funds whereas nonprofits survive primarily on charitable contributions. In addition, nonprofits employ a larger number of part-time workers and women, and they pay lower salaries than do government agencies (Hodgkinson and Weitzman 1986). There is little question that altruism is a motivating factor in the agency/employee relationship in the voluntary sector. A great many of the jobs in the nonprofit subsector, especially in human services, appeal to individuals having a special desire to help others. Significant differences also exist in organizational structure. There appears to be more bureaucracy within government agencies than in nonprofits, where management responsibility rests with boards of trustees.

Differences in size are apparent from the statistics in Table 2.1. The nonprofit sector contains a great many more individual agencies than government, and these agencies are obviously smaller in size, on average. In fact, the budget of either of the two largest federal agencies, Social Security or Defense, is greater than the combined expenditures of the entire nonprofit sector, including hospitals, schools and colleges, religious institutions, social service agencies, fraternal organizations, public broadcasting, museums, and foundations—again, combined.

P&NPOs COMPARED WITH PRIVATE SECTOR FIRMS

How do these two subsectors as a unit compare with the commercial sector? Marketing thought and practices are not entirely identical in the profit and the nonprofit sectors, but the similarities outweigh the differences. In both cases, customer satisfaction is paramount; all ideas, services, and goods are presumed to either fill a need or solve a problem. Exchange always takes place, even in the case of philanthropy (see Chapter 13). Something is transferred and a price is paid in return. Once satisfied, the customer tends to come back for another purchase. Marketing plans for child care, energy conservation, and manpower training programs are just as effective as those for food, automobiles, and designer jeans.

One obvious difference, as stated earlier, is that the social marketer is more altruistic than his or her commercial counterpart. Certainly, P&NPOs are duty-bound to render some services that are not cost-effective, a rare phenomenon in the private sector. Goals and mission statements, standard fare in corporate planning, are less clear in social marketing. This is particularly true in government (Enis 1981), where vague and ill-defined objectives are common (Yorke 1984). Furthermore, government markets are difficult to analyze because high-quality data are scarce and the marketing strategy may be impossible to assess. Price may not be as salient a factor as it is in traditional product marketing. Communicating the information may become difficult. Since governments often are required to promote an idea in a community consisting of many diverse groups, the message cannot be aimed at a particular audience or contain specific information. As a result, what does get through is often a weak message.

The nonprofit sector is also known for the vaguely defined character of its product offerings, absence of competition, short-term planning, and difficulty of measuring performance or cost benefits (Brady 1984). In particular, concept sector institutions and commercial firms differ in the way they measure performance: Private sector firms measure performance by the number of customers satisfied, whereas public and nonprofit agencies usually measure performance by the size of their budgets (Drucker 1973).

Marketing Budgeting. There are also significant differences in allocations for the marketing budget. Private sector firms spend a considerably higher proportion of their total operating expenditures on marketing than P&NPOs do—an estimated 15 percent versus less than 1 percent. Remember, however, that these statistics are little more than conjectures (see Table 2.1). For example, it is impossible to determine how much of the federal government's trillion dollar budget is spent on advertising, public relations, and marketing. One analyst estimates the public relations budget alone as "running into the billions" (Palmer 1985).

Certain details are known. The largest spender is the Defense Department, which has 1,066 full-time employees in public relations. The Department of Agriculture has a public relations staff of 144, with a budget of $6.5 million; the Department of Education has a staff of 46 and a budget of $2.4 million; and the Department of Transportation has a staff of 21 and a budget of $1.5 million. Note that these are only four of 128 departments and agencies.

In general, most expenditures for advertising, public relations, and marketing are hidden under other budget categories, but at an estimated two-tenths of 1 percent, the government spends a total of 2.7 billion dollars to promote itself.

Thus, the P&NP sector in the United States spends roughly 5.2 billion dollars annually on marketing, half of which is spent by government agencies and half by private NPOs. That estimate has increased two and a half times in the past decade (Fine 1981, chap. 3). Nevertheless, it is undoubtedly a conservative figure, if one considers the recent jump in heavy advertising campaigns by hospitals and universities. Despite the vagaries in making such heroic estimates, these figures do confirm that the social and the commercial sectors differ in the extent of their marketing expenditures.

PRODUCTS OF GOVERNMENT AGENCIES

Three Categories. By and large, the products (programs) marketed by governments fall into three categories—informational, educational, and political. Informational marketing is used to bring important facts to the public's attention, for example, information about a change in tax laws or speed limits, the announcement of a public auction of surplus goods, and so forth. Educational marketing is used to disseminate public interest programs, such as those concerned with promoting energy conservation or increasing seat belt use. Political marketing is intended to enhance the image of the party in power.

What Is and What Is Not Marketing. Sometimes an agency offers a product that is more likely to fulfill its own desires than the consumer's. That agency is demonstrating producer orientation, and therefore is said to be violating the marketing concept. Whether a government program falls into the former or the latter class may not be readily apparent. One must inquire whether an agency is promoting a product for the benefit of society or for its own ends.

Every institution, social marketer or otherwise, no doubt believes, and shouts from the rooftops, that its programs are designed for the commonweal: "What is good for General Motors is good for America." And administrators of a nonprofit hospital are surely convinced the health of the community will fall into ruin if it should cease to exist.[1] Whether a government program is designed to aid the poor, lower the capital gains tax, or overpower the opposition party, it will likely be promoted and defended as being in the public interest. But that alone does not mean it is being marketed. Suppose that a political entity offers some parcels of public land for sale, as part of a scheme that will fill the coffers of private land speculators, or that a government campaign promotes the idea of subsidizing tobacco growers. In each of these cases, surely some people—although they may be few in number—will be satisfied, but not the general public. A program might be seen as chicanery or edict, but not marketing. By omitting malevolent products from the social marketing appellation, we enhance the marketing concept. Indeed, there is justification for using the term *antisocial marketing* to denote efforts to promote such programs.

There are borderline cases: Some believe that promoting the space program has societal value, others think it does not. Thus, promoting the idea of space exploration might be a "product" to some, but not to others. The same is true of the direct deposit of federal payments, and many other controversial activities.

One may ask, "What does it matter whether a product does or does not warrant the social marketing label?" Analogously, does it matter whether "Hug your child each day" is or is not propaganda? Or whether acupuncture is called medicine? A discipline needs to make clear what phenomena are included in its domain. Why? For one thing, if a program conforms to marketing criteria, the agency may wish to be certain its staff includes a marketing expert who can promote the agency's products by drawing on experiences, processes, language, functions, and forms common to other marketing activities. Some parsimony and efficiency are thus obtained. By examining a situation through a different lens, one also sees dimensions otherwise overlooked; this is the philosophy behind an interdisciplinary approach to a situation.

Finally, to mention a point developed by Stanley Shapiro in Chapter 21, for a program to be marketed, it must stand the test of changeability to suit the customer. He argues that product immutability belies the marketing concept. Conversely, a product can often be better marketed if it can be differentiated, as all marketers know.

So it is important to have some criteria by which to determine whether a (primarily government) program falls under social marketing. For example, coercion is not marketing; to fit the definition, the exchange must be voluntary. The government possesses the power to pass and enforce laws, and therefore has the capacity to force an exchange transaction upon an individual against his or her will. Perhaps the most striking example is the Chinese population control program (Cho 1986) (which was discontinued in 1988). Still more insidious is Singapore's "voluntary" program, under which college-educated women were paid to have children and other women were paid to be sterilized (Belk 1988). Or consider the approach to food safety in the Peoples' Republic of China: A public health official told me they have no such problem. If a street vendor is found to be selling tainted food, his license is summarily removed forever—no problem. And pimps there are executed.

PRODUCTS OF NONPROFIT ORGANIZATIONS

Whether grouped on the basis of operating expenditures or employment, the categories of NPO products may be ranked in the following order, beginning with the largest category:

1. Health services
2. Education/research
3. Religion
4. Social services
5. Civic and fraternal services
6. Other (arts, public broadcasting, etc.).

Health services are covered in Chapter 16 and education in Chapter 1, through the example of the university. Chapter 18 discusses a social service organization, and those in the "other" category are dealt with throughout the book (for a thorough statement on promotion of the arts, see Semenik 1987). This section focuses on the social marketing situation with respect to religious organizations, research institutions, and civic groups.

Religion. "For Fast, Fast, Fast Relief Take Two Tablets," reads the headline of an advertisement by the Saints Martha and Mary Episcopal Church in Eagan, Minnesota. The layout contains a picture of the Ten Commandments on two tablets engraved in Hebrew letters with a finger pointing to the second commandment, "Thou shalt have no other gods before me." "Few businesses," notes McDaniel (1986, p. 24), "employ better marketing techniques than churches such as Jerry Falwell's Liberty Baptist Church, Robert Schuller's Garden Grove Community Church, James Kennedy's Coral Ridge Presbyterian Church or Charles Stanley's First Baptist Church of Atlanta." Although these are notable exceptions in a class of NPOs that have otherwise been aloof from such promotion techniques, the practice is growing. Ministers are perceived as highly credible sources of promotion messages. And behind them, is the Source even the strongest nonbeliever may have difficulty disputing!

A major concern of every marketer is whether promotion messages should be designed to appeal to existing customers or to new ones. It seems that religion, plagued with a few decades of membership decline, has in the main, adopted the latter strategy. To lure nonpracticing potential members to the church and synagogue, advertisements have appeared bearing such headlines as, "Moses Never Had a Bar Mitzvah" (Stern 1987) and "In the Church Started by a Man Who Had Six Wives, Forgiveness Goes without Saying" (Neff 1987).

Comical aproach

Churches are relying more and more on research to gain insight into their markets, and on segmentation schemes to plan their promotion strategy. One church, for example, segmented nonmembers into three classes called resisters, disinterested, and uninformed (cited in Fine 1981). Meanwhile, the Presbytery of Minneapolis–St. Paul found its advertising made a greater impact on younger, middle-class suburbanites than on older, more conservative and retired individuals (Stern 1987). Interestingly, clergy themselves appear to be more approving than the general public of the "commercialization" of religion (McDaniel 1986), in contrast to lawyers and accountants, many of whom are opposed to the idea of "snake-oiling" themselves.

Just what should the church promote? Membership, attendance, support, and building-fund messages are producer-oriented and likely to fall on deaf ears. More in keeping with the marketing concept are appeals to tranquility, security, sociability, and the entire gamut of church programs through which these goals are obtained. McDaniel (1986, p. 25) suggests a church should stress three factors in its appeal:

1. Individual behavior (e.g., "Spend more time with your family").
2. Benefits of involvement (e.g., "Find answers to your questions about life").
3. Institutional characteristics (e.g., "We preach the Bible as the inspired word of God").

However, church marketers should avoid any product that may be perceived as a political issue. Tax laws specifically forbid exempt institutions from participating in political campaigns or "devoting a substantial amount of their activities to influencing legislation" (Burnham 1988, p. A27). The courts have ruled that while the First Amendment protects the right to practice religion, tax exemption is a privilege granted by government under a set of rules of law; the Internal Revenue Service may revoke the tax-exempt status of any NPO violating that law. A case in point has to do with the recent attacks on the Roman Catholic church by abortion-rights groups arguing the church had distributed antiabortion literature designed to sway legislators to its point of view. Some other controversial social products that are potentially incriminating include U.S. membership in the United Nations, the nuclear test ban treaty, Medicare, and various forms of civil rights.

The channel for the religion product will likely become longer with time. Always mainly direct—that is, a producer-to-consumer process in the form of the Sabbath sermon—the channel now includes the media and an increasing number of word-of-mouth components, as illustrated by the Southern Baptists, the largest Protestant group in the United States, who have "just instituted a seminary curriculum with a specialty in media and promotional activities for the purpose of training 'Media Ministers' in some of its larger churches" (McDaniel 1986, p. 25).

Note, in passing, that the term *propaganda*, discussed in Chapter 10 as an important element in the marketing channel, came into being in 1622 when the Roman Catholic church mounted a fierce countermovement to the Protestant Reformation, calling the movement an institution for the propagation of the faith—hence propaganda.

The results of church marketing have been impressive. The Reverend George Martin, rector of Saint Luke's Episcopal Church in Minneapolis reported sharp increases in membership and attendance and a drop in the average age of congregants from fifty-five to forty. And for the first time in many years, baptisms outnumber funerals. Martin attributed all of this to advertising. In Miami, Temple Beth David appealed to the younger segment with such messages as, "Ruth Was Single Too," and "Moses' Mother Couldn't Find a Day-Care Center Either." The ads were timed to precede the Jewish High Holidays in September or, what the congregation's Rabbi Jack Riemer called "the mating season between Jews and synagogues." Membership increased 50 percent as a result of the campaign (Stern 1987). Rev. Martin has summed up the marketing of religion: "Some church people just can't imagine advertising the church. Yet the Bible says everywhere Jesus went, great crowds followed him. There just had to be some kind of advance PR" (Neff 1987, p. 13).

Marketing's place in religion in the United States may be better appreciated when one realizes that this is the first country in which religious organizations became voluntary. It would seem natural that the first society to separate church and state would later be at the forefront of unique and innovative initiatives to further the goals of the church.

Research Institutes. One group of NPOs that has received little publicity consists of such independent nonprofit research institutes as Battelle Memorial Institute, Columbus, Ohio; SRI International, Menlo Park, California; IIT Research Institute, Chicago, Illinois; Southwest Research Institute, San Antonio, Texas; and Research Triangle Institute, North Carolina. Typically, the institute is not affiliated with a university, firm, or government and conducts research for, and consults with public agencies and corporate firms on the development of new technology. Their combined billings are reportedly about two billion dollars per year with

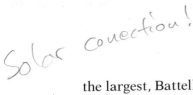

Solar connection!

the largest, Battelle, enjoying more than a quarter of that amount. Over half of the contracts come from U.S. and foreign governments (Feder 1986). Some contracts are for the overall management of huge projects such as the U.S. Solar Energy Research Institution in Colorado, which is operated by Midwest Research Institute in Kansas City, Missouri.

As with NPOs in general, research institutes are creating more of their own profit-making, tax-paying subsidiaries to market their inventions. They do so at the risk of losing their qualifications for tax exemption with the Internal Revenue Service. In addition,

> Debra Fassnacht, head of public relations for IIT, pointed to another telltale sign that institutes have been getting more commercial-minded. "I've noticed them advertising," she said. "That's something new for the not-for-profits." She pointed out that IIT placed its first ad last August in *Railway Age*, a trade publication, to call attention to its new locomotive simulator for training engineers. (Feder 1986, p. 23)

Public interest research groups (PIRGs) are carving out a formidable niche in the P&NP sector as this book goes to press. Citizen's advocacy organizations have always existed but now seem to be recognized to a greater extent than ever before, virtually as a sector in themselves. Certainly they constitute a growing movement, which has expanded by 25 percent since 1980. The pronounced goal of the movement is to bring about social change through citizens' lobbying efforts in such areas as voter registration, campaign financing, military spending, community right-to-know, pesticide control, credit card interest rates, toxic use reduction, lemon laws, and bank check–holding delays (float). Indeed, PIRGs lobby for practically every cause that some legislator must make a decision on at one point in time or another. Broad areas include politics, government, community, ecology, business, and economics. With such a formidable product mix, it is small wonder that groups have succeeded in enlisting large numbers of volunteers to participate in fundraising and consciousness-raising.

The "probing" component of our 7P's marketing model is well advanced in the PIRG phenomenon, in part because of the initiative of the Foundation for Public Affairs in Washington, D.C. The foundation publishes *Public Interest Profiles*, which contains a wealth of data on the larger of the individual groups, as well as general information about popular causes and concerns in the public interest. The 1986–87 edition, the fifth to be published, contains data on 250 groups as well as 13 commentaries by policy experts. For each group, a profile provides identifying demographic facts, the group's purpose, scope, political orientation, method of operation, current concerns, a list of its publications, and a statement describing its effectiveness.

PIRGs range in size from small groups concerned with issues that affect local communities to such national organizations as the Center for

National Policy, People for the American Way, the United States Public Interest Research Group, and perhaps the largest of the political action groups—the Fund for a Conservative Majority. About 40 percent of them have international orientations. Military spending is the focus of the largest concentration of newer groups, particularly the "grassroot networks" (Bergner 1986). According to *Profiles*, 250 of these groups have an aggregate budget of close to $1.5 billion, which represents a 50 percent increase since 1984, and about 60 percent of them have budgets in excess of $1 million. The average staff size is slightly more than sixty persons. Furthermore, "Many groups are now increasingly concerned with internal questions related to management: keeping good people on staff, retirement programs, benefits, and all the peripheral concerns that would allow professional staff to make career commitments to public interest jobs" (Bergner 1986, p. 16).

As with all markets, purchasers of the specialty products of PIRGs need to be segmented. One scheme for doing so may be based on the "expanded and highly educated professional stratum [which is] more concerned with political issues, with the culture of society. They divide between liberals and conservatives, largely linked to the subjects they chose to study in university: social scientists more to the left . . . business and technologists to the right" (Lipset 1986, p. 13).

Producers of public interest products—the sources of the promotional messages—range from advocates of leftist causes having roots in the activism of the 1960s to conservatives fostering preservation of free enterprise and strong government. The PIRGs' promotion media, apart from the usual print and broadcast vehicles, include fact sheets, newsletters, articles in appropriate publications, training and technical assistance seminars, and conferences.

Just as marketers use various models to plan strategic programs, public interest lobbyists may borrow a fascinating and provocative framework from the martial arts, to "capture the essence of the citizens' lobbying art" "for characterizing key recurring elements in the successful public interest lobbying campaign. Of particular relevance are the central concepts relating to the marshalling, transforming and focusing of energy (T'ai C'hi); the importance of moderation and balance, the avoidance of excessive aggressiveness (Yang); or yielding (Yin)" (Pertschuk 1987, p. 5).

The public interest lobbyist's raw material, says Pertschuk, is "the unfocused energy of the public will." The lobbyist refocuses that energy on specific targets, usually legislators, for a specific cause, with measured intensity, planning when to advance and when to withdraw. In addition, "movement" lobbying can be related to hope, which is "neither passive waiting nor is it unrealistic forcing of circumstances that cannot occur. It is like the crouched tiger, which will jump only when the moment for jumping has come" (Pertschuk 1987, p. 11). One sees an analogy

to the advertising theory of "pulsing." That is, ads may be scheduled to appear at just the optimum points in time to maximize overall retention of the message by target audiences (see the section on budgeting in Chapter 12).

The concept sector is complex, as it consists of all agencies at the federal, state, and municipal levels of government, along with NPOs in half a dozen different product categories. A true compendium of the industry's organizations would include all these entities. The purpose here, however, is to show how they do, or might do, their marketing tasks. Actual agencies, whether individual ones or groups, are only mentioned by way of examples.

CONTROVERSIAL ISSUES IN THE INDUSTRY

Several controversial issues have arisen in connection with the P&NP sector, notably in connection with the Fairness Doctrine, privatization, and unfair competition.

The Fairness Doctrine. A long-standing debate within the concept industry concerns the Federal Communication Commission's (FCC's) intervention into issue advertising on broadcast media. Under the Fairness Doctrine, a broadcaster must cover matters of public importance in a way that fairly reflects a balance of viewpoints. Otherwise, the radio station or television channel risks having the FCC challenge its license and right to continue operating. This regulation is based on a purported scarcity of airwaves—one of the controversial issues involved (controversial because print is also scarce). Opponents argue that airspace is more available than newspapers, yet print media are exempt from the doctrine. A stronger point is that the doctrine violates the First Amendment's guarantee of free speech to broadcasters.

An anomaly was pointed out by Beilenson (1987, p. A31):

> In 1967, the FCC ordered radio and TV stations to provide free air time for public service announcements depicting the health hazards of smoking. [The order] sought to counter cigarette ads. Curiously, Congress's ban on cigarette advertisements in 1971 was engineered by the tobacco companies. It was a smart move on the industry's part, though, because the FCC's counter-advertising requirements had resulted in a drop in cigarette sales. Once the ban took effect, and broadcasters were no longer required to carry antismoking ads, cigarette consumption again started climbing.

Consequently, Beilenson argued for the resumption of antismoking ads, which have all but disappeared by reason of the Fairness Doctrine itself—all of which is history. On August 7, 1987, the Fairness Doctrine was repealed. At this writing it remains to be seen whether the repeal will have any impact on social promotion. Indeed, one may predict that broadcasters will feel freer now to air issues they might previously have avoided for fear of the equal-time restraint. And they are likely to invite opposing views if only for enhancement of their own image of fairness—without the doctrine.

Privatization. The nature of the P&NP sector is such that its members' functions sometimes face the prospect of being transferred to private ownership and management. The question arises as to whether a for-profit firm may better serve society than a public or nonprofit organization, where a given product is concerned. The ability to "better serve society" is judged by such usual consumer choice criteria as quality of product, price or value, and delivery. For example, it is not uncommon for an instrumentality to change from supplying trash pickup service itself to purchasing that service from a private contractor. The same can be said for education, health care, social welfare, prisons, and other social products. As to which is more cost effective, the debate rages on.

The increasing trend toward privatization is due in part to the fact that the public sector has grown too large and too inefficient (Pack 1987, p. 256). Another powerful statement in favor of privatization comes from a study of nonprofit and for-profit hospitals: "Along each dimension studied, neither society as a whole nor individual patients benefit from the nonprofit form. Quite the contrary: for most variables the performance of the for-profit hospital is superior" (Herzlinger and Krasker 1987, p. 100).

It is a one-sided view; some of the assumptions and assertions of these researchers are open to criticism. For example, in stating "Nonprofits clearly give their professional employees a perfect environment in which to practice" (p. 94), Herzlinger and Krasker omit the crucial reality that nonprofit employees earn significantly lower salaries than their commercial counterparts.

In the domain of public agencies, privatization is often a political matter. Early in 1988, against outcries of public advocates, the Reagan administration weighed a proposal to privatize the country's main health research institution, the National Institutes of Health. An opponent to the scheme wrote:

> As a funding agency, N.I.H. has, with taxpayer money, supported the bulk of the biological research of the last 40 years. . . . With the latest proposal the corporations, via the Reagan administration, are moving to privatize the N.I.H. directly by transforming its research laboratories into a private—but still publicly funded—university . . . further reorienting the nation's research agenda from public need to private gain. (Noble 1988)

The other side of the argument was given by Savas (1988): "Japan's National Railways lost $14 billion in 1985; this was the last straw leading to its privatization. Private railroads in Japan employed fewer workers, charged lower fares and made money on routes that paralleled J.N.R.'s."

It is probably true that in some situations social goods may be provided more efficiently and with resultant greater satisfaction to consumers, if marketed commercially. The testing ground is the free marketplace. With rare exceptions, nonprofits hold no monopolies; there is little to prevent a profit-making group from going into the social business, as many have done. But results vary.

Finally, the privatization trend appears to be gaining a foothold in Europe as well. The situation in the Netherlands, for example, is described in Chapter 5, with respect to the matter of health insurance.

Outcries of Unfair Competition by Business. The tax-exempt status of an agency places it at a distinct competitive advantage over businesses marketing similar goods or services. And that advantage is compounded by lower postage rates and a supply of free labor in the form of volunteers and donated supplies. At the extreme, such competition could pose a threat to a small business. One group of private business associations has banded together to form the Business Coalition for Fair Competition with the express purpose of lobbying for fairer competition between organizations in the social and commercial sectors.

They are not alone. The National Tax Equity Association and the National Dairy Foods Association typify groups crying out against nonprofit farm cooperatives, which, they argue, are powerful drains on tax revenue while competing unfairly with taxpaying farm suppliers. The Northwest Alliance for Market Equality in Gresham, Oregon is a group of owners of health and racquetball clubs complaining of unreasonable encroachment by the YMCA's nonprofit competition. The Y centers are tax exempt, have lower postal rates and some volunteer help, yet compete with the private clubs on many services rendered. Considerable attention was drawn to the debate in July 1983, when the Small Business Administration (1984) staged a symposium on nonprofits' competition with small business, and later issued a report called "Unfair Competition by Nonprofit Organizations with Small Business: An Issue for the 1980s."

That such complaints are at least partly legitimate is indicated by recent court actions. A nonprofit Connecticut school operating a summer camp was challenged by a taxpaying competitor, and the school forced to close the camp (Williams 1982). Several such cases have been reported, one involving a commercially oriented publication service by the University of Tulsa and another Yale's income from its computer center and its football stadium (Kelly and Quick 1984). In still another, California revoked the property-tax exemptions of a large church that staged non-religious events featuring works by performing artists.

SUMMARY

In many respects, the public and nonprofit sectors of the U.S. economy are not too different from the industrial, or business, sector. Data were presented comparing the P&NP sector with its commercial counterpart and the public and nonprofit subsectors were themselves contrasted. The Advertising Council was introduced to readers as the sector's leading promoter of P&NP causes. Some characteristics of the industry were mentioned to the extent these relate to material in the remaining essays in this book. The chapter also touched upon several controversial issues affecting the industry such as the Fairness Doctrine, privatization and charges of unfair competition made by private sector firms.

NOTE

1. The notion that the social marketer must never be producer oriented may not be taken as unequivocal. I am grateful for being reminded of this by Belk, who wrote me, "Consider a nonprofit symphony orchestra that is the only one in town. Whatever portion of its program the audience will tolerate ought to be devoted to a total producer orientation. The ends of directors, composers and musicians rather than those of the audience (who must be 'educated') should dominate in order to enhance creativity, musical development and non-stagnation of culture. Otherwise mass tastes prevail, the Boston Pops flourishes and art dies." For more on this issue see Belk and Zhow (1987).

3

THE INDEPENDENT SECTOR

An American Phenomenon and a Coalition Created to Preserve It

JOHN H. THOMAS

Communications, INDEPENDENT SECTOR

Practically every industry has a trade association. The nonprofit sector has one as well. The national coalition of nonprofit organizations is known as the INDEPENDENT SECTOR. Americans are urged to recognize, participate in, support, and serve voluntary groups. In addition, providers and seekers of resources are urged to meet more often in order to promote mutual understanding. It is also important to recognize that marketing plays a significant role in the INDEPENDENT SECTOR.

Since colonial days, foreign visitors have commented on the extraordinary impulse of Americans to form voluntary groups and devise nongovernmental institutions to serve community purposes. Out of that impulse has come an incredible variety of American institutions. Taken all together, the groups and organizations number in the millions. These causes and the giving that supports them are as much a part of America as our democratic form of government and our free enterprise system. For that reason, this segment of our society is sometimes referred to as the "third" or nonprofit sector. It has also become known as the INDEPENDENT SECTOR.

The INDEPENDENT SECTOR includes not only a broad and diverse number of nonprofit organizations but individual donors and volunteers, foundations, and corporate public service groups. Many services of the sector—food, clothing, shelter and counseling, to name a few—are provided through religious institutions. Beyond that, there is a multitude of people and organizations that can help us stay physically fit, enjoy our natural resources, help us through personal crises, involve us with the arts, provide formal or informal education, and more.

Imagine, if you can, an America without the scouts and churches, without the Red Cross, United Way, National Association for the Advancement of Colored People (NAACP), American Association of University Women (AAUW), our community orchestras, the National Conference of Christians and Jews, the Cancer Society, Cooperative for American Relief to Everywhere (CARE), our private schools and colleges, and the thousands on thousands of other local, state, and national organizations.

This sector is made up of citizens caring about causes and people, often without pay and usually without much recognition. They usher, collect, inform, protest, assist, teach, heal, contribute, build, advocate, comfort, testify, support, solicit, mimeograph, canvass, demonstrate, guide, feed, criticize, organize, and appeal. The multitude of delightfully different organizations in this sector provide opportunities for creativity and freedom, but—as Senator Patrick Moynihan has said—they are also "outlets for outrage."

Waldemar Nielsen, author and international consultant on philanthropy, has provided an overview that captures the enormous breadth of this sector:

> If your interest is people, you can help the elderly by contributing to the Grey Panthers; or teenagers through the Jean Teen Scene of Chicago; or young children through your local nursery school; or everyone by giving to the Rock of All Ages in Philadelphia. If your interest is animals, there is the ASPCA and Adopt-A-Pet; if fishes, the Izaak Walton League; if birds, the American Homing Pigeon Institute or the Easter Bird Banding Association.
>
> If you are an old WASP there is the English Speaking Union and the Mayflower Descendants Association; if you have a still older association with the country, there is the Redcliff Chippewa Fund or the Museum of the American Indian. If your vision is local, there is the Cook County Special Bail Project and Clean Up the Ghetto in Philadelphia; if national, there is America the Beautiful, if global, there is the United Nations Association, if celestial, there are the Sidewalk Astronomers of San Francisco.
>
> If you are interested in tradition and social continuity, there is the society for the Preservation of Historic Landmarks and the Portland Friends of Cast Iron Architecture; if social change is your passion there is Common Cause; and if that seems too sober for you, there is the Union of Radical Political Economists or perhaps the Theatre for Revolutionary satire in New York. If your pleasure is music, there is a supermarket of choices, from Vocal Jazz to the Philharmonic Society to the American Guild of English Handbell Ringers.
>
> If you don't know quite what you want, there is Get Your Head Together, Inc. of Glen Ridge, New Jersey. If your interests are contradictory, there is the Great Silence Broadcasting Foundation of California. If they are ambiguous, there is the Tombstone Health Service of Arizona. The landscape

of the third sector is untidy but wonderfully exuberant. What counts is not the confusion but the profusion. There is literally something in it for everyone. (Nielsen 1980, p. 5–6)[1]

Almost everyone who supports the independent sector is a donor or volunteer, working either alone or through organizations, corporations, and foundations. In 1987, according to *Giving USA*, published by the American Association of Fund-Raising Counsel, total private support of this sector was $93.7 billion. That's billion with a "b." Now comes the real shocker. Of that total, $82.8 billion, almost a full 90 percent, came from individuals! Added together, the total support from corporations and foundations—vitally important as it is—amounted to just 10 percent of the total (Weber 1988).

Nowhere else on earth can one find giving and volunteering of this extent at all socioeconomic levels—in truly all demographic categories. According to a 1986 survey by Yankelovich, Skelly, and White, conducted for the Rockefeller Brothers Fund and published by INDEPENDENT SECTOR, almost 90 percent of Americans gave to some cause or causes. Eight out of ten Americans believed that one should volunteer time to help others. And this is not just casual giving and volunteering. The same survey indicated that twenty-three million Americans gave five or more hours each week in volunteer time and twenty million gave 5 percent or more of their income. And nearly 40 percent of those surveyed felt they should have given and volunteered more than their current levels (Yankelovich, Skelly, and White 1986).

In 1987, the National Center for Charitable Statistics, a subsidiary of INDEPENDENT SECTOR, published the first "National Taxonomy of Exempt Entities," a system for classifying nongovernmental, nonbusiness tax-exempt organizations in the United States with a focus on the nearly half million philanthropic organizations under IRS Section 501(c)(3). The major headings of that taxonomy alone indicate the breadth and diversity of America's independent sector:

A. Arts, Culture, Humanities
B. Education/Instruction
C. Environmental Quality, Protection/Beautification
D. Animal Related
E. Health: General and Rehabilitation
F. Health: Mental Health/Crisis Intervention
G. Health: Mental Retardation/Developmentally Disabled
H. Consumer Protection/Legal Aid
I. Crime and Delinquency Prevention/Public Protection
J. Employment/Jobs
K. Food, Nutrition, Agriculture
L. Housing/Shelter

      M. Public Safety, Emergency Preparedness, and Relief
      N. Recreation, Leisure, Sports, Athletics
      O. Youth Development
      P. Human Service/Social Services
      Q. International/Foreign
      R. Civil Rights, Social Action, Advocacy
      S. Community Improvement, Community Capacity Building
      T. Grant Making/Foundations
      U. Research, Planning, Science, Technology
      V. Voluntarism, Philanthropy, and Charity
      W. Religion Related/Spiritual Development.

With such a variety of nonprofit organizations and activity and with such impressive figures in giving and volunteering, it is easy to become a cheerleader for this American phenomenon—sometimes to the extreme. This can be dangerous. As Brian O'Connell, president of INDEPENDENT SECTOR, points out,

> We lose our perspective on the sector and society when we exaggerate the importance of private philanthropy and voluntary organizations, particularly when we put them ahead of our responsibility to democratic government. An active voluntary sector can help preserve and enhance our democratic principles, but is doesn't transcend them.
>
> More attention by the schools and the public at large would help people sort out and understand how this country does its public business. In some quarters, there is an exaggerated interpretation of what voluntary organizations should and can do and what government should not do. Some see voluntary effort as getting in the way of governmental responsibility. Others preach that voluntary organizations should do it all. Obviously, we need both strong government and a strong voluntary sector, but we won't have either if the public does not understand the relative roles and its responsibility to each. (O'Connell 1984, p. 5)

Helping the public understand, appreciate, and support the independent sector is part of the mission of an organization conceived in the 1970s, formed in 1979, and launched in 1980. One might say that the organization is marketing the national lifeblood to the nation.

THE COALITION ESTABLISHED TO PRESERVE THE SECTOR

"Such a forceful entity is long overdue. Those who study the field almost invariably conclude that such a body must be created to help establish sensible national policies and attitudes relating to the preservation of the independent sector." So stated John W. Gardner—former secretary of health, education, and welfare and founder of Common Cause, the National Urban Coalition, and numerous other efforts—in a 1979 letter to the leadership of the National Council on Philanthropy (NCOP) and the Coalition of National Voluntary Organizations (CONVO). The two organizations had been exploring the possibility of something rare among associations in this country—going out of business. But central to their exploration was the plan to bring into business an organization encompassing giving *and* volunteering, those who give *and* those who receive, corporations, foundations *and* national nonprofit, voluntary organizations—working together as a single, national coalition.

John Gardner, chairman of the organizing committee, whose task was to lay the groundwork for this new coalition, became the organization's first chairperson. Brian O'Connell, the most recent staff head of both NCOP and CONVO, staffed the organizing committee and was named president of the new organization. INDEPENDENT SECTOR was launched on March 5, 1980, in Washington, D.C. As part of his remarks at the charter meeting, John Gardner said, "You have just witnessed a significant act of creation. If it were notable for nothing else, it would be notable in that it has not resulted in 'just one more organization' but, in fact, in one less organization." Members considered numerous titles for the new body and finally settled on the one that was becoming a popular name for the sector itself. To distinguish the organization from the sector, members decided to spell the name entirely in capital letters. This practice, incidentally, has been successfully carried out in the organization's own materials and in those of other sector groups, but is seldom followed by editors and journalists.

So why form such a group? The final report of the organizing committee, "To Preserve an Independent Sector," stated, "America's independent sector is a long way from extinction and could generally be described as alive and well. However, problems have been developing which need the attention of everyone interested in maintaining and increasing the place of the sector in American life."

The report listed several potential problems, including the relative decline in giving, encroachments on the freedoms of citizens to organize, negative impacts of changes in tax policy, greater dependence on government funding by independent institutions, governmental influence on the agenda of the independent sector, the limitations of the organizations in the sector, limited public understanding of the sector, and inadequate recognition of the importance of having alternatives and multiple sources of support. The "relative decline in giving" obviously did not refer to dollar amounts, which have continuously increased, but to the percentage of gross national product and percentage of personal income.

The report came to the general conclusion:

Despite how very real the obstacles are, they are balanced by a growing conviction that if the independent sector is to continue to serve society well, it must be mobilized for greater cooperation and impact. Despite all the differences, antipathies and antagonisms which may exist in this quarrelsome, competing and truly independent sector, there are even stronger forces pulling it together. However different all the other beliefs, there is a shared understanding of the sector's capacity to serve human values and a shared stake in the fundamental relationship between the freedom of citizens to organize themselves and the freedom of citizens.

INDEPENDENT SECTOR operates through six program areas: public education, government relations, research, measurable growth in giving and volunteering, effective sector leadership, and management and communications/meeting ground. Each program area is guided by a committee, consisting of IS board members, member representatives, and others. INDEPENDENT SECTOR members are involved in, and interested in, all of the program areas, each of which, in addition, oversees separate markets and separate marketing efforts.

For example, the research arm of the organization holds annual meetings, which have been attracting a growing number of persons involved in research into this sector. At these "research forums" individuals studying various aspects of the sector or the basic patterns of giving and volunteering behavior of Americans come together in a heretofore unavailable opportunity to learn from each other and to share their findings. At the base of such activity is an effort to promote even more research. The growing number of projects, listed each year in the IS publication *Research in Progress*, is proof that the effort is succeeding.

The division that is concerned with effective sector leadership and management area tries to foster greater awareness and observance of the principles and practices of effective operation, leadership, and management of philanthropic and voluntary organizations. The division not only works with existing programs—be they college-degree programs or in-service programs—but also makes an effort to create more of both. Here too, INDEPENDENT SECTOR has played a convening role, bringing together those responsible for these programs in a forum where they can learn from each other. These activities in research and effective leadership and management have created specialized networks, which are maintained to further the efforts.

Perhaps the most "market-driven" program area—where nonprofit organization members look to INDEPENDENT SECTOR for help in ensuring their freedom, if not their very survival, is government relations. Whether it's an effort to maintain the rights of nonprofit organizations' to lobby and be actively involved in advocacy or a struggle to keep charitable contributions deductible for all taxpayers, INDEPENDENT SECTOR pulls together ad hoc coalitions with the widest possible sector representation to wage the fight.

It's a constant roller coaster of successes and setbacks. During the first decade of the organization's existence, IS succeeded in bringing into being a deduction for charitable contributions for taxpayers who don't itemize, only to see it die in the tax reform legislation of 1986. Almost immediately, the IS initiated efforts to reverse that action. It takes time. And, over time, it takes hundreds of letters and phone calls and congressional visits from hundreds of persons representing thousands of organizations. But the need to orchestrate those letters and phone calls and visits is one of the primary reasons INDEPENDENT SECTOR was formed. And the combination of that action and vigilance is one of the primary reasons organizations pay dues to belong.

AMERICANS DON'T APPRECIATE, OR EVEN KNOW, WHAT THEY'VE GOT

In the 1970s, one foundation executive scanned almost one hundred high school and college social studies textbooks in search of some mention of this sector—of the history and contributions of philanthropy and voluntary initiative. He found none. Others have complained that this sector gets practically no news coverage. Actually, this is highly arguable. There is probably far more news coverage than most people realize, particularly when one considers the reporting of local community activities. Nevertheless, a good case can be made that many Americans don't know or appreciate what they've got in this unique third sector of our society.

The task of increasing public awareness, appreciation, and support of the independent sector—a task destined to take many years—is being pursued by INDEPENDENT SECTOR's public information/education/communications arm. To reach this goal will take far more than just wider media coverage, although that would certainly be welcomed. It consists, first, in expanding the literature on this sector. Not only have the textbooks been void of information on this subject, the library shelves have been void of publications on this subject—mainly because the books either don't exist or have long been out of print.

An effort has been mounted to encourage people to write more books, reports, monographs, and articles on the sector. Realizing that libraries and librarians constitute an important market, the organization has begun a marketing effort to libraries and is regularly convening selected groups of librarians. As the projects and studies on research, effective sector leadership and management, and government relations move forward, the results are providing more and more valuable publications and increasing the organization's publications program. But a better marketing job is needed to encourage more graduate students and scholars to make this sector the subject of their studies and research.

The organization is working to make the sector known in schools through its appeals to curriculum specialists and textbook publishers and is promoting more student community service activity, preferably in association with course work. The day may not be far off when an educated person will be required to have an understanding of this sector and one criterion of good citizenship will be active community service.

Through increased literature, additional study and research, placement within the nation's school curricula, and integration in the minds and files of writers, editors, and producers, the independent sector may indeed become better known, more appreciated, and better supported in years to come. Not just more, but measurably more.

Perhaps the greatest marketing challenge facing INDEPENDENT SECTOR lies in the area of measurable growth in giving and volunteering. There is a strongly held belief within the sector that, great as the giving and volunteering records have been in this country, there is much room for growth.

Efforts at achieving measurable growth began in 1986 with the campaign "Daring Goals for a Caring Society," the overall goal of which was to double giving and increase volunteering by 50 percent in five years. What is more interesting and perhaps more significant for the long-term, the campaign included a new personal goal for Americans—to give 5 percent of their annual income and five hours of volunteer time each week to causes of their choice. Thus, new terms have been introduced to our society—terms like *fiving, fivers*, and, as the result of a national INDEPENDENT SECTOR/Advertising Council campaign, *Give Five*.

The organizers of the "Daring Goals" program recognized that tithers, those who give 10 percent, are still the true caring leaders of our society. But they also realized that today it is more realistic to ask all Americans to stretch toward the 5 percent mark. The extent to which the reader of this book is aware of the 5 percent target and Give Five reflects the extent to which the campaign has been successful. The effort continues.

THE MEETING GROUND AND COLLECTIVE PRESERVATION

David Mathews, president of the Kettering Foundation, tells the story of how Dorchester, Massachusetts, in 1633 dealt with its "serious problem" of cows and goats that kept straying from the grassy hillside onto the village green. John Maverick, a minister, intervened with words that, according to Mathews, "should be immortal in American history—'We have a problem. We need to talk about it; let's meet on Monday.' " We are taught many phrases, but, as Mathews says, " 'We have a problem; let's meet and talk about it' should go down in our history as the quintessential American political expression" (Mathews 1987, p. 3).

Whether such a phrase should rank right up there with "Give me liberty or give me death" is up to each of us to decide. Whatever the case, we've been meeting ever since—in town meetings, employee meetings, church meetings, school meetings, neighborhood meetings, family meetings, and yes, in nonprofit association meetings.

And now, we have an even broader meeting ground for the tremendous variety of nonprofit organizations and corporations, and foundations. As the independent sector struggles to remain independent and safeguard its future, perhaps the most important service INDEPENDENT SECTOR can provide is to do what most of its founders had in mind—to convene meetings.

Association executives can learn management techniques from one another. Educators can learn methods of integrating the American philanthropic experience into the curriculum from one another. Researchers can advance and broaden their work by meeting together. Organizations with similar concerns can mount appropriate responses by meeting together. Those seeking private funds can learn of the opportunities, limitations, and funding policies of those providing those funds—and "the providers" can learn more of the valuable work provided by "the seekers"—through a common meeting ground. It is amazing to see how much learning can take place simply when such groups convene in one room. Provide the opportunity and progress is a given.

Marketing will always have a place here. Numerous groups within the sector must be targeted with appropriate messages; with strategic calls to collaboration and action. Of course, the country and the world provide additional, targeted audiences—audiences that must constantly hear and know of the value of America's independent sector, and experience it.

Perhaps INDEPENDENT SECTOR's president, Brian O'Connell, has summed it up best: "Through our voluntary initiative and independent institutions, ever more Americans worship freely, study quietly, are cared for compassionately, experiment creatively, serve effectively, advocate aggressively and contribute generously. These national traits are constantly beautiful and hopefully will remain beautifully constant" (O'Connell 1984, p. 8).

What a special commodity—a commodity eminently marketable, and eminently worth marketing to our American society.

SUMMARY

The INDEPENDENT SECTOR is the trade association for a group of nonprofit organizations. It also includes individual donors, volunteers, foundations, and public service groups. Participants of all economic levels care about causes and people and work without pay or recognition. The INDEPENDENT SECTOR, operating through six program areas, strives for greater awareness and continuing giving among the American public.

NOTE

1. Reprinted by permission from Waldemar A. Nielson, *The Third Sector: Keystone of a Caring Society*. (Washington, D.C.: INDEPENDENT SECTOR, 1980) pp. 5–6.

4

The Policy Characteristics and Organizational Dynamics of Social Marketing

MICHAEL P. MOKWA

Arizona State University

Marketing experts have asserted that marketing philosophy and methods can improve the effectiveness and social performance of public and nonprofit organizations. They have used conventional marketing management perspectives to frame their analyses and suggestions. However, P&NPOs possess varying ideologies and unconventional policy dynamics that can inhibit the adoption and development of social marketing orientations and practices. These characteristics must be taken into account in integrating conscious social marketing practice with organized social action. These forces, taken together, constitute the "dynamics" of social marketing and they are of interest to social marketers and social workers alike. Although most of the observations in this essay pertain to the nonprofit sector, they also apply to public agencies.

Social activism, organized voluntarism, and humanitarian involvement are vital dimensions of a democratic culture. Public and nonprofit organizations embody and manifest these important values.[1] The basic purpose of a P&NPO is to organize and oversee voluntary social action directed at humanitarian problem solving. As a result, P&NPOs usually embrace significant social ideas and perform critical social functions. They pursue lofty missions, serve important human needs, and try vigorously to enhance the quality of life. But, typically, P&NPOs approach their missions and markets with indeterminate technologies, severely constrained resources, extensive volunteer involvement, and informal management styles.

Management of the contemporary P&NPO is demanding. To fulfill its mission, a P&NPO requires active social conviction, a strong collaborative orientation, a healthy competitive spirit, trust in professional capabilities, and strategic competence. Each P&NPO must transform its ideas and ideals into causes, services, and products that offer genuine value to its public and motivating benefits to its members.

Marketing can provide management orientation and policy frameworks that are compatible with P&NPO perspectives. Marketing encourages P&NPOs to consider their ideologies, missions, problems, and opportunities strategically, and to manage their activities and performance carefully, responsively, and effectively. Fundamentally, marketing enables a P&NPO to develop exchange relationships that can improve its chances of fulfilling its mission.

P&NPO managers, like marketing experts, have recently become interested in stepping up the quality and impact of social marketing practice. Before this can take place, however, both groups need to develop a better understanding of the policy characteristics and organizational dynamics of P&NPOs.[2]

THE THIRD SECTOR AND P&NPO POLICY DEVELOPMENT

Policy Development by the P&NPO

P&NPOs are the prevalent form of third sector organization, which McGill and Wooten (1975) describe as "transorganizations." This term reflects the complicated interdependence that exists between P&NPOs and their environments, not to mention their complex character, which transcends traditional notions about organizational taxonomy, management theory, and practice. McGill and Wooten find that P&NPOs are characterized by inherent goal ambiguity, process-dominated policy-making, existential policymakers, and indeterminate core technologies.

Goal Ambiguity and Process Domination. Most P&NPOs are strongly committed to combining societal reform and human service, and to involving organizational members and nonmembers (who possess important resources) in the management and operation of the organization. Given the uncertainty of social change, the complexity of human services, and the multiplicity of values and desires of relevant organizational actors, the most fundamental and pervasive characteristic of P&NPOs is their ambiguity, particularly goal ambiguity.

P&NPOs appear to adapt by becoming "process" dominated—that is, they tend to focus on what they are trying to do and are doing, not on explicit accomplishments. The P&NPO accepts and even promotes widely differing personal goal conceptualizations, and these are in constant flux. Goals, as such, are used as guideposts and directives, but not as explicit evaluative criteria. Situational demands and opportunities are the basic cues used to orient P&NPO policy development and behavior. Policy varies from one situation to another, and thus it is usually difficult to identify a coherent policy thrust.

P&NPO Policymakers. Responsibility for policy development and management is often decentralized and diffused in and around a P&NPO. Its policymakers appear to thrive in unstructured environments and have a high tolerance for uncertainty and indeterminacy. They perceive their role to be that of a conduit, facilitator, and enabler. Their basic resources are information about situations and knowledge of human service and social action methodologies. They require considerable feedback, encouragement, and recognition. However, they prefer informal control mechanisms. They are not highly sensitive to direct economic incentives and rewards, although thresholds are usually present. Above all, they are highly involved and deeply committed to their organizations, clients, causes, and professions.

Core Technologies. The term *core technologies* has a rich history in the literature of organizational behavior. It relates closely to what Fine calls (in this book and elsewhere) the agency's product offerings or the actions and "things" that satisfy consumer wants and needs. P&NPOs attempt to "change" human beings and social conditions as their core technology or product (see Hasenfeld and English 1975; Sarri and Hasenfeld 1978; Hasenfeld 1983). Moreover, P&NPOs attempt to enhance personal well-being and social quality simultaneously. Most core technologies used for this purpose are indeterminate—difficult to identify, and unreliable in linking causes and effects. Thus, human and social service disciplines are called upon to formulate the methodological norms for social action. These become closely protected by the practitioners of those disciplines. Professional norms, service interactions, and indeterminate processes are therefore the critical parameters in the P&NPO policy context.

Policy Characteristics of P&NPOs

Table 4.1 presents an outline of the main policy characteristics of P&NPOs. Many P&NPOs strive for unique qualities and policy processes and thus differ along many policy dimensions: fundamental social ideology, guiding profession, scope and size of the operation, level of funding and support, quality of leadership, comprehension of core technologies, and so on. Moreover, not all P&NPOs are third sector organizations. Some are units of a commercial business, and others are government agencies. Some that were born in bureaucracies are becoming autonomous whereas others are becoming more bureaucratic. However, the outline identifies the important features of the P&NPO policy context that challenge the conventional precepts concerning management and marketing.

In summary, P&NPOs formulate lofty goals, but recognize that they may be difficult to reach and that the pursuit will be complex because it is conducted in an open and turbulent context. The ambiguity of goals, informality of management, indeterminacy of technologies, and the reflexive approach to policymaking must be considered basic conditions—the *foundations* on which one hopes to construct novel policy prescrip-

TABLE 4.1   Policy Characteristics of P&NPOs

1. Organizational purpose is defined in terms of social ideals and refined by professional norms. There is a constant struggle for organizational legitimacy.

2. Organizations adopt an open systems policy, which includes a high degree of involvement and choice for organization members and open access to the policy process for nonmembers perceived as possessing critical resources for the organization.

3. Goal formulation is a bargaining process involving many organizational members and nonmembers. Frequently, this occurs during or even after organizational performance.

4. Goals are ambiguous and can be mutually incompatible. Goals fluctuate from member to member, time to time, and across relevant segments of the public.

5. The organization attempts to generate an informal management climate around the personal characteristics of leaders, the processes of social action, and emergent situations.

6. The policy development system is oriented toward general activity domains, thrusts, or directions. It is incremental and contingency based. Situational opportunities and demands are the critical determinants of choice.

7. Organizational technologies are indeterminate, given the level of knowledge concerning interactive social and individual processes of change. Performance is oriented toward the efforts and processes of social action.

8. Success (performance evaluation) is defined by effort and formative criteria, rather than by the achievement of explicit outcomes or specific goals.

Source: Michael E. McGill and Leland Wooten, "Management in the Third Sector," *Public Administration Review* 35 (1975): 444-455. Reprinted with permission from *Public Administration Review.*

tions. Marketing experts and analysts need to understand this policy context and its implications for diffusing and generating marketing thought and practice. P&NPO managers and operating personnel need to understand and appreciate marketing and its potential for increasing organizational effectiveness and social performance.

P&NPO MARKETING

Marketing involves a proactive and responsive organizational orientation. Simply expressed, marketing philosophy and practice are concerned with the development and management of exchange relationships through purposeful benefit configuration, communication, facilitation, and evaluation processes (see Bagozzi 1975; Kotler 1973). As such, marketing is compatible with basic ideologies and methods of social action (Kotler and Levy 1969; Kotler and Zaltman 1971; Shapiro 1974; Kotler and Murray 1975; Fox and Kotler 1980; Fine 1981; Rothman et al. 1983; Lovelock and Weinberg 1984; Belk 1985; Crompton and Lamb 1986). P&NPOs strive to be innovative, flexible, and responsive. They must rely on their own initiatives to generate sufficient resources and respond to appropriate societal needs and opportunities. These organizations are constantly struggling for legitimacy and for the resources accompanying social acceptance and approval. P&NPOs thus deal with a great array of social demands and opportunities and serve diverse constituencies. Despite a strong sense of purpose and vitality, most P&NPOs have to struggle and many do not succeed.

Marketing as a policy framework for P&NPOs does not ensure success, but can improve the chances of achieving it. Marketing can provide responsive and adaptive perspectives and decision frameworks to help P&NPOs understand and better articulate their goals; to find and develop the opportunities that most closely relate to a P&NPO's purpose and competencies; to design and implement more integrated and sensitive social action and human service programs; and to control, or at least, to learn about complex social efforts and their outcomes and impacts. This creates a bold challenge for both marketers and P&NPOs. A study of the areas in which marketing principles coincide with current P&NPO policy dynamics can suggest where these principles can best be applied and how to encourage more P&NPOs to adopt them (e.g., Bloom and Novelli 1981; Hirsch and Davis 1981; Murphy 1980; Mokwa and Permut 1981; Rothschild 1979).

1. *P&NPOs are involved inherently in an implicit process of marketing policy development.* Marketing is a generic organizational process that cannot be ignored. However, most marketing issues within P&NPOs are not consciously identified or managed technically as such because few policymakers have been exposed to formal marketing concepts and methods in depth. Many associate marketing with commercial activities, and some reject it on ideological grounds. Even board members with strong business backgrounds may not see the relevance of marketing to P&NPO activities. There is a vast potential for raising marketing awareness and increasing technical precision.

Before an organization is ready to accept and apply the marketing approach, it may have to change certain values and attitudes and build up its technical marketing skills. Marketing consciousness can be increased through educational programs or changes in P&NPO policies and programs. Relevant marketing concepts, terms, and methods can be defined to take into account the perspectives and policy orientations of P&NPO policymakers. However, marketing should be considered a generic organizational process, rather than a business activity that can be transferred to P&NPO contexts. When marketing is introduced through direct policy or program changes, the total experience must be carefully managed.

2. *Social ideals, "professional" service norms (from human and social action disciplines), and counterconventional organizational behavior provide the internal basis for generating P&NPO missions and policies.* Social problems are by nature difficult to define and to resolve. Thus, P&NPOs formulate missions that are idealistic. However, these missions are built upon important aspirations that evoke strong emotional commitments. Norms from human service and social action disciplines provide the action parameters needed to work toward the inspirational missions. Both social ideals and action norms tend to ignore organizational and management issues. A distaste for bureaucracy and a strong desire for a responsive and sensitive climate exists.[3]

An organizational "anarchy" often emerges owing to extensive decentralization and the decoupling of internal units, programs, and personnel, the purpose of which is to generate and protect organizational discretion and operating autonomy from potentially intense internal or external demands. This breeds and spreads policy ambiguity throughout the organization and its relevant context. As policy ambiguity becomes accepted, substantial power is anchored in the autonomous units or programs of an organization and in individuals. A benevolent anarchy protects ideals and action norms and personalizes responsibilities. However, it also produces extensive policy drift, which can result in conflicting, myopic, and reactive policies that counteract the commitment to responsiveness and accentuate ambiguity.

The organizational dynamics of P&NPOs can frustrate marketing analysts, but can also frustrate P&NPO personnel and their public.

Fundamentally, P&NPOs are committed to an ideology and are therefore charged with emotion. Policy ambiguity is a natural outgrowth of this situation, and suggests that professionals and qualified volunteers should have a certain degree of autonomy. Yet, P&NPOs often crave more systematic, coherent organizational dynamics. Thus, organizational development using a marketing perspective should precede program changes. A marketing perspective can be used to help P&NPOs articulate their basic missions and to identify the competencies that need to be improved and expanded.

3. *The responsibility for P&NPO marketing policy is widely diffused and shared among organizational members and relevant external publics.* Social action is value-laden and broad in scope. It is carried out by many participants who have many different roles. Despite efforts to gain internal control and autonomy, P&NPOs become highly dependent on their environments for support. Thus, P&NPOs open their organizational boundaries to include representatives from the environment in their policymaking. This may be largely a symbolic maneuver, or the public may become directly involved. Whatever the case, power becomes diffused and responsibilities are fragmented. Organizational dynamics and structures, as well as informal internal and external networks, reinforce this process. Nonetheless, dominant power centers can be identified. For example, the bases of power may lie with the executive director, key action personnel, powerful board members, select community elites, or decisionmakers in the funding network. Policies are developed through substantial bargaining, coalition building, and the acceptance of the inherent value plurality. A "political" style of policy development emerges.

4. *P&NPOs must deal with a varied external public, serve many markets, and constantly demonstrate their legitimacy.* Volunteers, clients, influential participants in clients' lives, funding agents, community elites, the media, other P&NPOs, and the general public coalesce in the P&NPO policy context. Consequently, P&NPO policy must apply to more than one public if the organization is to survive and be effective. P&NPOs must accommodate the plurality of values and diversity of expectations of their multiple public in order to survive.

P&NPOs must devise a multifunction, multimarket, and multisegment marketing strategy as their success depends on the ability to generate consensus and support for or tolerance of their policy across their markets. A challenge for P&NPOs is to expand marketing beyond the public relations function and beyond communication dimensions into a coherent philosophy and methodology for effecting and integrating multipublic exchange relationships.

5. *Many P&NPO policymakers engage actively and aggressively in market intelligence activities*. Many policymakers seem to prefer personal communication and informal means of gathering the information they need to reach policy decisions. Thus, they encourage intelligence activities, but seldom coordinate or systematically manage these activities. However, formal market research consisting of "needs assessments" or client feedback studies is not uncommon, although the technical quality of this work is often suspect. Even so, the data can be revealing. Research appears to be used mainly to justify or block policy decisions, rather than to reach the decisions. General studies, such as government reports and professional literature are used in conjunction with intelligence data to support personal experience and intuition. The credibility of the source and supportive value of the information appear to determine whether it will be used. Thus, although considerable information is collected in the P&NPO policy context, it is not the precise, situation-specific information marketing analysts have come to expect from consumer research.

The task for P&NPOs is to organize the available information and to improve the quality of the intelligence system before demanding or conducting client research. The personnel of an organization are capable of initiating efficient client research. Service professionals often interact closely with individual clients in a cooperative problem-solving effort and thus can help generate useful models of client behavior and satisfaction. In turn, this can be a beneficial policy experience for action personnel and it can contribute directly to their personal work. However, this approach requires sensitive design, elicitation, and analytical procedures that must be managed by the marketing analyst.

6. *P&NPO policymakers tend to identify significantly more mission-related program opportunities and demands than they have the resources to meet*. This problem is common in three interrelated areas of P&NPO policymaking: (a) resource attraction strategies; (b) priority establishment for action programs; and (c) resource allocation policies.

Resource attraction, which includes both fund and volunteer development activities, is seldom managed strategically. Many P&NPOs prefer to develop captive relationships with large funding organizations and volunteer bureaus that provide a steady flow of resources but usually limit a P&NPO's activities with respect to attracting and allocating discretionary resources. Other P&NPOs grope for funds and volunteers without any sense of direction. In general, P&NPO efforts to attract resources focus on the near term and tend to pick up whenever there is a strain on the budget or a specific situation warrants it—such as a local fund drive or volunteer fair. As a result, resource requirements and flows are matched poorly. The greatest problem for most P&NPOs, however, is how to raise funds and build a stable of volunteers.

When resources are scarce, P&NPOs must rank their action programs in order of priority. Usually this is done subjectively, without applying consistent or formal criteria across problems, proposals, and programs. This approach merely accentuates policy drift and makes it impossible to coordinate action programs, which end up competing for resources.

A P&NPO with a poor system of attracting and allocating resources cannot last long. Its programs cannot exist without an adequate resource base. Admittedly, the benefits and costs of social programs are particularly difficult to predict. That is why P&NPO efforts tend to be unprofitable. However, the lessons of strategic marketing can be useful for developing resource attraction strategies and for defining program parameters and priorities.

To attract resources, the P&NPO must be able to identify prospective donors, develop or accentuate appropriate benefits that can be tailored to prospective donor targets, and then implement coordinated resource market programs. The entire process can be conducted from a marketing perspective, but this requires significant redirection for most P&NPOs. First, they have to shift their attention from the short term to the long term. Second, they have to carefully assess the amount that will be needed and when. Finally, a P&NPO must thoroughly understand and be ready to manage its programs with full awareness of their opportunities and pressures. Resources are difficult to inventory and store in a P&NPO and thus must be carefully linked to the appropriate program. Moreover, different programs are attractive to different donors, many of whom want a say in the allocation of their funds. A strategic marketing approach to resource attraction can alleviate many such pressures and allow a P&NPO to focus on the action programs instead.

Product/market analysis can provide a sound basis for resource allocation, but the approach has not been widely adopted by P&NPOs. Perhaps some of them might object to having to articulate the conditions of social action market attractiveness (benefits) and the conditions of developing competencies (costs). Product/market analysis would also force them to define the role of each of their social action programs and to consider their comparative benefits in allocating resources. A P&NPO must also define its basic action programs, and the related resource requirements. According to the Boston Consulting Group commercial model of product/market portfolio analysis, most social action programs would be classified as "dogs" or "problem children" (see Chapter 7). All the same, the P&NPO's typical strategy will be concerned with development, rather than divestiture or deletion. Thus, the techniques of product/market strategy analysis require careful consideration and possibly reformulation for the P&NPO context.

7. *P&NPO action program policies are grounded in human and social service professional norms that emphasize the product/process dimension of the program.* The product is usually defined and developed from a paternalistic producers' perspective. Client involvement and the valuation, communication, and implementation aspects of an action program may receive little attention in the design stages. Many P&NPO professionals and researchers are defining human service and social change "product technologies" in terms of exchange relationships. This concept provides an excellent bridge between service marketing and generic marketing theory on one hand and social action problems and methodologies on the other.

Marketing concepts are particularly applicable to questions of product mix coordination, communication and facilitation, and test marketing methods can be used to improve product and program design. To have an impact, these tests must be sensitive to the P&NPO product ideology and to the relevant technical dimensions of the social action product.

One of the first steps in adopting a marketing perspective is to establish a center of responsibility for initiating, coordinating, and adjusting marketing activities. Strategic planning or marketing committees are usually set up and a director of marketing named. The person(s) responsible for marketing usually must serve as change agents in their organization. They must have the support of the board and executive staff (or policymaking body), and they must be able to work across a broad spectrum of organizational personnel and relevant sectors of the public. A serious marketing orientation must also be introduced into the entire organization.

Marketing programming means transforming the P&NPO's special ideas, functions, and values into offerings—specific causes, places, people, incentives, services, and/or goods. And, it means developing integrated promotion, distribution, and pricing strategies for augmenting the basic offering and facilitating an exchange. Marketing programs must be predicated on sensitivity and responsiveness to consumer values, needs, behaviors, and desires, and on analyses of competitive and environmental factors. Marketing programs can be tailored to specific consumer targets, or to a broad market. Market implementation occurs when the P&NPO—its contact personnel and agents—interacts with its consumer public.

8. *Evaluation is a critical, yet highly sensitive policy issue for P&NPOs because social action performance is difficult to define, identify, measure, and interpret with precision and without bias.* The current public demand for greater accountability within the social sector has created pressure for formal evaluations of P&NPOs. Many such evaluations have been critical of P&NPO efforts and effectiveness. Consequently P&NPO

policymakers see these assessments as a threat, even though they may otherwise insist on feedback, both for personal reinforcement and encouragement and for information that can be used to guide the behavior of their organizations. The evaluation climate is such that external demands for summative evaluations which attempt to measure composite levels of P&NPO effectiveness are at odds with internal concern for constructive feedback that can be used to structure a process of organizational learning. Too many of the recent evaluative efforts have generated conclusions and recommendations that are underutilized or not utilized at all, or that amount to symbolic gestures that provide little information of operational value.

Marketing evaluations are particularly useful for raising an organization's sensitivity toward its clients and other audiences and for increasing its understanding of consumer perspectives, behaviors, and contexts. Composite evaluations can also be used to establish a consumer frame of reference or baseline data, but these studies often take time to develop, replicate, and apply longitudinally in order to capture and present valid assessments. Thus, a framework establishing an ongoing consumer information program can often be a more valuable evaluative outcome, than the conclusions of a one-shot, sophisticated composite consumer evaluation.

The marketing audit contains an articulation of social missions, an analysis of the action contexts, and a review of social action program designs and implementation, with suggestions for improving each and the linkages of them. The audit can be tailored to different organizational needs and capabilities. In its simplest format, it can be used to show how marketing applies to the social action context. The marketing audit may be the most powerful marketing-oriented evaluative methodology for P&NPOs. The audit is diagnostic, constructive, and formative. It is also systematic, integrative, and comprehensive. Thus, it reflects the basic concerns of P&NPO policymakers. Yet, it provides a coherent policy framework blending social ideals and action with strategic marketing principles and methods.

9. *Marketing issues span the entire P&NPO policy process.* Marketing perspectives and methods can be incorporated in articulating organizational purpose; designing decision systems and structures; in attracting and allocating resources at the strategic, administrative, and operating levels in implementing action and service programs; and in managing program elements. There are many points at which marketing can be introduced into P&NPOs and places where marketing efforts can be extended once introduced.

P&NPOs usually adopt marketing efforts to support established programs or to attract funds, but the commitment to these efforts quickly dissipates. The power of marketing can be best employed in helping policymakers articulate basic missions, systematically organize programs around relevant markets and then initiate information systems and evaluation-driven planning processes. Despite the P&NPO's penchant for loose policymaking processes, there are strong pressures to strengthen these processes without generating insensitive bureaucratic structures. A responsive, strategic marketing perspective can be used to develop fundamental P&NPO policy processes that guard against bureaucratic insensitivity and inflexibility. However, policy processes anchored in a genuine social action/marketing perspective will be more enduring and have greater impact than incremental marketing program adjustments.

SUMMARY

Marketing concepts can be applied to P&NPOs, but will not be consciously accepted on merits earned largely in the business sector. P&NPOs formulate distinctive organizational philosophies and generate policy processes to enact and protect their idealistic purposes and operations. Despite lofty missions and responsive orientations, many P&NPOs do struggle to survive and to enhance the human social condition. Marketing concepts and methods can be helpful, but must meld with the P&NPO style and dynamics. Marketing perspectives can improve P&NPO policy development, but marketing must be understood and accepted by P&NPO policymakers in their own context. In addition, marketing analysts must become more sensitive to the P&NPO policy context.

Marketing offers P&NPO policymakers innovative thinking and inventive ways of doing. The organizational context and policy style of P&NPOs are novel and even uncomfortable for many marketing experts and analysts. Therefore, there is an opportunity and genuine need to exchange ideas, methods, and ideals in these two areas.

NOTES

1. There is no standard way of defining, describing, or differentiating P&NPOs. In the broadest sense, there are two main types of P&NPOs: government agencies and voluntary action organizations. Government agencies receive legal mandates and concomitant coercive powers to do the business of government. Most government agencies can be characterized as bureaucratic administrative cultures that are sanctioned and sustained to balance the public interest, productive service delivery, and intrusive political interdependencies.

"Government marketing" is the field of study relating primarily to these bureaucratic agencies and other politically driven organizations (see e.g., Mokwa and Permut 1981; Crompton and Lamb 1986).

The other type of P&NPO is the voluntary action organization. The members of this group are public but not governmentally administered, and they are dominated by ideologies other than "profit motivation" and "political action." These organizations are called nonprofits and are said to make up the "third sector." They embody "social marketing" practice and potential. These third sector P&NPOs are the subject of this chapter. However, many third sector P&NPOs drift away from their social action ideology toward political, economic, or bureaucratic goals. Moreover, within government and business, organizations or units often emerge that embody the ideals and characteristics of third sector P&NPOs and engage in social marketing. Thus, any simple demarcation is not really adequate. The tension of discovering, enacting, and maintaining the ideologies of organized voluntary social action should be the determinant factors in defining and identifying a P&NPO.

2. *Policy* is an umbrella term used to indicate the comprehensive strategic responsibilities, decisions, and actions of an organization's personnel. Simply, policy development involves the dynamic and complex processes of strategic analysis and decision making within an organization. These decisions focus on aligning internal dimensions of an organization with its external context and total environment. Fundamental elements of a policy development system include goal formulation, planning, operating, and control processes.

3. The idea of organizational anarchy is not meant to be negative, although it is counter to most managerial thought (Weick 1976; Cameron 1981). Organizational anarchy appears to be a typical path and natural strategy to protect and enhance individuation in organizational environments.

5

The Public and Nonprofit Sector in The Netherlands

GARY J. BAMOSSY

Vrije Universiteit, Amsterdam

Marketing thought and practices in the public and nonprofit sector are being accepted more slowly in Europe than in the United States. One possible explanation is that European countries have smaller markets and a stronger socialist orientation than the United States. Certainly, countries with different political and socioeconomic philosophies will have different definitions and priorities for the public and social services they offer their citizens. As a result, marketing practices are difficult to compare. Nonetheless lessons can be learned from the experiences of each in implementing marketing across different cultures.

Unfortunately, published empirical studies on social marketing in the P&NP sector outside the United States are difficult to find. Studies that are commissioned are usually conducted jointly by government agencies and commercial research firms, and the knowledge gained is seldom shared by countries. One recent example was a national survey on the perceptions and uses of marketing as a management tool by P&NPOs in one of Europe's wealthiest and most generous welfare states, The Netherlands. Marketing seems to be conspicuously absent from the Dutch P&NP environment for a number of reasons.

BACKGROUND

Since the end of World War II, the Dutch government has offered its citizens and resident noncitizens one of the most comprehensive and generous programs of public welfare in the world. (The Dutch word *welzijn* is more accurately translated into English as "well-being," rather than "welfare.") A constitutional monarchy, Holland has blended a rather unique socioeconomic structure of free market capitalism based on a long tradition of international trade with a strong commitment to public welfare. This "cradle-to-grave" welfare philosophy is administered and financed almost entirely by the federal government. All citizens and residents are entitled to a minimum wage, health care, housing, and cultural offerings. The Dutch enjoy one of the highest standards of living in the world.

Table 5.1 compares social expenditures of select countries of the Organization for Economic Co-operation and Development (OECD). Social expenditures is defined here as "direct public expenditures on education, health services, pensions, unemployment compensation and other income maintenance programs, and welfare services" (OECD 1985, p. 18). Table 5.1 does not represent the full extent of social expenditures in these countries, some of which have large private sectors in social provision—private health care systems and related insurance arrangements, private schools and universities, private pension, sick care and disability insurance programs, and flourishing charitable sectors. To present a full picture of social provision would require detailed data, which are difficult to obtain from these sectors. Nonetheless, Table 5.1 does give an idea of each country's commitment to social expenditures and does point out the high priority accorded social welfare in The Netherlands.

Government financing of Dutch welfare programs as well as other public programs for maintaining such infrastructure as the railway sys-

TABLE 5.1   Social Expenditures in Selected OECD Countries (percent)

Country	Expenditure Share as Percentage of Gross Domestic Product	
	1960	*1981*
Canada	12.1	21.5
France	13.4	29.5
Germany	20.5	31.5
Italy	16.8	29.1
Japan	8.0	17.5
Sweden	15.4	33.4
Switzerland	7.7	14.9
United Kingdom	13.9	23.7
United States	10.9	20.8
Average of the above countries	13.2	24.6
The Netherlands	16.2	36.1

Source: OECD Social Expenditure Statistics.

tem, comes primarily from two sources: corporate and personal income taxes (among the highest in the world), and foreign exchange revenues derived from export sales of Holland's large natural gas reserves. In recent years, the drop in the world price of oil has led to a drop in the price of natural gas. This trend, coupled with some basic demographic trends in the population, has caused the Dutch government to shift to a policy of fiscal conservatism in recent years. Many government agencies that administer public programs are now operating on reduced subsidies and budgets, and are learning to cope with austerity.

Like several other developed Western economies, the Dutch are faced with the dual demographic trends of the "greying" and "degreening" of the population. In 1984 one in nine residents was sixty-five or older; in 2030 this figure will be one in five. In addition, the number of young people will continue to decline. In 1984 there were 4.3 million people under the age of nineteen, and in 2030, the number is expected to drop to 2.8 million. These demographic trends have a direct influence not only on the government's tax base revenues and pension payments, but also on the demand for a variety of government subsidized services.

Some of these socially administered programs are already showing signs of stress. There are, for example, no commercially operated hospitals in The Netherlands. The Dutch Ministry of Health, through its national socialized health care program (*ziekenfonds*), controls the number of physicians, hospital beds, and other health care facilities throughout the country. Although basic and advanced health care facilities are available to everyone, there are critical shortages of facilities for certain types of cancer and heart surgery. For some procedures, there is a waiting list of two to three years before the patient can be treated in the government-sponsored health care institution. Growing dissatisfaction with the public offering of health care has created new market opportunities for the private sector. As a result of not having any domestic substitutes for this excess demand, specialized commercial travel agencies have grown up in Holland to book flights and schedule appointments for their clients with medical specialists in the United Kingdom and the United States. Other public programs such as those administering retirement homes, schools, culture, recreation and sports organizations, and employee unions will also be facing turbulent times, and will need to reorient themselves with respect to their product offerings and target markets.

Although many government-operated institutions are said to be rigid in structure and slow to respond, the environment in which they operate is usually dynamic, and often unpredictable. Some changes in the P&NP sector environment, for example, in demographic characteristics, are fairly predictable. Other changes, such as the price of natural gas and other economic factors, technological advances, and consumer attitudes and expectations are less predictable. This combination of decreasing government revenues and the subsequent shift toward fiscal conservatism, coupled with increasingly unfavorable trends in the environment, calls attention to the need for more efficient and effective management of Holland's social institutions. It is against this background that a field study was undertaken of a large number of P&NP organizations to determine their uses and perceptions of marketing as a tool for management.

THE STUDY

The Sample. The Dutch Central Bureau for Statistics lists more than 40,000 P&NPOs in its yearbook. The majority of these registrations consist of small clubs and neighborhood houses, and were not relevant to the study. Of the seven principal welfare categories of P&NPOs listed, a judgment sample was used to select 436 organizations for study at the national and provincial level throughout Holland, in both rural and urban locations. In addition, a cross section of organizations was selected within each P&NP sector (e.g., in health care the selected organizations included hospitals, policlinics, mental health organizations, and green cross). "Social work" and "cultural work" institutions are among the most numerous of the P&NP organizations in Holland, as is reflected in the sample. Table 5.2 lists the P&NP categories chosen, the number of organizations selected in the sampling frame, the number of respondents per category, and the type of nonresponse.

A personal letter on university stationary was sent to the managing director of each organization, explaining the purpose of the study, and informing him or her that researchers would be calling within a few weeks for a telephone interview. During the personal interview, the interviewer asked for the managing director. In some cases, the interviewer was referred to another staff member at the managerial level within the organization. Three unsuccessful callbacks were recorded as a nonresponse. Respondents who thought the study was irrelevant for their organization or who were unwilling to participate for other reasons were recorded as refusals.

The Questionnaire. A semistructured questionnaire consisting of three sections was administered over the telephone. The first section sought the usual demographic information. The second contained a list of potential marketing problems likely to be encountered in organizational operations. The third section asked about marketing personnel within the organization, whether or not external marketing consultants were used, and the reasons why or why not. The length of the interviews averaged twenty minutes each, varying from ten minutes to eighty minutes. In addition to the structured questions, the interviewers also noted

TABLE 5.2 Sampling Frame and Response Rate

Type of Organization	Sampling Frame	Responses[a]	Reason for Nonresponse	
			Unavailable	Refused
Religious organizations	23	10 (44)	4	9
Educational organizations	39	17 (44)	11	11
Health care organizations	78	18 (23)	13	47
Social service organizations	141	80 (57)	29	2
Social-cultural work organizations	104	55 (53)	19	30
Sports and recreation organizations	30	11 (37)	5	14
Employee unions	21	9 (43)	4	8
Totals	436 (100)	200 (46)	85 (19)	151 (35)

[a]Figures in parentheses are percentages.

general trends by verbal responses: the degree of interest in the survey exhibited by the respondent organization, eagerness to discuss reasons for the organization's use or nonuse of a marketing orientation in its strategic planning and daily activities, and whether a marketing orientation was actually needed in the operation.

RESULTS

Of the 436 organizations contacted, 200 completed the telephone interviews (response rate of 46 percent). Nineteen percent of the total sample was treated as nonrespondents (inaccurate address or unavailable after three recalls) and 35 percent of the sample was recorded as refusals (contacted, but unwilling to participate). The highest refusal rate (60 percent) occurred in the health care sector. The highest response rate was in the social service sector.

Chi-square analysis was performed to determine whether significant differences existed between respondents and nonrespondents in terms of organizational type, provincial location (rural or urban), and hierarchical level. The tests revealed no significant differences between the two groups on any of the factors *except* organizational type. Here, there was a significantly different (higher) nonresponse rate from the health care sector (chi-square of 26.3 with 6 *df* and $p > .001$). Running the analysis again excluding health care organizations produced no other significant differences (chi-square of 6.4, with 5 *df*, $p < .2$).

Nature and extent of marketing problems. Seventy percent of the responding organizations felt they had one or more marketing problems that needed to be addressed if the organization was to reach its goals or satisfy its public mandate. In many of the interviews the marketing term was explained, and this helped improve the interviewee's ability to respond. Table 5.3 presents the percentage of organizational types naming one or more marketing problems, and the most frequent type(s) of marketing problem encountered.

A few other findings emerged from personal interviews besides the results presented in Table 5.3. First, the organizations that showed the greatest interest in the survey were those in direct contact with their clienteles, and they provided the longest interviews. For example, even

TABLE 5.3 Types of Marketing Problems

Type of Organization	Percentage Listing One or More Problems	Most Frequent Type of Marketing Problem
1. Sociocultural goals not achieved; work	94	More/different target markets
2. Religious organizations	89	More users; more/different target markets
3. Sports and recreation	82	More users; more/different target markets
4. Employee unions	71	More users
5. Educational organizations	69	More users
6. Social service organizations	39	Goals not achieved; more/different target markets; need new products
7. Health care organizations	39	More/different target markets

though only 58 percent of the organizations from the social services sector mentioned having any marketing problems, those that did were likely to mention multiple problems. Second, respondents disagreed as to whether the problem facing the organization should be considered a marketing problem. While conceding that marketing problems existed (as defined by three researchers), "no marketing problems" organizations (about one-half of the 30 percent reporting no problems) tended to blame the sponsoring agency for the problem. For these organizations, "too few users" or "more or different target markets desired" was a consequence of another problem, such as declining subsidies, inability to innovate owing to a rigid bureaucratic structure, and so on. Taking the sample as a whole, the following types of marketing problems were mentioned:

Type of Problem	Percentage of Total Sample
Desire more or different target markets	39
Need more users	33
Suffering fiscal cutbacks from sponsoring institutions	26
Unable to reach goals	26
Have problems in assessing effectiveness of programs or services offered	21
Need new products/service offerings	10
Need to improve current offerings	9

It is interesting to note from this list that the need for new/improved products and service offerings ranks last among the potential marketing problems. These results reflect an attitude apparent during many of the interviews, which may be summarized as "We have appropriate products and services, but we're just too restricted in our ability to offer them to our clientele." The source of this sense of inflexibility was often the sponsoring institution, which, in assuming the role of "channel captain," set not only budgets, but policies and procedures under which other channel members are to operate. (A marketing channel is the system of organizations involved in the marketing of a product, the parties to the process. The dominant agency is called the "channel captain." Channel concepts are elaborated in Fine and Fine 1986.) A recurring theme during the study was that these government mandates precluded or preempted innovative marketing tactics.

Apart from the rank ordering of types of marketing problems mentioned by these P&NPOs, it is also interesting to note the different types of problems mentioned by the various P&NP sectors in the sample. First, the social/cultural, social service, and health care sectors represent organizations that are already seriously overburdened by a combination of high demand and limited resources. These are also the only three types of P&NPOs that failed to mention having the problem of "need more users"! Several conclusions can be drawn from forecasts for *increased demand* in these sectors based on demographic trends alone. As the population ages, the nature of the services demanded from these organizations will change. Furthermore, the "greying" of the population will also increase the demand for services in these sectors. These trends will only serve to aggravate the types of problems already mentioned by these groups: a feeling of not being able to achieve their goals, a need to serve more or different target groups, and the need to develop new service offerings.

At the same time, the organizations representing the other four P&NP sectors that responded affirmatively to the question on types of marketing problems *all* mentioned the need for *more users*. Attendance, membership, and enrollment figures in general are declining for organizations representing religious groups, sports and recreation clubs, employee unions, and educational institutions. This decline is due in part to the changing demographic profile of the population, and in part to changing social values.

Marketing Audit Results. While 70 percent of the responding organizations mentioned having one or more marketing problems, only 5 percent of the organizations reported having any individuals with formal marketing training on the policy board or in key management positions. Another 20 percent of the organizations had personnel who had participated in a marketing workshop, or through self-study had acquired some marketing skills beyond the level of public relations and advertising. These so-called amateurs were most often found in the education and sports and recreation sectors. The remaining 75 percent had no in-house marketing management skills.

P&NPOs without in-house marketing talent did not necessarily seek outside marketing assistance on a contract basis. Occasionally, they mentioned using an advertising agency or public relations firm, but given the limited marketing functions performed, these responses were not included in the analysis. Only 8 percent of the organizations reported using an external marketing consulting firm in the past three years, and in 80 percent of these cases, outside consultants were used only one time. Reasons offered for not using external consultants included "We don't have any marketing problems" (37 percent), "Consultants are too expensive" (31 percent), "It is not our habit/never thought about it" (25 percent), and "Our sponsoring institution has internal advisors" (20 percent). These results are consistent with the results of a 1985 field study carried out by a commercial market research firm investigating the use of external marketing consultants in the Dutch P&NP sector. In the 1985 study, the predominant reasons for not using marketing consultants were "Nonprofit organizations do not have to be market oriented" and "Consultants are too expensive" ("Markt in Kaart" 1986).

DISCUSSION

The results of this study clearly indicate that a large number of organizations in the sample are facing a variety of marketing problems. With the possible exception of the health care sector, most of the respondents were able and willing to identify and discuss at least one or more of these. One would have thought that nonprofit organizations operating in a sector that was completely or heavily subsidized would provide the perfect seedbed for the marketing concept. Why, then, have so many of these organizations failed to adopt a marketing perspective at either the strategic or tactical levels?

First, the interviews with various organizations across all sectors clearly indicate that *marketing itself* has a bad image. At best, marketing was equated with advertising, and at worst it was associated with aggressive attempts to stimulate the demand for and increase the market share of commercial, tangible products. A number of respondents expressed concern that the application of marketing methods "would damage the culture of their work environment." At the end of each interview, the interviewers subjectively evaluated the respondent organization's attitude toward the concept of marketing (not to be confused with the marketing concept). Only 25 percent of the P&NPOs interviewed were positive about the use of marketing (as they understood it); an additional 35 percent were neutral or open, and 40 percent had a negative attitude toward marketing. (There are striking parallels between these results and those of a similar study by Fine 1983, of P&NPOs in the United States.)

Herein lies the irony of the situation: Both the P&NPO service providers and the general public would agree that the social welfare sectors in Holland are under stress owing to the increasing and changing nature of demand, coupled with declining resources (subsidies). Both parties in the exchange process would welcome a more effective and efficient market, if for no other reason than that it would be consistent with the emphasis that the Dutch culture places on providing adequate levels of "well-being" for all its citizens.

Although a marketing management orientation applied to the P&NP sector in Holland would obviously not immediately cure all the complex financial and social problems there, it would add new perspectives to the analysis, planning, and control evaluation activities of organizations operating in these sectors. To date, a marketing perspective has not had much of a chance to evolve. One reason is that the potential contribution of the marketing management concept is not well understood. In a field study (Van Leeuwert 1977) of the public's perceptions of the role of marketing researchers, 80 percent of the respondents had absolutely no idea of what a marketing researcher did (25 percent of the respondents thought that a market researcher was a *keurder van waren*—a civil servant who makes inspections of the quality of goods sold from stands in the open-air markets!) A second reason, already mentioned above, is that marketing has a negative connotation to employees in the Dutch P&NP sector. Thus, marketing is not just poorly understood, it is misunderstood.

A second, related explanation for the sparse use of marketing is that very few of the responding organizations have any personnel with marketing training. Given marketing's image in this sector, it is not surprising that it lacks torchbearers! This is an unfortunate situation, particularly at the higher levels of the larger, sponsoring institutions that set policies and procedures for others to follow. Of the various managerial skills needed to run any organization, professional marketing skills seem to be in the shortest supply in firms in the P&NP sector. They are otherwise well staffed with personnel managers, general managers, office managers, accountants, and volunteers. There are more than enough people to handle "daily administration" types of management functions. *Some* of the long-range planning activities are also well managed. For example, the Dutch Civil Servants Union has what is believed to be the largest pension fund reserve in the world, and this fund is managed by a professional team of investment counselors.

Third, although P&NPOs may be short on marketing personnel, they are not short on professional bureaucrats, or on rigid, bureaucratic procedures. According to Mintzberg (1979, 1983), professional bureaucrats are inflexible, not dynamic, and they set highly standardized policies and procedures. A number of authors have criticized the Dutch P&NP sector for being too bureaucratic, for ignoring strategic market planning, and for paying more attention to the hiring of personnel and the quality of their labor conditions than to the quality of service offered to clientele (van Reekum and Van der Velpen 1985). Subsidized nonprofit organizations in Holland use about 70 percent of their budget on overhead and personnel costs.

Finally, it can be argued that the lack of a competitive environment in the P&NP sector reduces the need for a marketing perspective. If clients are dissatisfied with the benefits derived from organizations in the P&NP sector, the "privilege" of going to the competition oftentimes simply does not exist. Although 72 percent of the sample reported having paying customers, this payment is often in the form of a nominal service charge, or direct payment in some insurance arrangement. Customer revenues in these sectors seldom cover operating expenses; 90 percent of the sample reported that their principal source of revenue was direct subsidy from the government (religious organizations and labor unions most often being the exceptions). This finding lends credence to van Reekum and Van der Velpen's assertion (1985) that subsidized organizations pay more attention to the wishes of the subsidy giver than to the groups they are mandated to serve.

One cannot conclude, however, that organizations in our sample are totally insensitive to their clientele. The two most frequently mentioned marketing problems were a need for more or different target markets, and a need for more users. This would suggest that, at least for the firms mentioning these problems, there is a willingness to do more than they are currently able to do.

SUMMARY

Public and nonprofit organizations that have already adopted the marketing concept and have successfully used marketing applications in their markets have found it to be a viable management tool for enhancing the exchange process between supplier and client, and an efficient and effective method of allocating their limited resources. Both the Dutch railway (still heavily subsidized) and the soon-to-be-deregulated telecommunication branch of the PTT (Post, Telephone, and Telecommunications) have adopted marketing orientations and are doing well in their respective competitive markets.

Early efforts at opening up service markets to commercial offerings have met with resistance. Entrepreneurial attempts to set up a commercially operated health care organization (an outpatient policlinic) were opposed by the government Ministry of Health (there have been long-lasting parliamentary debates and delays in granting the operating license), by health providers in the nonprofit sector who were apprehensive of the new competition, and by special interest groups (primarily women and senior citizens) who were concerned about rising costs and reduced care.

Much of this public opposition was not directed at marketing per se, but at the notion of changing the structure of health care, and at change itself. To the majority of the service providers and the public, marketing represents a move toward commercialization (with all its negative connotations). The image of marketing simply does not project a managerial philosophy that is considered to be compatible with the "culture" represented in the nonprofit environment.

What can be done to improve the image of marketing and increase its acceptance as a management tool in the P&NP sectors of The Netherlands? First, it is necessary to clear up some of the misunderstanding about the potential impact of marketing and about the concept of marketing management itself. The usefulness of marketing to the PNP sector needs to be explained to managers at the national, regional, and local levels. In addition, clear examples of how marketing can enhance the allocation of resources and help managers develop tactics for improving their organization's services should improve the image and acceptance of marketing.

Second, selected P&NP sectors should be opened up to more competition. Over the past decade there has been a growing trend toward "privatization" of government-subsidized industries throughout Europe. In particular, there has been a shift away from socialized or public health care systems (*ziekenfonds*), as more individuals are paying their own premiums for health insurance. As a result, commercial insurance firms and banks are taking a more active role in competing for this large market. This increased interest in the market has led a number of commercial firms to propose alternative health care programs for Holland, similar to the Health Maintenance Organization model popular in the United States. Although the trend of health care in the United States has been one of market aggregation (from individual policies to group insurance policies to HMOs), the trend in Holland is toward privatization (from a national plan of socialized medicine toward the HMO model). Both Holland and the United States are moving toward similar health care models, albeit at different speeds and from opposite directions. Surely there is much to be learned from the experiences of each. Perhaps introducing an element of competition into the Dutch P&NP sector will further highlight the usefulness of marketing as a strategic and tactical tool. At the same time, a marketing philosophy could improve the P&NPOs' chances of surviving and growing into a dynamic market, and could help to strengthen their contribution to the general welfare.

NOTE

1. The author acknowledges the data collection assistance of H. Griffioen, management consultant at KPMG KLYNVELD and E. Molenaar, project manager of the Science Shop, Vrije Universiteit. He is also grateful for their suggestions on an earlier version of this chapter.

6

Ethical Issues in Social Marketing

PATRICK E. MURPHY

University of Notre Dame

PAUL N. BLOOM

University of North Carolina, Chapel Hill

The late 1980s have been a time of intense analysis of ethical issues. Ethical abuses have touched almost all sectors of society, including business, government, the media, and even television evangelists. Whether these occurrences are due primarily to an erosion of the moral fabric of society, a relaxed view of regulation by government, more aggressive reporting by the media, or other factors is uncertain. However, the subject of ethics is discussed almost daily on all communication fronts. In fact, Time *magazine introduced an ethics section as a regular feature.*

Social marketers should not consider themselves immune from ethical scrutiny. Public and nonprofit organizations face a number of ethical dilemmas in promoting social causes. They will find it better to deal with such issues in the planning stages than to be forced to do so under pressure of crisis.

What is ethics? Some theoreticians consider it a branch of philosophy concerned with morality—"a systematic attempt, through the use of reason, to make sense of our individual and social moral experience, in such a way as to determine the rules that ought to govern human conduct and the values worth pursuing in life" (DeGeorge 1986, p. 15). The word "ought" in this definition indicates that ethics is a normative science. Marketing ethics, as a subset of business ethics, is concerned with moral issues arising from marketing practices, including advertising, selling, product management, and pricing.

Ethics is closely linked to marketing in the sense that exchange, the central concept of marketing, is said to be based on "fairness." Three conditions must be met for a fair exchange (DeGeorge 1986). First, the transaction must be entered into freely by both parties. A coerced exchange, then, is unfair. Second, the marketer and consumer both expect to benefit from the exchange. For example, the hypertensive consumer expects to benefit from dietary changes advocated by the American Heart Association, which fulfills its mission by promoting these changes. Third, both marketer and consumer must have access to appropriate levels of knowledge concerning the exchange. For instance, the problem with marketing the idea of using infant formula in underdeveloped countries is that most consumers do not have appropriate levels of knowledge concerning the use of the product.

We believe that social marketers should be held to an even higher ethical standard than commercial marketers. Because they are usually promoting the "social good" (e.g., the use of seat belts, the cessation of smoking, donations to charity), it is imperative that organizations marketing ideas and causes not run close to the ethical line. If potential consumers feel coerced or are not given complete information, the fallout in terms of goal attainment and public scrutiny can be great. Another compelling reason why social marketers should have a higher standard is that more *harm* can come to consumers and society from unethical social marketing (e.g., infant formula) than from unethical commercial marketing (e.g., puffery in advertising detergents). Therefore, the topic of ethics is one that should be foremost in the minds of all social marketers.

PAST RESEARCH

Little more than cursory attention has been given to the ethical dilemmas faced by social marketers. The first study on the ethical dimensions of both business and social marketing was published ten years ago (Murphy, Laczniak, and Lusch 1978). Using a typology developed by Kotler (1973a) to classify social causes, the authors concluded that the potential for ethical abuses by social marketers increases as one moves from beneficial social marketing to protest social marketing to revolutionary social marketing. Table 6.1 lists the types of ethical questions that may arise in certain programs.

In subsequent studies (Laczniak, Lusch, and Murphy 1979; Lusch, Laczniak, and Murphy 1980) it was found that social marketing can be a doubled-edged sword that has considerable benefits as well as some potentially harmful consequences. Specifically, there appears to be a connection between the techniques used to market social ideas and the ethical sensitivity to the ideas themselves. For example, individuals who

TABLE 6.1 Ethical Issues in Social Marketing

Type of Social Marketing Program	Example	Potential for Ethical Abuse	Possible Ethical Questions
Beneficial	Preventive health care program	Low	Is the information about the soliciting organization clear?
	United Way		Are fear appeals appropriate in promotional efforts?
Protest	Environmental protection	Moderate	Should attempts be made to present an objective argument?
	Campaign for improved TV viewing		Should certain individuals or organizations be singled out as targets?
Revolutionary	Pornographic marketing	High	Are the mass media appropriate promotional vehicles?
	Euthanasia		Should individual program developers be required to identify themselves?

Source: Reprinted with permission from Patrick E. Murphy, Gene R. Laczniak, and Robert F. Lusch, "Ethical Guidelines for Business and Social Marketing," *Journal of the Academy of Marketing Science* 6 (Summer 1978): 199. © Academy of Marketing Science.

view legalized gambling as an unethical product will say that promoting it is unethical as well. Despite these potential problems, governmental review and licensing of marketers is considered premature and probably undesirable.

The neglect of ethics in the social marketing literature is somewhat surprising bcause its "products affect the human condition more profoundly than tangibles do" (Fine 1987, p. 88). At least, an attempt has been made to construct a theoretic framework of philosophical orientations for analyzing behavioral change (O'Connell and Price 1983; Fine 1987). That framework provides a convenient base for discussing the ethics of social marketing.

THEORIES OF ETHICS

Four theories of ethics are said to be applicable to social marketing: natural law, utilitarianism, paternalism, and distributive justice (Fine 1987). We would add the theory of rights and the theory of virtue.

The theory of *natural law* has to do with peoples' self-determination. It posits that every individual should be permitted to choose what he or she believes is best for him or her. According to this theory, decisionmaking rests with the individual and not with the government or social marketer. Therefore, a decision to submit to a vaccination or a medical test should rest with the individual, and it would be unethical to force people to be vaccinated or tested. Food distribution to Third World countries without adequate education on preparation and use is an example of a social marketing effort that may have unethical aspects under the theory of natural law (Fine 1987).

The central tenet of *utilitarianism*, as originally conceived by Jeremy Bentham and John Stuart Mill, is that the right choice is the one that produces the greatest good for the greatest number. Commercial and social marketers often use cost-benefit analysis as an example of the application of this theory. Seat belt laws, water fluoridation, and the administering of swine flu vaccine could all be justified on utilitarian grounds, but not on the principles of natural law. Most social marketing programs and the promotional campaigns supporting them attempt to benefit large sectors of society. The question that some politicians and critics ask is: At what cost?

Utilitarianism also has its flaws (Robin and Reidenbach 1987). The "greatest good" notion may deny certain segments of society access to social goods. Since sickle cell anemia only strikes blacks, a strictly utilitarian argument might be used to oppose programs aimed at this disease. Second, at the individual level, a marketer may feel that an unclear or potentially deceptive advertisement is acceptable as long as someone might benefit from it, never mind the larger context. The current tactics some marketers use in the AIDS market, in promoting tests that may only help a few patients, are justified on these grounds.

The theory of *paternalism* states that authorities such as the government or educational and other institutions have a right to intervene if they feel that they are advancing the good of society. Much of social marketing seems predicated on the view that the marketer is more competent and better informed than the consumer. Many ills throughout the world are perpetuated on this basis, particularly where free speech and access to information are controlled. At the same time, mandatory public education in the United States stems from a paternalistic attitude, and obviously social marketers will not be effective unless they can convince consumers of their superior knowledge—otherwise, the marketer will "likely run the risk of alienating its audience and facing subsequent failure in disseminating its message" (Fine 1988).

The best known proponent of the theory of *distributive justice* is John Rawls (1971), who argued that both rewards and burdens should be shared by all citizens (for a summary of Rawls, see Laczniak 1983). However, some would argue that it is ethical to impose higher burdens on certain people such as smokers, alcoholics, and those in high-risk categories because there is higher risk in serving them. Distributive justice is appealing to social marketers because one of their goals is to "distribute" their programs and campaigns equally to their respective markets.

Moral *rights* are justifiable claims or entitlements, a classic example being those embodied in the Declaration of Independence. Ross (1930) is one of the most frequently cited advocates of the rights principle. Individuals have the right to receive an education, earn a living, maintain their privacy, and so on. But rights are counterbalanced by obligations. Social marketers have the right to convey their messages to the market, but they also have an obligation to do it in a truthful manner. The rights of individuals—especially those who are poor, uneducated, and illiterate—must be understood by social marketers. For example, a family planning agency promoting vasectomies must make sure that target markets understand the side effects and possible irreversibility of the procedure.

The theory of *virtue* was first suggested by Aristotle. Certain virtues such as honesty, compassion, loyalty, and justice are required in order to live a humane life in society. This theory states that only a good person knows good, can perceive moral dilemmas, and make proper ethical judgments (Williams 1986; Williams and Murphy 1988). When a person is described as an "ethical" business executive, the speaker is implicitly using the theory of virtue as a standard. The marketing application of this theory can be seen by looking at how a particular program or campaign will shape consumers. For instance, if social marketers raise the level of public fear through programs on the ill-effects of high blood pressure or cholesterol, they must recognize that they may be contributing to a consumer paranoia and therefore may not be acting in a virtuous way (Wassersug 1988).

These theories are not mutually exclusive and almost any action a social marketer might take can be rationalized by at least one of the theories. They are not meant to suggest "right" answers to moral dilemmas; they serve as a means of evaluating the promotion activities of social marketers.

GENERIC ETHICAL PROBLEMS FOR MARKETERS

Table 6.2 lists five generic ethical problems facing all marketers and three specific ethical questions associated with each problem—questions social marketers should ask themselves. Because marketing is the business activity with the greatest public contact, the potential for ethical abuse is great. Furthermore, since so much money is spent by the commercial sector on advertising, selling, and developing new products and on other "expensive" marketing activities, many individuals and social critics are skeptical about the value of marketing. They complain that marketing is unfair, manipulative, wasteful, and that it plays favorites and is intrusive.

Marketing Is Unfair. Some people believe that marketers lie, do not fully disclose relevant information, and are guilty of collusion, extreme embellishment, and planned obsolescence. If marketing and promotion are viewed as a continuum from absolute truth to complete lie, much of marketing activity falls in the middle, which can be labeled persuasion and embellishment (Murphy and Enis 1985, p. 434). Some of the best-known situations of this type are found in the marketing of insurance, encyclopedias, and toys to children. The famous Listerine deceptive-advertising case of fifteen years ago is a documented example of unfair marketing, and several recent cases involving collusion among soft-drink bottlers illustrate other forms of unethical marketing.

TABLE 6.2 Generic Ethical Problems for Marketers

Problem	Social Marketing Question
Marketing is unfair	How much disclosure is enough? How much fear is reasonable? Are appropriate selling tactics being used?
Marketing is manipulative	Is the idea/cause worthy? Will successful marketing of the primary idea/cause produce for an unworthy secondary idea/cause? How are competing wants judged?
Marketing is wasteful	Should scarce resources be used to promote offerings that are intrinsically valuable? How much should be spent on reluctant consumers? Would the cause be better off without raising the ante?
Marketing plays favorites	Do the social benefits of segmenting outweigh the costs? When has enough been done for a less-advantaged group? Who speaks for the mass market?
Marketing is intrusive	Is the cause being promoted in "good taste"? What information is appropriate and reasonable to seek from people? How can confidentiality of research results be maintained?

All social marketers should be concerned with the questions relating to unfairness shown in Table 6.2. Marketers must decide how much information should be disclosed to consumers. Vasectomies, the use of condoms, and high-fiber diets all have potential risks associated with them that social marketers need to consider. Sometimes, only the beneficial effects of such products are disclosed, and that may not be enough. The second question deals with fear. Social marketers can and have raised the level of fear in consumers and thus induced a behavior change. The marketing of cholesterol testing, long-term care insurance, and the use of seat belts can generate high levels of fear (Wassersug 1988). Our question is: How much is reasonable?

The final question concerning unfairness in social marketing pertains to the appropriateness of certain selling tactics. The selling approach (which may simply mean providing information) is often necessary to make consumers aware of certain social problems such as the need for high blood pressure screening and breast self-examination. However, certain selling tactics are less appropriate in the nonprofit sector than in the commercial sector, such as fund-raising "door-in-the-face" approaches, whereby a request is first made for a large donation, followed by a request for a smaller one. Although such subterfuge frequently is effective, do the ends justify the means?

Marketing Is Manipulative. Some critics believe that marketing's greatest sin lies in manipulating the consumer. Many of the ills of our consumer culture and consumption-oriented society are blamed on marketers, who persuade people to buy things they would not otherwise buy and do not need. Conventional marketing has been blamed for the high use of cigarettes and alcohol, especially among people, and for the popularity of junk food, expensive automobiles, and lavish homes. Marketing of fad products, an extreme example being pet rocks or radical new styles of clothing, also fall in this category.

To avoid this pitfall, social marketers need to examine the worthiness of the cause or idea. For example, drink milk, eat beef, right-to-life, right-to-bear arms, and not developing real estate have all been marketed as positive social causes. For at least some segments of the population, however, these ideas create economic, physical, or emotional problems. Others see them as worthwhile. Another question to consider is whether the successful marketing of certain social ideas can lead to unworthy secondary results. For instance, does the promotion of breast feeding among poor single mothers lead them to want more children; do antidrug campaigns lead to more alcohol abuse; do smoking cessation programs lead to eating disorders or dependence on drugs or alcohol; does condom use lead to more promiscuity? These are extremely difficult questions to answer, but certainly social marketers must grapple with them.

Still another question concerning manipulation is how can one judge competing wants? The age-old economic argument is that consumers have insatiable wants. Even in the social marketing sphere, consumers probably want more of a good thing. Does the active promotion of one cause or idea mean that others will be ignored? Every social marketer—whether a blood center, church, or social service organization—believes that its cause is most important. Aggressive marketing and promotion may manipulate consumers by placing undue emphasis on one cause to the detriment of another. One advantage of the United Way is that it has attempted to balance the needs of various social agencies.

Marketing Is Wasteful. Wastefulness is another problem plaguing marketers. The question here is how expensive is it to differentiate offerings and to communicate persuasive messages through personal and mass media? This problem can reach large proportions when "warfare" erupts in a market. Packaged consumer goods such as soft drinks, beer, breakfast cereals, and detergents are often cited as examples in this respect. The personal care products industry, which markets products having much more social than functional value, also come under fire from such critics as Ralph Nader for wasteful spending on marketing.

Wastefulness should also be a primary concern of social marketers, who have long been called to task for spending money on marketing social causes, even though they may have valuable goals. Health care providers have resisted social and nonprofit marketing for this reason. Beneficial causes such as drug abuse counseling and proper nutrition during pregnancy may not need to be marketed per se, but left to counselors and agencies. A related question is how much should be spent on converting "reluctant consumers." Some individuals will simply not fasten their seat belts, go for blood pressure or cholesterol testing, or engage in other behavioral changes that social marketers advocate. High levels of marketing effort may then be wasteful, and resources could be more effectively spent in other endeavors by the organization.

Perhaps a fundamental question to ask is whether causes are always better off after they have been marketed. A good example of protest social marketing can be found in the social causes advocated in the 1980s. There are groups for and against smoking rights, gun and arms control, abortion, and alcohol use. Nonprofit organizations sometimes raise the ante on the cause with modest marketing efforts and thus incur the ire of affected industry or social cause organizations. Self-interest then takes over, and all the conflicting messages merely confuse consumers and sometimes make them cynical about a particular social cause. Negative advertising does little for consumers or the organization.

Marketing Plays Favorites. One of the hallmarks of marketing is its use of market segmentation and targeting strategies. By focusing on potentially "profitable" markets, marketers may overlook or give second-class treatment and may neglect services to other segments of society, such as minorities, the poor, and the elderly (see Chapter 11). Like physicians, attorneys, and accountants, many modern marketing institutions such as supermarkets, shopping malls, financial service institutions, and others situate themselves in the more affluent sections of cities so that they can serve these market segments.

Most social agencies are generally egalitarian in nature and find such favoritism foreign or even repulsive. Still, they face the conflict of whether to cater to profitable audiences or to those most in need. The first question listed in Table 6.2 poses the classic utilitarian question. For example, is the benefit of helping teenage mothers worth the cost of allowing other parts of the market (older, but yet indigent pregnant women) to go underserved? The second question asks the potentially unanswerable question, "When have we done enough for less advantaged groups?" For instance, in programs to aid the education and health care of native Indians, how much should be spent to deal with the problems they have experienced for many, many years? Similar questions may be asked about new immigrants to the United States. How much should and can be done for them?

Another question concerns the "mass market." Recent literature on commercial marketing refers to such phenomena as the "mass market splitting apart" and the "vanishing mass market"—which suggests that more and more segments are coming into existence. In social marketing there is a potential danger of catering only to the most demanding and strident segments of the market. Many elderly and minority groups are afraid to ask for help even when they need it. How can social marketers overcome this tendency toward favoritism to reach large needy populations? Or, does the mass market even exist for some social causes?

Marketing Is Intrusive. The final question identified in Table 6.2 deals with marketing's intrusive nature. This intrusion can take two forms: the invasion of privacy, and the invasion or spoiling of the physical environment. The statement "marketing is everywhere" is sometimes made to reinforce this point. Advertising in all media (especially television), outdoor advertising, and direct "junk" mail, are the most conspicuous examples of the intrusive nature of marketing. Telemarketing, which is the new label for telephone sales, is viewed by many as an irritant. Even survey and qualitative marketing research can be potentially intrusive. At the same time, packaging that ends up as litter or waste in our oceans and rivers is intrusive to all who enjoy an uncluttered physical environment.

Social marketers need to be aware of the intrusiveness of their messages. Is the cause being promoted by methods that are in "good taste"? Do family planning agencies, for example, use good taste in promoting condoms and other birth control methods? Other organizations must also make sure they meet the standards of propriety. For example, smoking cessation programs should avoid calling smokers "butt-heads" and breast self-examination programs must exercise caution in considering the use of nudity in messages.

Those engaged in marketing research for social causes should also be aware of the particular ethical issues they may face over and above those experienced by commercial marketing researchers. For example, they must establish standards of reasonable and appropriate information demands. Marketing researchers need to recognize that some information they seek is highly sensitive—such as past sexual history, donation to social causes, and for some, membership in social clubs or organizations. Even if these data can be obtained, the researcher has an ethical responsibility to protect the identity of the respondents. Difficult questions arise when the respondent is a teenager who is sexually active or an employee who is a drug abuser.

The generic problems summarized in Table 6.2 are those faced by all marketers and require their close attention. Although there are few easy answers to these questions, it is important to ask them. Just raising them will help the social marketer become more attentive to ethical concerns and reduce the risk of violating ethical norms.

EMERGING ETHICAL CONCERNS

The ethical problems described in the preceding section have troubled social marketers for some time. In addition, we see new ethical concerns emerging from social marketing practices in the 1990s, particularly as a result of the growth of cause-related marketing (see Chapter 14 for additional discussion).

Cause-related marketing has been defined as follows: "Cause-related marketing is the process of formulating and implementing marketing activities that are characterized by an offer from the firm to contribute a specified amount to a designated cause when customers engage in revenue-providing exchanges that satisfy organizational and individual objectives" (Varadarajan and Menon 1988, p. 60). Ideally, both commercial and social marketers benefit from this partnership. The name "cause-related marketing" originated with American Express's contribution to the Statue of Liberty restoration. One ethical issue that arises here is the conflict of interest between the causes and the participants (Varadarajan and Menon 1988, p. 72). Another is whether P&NPOs promoting social causes are willing to pair up with just any willing corporate sponsor. For example, an ad campaign running in late summer of 1988 stated that for each purchase of Bud or Bud Light beer during a specified period of time, a donation would be made to the Muscular Dystrophy Association (MDA). The question is whether Anheuser Busch and the MDA have the same goals, and whether the MDA wants to be associated with a product having potentially harmful side effects.

Another emerging ethical issue relates to the promotion of controversial ideas such as drug and AIDS testing in the workplace. The risks to companies and organizations are great in terms of lost time from work and ineffective employees. However, those advocating the widespread use of involuntary testing must recognize that such procedures violate the rights of individuals. The larger question here concerns the common and social good versus the individual good. This is a classic case of utilitarian/paternalism versus natural law/rights. Whether this cause should be promoted is being studied by medical ethicists, but marketers must also recognize the ethical dilemmas such programs can cause.

SUMMARY

Social marketers cannot ignore the ethical issues of their discipline. The principal ones have to do with the marketer's obligation to be fair, truthful, and open in their exchange relationships, and not to be manipulative, wasteful, or intrusive. P&NPO administrators must be prepared to grapple with these questions if they hope to maintain high standards of behavior for their profession.

PART TWO

Social Marketing Processes

7

Product Management in Social Marketing

SEYMOUR H. FINE

Rutgers, The State University of New Jersey

A key position among commercial marketing executives is that of the product manager who is responsible for overseeing one or more items in the firm's product assortment, its "product mix." The product is defined as something having the ability to satisfy human needs or wants; it is a tangible thing marketed by a business firm or a social cause or a program offered by a public or nonprofit organization. Overseeing includes all planning and control functions associated with the marketing of that product. The product manager's role is to ensure that a product being offered meets several requirements:

1. *The criteria by which consumers will choose.*
2. *The marketer's own standards.*
3. *A niche within the organization's existing "product portfolio" and its supply capabilities.*
4. *Legal, moral, ethical, and public opinion codes and mores.*

The manager is also responsible for segmenting the market and for creating the marketing plan. It is an awesome responsibility.

PRODUCT MANAGEMENT

Product management consists of numerous tasks: overseeing market segmentation; making decisions on brands and package designs, product positioning, product safety, the product mix, product form, and product differentiation; studying the product life cycle; and developing new products.

Market Segmentation. This refers to the partitioning of a market of consumers according to some criterion so that marketing planning may be custom-tailored to suit the unique needs of each segment. By catering to differing characteristics possessed by several submarkets, the organization hopes to penetrate the overall target population.

An effective segmentation program must ensure that

1. The segmentation criterion selected is appropriate for the particular product.
2. Individuals belonging to different segments are likely to react differently to one or more marketing policy instruments.
3. Those within a given segment demonstrate relatively homogenous behavior.
4. The number of segments formed is such that it is economically feasible to reach the most important target groups.
5. Segments are sufficiently large and reachable to warrant individualized cultivation.
6. The program will enable the organization to modify or manipulate one or more of the marketing-mix components. In other words, the newly identified segments will be addressed by modifying the product, the price, promotion, or distribution strategies.

The marketing scenarios painted throughout this book provide numerous illustrations of segmentation within the public and nonprofit sector (for example, see the discussions on segmentation in government marketing and in health care marketing in Chapters 8 and 11, respectively).

Branding. The objective in branding strategy is to encourage consumers to purchase the product habitually. A brand name, once remembered, increases the chance of repeat purchase because the product and its name become closely associated in the consumer's mind. At the same time, by assigning a brand name to a product (or a concept) the sponsoring organization implies that it intends to create and maintain high standards. For the sake of the long-term welfare of the firm, the producer of a branded item tolerates nothing but high-quality output.

The name of the sponsoring organization or movement itself may be a suitable brand name for a cause, as in the case of the Boy Scouts, Goodwill Industries, ERA, Gay Rights, and I Love New York. The appropriateness of the brand name cannot be emphasized enough. Thus an organization promoting education for Hispanics is called Aspira, Spanish for "aspire," and a museum in San Francisco calls itself the Exploratorium. There is an old saying that if you can't name something, you don't know what it is.

Packaging. A good description of the value of packaging causes was given to me many years ago by a public health official from India: "You can't sell sound nutrition practice in a vacuum; you must package it together with such ideas as clean water, sanitation, and preventive medical care."

Product Positioning. This is the strategy by which the marketer attempts to carve a unique niche for a product in a market of competing products. Product positioning consists of the following activities:

1. Listing the competing products. They could be other brands of the same class, or they might be substitute or alternative things vying for the consumer's attention. Thus, a high school graduate in pursuit of a career can choose between two competing universities, or between going to college and postponing higher education in favor of a job. The latter, too, is a competitive situation that the university must contend with.
2. Determining the most important criteria by which consumers choose the products under study.
3. Locating the "position" of the product in relation to its competing products according to these criteria.
4. Locating the position consumers consider their most desirable choice, the *ideal point.*
5. Examining the relative positioning of the focus product, competing offerings, and consumers' ideal, and using that information to frame strategic plans for product design as well as the other marketing factors (promotion, pricing, distribution, and research).

To illustrate, research has revealed that many vacationers seeking warm weather, the wild West's scenery, and recreational facilities perceive the town of Yuma, Arizona, as "a gas stop between Phoenix and San Diego." Since Yuma itself is blessed with all these attributes, it has positioned itself against Florida, Phoenix, and Scottsdale with campaigns featuring such slogans as "Where's your sense of Yuma?" The strategy has not only been successful, but the ads have captured several awards and brought the town publicity on national network media (Bearden-Mason 1985).

The key task in product positioning is to select the most appropriate criteria on which to position the product. Rogers and Shoemaker (1971, pp. 22-23) suggest five "characteristics of innovations" which may fit virtually any product:

1. *Relative advantage* is the extent to which an innovation is perceived as better than the one it is to replace. Acceptance is facil-

itated if people see the new idea as advantageous over its predecessors.

2. *Compatibility* is the extent to which an innovation is seen as consistent with peoples' current values, needs, and past experiences.
3. *Complexity* is the extent to which an innovation is seen as difficult to understand and use. Obviously, the more complex the new idea, the less likely it will be adopted.
4. *Trialability* is the extent to which an innovation may be adopted partially rather than in its entirety.
5. *Observability* is the extent to which the outcome of adoption is visible. Thus it is easier to adopt the idea to stop smoking than it is to appreciate its long-term benefits.

Product Differentiation. This is the strategy of rendering one product different from another in order to

1. Justify a difference in pricing or method of promotion.
2. Cater to unique needs of some particular segment of the market.
3. Improve the product with a view to attracting a more desirable clientele. The widely held misconception that advertising is the major, or only important component of the marketing mix often diverts attention from the design of the product. It is a waste of resources to invest in an ad campaign until and unless the product being offered is perfected, that is, to suit consumers' needs and wants. Sometimes the zeal and enthusiasm of the organization must be held in check lest an inadequately designed offering is provided prematurely.

The U.S. Army's recruitment program provides an example of point 3. In 1979 the number of recruits entering the army was far below the level desired and, what was worse, those signing up had a very poor education. Less than 55 percent had graduated from high school. An intensive product improvement campaign was undertaken to raise the pay and put greater emphasis on education and career opportunities. This was the "Be All You Can Be" campaign, which replaced earlier patriotic themes. By 1985, a few year later, the army had not only increased the number of recruits, but 91 percent of enlistees had graduated from high school (Achenbaum 1986).

Product Form. Product form follows differentiation. A social product is available in various forms just as an automobile, for example, may take the form of a sedan, compact, and so forth. Health services may take preventative, ambulatory, or recorded (Tel-Med) form. Product form enables the consumer to distinguish among several types of product offerings. The marketer's goal is to make a specific product type available to suit the distinct needs of each market segment.

Product Safety. The rules of ethics and of law have been established to protect consumers from potentially harmful products such as electrical appliances, fondue dishes, stepladders, and certain foods and drugs. Manufacturers need to be on the alert for possible hazards to consumers, no matter how remote. Similarly, the "producers" of certain social causes must make sure that they do not infringe on civil liberties or cause bodily harm. Examples are the abortion and antiabortion movements, pornography, the exclusivity of men's clubs, and numerous other feminist and civil rights causes.

When seat belts were first advocated, some feared that an accident victim might be worse off if locked in place. National Rifle Association supporters are constantly urged to consider the dangers of indiscriminate firearm sales. Product safety may be a concern in the deinstitutionalization of mental patients released into residential communities, particularly when a main-streamed individual demonstrates antisocial behavior. And the 911 emergency number is constantly plagued with calls about trivial matters.

Marketers of social products, especially controversial issues, must design their offerings and the messages to be used in promoting those offerings with the potential repercussions in mind.

The Product Life Cycle (PLC). Like living organisms, most products follow a cycle from their inception, which takes them through periods of growth and saturation and ends in their eventual demise. Marketers need to know what stage of the life cycle a product is passing through at any given point in time. Each stage may require a specific "marketing mix" with some optimum combination of promotion, pricing, distribution, and research resource allocation. The stages that social products pass through resemble those typical of ordinary products.

Suppose that the "cold war" is considered a product in a marketing analysis of foreign policy. Then, according to PLC theory, "The concepts, issues and positions marketed by the U.S. should not be approached as static phenomena. They envolve, and many eventually become obsolete. Possible examples are free trade and the gold standard. As the product evolves, the appropriate marketing strategy will change" (Morris 1985, p. 57).

A great many concepts are such that the more rapidly they move through the PLC, the sooner they decline. That is, the wider their acceptance, the sooner does the need for them cease to exist. Concepts in this category include population control, the prevention of shoplifting, foreign aid, cancer research, and literacy, to mention a few. They may be described as *self-terminating* in that their rate of decline are directly proportional to their rate of adoption. Hence their adoption automatically implies their demise.

Organizations sponsoring self-terminating ideas, like commercial product managers, must take the time to consider what they will offer for an encore. Moreover, they must do this early in the life cycle of a product, long before the product enters its phase of decline. When the need for military recruits drops, one wonders why the elaborate apparatus that has been established to attract attention—the kiosks, the personnel, the advertising programs and so forth—are dismantled. These facilities could, with little effort, be used in promoting any of a large number of new causes.

The stages of a PLC are by no means discrete, as is usually assumed. The process is continuous and its pattern often erratic and difficult to predict. Thus PLC theory is more effective as a measure of the value of planning rather than a basis for planning.

The Concept of a Product Mix: New Product Development. The mix of products offered by an institution to its consumers should be carefully examined to determine if it is too wide, too narrow, or just right. Although it may be difficult to say what is "just right," good business sense generally argues against operating a "one-product house." Sometimes only a small additional investment is required to broaden the product mix. At the same time, if the product mix is too broad, it can become unwieldy and difficult to manage. But if it contains too few items, the organization could become overly dependent on one of them.

The Institution as a Product. Commercial firms speak of corporate image, the impressions or perceptions people have of the firm or of its "personality." And their use of mass media to promote that image is called institutional advertising. Otherwise, one does not ordinarily refer to the company as a product. In the social sector, however, especially in the case of nonprofits, the product sometimes *is* the organization. As mentioned earlier, the Red Cross, museums, and Boy's Town are "purchased" by people deciding to contribute to, or to participate in them in some way. The effort put into image enhancement should be no less than that devoted to promoting the agency's programs.

These then, are the principal aspects of product management. Now it is time to look at two cases that illustrate these points.

A SUCCESS AND A FAILURE

The annals of social marketing are replete with sagas about programs that succeeded and some that failed. Two examples that are particularly interesting represent the best and the worst cases in social marketing. They are analyzed here in terms of the 7P's model.

The success case is that of *Save the Children Federation of America* (SCF), whose principal *goal* is to reduce human suffering throughout the world by means of self-help techniques. This organization has been operating continuously since 1932 and has offices in most of the countries it serves, and therefore is a highly credible source. The federation not only has presence, but it also tries to act as a liaison with local governments, to further enhance its credibility and overcome cultural resistance to its programs.

SCF has two *markets*. One consists of the needy, the hungry, the illiterate, and people suffering devastation of all kinds; the other consists of contributing organizations and individuals. The *product* in the former is assistance in which the consumer, that is, the host population, participates. The resulting partnership gives the "customers" a rare feeling of independence, which does not exist in many other aid programs. The other market, the donors, buy the good feeling associated with contributing to a worthy cause, as well as the inevitable tax deduction. Donors pay an appealingly low *price* in the form of an unusually low expense factor—12 percent of all funds collected is used for operating expenses. Beneficiaries pay a low "mystery price," the uncertainty ordinarily associated with receiving assistance when they do not participate in the program.

Federation management allocates some 5 percent of its budget to *promotion*, for advertisements in the style of documentaries and "specials" up to one-hour long. This produces an "avalanche effect" in contributions. The *channels* used are broadcast and print media, wherein the "sponsor a child" theme has "captured the eyes, hearts and dollars of hundreds of thousands of Americans" (Gilbert 1986, p. 51).

Probing is not given a great deal of attention because the emergency nature of the federation's products makes extensive research unnecessary. Decisions must often be made quickly. Save the Children usually bases program design on informal research and intuitive, on-the-spot interviews. Evaluation, too, is based on first-hand inspection by regional personnel:

> One measure of efficiency is the ratio of administrative and fund-raising costs to total expenditures. Another is the drop in infant mortality in target areas. A third is how quickly the agency can enable an impact area to become independent of its services. And in the broadest sense, the evaluations of USAID, the United Nations and other governments and multinational agencies, which give large contracts and grants to STC, are a significant measure of the charity's performance. (Gilbert 1986, p. 51)

What a sharp contrast to the often-quoted, and generally valid observation that nonprofits typically measure performance by the size of their budgets (Drucker 1973).

Another contrast is the following case, the failure, again described with reference to specific points of the 7P's model. On every point, glaring differences highlight reasons for lack of success. Admittedly, these two cases are extreme and the comparisons are "pat." The reality that both refer to very large institutions might make translation to the reader's own situation somewhat suppositious. Yet the philosophical concepts are apparent and one hopes the few lessons contained therein may be carried away.

The example of failure is the *Susan B. Anthony coin* introduced on July 2, 1979. The U.S. government had already made several attempts to put a one-dollar coin into circulation. The *goal* in this instance was to cut $50 million a year from production costs by taking advantage of the fact that coins last much longer than paper. However, this was the marketer's goal, not the customer's, as in the SCF case. That factor alone is a frequent cause of marketing failures, and hence should be considered an early warning sign when one is examining a program.

The marketer of the coin idea was, of course, the government, usually not one of the more trusted *sources*. Better results would no doubt have been obtained if the campaign had been designed so that banks were the source of the program. Consumer goods are usually promoted through retailers and banks are retailers of money. Yet, at a congressional hearing on the proposed coin, it became evident that 70 percent of U.S. bankers had never heard of the Susan B. Anthony dollar (U.S. Congress 1979). Officials made the mistake of ignoring what marketers call the "primary level of acceptance" and appealing prematurely to the consumer *market*.

The *product* itself had several flaws. It was too similar to the twenty-five-cent coin, and thus was not in tune with the concept of product differentiation. In addition, some individuals considered the feminist theme too controversial. The coin was also too heavy; Congressman Frank Annunzio of Illinois quipped, "The treasury would be required to issue every American a pair of suspenders" (Greene 1981, p. 12), which reflected the high *price* of adopting the idea. When elaborate *promotion* efforts failed, the government, in desperation, engaged a New York public relations firm (at a fee of $150,000) to enhance the coin's image. Not surprisingly, little could be done to correct a badly designed product and a neglected channel of distribution (see the discussion of public relations in Chapter 10).

Research into the idea proved sorely misleading, even though it had been conducted at several levels of the channel:

> There were studies and surveys conducted addressing the obvious questions of usefulness, circulation prospects, savings to the American people, as well as the image of Susan B. Anthony. . . . Our subcommittee heard testimony from the U.S. Treasury officials, the Bureau of the Mint, . . . the Fed-

eral Reserve Board, the National Automated Merchandising Association, the National Association of Retail Grocers, the American Bankers Association, the National Organization of Women. Other groups who submitted letters in support of the coin legislation include: The Daughters of the American Revolution, the League of Women Voters, the Women's Political Caucus, and Women's Lobby, Inc., as well as groups representing the elderly and the handicapped. (U.S. Congress 1979, p. 3)

How similar this case is to that of the Ford Edsel, except that the Treasury ignored history! The same year the Anthony coin appeared, the Treasury withdrew the Eisenhower one-dollar coin, which had been introduced a decade earlier with the same hoopla as its successor.

These two cases illustrate how the 7P's model can be used to analyze marketing phenomena. The model makes it possible to evaluate the program after the fact, as well as plan it.

THEORIES AND MODELS FOR MARKETING PLANNING

The principal tool of the product manager is the marketing plan, which transcends product considerations because it extends beyond the product, into the entire set of strategic marketing variables. It is often constructed from an outline similar to the 7P's model proposed in Chapter 1. One explores and analyzes the marketing situation in terms of each of the 7P's, thereby creating the marketing plan. The plans in Chapters 1 and 22 were developed in that way.

In addition to such concepts as the product life cycle and product positioning, mentioned in this chapter as well as elsewhere throughout the book, several theories and models from marketing and other social sciences can provide considerable insight into the analysis of marketing situations. As Kurt Lewin has observed, "Nothing is as practical as a good theory." In this approach, the marketer begins with the conventional 7P's marketing plan and then expands on it by incorporating other models in the analysis. The following paragraphs identify several such models and suggest how they might be incorporated into strategic plans for public and nonprofit organizations (P&NPOs). The title of each model is followed in parentheses by the name of the most relevant "P" of the 7P's model. The reader should be aware that these are mere thumbnail sketches.

Product Portfolio Model. The product portfolio model (product) is widely known in commercial marketing; it is based on the idea that an organization should balance different types of product offerings in some way so as to optimize cash flow. The model is the brainchild of the Boston Consulting Group and thus is often referred to as the BCG model. Four product categories are specified:

1. Stars—require high investment of resources to support high growth potential.
2. Cash cows—currently generate excellent returns but have questionable future.
3. Question marks—somewhat uncertain future makes the need for high investment questionable.
4. Dogs—probably not self-supporting and should be dropped unless needed to "round out" the total mix of offerings.

Briefly, the idea is that if one product is not profitable, it may be supported by the income from one that is more profitable. In the context of the P&NP sector,

> An investment is undertaken to enter a product market segment in its introductory (question mark) stage. This segment should gain market share and profitability in its growth (star) stage, and then settle into its maturity (cash cow) stage where it will generate high cash flows that can be used to finance new potential "stars." In the last stage of the cycle, the segment gradually loses market share and profitability and enters the decline (dog) stage. (Nielson 1982, p. 66)

Two notable examples from the social sector are the Boston Symphony Orchestra and Christ Hospital in Jersey City, New Jersey. The orchestra's main mission is to perform classical music. The organization also invested in the development and presentation of an ancillary product, popular music, offered along with food and drinks. Profits from the latter subsidized the main product, which was being provided at a loss. In a similar vein, Christ Hospital has opened nursing homes in order to generate profits to support the hospital's main mission, primary health care. These homes are cash cows that pay for the problem child. Nielsen cautions that an agency should not engage in this practice, which he calls strategic piggybacking, unless it is capable of effectively managing relatively unrelated businesses.

Growth Strategies Model. The growth strategies model (products and purchasers) was proposed by Igor Ansoff (1957), an industrial engineer. According to this model, the marketer has four possible growth strategies to choose from:

1. Penetrate existing markets deeper with existing products; for example, a conservation organization could initiate a direct-mail "reminder" campaign to encourage its members to participate in a trail clean-up program.

2. Develop new clientele for existing products; for example, municipal police could promote the crime-watch program to new homeowners.
3. Develop new products for existing customers; for example, a state park could institute a band concert series.
4. Diversify by putting new products into new markets; for example, a university could offer a discussion-group program for senior citizens, led by renowned professors.

Theory of "Chunking." The theory of "chunking" (promotion) evolved from the observation that short-term memory retains only five to nine "bits" of information for eighteen seconds. Therefore it is argued that brevity is needed to achieve high impact in communications.

AIDA Model. The AIDA model (promotion) is concerned with attention, interest, desire, and action. It is based on the premise that human behavior does not change unless a desire to change is present. However, that desire only arises if the individual is interested in the idea behind the program. That interest must be cultivated by capturing the individual's attention. Thus a campaign goal must be specified in terms of the level at which the marketer wishes to bring the potential purchaser into this hierarchy. For example, a church must decide whether to design advertising copy to merely attract attention, stimulate interest in religion, generate earnest desire, or actually invite church attendance. A different appeal is called for to attain each goal of the model.

Role Theory. Role theory (producer, place) holds that the typical occupant of a given position and in a given context is expected to behave in a certain manner. Because it focuses on interpersonal behavior, its marketing applications have been primarily in the study of buyer-seller "diadic" relationships (Solomon et al. 1985). It is obviously useful to the political candidate or to any other figure in the P&NP domain who is charged with creating desired impressions on others. That individual must study the context in which the appearance is to be made, in order to play the expected role. If I visit the offices of a public interest group espousing free enterprise, for example, and I encounter a receptionist who is sloppily dressed, I may be confused by this apparent "role ambiguity" and leave with a poor impression of the free enterprise concept. Similarly, an agency serving the needs of the handicapped would certainly be expected to employ handicapped individuals.

Cooperative Egoism. According to the theory of cooperative egoism (product) (Wintrobe 1983), philanthropy is based on the expectation that the gift will be reciprocated. Thus it is the opposite of true altruism, and is said to describe a stronger motivation than pure altruism. Furthermore, some would argue "that when a community becomes more altruistic, the welfare of everyone in it declines" (p. 255). This notion has bearing on social marketing because fund-raising is an important component of the P&NP product mix. And it does suggest that one approach to the framing of fund-raising messages is to stress donor benefits.

Hierarchy of Needs Theory. The Hierarchy of Needs theory (purchasers) lists human needs that must be satisfied in sequence. Until a lower order need is satisfied, there is little point in appealing to one above in the hierarchy (Maslow 1970, Chapters 3–7):

> Psychological (food, water, sex, shelter)
> Safety (security, protection, order)
> Belonging (love, acceptance by a group)
> Esteem (self-respect, status, reputation)
> Self-actualization (self-fulfillment)
> Knowledge (need to understand)
> Aesthetics (beauty, art, music)

I have often thought an eighth rung should be added to this "ladder"— fun, the need for exhilaration.

A society may be identified by the type of *social character* (purchasers) with which it enforces conformity to social norms (Riesman 1950). Three principal types have been identified:

1. A tradition-directed society ensures conformity by instilling a strong tendency to following tradition.
2. An inner-directed society ensures conformity by following an internalized set of goals.
3. An other-directed society ensures conformity through sensitivity to the expectations and preferences of others.

Zinkhan and Shermohamad (1986, p. 127) have concluded that "the United States is moving from a stage of inner-directedness to a stage of other-directedness. This suggests a trend toward consumption for the sake of others' approval and the development of an attitude-value system that is very sensitive to the standards of peer groups." For program promoters, the theory suggests segmentation is needed to discriminate between the three Riesman types and then each should be approached by means of a distinct strategy, message, media and so on. Other-directedness, for example, can be treated as the "keeping up with the Jones's" syndrome, which will provide a clue to the appropriate promotional design.

Social Exchange. Social exchange (price), the theory propounded by George Homans (1950), states that individuals engage in social activities only to the extent to which the perceived rewards are greater than the perceived costs. This probably best explains the underlying philosophy of all marketing transactions. For example, Alcoholics Anonymous has convinced many individuals that the benefits of participating in its program far outweigh the social cost in time, effort, and life-style change.

Systems Theory. Systems theory (probing) posits that any entity, of any size whatsoever, consists of a boundaried system with certain elements inside the boundary and other elements outside it. A typical agency, for example, is a system with people and processes within and a host of environmental factors outside the boundary. The latter include clients, competition, regulatory forces, economic conditions, and so on. The basic assumption of the theory is that the boundary is permeable, and the degree of permeability determines the ease with which energy (e.g., information) passes in and out of the system. If a federal agency permits ready access and response to inquiries, its system is said to be relatively "open" and thus its programs can be readily promoted. On the other hand, if its public perceives a closed-system atmosphere, its programs will be met with greater resistance. For optimum effectiveness, P&NPO policy must create a boundary that is sufficiently closed to protect confidentiality and resources, but open enough to allow certain information to flow to gatekeepers, opinion leaders, and other parties involved in the marketing process.

As such, systems theory may be used to analyze the "place" component of the marketing model—to examine interactions between and among the members of the marketing channel. However, it is listed here as a "probing" tool because it provides an overall view of the factors (variables) affecting the system's operation. One thus has a convenient checklist for implementing the two main tasks of a research project: preparing the questionnaire and identifying potential respondents

Reinforcement Theory. Reinforcement theory (purchasers) stems from the idea that any event (stimulus) that produces a satisfying response, whether by chance or design, creates habitual desired behavior—hence the notion of "stimulus-response." Usually credited to psychologist B.F. Skinner, this theory is virtually synonymous with the marketing concept that profit derives from the pleasing of customers. A warm, personalized letter or telephone call acknowledging a contribution to a fund-raising appeal is a reinforcing action in obtaining "brand loyalty."

Push/Pull Marketing. Push/pull marketing (promotion) refers to two strategies used in the promotion mix. Push refers to sales promotion and personal persuasive effort. Pull implies preselling by means of mass media to stimulate demand (pull) for the product. Some programs require more of one and less of the other. In the seat-belt campaign, the threat of a fine (push) seems to have been more effective than the extensive advertising carried out during the 1970s. On the other hand, interest in continuing education is generated by print and broadcast promotion, which appears to instill and further another important element in peoples' value systems.

Multiattribute Model. A multiattribute model (probing) is a hypothetical mathematical formulation representing the total set of beliefs a consumer holds about a product. A survey is taken of a sample of consumers. The questionnaire asks respondents to rate several specified attributes (of a given product) according to their importance and to estimate the extent to which the product is affected by each attribute. Its typical format is:

$$A_k = \sum_{j=1}^{n} (I_{jk} B_{jk})$$

where j = an attribute or characteristic of the product (a total of n attributes are specified), k = a consumer responding to the survey, A_k = consumer k's total attitude score, I_{jk} = the importance weight assigned to attribute j by consumer k, and B_{jk} = consumer k's estimate of the extent to which the product is affected by attribute j. A total score is obtained of all attributes (each multiplied by its corresponding weight) that the respondent believes is affecting the product. From these scores, the marketer obtains a diagnosis of the product's strengths and weaknesses and learns which product attributes to emphasize in the promotion campaign. The responses might provide clues for segmentation criteria. Finally, total scores may be compared across several products.

Product/Market Scope. The product/market scope (products, purchasers) is a listing of the organization's markets (publics, stakeholders, clients, etc.) and channel members, together with a list of products to be offered to each (see Table 1.2).

The foregoing is hardly a complete compendium. The literature in the various social sciences contains many other theories and models that have already been adapted, or are suitable for adaption to the 7P's. Although all models do not apply to every situation, the product manager should be aware of their potential.

SUMMARY

The marketing planning process consists of two main stages. First, the marketer constructs a plan using the 7P's model of Chapter 1 for the basic outline. Next, one incorporates theories and models such as those suggested above, where applicable. The plan emerges from the overall exercise. This plan applies to social products and programs of P&NPOs as much as other products and programs. Remember, social and business marketing have many features in common. The product management functions of market segmentation, branding, packaging, product positioning, product differentiation, product form, the product life cycle, the concept of a product mix, new product development and product safety apply equally well to ideas, goods, and services.

A brief compendium of models and theories was suggested for analyzing the agency's situation well beyond the standard marketing mix, such as that in the 7P's model. These models and theories can be used in enhancing the level of sophistication of the marketing plan.

8

The Role of Consumer Research

SEYMOUR H. FINE

Rutgers, The State University of New Jersey

The most characteristic aspect of marketing as a business activity is, of course, its close tie to the wants and circumstances of prospective customers. Marketing research plays a vital role in determining the nature of those wants and circumstances. Institutions in the public and nonprofit sector have begun to use marketing research in much the same way that corporations do now that more and more public and nonprofit organizations are attempting to learn how consumers feel about the design and delivery of existing programs and to obtain suggestions for new offerings. Agencies are also becoming increasingly aware of the need for surveying trustees, donors, businesses, the press, special-interest groups, and other organizations. Marketers use information on these audiences not only to design their programs, but also to plan promotion strategy. Considerable research is also devoted to the testing and evaluation of advertising effectiveness.

Research supplies not only valuable information, but also favorable publicity. That is to say, every questionnaire is a potential promotional piece and should be designed as such. When it reaches the group to be surveyed, it carries a message about the agency's mission and an opportunity for enhancing the agency's image. Even those individuals who do not respond to the survey might read it and applaud the agency's sincere effort to obtain feedback. Most individuals appreciate having their opinions sought out.

Plans based only on the initiatives of professionals are "producer-oriented." But the marketing approach, or consumer-oriented planning, implies that input will be obtained from those who are to be served. That notion is predicated on the philosophy that such individuals are best qualified to say what their needs are and how those needs should be met.

Marketing research may be conducted at any stage in the strategic planning process. Obviously, its results will be more useful to the organization the earlier it is done. Ideally, research should be performed before an organization opens its doors or before a new program is created. However, even if research is overlooked at the outset, it is never too late to generate data that may be used to make subsequent decisions and to modify plans (for an example of this type of neglect in a hospital and a university, see Murphy 1980).

In that connection a point made in Chapter 1 warrants reiterating: Consumer research is the most powerful and yet the most abused item in the marketer's tool kit. All too often it is either overdone or underutilized. Universities, as well as their constituents, have been surveyed themselves and have conducted surveys on others, ad nauseam. Yet, in this era of sophisticated computerized data analysis, it is frustrating to see data of poor quality or a year old or more that have not been analyzed or whose findings were never translated into action.

Probing, or research, is one area in which the public sector has some advantages over nonprofits and over the private sector as well. Government consumer research is often liberally funded, and thus makes it possible to create national samples (Bernhardt 1981). By contrast, most research, private and nonprofit, is usually conducted in a few select markets in order to conserve scarce budgets. For the same reason, sample sizes in government studies are typically larger. Furthermore, because results of public sector research must be made available to the general public, greater emphasis is placed on in-depth reports.

CASE STUDIES

Many cases can be cited to illustrate the way research has been applied in the social sector, but the four presented here show how the three standard methods of data collection can be used—mail questionnaire, phone survey, and personal interview—and how the marketer obtains both qualitative and quantitative information with each. These cases also reflect three common research objectives: assessment of consumer attitudes, testing of proposed advertising copy, and evaluation of advertising effectiveness.

Attitude Assessment. The marketing concept, as already mentioned, rests on the assumption that the marketer needs to be aware of consumers' needs, desires, attitudes, and perceptions relative to the particular product offering. In fact, consumer research is sometimes known as attitude research.

An example of how to approach this task is taken from hospital-based ambulatory care services (Flexner and Berkowitz 1979). Using a conventional methodology, the survey team first contacted focus groups in order to determine the most important attributes of hospitals in general. These attributes were later used in designing an instrument for a mail survey. The focus groups were made up of individuals who had not been exposed to hospital care in the previous six months and who had no relatives employed in the health care industry.

Next, some 5,000 questionnaires were mailed to randomly selected households in the area under study. Respondents were asked to rank the attributes in order of personal preference and to provide certain demographic information.

Results of the study enabled the researchers to prepare several strategies for developing hospital-based ambulatory care services for selected groups. They also suggested criteria for segmenting the market for these services in such a way that each segment could be appealed to on the basis of its own particular needs.

Copy Testing. The second case involved motivation research. This time the focus groups were the main source of the data.

In 1980, the Interfaith Hunger Appeal called upon the Marketing and Research Department of Ketchum MacLeod and Grove (1980) to test three proposed copy appeals for an upcoming fund-raising campaign. The objective was to determine which appeal women perceived as most effective. The researchers conducted two focus group sessions, each with twelve female participants who were heads of households in the greater Pittsburgh area. Half the participants were between the ages of eighteen and thirty-five, and the other half were between thirty-six and sixty. Each group contained at least three representatives of the three major religious faiths: Catholic, Protestant, and Jewish.

Copies of the different appeals were shown to participants, who were asked which did the best job of motivating them to contribute. Using the resulting information, the researchers were able to predict certain attitudes and behavior.

However, the methodology of this study is open to criticism. Focus groups constitute a very small sample, and results based on such a small sample are too tenuous to apply to a broad segment of the population. The next case demonstrates how to overcome that problem.

In 1981, the J. Walter Thompson Co. and ARS (1982), a service of Research Systems Corporation, performed research designed to measure the recall of a new Red Cross commercial. The commercial, featuring television personality Carol Burnett and a three-year-old boy whose life was saved through blood donations, urged consumers to donate blood and to encourage friends to donate as well. The ad was shown to 187 men and women selected randomly from the Chicago and Boston telephone directories and invited by mail to attend focus groups where they would watch an hour of television programming. The spot for the Red Cross was shown along with twelve unrelated commercials. Three days later, participants were telephoned and asked questions about the test program they had viewed, the overall goal being to determine the number of people who said they remembered seeing the commercial, with or without several clues to its content. When results were tallied, it was found that the commercial surpassed the average recall scores of other commercials. Besides creating a memorable impression upon viewers, it also communicated key messages to them effectively.

As in the Flexner and Berkowitz example, this project combined quantitative analysis of data generated by phone interview, in addition to the focus groups.

Evaluating Advertising Effectiveness. Copy testing seeks information about a promotion in its planning stages, but advertisers also need to know the effect of a campaign that has already been run. This is difficult to do because consumer response to an ad may depend on extraneous factors such as the state of the economy, the weather, competition, and so on. Nonetheless, advertisers keep trying to measure advertising effectiveness.

The U.S. Treasury Department would like to encourage older Americans to use the "direct deposit" scheme of handling social security payments. The department had been marketing the concept for some time and in 1983 asked the McCann-Erickson (1984) agency to evaluate the effectiveness of its "Money in the Bank" campaign and to determine whether consumers in northern and southern parts of the country expressed different reactions to the program. The latter was of interest to the Treasury because it had been suggested that Northerners feel more comfortable about having monetary transactions handled for them, whereas Southerners generally prefer to handle their own affairs.

To test that hypothesis, the research staff interviewed 150 individuals over the age of sixty. The group was divided evenly between males and females and between Northerners and Southerners. The study only examined individuals who received government checks on a regular basis but who did not use direct deposit at the time. Interviews took place in two northern cities, Pittsburgh and Baltimore, and two southern cities, Memphis and Roanoke. Respondents were shown copies of the campaign's printed ads and asked several questions about how they interpreted the advertising messages, what they liked and disliked. Certain demographic information was also requested. The results showed that the campaign had been more favorably received than a previous one used by the Treasury Department and that it had been more effective in getting its message across. The study also revealed that Southerners found the idea of direct deposit less attractive than did Northerners. It was therefore recommended that a special print campaign be targeted specifically to the southern market—a market segmentation approach.

SUMMARY

P&NP organizations can use marketing research to assess consumer perceptions and to evaluate promotion efforts, both before and after execution. Marketing research provides valuable information about how an organization may improve the way it serves the public, as well as direct contact between the group and its constituents. By matching the needs and wants of consumers with the mission of the organization, the agency can make intelligent strategic decisions that may determine whether it survives.

Such research need not be confined to large, well-funded organizations. Those associated with small agencies can replicate the methods. Scaled-down versions of these techniques need be no less effective than those used in the more elaborate projects.

9

Pricing Considerations in Social Marketing

MARY L. JOYCE

San Francisco State University

MICHAEL H. MORRIS

University of Central Florida, Orlando

A common misconception is that social marketing campaigns do not involve price, at least not one that can be managed. Although not measured in terms of cash, the costs of social marketing are significant when one tallies the time, effort, and life-style changes that go into this endeavor. Social marketing programs could be significantly enhanced if more attention was paid to identifying and managing these components of price.

First, however, the marketer of ideas and causes must recognize that not all aspects of traditional pricing theory apply to social products. The social marketplace is unlike the traditional marketplace in that the price mechanism fails to efficiently allocate resources or produce a balance between the quantities demanded and supplied.

These conceptual difficulties purportedly lead to practical problems for the social marketer attempting to determine and manage the price variable. One method that might be used to address such problems is the "public-social exchange perceived cost segmentation," which requires marketers to design marketing programs so as to reduce the perceived prices of specific social exchange transactions for specific segments of the public.

Those developing social marketing programs must employ creativity and flexibility to meet the special demands of price management, especially since price is usually intangible and the marketer does not control price levels.

Although social marketing is concerned with each element in the marketing mix—product, price, promotion, and distribution—marketers have focused largely on promotion up to now. It is easier to see how promotion functions in social change efforts, than to specify how to apply pricing theory to social marketing. The problems in this task are numerous.

PROBLEMS IN DETERMINING VALUE WITHIN SOCIAL MARKETS

Marketers bring a fragmented approach to the pricing of social products, in part because the tools and techniques they use, which are effective in a competitive marketplace, do not fit the requirements of social marketing. Prices have an allocative function in economic (capital, resource, and product/service) markets. Quantities supplied and demanded are functions of price, with markets clearing at some equilibrium price level. This suggests that the going market price is an objective measure of the value consumers place on a particular commodity. The question is, does some type of marketplace exist for social goods, and to what extent is the value of these goods determined objectively by a price mechanism (Kotler, in Foreword to Fine 1981)?

It is sometimes difficult to find in a social marketplace such phenomena as consumer needs and wants, a profit motive, an efficient price mechanism, forces of competition (supply), and a set of utility-maximizing consumers (demand).

Consumer Needs and Wants. Perhaps the most basic principle of marketing is that an organization must recognize the importance of concentrating all of its efforts on creating value for users. Value, in this case, is perceived in the minds of customers. The desire to identify and satisfy customer needs is the driving force that leads an organization to develop a coordinated set of product, price, promotion, and distribution programs.

Those who market social products attempt to convince people that they have certain needs they may not acknowledge, and should engage in behaviors they currently resist. Social marketers are, in general, more concerned with long-term societal welfare than with satisfying a particular customer at a given point in time.

Profit Motive. Economic markets are predicated on the concept of "enlightened self-interest." The efficiency of such markets is a function of the sellers' ability to maximize profits and the buyers' ability to maximize utility per dollar spent. But the social marketer has little desire to promote self-interest. There is no profit motive in social markets, other than a qualitative sense of social well-being. In contrast, profitability plays a central role in economic markets, both as an incentive for competitors to enter the market and as a means of monitoring or controlling performance. In the absence of a profit motive, the programs of the social marketer are subject to less competition from those holding alternative viewpoints. At the same time, the social marketer has no definitive measure of the quality of marketing performance.

Efficient Price Mechanism. Even where there is some competition among viewpoints—for example, concerning whether people should drive below fifty-five miles per hour, there is no price mechanism that assigns values to social concepts and efficiently allocates them. For example, to what extent is "practicing safe sex" more or less worthy of resource support than the "don't drink and drive" campaign? This is not to say no price is involved with ideas (see Fine 1981 on consumer adoption of ideas), but merely that social price is difficult to measure, as it is a highly subjective concept.

Supply and Demand. The concept of social price does not involve a supply and corresponding demand of ideas and therefore is considered a weak criterion of the value of an idea. Supply could be equated with the commitment of resources to programs directed at accomplishing a particular category of social change. Perceived in this manner, supply is not positively related to the price (economic and social) of social change for the target audience. If anything, supply should be a function of the perceived long-term costs to society of forgoing the social change—that is, of *not* getting people to give up smoking, to vote, or to stop littering.

Demand is equivalent to the willingness and ability of members of the target audience to engage in attitudinal and/or behavioral change at various price levels. It is not apparent, however, whether the actual tendency among members of the target audience to embrace such change is primarily a function of the perceived price. Also unclear is whether the demand function is inversely related to this price, as is true with conventional products.

These difficulties have important implications for social marketers, who must discard their traditional assumptions regarding the existence of a free market for ideas and concepts. What, then, is the role of price and the nature of pricing management in social marketing programs?

THE MANAGEMENT OF SOCIAL PRICES

The key managerial differences between conventional and social prices are summarized in Table 9.1.

TABLE 9.1 Comparing Price in Traditional Markets and Social Markets

Pricing in Traditional Markets	Pricing in Social Markets
1. Price directly benefits the seller.	1. Price benefits society at large.
2. Marketer controls price.	2. Marketer may have a minor influence on price.
3. Marketer attempts to maximize price.	3. Marketer often attempts to minimize social price (i.e., perceived costs) to the target audience.
4. Price is primarily monetary.	4. Price is primarily nonmonetary.
5. Price is quantified.	5. Price is qualified (perceived).
6. User typically pays price at time of purchase.	6. Price is incurred over time (cumulative).
7. Standard list prices are generally used, with some variation by market segment.	7. Price is different for every customer.
8. Higher prices generally discourage consumption.	8. Higher prices generally discourage social change.
9. Price is used to reflect quality.	9. Prices reflect the incompatibility of the social concept with currently held norms and values.
10. Price is strongly affected by competitor actions, with increased competition resulting in lower prices.	10. Competition is limited, but increases in competition are likely to drive up the perceived cost of a particular social change.

Costs and Benefits. Pricing strategists generally focus on the monetary costs incurred by the consumer, and give little attention to the nonmonetary costs inherent in every exchange. Monetary payments are indeed much easier to operationalize in commercial settings than in social settings. Similarly, available pricing theories concentrate on monetary payments.

Social marketers are not primarily concerned with determining acceptable monetary prices, or with maximizing monetary gain. Their task is to reduce the nonmonetary, psychic, energy, and time costs incurred by consumers when engaging in the desired social behavior (Bloom and Novelli 1981). However, they are constrained by a lack of information on these prices. Although monetary prices are certainly inherent in the desired social behavior (transportation costs, forgone income, etc.), these are minimal compared with perceived nonmonetary prices (Rothschild 1979).

Some consumers may view nonmonetary issues as benefits rather than sacrifices. For example, giving blood, exercising, or voting may initially be resisted because of high perceived social prices, but in time these may be seen as utility-generating benefits. This is unlikely to occur with monetary prices. Further, the perceived cost of social change activities is likely to vary among target markets. Consequently, it may be useful to segment the markets, as discussed later in this chapter.

In traditional markets, price represents revenue to the seller. Marketers attempt to maximize price subject to the constraints of demand elasticity. They are able to do so because they usually have direct control over the prices charged to customers.

Unlike conventional goods, social exchanges have benefits that take time to accrue to society at large. For example, an individual will readily understand the personal utility received from purchasing gasoline at one dollar per gallon—it will allow that individual to travel to a specified destination at will. The same individual, when asked to carpool two days a week, will see little direct personal benefit in helping to reduce atmospheric pollution because the results of having fewer people drive automobiles are only evident over the long run.

Control and Variability. Social marketers have little control over nonmonetary prices, except to influence how high or palatable social prices are perceived to be, and the social marketer's goal is usually to minimize rather than maximize the social price. In contrast, the marketer who manages traditional prices frequently establishes standard list prices, and may alter the price charged to particular segments of the market through discounts, rebates, and special deals. Also, the price will vary to reflect competition. Competitive pressures often lead to price reductions. At the same time, higher prices will be used to reflect product or service quality.

In the social marketing arena, a standard price rarely exists. Instead it varies from segment to segment and from situation to situation. Furthermore, the pressures of competition are not as significant. For instance, there are no programs encouraging people not to vote, to start forest fires, or to drink and drive. However, where competition is present, it may serve to raise the perceived price of social change. The more that people are encouraged through advertising to smoke, or through movies to be promiscuous, the greater may be the perceived price of not smoking, or of practicing safe sex.

In the last analysis, social marketers have fewer opportunities than their commercial counterparts to use pricing as it is defined in available price theories. As a result, they must concentrate on developing innovative pricing strategies that manage price as nonmonetary sacrifices or benefits—to the individual as well as society. It is a process that begins with the delineation of the various segments of the public that the social marketer must interact with.

PRIMARY AND MULTIPLE SEGMENTS

Types of Consumers. To understand how consumers view the nonmonetary component of social price one must identify these perceptions across the social groups affected. Each group may be considered a particular type of public, in other words, "a distinct group of people, organizations, or both whose actual or potential needs must in some sense be served" (Kotler and Andreasen 1987). A public can be categorized as an input, internal, intermediary, or consuming groups. An input public generates resources that are converted by intermediary groups to delineated consuming groups. An input public includes donors, suppliers, and regulatory groups; an internal public comprises management, board members, staff, and volunteers; an intermediary public includes merchants, agents, facilitators, and marketing firms. A consuming public consists of clients, the local public, activist public, general public, and media public.

Social price varies for each type of public. The appropriate social price will be a function of the applicable costs incurred and benefits received by each public, at the personal or social level. Targeting the appropriate public and delineating social price for each is difficult, because the exchange process that occurs in social marketing frequently involves multiple parties (Bagozzi 1975). Consider the following example.

The antismoking campaign has sparked a social revolution in America (Business Week 1987). Many segments of the general public have a stake in the campaign, but each may have a different view of the social price "paid" in "buying" the idea. The input public includes donors who give dollars to the American Cancer Society to help disseminate information about the effects of continued smoking. These donors could be private citizens or representatives of corporations who might view their social price as a monetary cost; for example, as a dollar contribution, just as much as nonmonetary benefit, helping to educate others about the effects of smoking. Regulatory agencies are also input groups that pay a social price in having to account to political constituencies for supporting legislation prohibiting smoking.

The American Cancer Society may rely on its volunteers as an internal public to attract more resources, educate groups about the effects of smoking, and help in mass mailings. These volunteers pay a social price in the form of a nonmonetary sacrifice or benefit, such as nonpaid time or altruism.

An intermediary public consisting of marketing firms, for example, might join the American Cancer Society in disseminating information by developing public service announcements (PSAs), often donating these services for the cause. The social price could be monetary, such as the loss of revenue from cigarette manufacturers who decide to take their business elsewhere, or it might be nonmonetary such as the time and energy spent on the activity.

Finally, the consuming public (i.e., the clients) constitute the primary public of the organization. The American Cancer Society would like to see a smoke-free society in which smokers pay a social price, for example, giving up the smoking habit in exchange for improved health.

Primary versus Secondary Public. In social marketing, the largest hurdles are usually associated with the primary public, the group that the organization is trying to convince to change its behavior, because the social price is deemed high. Social change evolves more rapidly when the public considers the social price to be low, or sees the price as a benefit rather than a sacrifice.

It is critical for marketers to identify the costs and benefits inherent in the social product through research, as this will enable them to better explain why the social price is "affordable" to the primary and secondary public. It is also important to communicate the social price in terms appropriate to each of the primary and secondary public segments, instead of blanketing the entire public with one social price message. There is little point in appealing to markets with different perceptions in the same way. Target markets with the greatest need for a particular social change are often most negatively disposed toward that change. Limited resources make it all the more necessary for the social marketer to identify the social groups being affected and their respective attitudes toward the social change effort. For that reason, social price management can benefit greatly from innovative uses of market segmentation.

A SEGMENTATION APPROACH TO SOCIAL PRICING

Our approach is based on Dickson's (1982) framework, which links personal traits and usage situations with benefits, preferences, utilities, and behavior. This framework is somewhat modified to link the primary and secondary public and type of social exchange with perceived costs, social product perceptions, and the resultant behaviors. The scheme is depicted in Figure 9.1.

Campaigns that address the rapid spread of sexually transmitted diseases (STDs) such as AIDS, herpes, and gonorrhea provide us with ex-

FIGURE 9.1 Public-Social Exchange Perceived Cost Segmentation

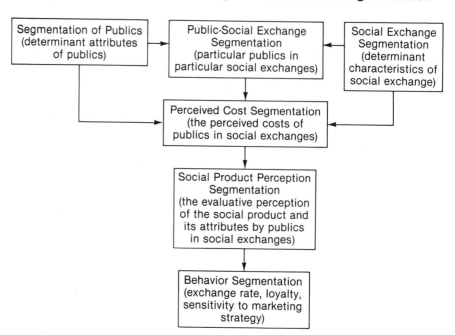

amples of social exchanges that could be facilitated by the framework proposed in Figure 9.1. For the sake of convenience, we use the university campus as an example. The framework can be implemented using the following six steps.

Step 1: Identify Relevant Public. The first step is to identify each public involved in the spread of STDs, both primary and secondary. This includes the input public (e.g., condom manufacturers), internal public (e.g., student volunteer groups), intermediary public (e.g., university personnel), and the consuming public (which in this case consists of the currently enrolled student population).

Each public must be studied to identify its distinguishing characteristics or attributes. A primary goal of such research should be to establish a better understanding of each public's level of involvement. For example, are condom manufacturers more highly involved in decisions regarding STDs than some other constituent of the input public, such as a local beer distributor who might sponsor a safe-sex day? Are faculty and administrators in the health care disciplines more positively disposed to implementing educational programs than those in the liberal arts? Are student volunteer groups concerned with the spread of STDs made up of more females than males, older or younger students? Are sexually active students more likely to seek information than sexually inactive students?

Step 2: Identify Social Exchange Approaches. The types of social exchange methods that need to be identified are the mechanisms available for bringing about social change. These can be legal, technological, economic, or informational devices (Fox and Kotler 1980). Legal methods are used where behaviors that can be mandated; for example, students may be required to undergo AIDS testing, or to attend an AIDS seminar. Technological methods are used where new knowledge and innovative developments can be applied, such as self-administered screening tests for STDs. Economic methods would attach a financial penalty or reward to undesirable or desirable behaviors. For instance, college credit might be awarded for attending sexual awareness courses. Finally, informational methods concentrate on information dissemination and education programs, such as brochures that are mass-distributed to the community.

Step 3: Assess Perceived Prices. Efforts should then be directed toward determining how each public perceives the price of different approaches to social exchange. For instance, students may conclude that programs encouraging sexual abstinence carry a higher price than programs that disseminate free condoms. University administrators, however, are likely to estimate the respective prices quite differently. This assessment also includes consideration of the likelihood that these prices will be paid.

Step 4: Construct a Segmentation Matrix. The social marketer is concerned not only with each public or with types of exchange, but with combinations of the two. A segment for a given exchange is one public involved in that exchange. The set of possible segments and related types of prices for our safe-sex example are presented in Table 9.2.

Step 5: Rank Segments on Acceptance of Desired Behavior. Having established these segments, the marketer attempts to prioritize them on the basis of his or her ability to reduce the perceived prices involved. The cells of Table 9.2 provide examples of monetary and nonmonetary prices for the possible segments.

Step 6: Determine Specific Pricing Programs. The final step is to move from social product perception to actual behavioral response. Social change is more likely to result if the social marketer can successfully reduce prices inherent in the social exchange, or encourage the public to replace present behaviors with proposed behaviors. In that way, the so-

TABLE 9.2 Perceived Costs of Social Exchange Programs Across Various Types of Public (A Safe-Sex Example)

Social Exchange Approach	Type of Public			
	Input (Condom Manufacturers)	*Internal (Student Volunteers)*	*Intermediary (University Administrators)*	*Consuming (College Students)*
Use of Condoms (Technological)	1. Monetary if manufacturer gives away	1. Time to disseminate information	1. Monetary to develop program	1. Monetary if not give away
	2. Time to plan program	2. Psychic Embarrassment Alienation	2. Psychic Angry parents	2. Psychic Machismo Embarrassment Fear of rejection
			3. Time to plan/ implement	3. Time Interruption
Promotion of Less Promiscuity (Informational)	1. Monetary if involved in program	1. Time to disseminate information	1. Monetary to develop program	1. Psychic Machismo Femininity Frustration Fear of rejection
	2. Time to plan	2. Psychic Embarrassment Alienation	2. Psychic Angry parents	2. Energy Restraint
			3. Time to plan/ implement	
Free STD Screens (Economic)	1. Monetary if involved in program	1. Time to disseminate information	1. Monetary to develop program	1. Psychic Fear of test positivity Admission of life-style
	2. Time to plan	2. Psychic Embarrassment Alienation	2. Psychic Angry parents	2. Time to be tested
			3. Time to plan/ implement	

cial product may be evaluated positively and the public is likely to adopt the suggested social behavior over time. Loyalty patterns to the sponsoring organization can be assessed, and social exchange rates can be monitored to determine if the segmentation analysis has led to the desired social change.

MEASURING THE EFFECTS OF SOCIAL PRICE

Once social price is defined for relevant segments, programs are developed to reduce the price, if necessary. Customer perceptions of reduced prices must be measured and desired behaviors adopted if social price is to be controlled. Limited budgets and significant measurement problems frequently dissuade the marketer from attempting to track marketing program performance. In the absence of follow-up research, however, the marketer has no evidence of the relative effectiveness of specific social price strategies.

The measurement process is concerned with two areas in particular: perceived price reductions and actual behavioral change. To assess price reduction, pre- and postprogram measures are needed to monitor changes in perceptions regarding the magnitude of the various social prices and benefits as the programs are implemented.

Social price programs may be evaluated by asking the following questions:

1. Have strategies been selected that can explicitly be used to reduce perceived prices?
2. What is the marketer's actual cost of reducing a perceived price to the customer?
3. How much of a change in perceived prices is desired?
4. To what extent are perceived prices of social change actually being reduced?
5. What is the probable response of the consumer to given levels of perceived price reduction by the marketer?
6. What is the actual extent of behavioral response to the marketer's social price efforts?

Unfortunately, social behavior is not readily measurable. Secondary data or direct observations cannot be collected for many social change phenomena. However, there are exceptions. For example, voting data can be used to assess the success of programs designed to encourage citizen involvement in the democratic process, and patterns in cigarette sales can be monitored to assess the performance of programs designed to reduce lung cancer. Also, behavior may be "spot-checked," for example, by randomly stopping drivers to see if they are wearing seat belts. Frequently, however, the marketer must rely on self-report measures of behavior and behavioral intentions.

TYPES OF SOCIAL PRICES

Once equipped with information about the perceived prices of a product offering, social marketers should be better able to develop appropriate social price strategies. Not only must pricing be singled out as a strategic variable, but it must be managed with creativity and flexibility.

Psychic Prices. Psychic prices are closely tied to attitudes and long-term beliefs that result from a multitude of sociocultural influences. A high level of involvement with an existing behavior affects the perceived prices of the suggested behavior. Therefore the social marketer might be well advised to approach targeted segments on one of the other nonmonetary prices. Another approach might be to give individuals the opportunity to engage in a desired behavior, so that in time the social product will be better understood and the perceived prices, psychic or otherwise, will become more tolerable. Opportunities to behave in a desired way have been provided by legal mandate and the introduction of an economic advantage. For example, seat belt usage increased as states passed relevant laws. Legal action appeared necessary because psychic prices related to freedom were apparently too high.

Time Prices. Time prices may be decreased by considering the following key dimensions of time:

1. Performance time. How much time does it take to carry out a social behavior? How much time does one think it takes to carry out the proposed behavior (objective and subjective performance time)?

2. Flexibility/fixity. Can the social behavior be carried out at any time within the existing time constraints and public's preference, or must it be scheduled?

3. Frequency. How often must the social behavior be performed to be effective?

4. Regularity. How critical is regular performance of a social behavior to obtaining the desired outcome?

5. Duration. Over what period of time must the behavior be maintained to produce the desired outcome?

6. Disruption/simultaneity. To what extent will the proposed social behavior require individuals to rearrange their current preferred allocation of time? Could the proposed behavior be done in conjunction with, or at the same time as other activities which are already part of that time allocation? To what extent is the new behavior perceived as disruptive?

7. Monitoring time. How much effort must be expended to remember to carry out the proposed social behavior? (Fox 1980)

Energy Prices. Energy prices can be reduced if the public perceives the seriousness of the outcome of not adopting a proposed behavior. For example, the physical exertion required to exercise regularly is discouraging to many. People must be made aware that the physical exertion required is minimal compared with the positive outcomes of exercise, such as a healthy heart and lower stress levels.

SUMMARY

Having recognized the need to "manage" or influence the perceived social price, the marketer will find it useful to assess specific prices as they apply to the various combinations of type of public and social change mechanisms. This exemplifies what is perhaps the most useful delineation of social price from a managerial perspective.

The main challenge for the social marketer is to quantify social prices and assign them to a particular social change program. Attempts at measurement must also reflect the temporal nature of adopting a given social change. At present, these efforts tend to rely heavily on self-report measures from the social groups of primary concern.

As the pricing variable receives more and more strategic emphasis, the need for creativity in pricing management will become paramount. The key lies in developing sensitivity toward those facets of consumer psychology that reveal "bargain hunting" with respect to social prices to be paid in the adoption of ideas.

The Parties to the Process

SEYMOUR H. FINE

Rutgers, The State University of New Jersey

It is often difficult for an agency to perform all its marketing functions by itself. If the agency is engaged in the marketing of commercial commodities, it can obtain assistance from various intermediaries—such as wholesalers, retailers, brokers, and agents—in what is called the channel of distribution. They are assumed to be knowledgeable not only about their particular role, that is, which marketing functions they are expected to perform, but also how best to perform them. The question of which functions are performed by which members of the channel is of lesser consequence than the strict requirement that all functions actually be performed. If a particular task is neglected by one member, then either that task is assumed by another, or the overall marketing process suffers because of the neglect.

In social marketing, the parties that assist the agency promoting a program consist of other agencies, various community organizations, the mass media, and a variety of key individuals and groups performing personal or word-of-mouth communication roles. These parties must be appealed to at the same that they function in the channel, alternatively called the system, network, or family of channel elements. They include governing boards, private sector firms, fraternal and service organizations, and a broad range of such word-of-mouth channels as gossip, rumor, publicity, public opinion, lobbying, advocacy, and propaganda.

MEANING OF "PLACE"

An important function of the channel is to ensure that the product offering is available at a time and place convenient to consumers. In fact, the distribution process is referred to as the "place" component of the marketing mix. Place is a measure of whether and to what extent the product will be accessible to the customer. Whatever the product offered—no matter how well designed, attractively priced, or elaborately promoted—the strategies and tactics leading up to the purchase are of no avail if the product is inaccessible at the crucial point in time and at the proper place to suit target consumers' needs and wants.

In economic terms, place imparts time and place utility to the product offering, just as the physical characteristics of goods add form utility. Furthermore, place adds value to a product. That is, accessibility enhances the price that consumers are willing to pay for the offering. A consumer derives more utility or satisfaction from an exchange if the product is available for purchase at a desired time and place, and with minimum difficulty. For example, under many circumstances, an individual will perceive an object to be more valuable if it is on hand at the point of purchase, than if it must be "special-ordered."

The "place" variable of the marketing mix (whether the popular 4P's or the 7P's advocated in Chapter 1) is properly executed if, and only if, all parties to the marketing process carry out their assigned tasks effectively and efficiently.

It should be noted that the channel belongs to the product, not to the institution. One does not speak of the channel of a hospital, of the Department of Health, Education, and Welfare, or of a physician; one refers instead to a channel for a health care product. Every product offering has, if only implicitly, a unique channel of distribution through which it is marketed.

IMPORTANCE OF THE STUDY OF CHANNELS

Marketing channels can provide a wealth of information about the institutions involved in the process, their roles and functions, and the quality of their performance. The particular arrangement of a channel might upgrade the place utility that customers enjoy for a product; that is, marketing through either a larger or smaller number of intermediaries could increase the efficiency of deliveries. So channel choice has a direct bearing on accessibility. By studying channel structure, the marketer will also learn about alternative modes of distribution, or alternative channels. For example, a producer might wish to sell through several intermediaries because each makes a unique and necessary contribution to the process. Or one might wish to shorten the channel by selling directly to consumers. Each arrangement has its advantages, while imposing certain constraints on the producer, who ordinarily designs the channel structure believed to meet situational requirements.

Channel design has been a concern of public and nonprofit organizations (P&NPOs) for sometime. Nearly two decades ago Taylor (1970) described a psychological rehabilitation project for the poor in which a network of organizations was responsible for the delivery of the social cause. Taylor attributed the success of the system to what he termed the "principle of coaptation," or an "interpenetration of personnel from other groups and agencies," such as local offices of the Division of Vocational Rehabilitation, the Office of Economic Opportunity, the Urban Renewal Agency, as well as health, school, and correction institutions (p. 74).

Channel Conflict and Leadership. Like the business marketing channel, the social network is at times beset by disagreement. The wholesaler may complain about the retailer's high markup and reluctance to carry adequate inventory, while retailers may bewail the wholesalers' neglect of sales calls. Similarly, collateral agencies may cry for better communication and reportage from one another and better follow-up; each may be seeking greater autonomy and more credit for the success of the program.

Conflict may also surround decisions on the functions assigned to channel members. Each may have a particular preference and be willing to vie with others for grants to be obtained, their image in the community, and the like. Conversely, certain undesirable jobs tend to be avoided and passed from one to the other. These include working with resistant clients or those with limited resources and playing roles with little status. Consequently, channel members should agree on the choice of a "channel captain," a person or agency whose competence inspires other members to look to it for leadership. Unless that role is filled, leadership is unspecified and fragmented, and no one, least of all the client, will know who to turn to for substantive decisions, and each member agency will behave autonomously. Confusion may increase if one party invites additional, and sometimes extraneous agencies to join the network, while another decides to drop out.

In the commercial sector, the channel captain often emerges in some natural manner. Motivated by profit, businesspeople have little difficulty agreeing on a leader. But in P&NPOs, leadership is frequently left to chance, and hence is overlooked completely. This is a serious problem that program producers must attend to if they hope to instill confidence in the consumer (for a comprehensive treatment of channel conflict in social marketing, see Andreasen 1984).

CHANNEL STRUCTURE FOR CONCEPTS

A host of community-based organizations (CBOs) participate in many ways in programs related to the spread of social causes. They include the entire gamut of private, governmental, and religious bodies, grass roots movements, and a variety of associations. Many are intermediaries as well as sponsors of ideas and issues; in social marketing it is often difficult to distinguish the producer from the wholesaler. The important consideration for the concept marketer is to determine which institutions are to be formally and appropriately included in the distribution scheme for a particular program. CBOs play a unique middle role in social marketing as *gatekeepers*. In that role, they can increase (or decrease) the credibility of the program.

Boards of Directors and Trustees. Although by definition members of a channel must not be part of the organization, they can be on the governing board of the P&NPO. (This applies almost exclusively to nonprofits and hardly at all to public agencies.) Directors and trustees are usually independent individuals whose functions are not administrative but advisory; they oversee operations and, of course, they participate in fundraising activities. Nevertheless, board members are "boundary people" in the system, with access to a wide range of contacts external to the agency (for details on board membership, see Haugen 1987).

Private Business Firms. The role of intermediary in P&NP programs is also handled by private business firms. Wholesalers and retailers are strategically situated to act as conveyers of ideas and social issues at the same time that they serve as conveyers of goods and services. Pharmacists, for example, have always given customers advice on health care. The pharmaceutical industry takes part in such health activities as the National High Blood Pressure Education Program, which promotes detection and treatment of hypertension. Indeed, it is surprising that book publishers are not involved to any great extent in the promotion of reading improvement domestically and in the upgrading of literacy worldwide. Business firms justify their involvement in idea marketing either on altruistic grounds or on purely economic grounds. Whatever the case, consumers are more eager to patronize establishments that offer access to the needed information. Moreover, the firm enhances its public image by participating in social programs.

More and more corporations are engaging in social marketing by sponsoring societal causes and programs (for example, Mobil sponsors Masterpiece Theatre). Whether they are doing so to create favorable institutional images or to improve the quality of the society in which they exist seems of little consequence. Both motives are entirely valid. What matters is that businesses partake of that mutuality. If they did not, a great many social products would be begging for sponsorship (see Chapter 14).

Fraternal and Service Organizations. Organizations like the Kiwanis and the League of Women Voters usually have one or more altruistic goals such as service to the community, in addition to their objective of socialization for members. Often they market ideas as well as services, and purport to be forums for the discussion of social causes, or to be vehicles for the dissemination of information on issues that the organization has taken a stand on. These groups adopt ideas they deem important and usually promote their adopted causes effectively, often through the sheer weight of numbers of well-motivated volunteers.

To a large extent, the intermediaries of distribution channels for ideas are the media through which information flows. The media are to concept marketing what wholesaler middlemen are in traditional marketing channels. In the latter realm, the media carry information *about* the product, whereas in the former context, information usually *is* the product. In fact, because a newspaper or a television screen cannot deliver a tangible good, media are entirely in the idea business. The most tangible good is reduced to two-dimensional ideas on the printed page. Media carry ideas.

Mass Media. Print media, and newspapers in particular, play a more prominent role than radio and television in advertising ideas and opinions. Social marketers have been attracted to print media because of relatively lower costs, as well as the desire for a high degree of audience involvement in an idea. Print advertising, by permitting repetitive reading, affords potentially deeper understanding of ideational messages than would be possible in a thirty- or sixty-second broadcast:

> Television seems particularly useful to the politician who can be charming but lacks ideas. Print is for ideas. Newspapermen write not about people but policies; the paragraphs can be slid around like blocks. Everyone is colored gray. Columnists—and commentators in the more polysyllabic magazines—concentrate on ideology. They do not care what a man sounds like; only how he thinks. For the candidate who does not, such exposure can be embarrassing. He needs another way to reach the people.
>
> On television it matters less that he does not have ideas. His personality is what the viewers want to share. He need be neither statesman nor crusader; he must only show up on time. Success and failure are easily measured: how often is he invited back? Often enough and he reaches his goal— to advance from "politician" to "celebrity," a status jump bestowed by

grateful viewers who feel that finally they have been given the basis for making a choice. (McGinnis 1969, p. 29)

Finally, broadcasters have been the target of the confusing Fairness Doctrine, which has, until recently, kept their interest in social marketing at a somewhat low level (see Chapter 2).

Many other media are employed in the social marketing channel—motion pictures, puppet shows, folk songs, telethons, bumper stickers, T-shirts, and a host of out-of-home vehicles.

Word of Mouth. Mass media such as the print and broadcast vehicles constitute channels for the rapid dissemination of innovations among large audiences in a one-to-many manner. The term *mass media* is synonymous with impersonal channels. In contrast, marketers are aware of highly effective *personal channels*, alternatively referred to as word-of-mouth (WOM), informal, or interpersonal media. WOM channels are especially useful to the social marketer because they are more trusted than mass media, being a two-way form of communication. (This is particularly true in less developed societies where the "interpersonal channel totally predominates in the diffusion of innovations" (Rogers 1976). But WOM is an expensive medium to use and the marketer is at the mercy of intervening salesmen to relay the idea effectively to the target audience.

A pivotal role in the WOM communication-influence process is played by certain individuals called *opinion leaders*, a term that usually refers to persons in a community whose opinions are respected, trusted, and sought out. Often the opinion leader is not a formal leader as such, in the way that a political figure is, but someone with no special "station" at all. More likely he or she is a well-informed, well-liked individual who keeps in touch with the relevant sources of information. In fact, the opinion leader is much like the channel captain. Both are intermediaries who, because of a dominant position, command a strong following above and below them in the channel hierarchy. Thus a nurse having a charismatic personality could emerge as a more important intermediary in the health care channel than the doctor. The hospital administrator and doctor, as well as patient, will consider his or her advice, clarifications, and interpretations of information authoritative. Again, a county agricultural agent is an official adviser to farmers, but the agent's position may well be preempted by a knowledgeable tractor mechanic who often transmits valuable farming ideas to customers. The challenge to the social marketer is to locate appropriate opinion leaders, to cultivate their interest in the cause to be promulgated, and to maintain satisfactory relationships with them.

OTHER CHANNEL MEMBER TYPES

Beyond mass and personal media, the social marketing network may contain other communication links not usually associated with marketing.

Information Dissemination and Education. In a broad sense, as already mentioned, virtually all marketing activity consists of the dissemination of information. No matter what the product, the marketer must inform the consumer of the benefits to be derived from an exchange transaction. The acquisition of information and education is a consumption process and includes not only formal schooling, but participation in lectures and seminars of all types.

The most obvious middlemen of ideas are the institutions in the educational sector. Students who attend schools (above the compulsory grade) have already purchased the idea that education is a good thing. But they are also being sold large packages of knowledge in various subjects, as well as extracurricular concepts. It is no wonder then, that many program promoters have asked educational institutions to act as intermediaries for ideas. One such promoter is the U.S. Agricultural Extension Service, which operates under university auspices.

Gossipmongering. "Gossip is a valuable social commodity," writes Rosnow (1977). "There is in fact, a close and very specific parallel between the functions and distribution of gossip and the patterns of marketing practices" (p. 159). Gossip comes in three varieties—information, influence, and entertainment—and there are three patterns of trade:

> *Redistributive trading* denotes that case in which resources are brought to a central operation and from there fairly dispersed, as when individuals make charitable contributions to some central collection agency which redistributes the donations to needy persons according to their requirements. *Exchange* is that case in which the value placed upon a commodity results from bargaining for economic advantage, as when goods or services are brought into the marketplace and sold to the highest bidder. *Reciprocative trading* refers to the establishment of an equitable ratio or balanced reciprocity in the giving and receiving of goods and services, as when farmers lend a helping hand to one another at harvest time.
>
> Informative gossip exists for news trading and to provide participants with a "cognitive map" of their social environment. Gossip exploited for purposes of influence is a manipulative tool with which A attempts to gain an advantage over B, or over C by persuading B to revise his opinion of C. Gossiping for entertainment is engaged in primarily for mutual satisfaction and amusement rather than to convince someone of a moral position or to

probe for news or confirmation of news. (Polanyi, Arensberg, and Pearson 1957, p. 159)

Other parallels have been drawn between gossiping and marketplace psychology:

> For example, it might be said that consumers of gossip, like consumers of any commodity in the marketplace, have their own brand of loyalties—columnists, tabloids, magazines. The consumption of gossip of all kinds may be analogous to the conspicuous consumption of goods and services in societies whose needs have been conditioned by competitive pressures; it also attests to the wide generality of a habit that ignores most sociological and demographic demarcations. Further, it can be observed that when news is scarce, the gossip-monger can exact a higher price for his tales. When the market for news expands, the amount of gossip in circulation will proliferate. If the transaction between A and B is mutually beneficial, whether equitable or not, it should result in some structural relationship in which future transactions can be more easily made. (Rosnow and Fine 1976, p. 162)

Rumormongering. Rumormongering is a form of exchange in the marketing channel similar to gossipmongering, except that a rumor usually refers to some specific episode; gossip is more general. Trade in rumors dates back to ancient Roman emperors who appointed public rumor wardens (called *delatores*) to act as agent middlemen who would bring rumors from the populace to the palace and then carry back other rumors to the people. "Psychological warfare is not new," as Allport and Postman (1947) have noted. The question is, "How much of history, . . . can be regarded as the reactions of important groups of people to current rumor?"

> A great deal, we suspect, for until very recent times the inhabitants of the world had little to rely on other than rumored information. Newspapers, the telegraph, the radio are late inventions. Before their advent the public had to rely upon some traveler to bring with him word-of-mouth reports, upon some Paul Revere to announce approaching danger, or upon the town crier to tell his own version of the day's news. Only a few statesmen and a few monarchs received written and sealed dispatches, and their source was not necessarily rumor free. (Allport and Postman 1947, p. 161)

For a rumor to exist, two conditions must be present: The tale must be *important* to both parties and the actual facts must be shrouded in some kind of *ambiguity* (Allport and Postman 1947, p. 33). Interestingly, both importance and ambiguity are key variables in the study of buyer behavior theory: A product's importance to a consumer motivates him or her to attend to advertising, while ambiguity in the promotion's message stimulates further search for information to clarify the ambiguity. What is particularly interesting is that people tend to recall the message of rumor while forgetting its source or the channels through which it was transmitted. One reason is that rumor, true to a cardinal rule of the advertising profession, typically is heard more than once. Redundancy and repetition make the message clearer and tend to mediate "noise in the system."

Probably the highest price one pays for adopting an idea arriving in rumor form is that it may contain inaccurate information. Another price is just the attention "paid" to the rumormonger who is in need of solicitude, possibly to fill an otherwise humdrum existence. In return, the rumor consumer obtains psychological benefits:

> In August 1945, a rumor spread to the effect that Russia declared war on Japan only because Russia received in exchange the secret of the atomic bomb. Those who believed and spread this tale were people who disliked the Russians and, perhaps to only a slightly less extent, disliked the Administration in Washington. Gnawing hatred motivated the rumor. But instead of saying candidly, "I hate Russia," or "I hate the Democrats," the rumor spreader seized upon a story that would *relieve, justify* and *explain* his underlying emotional tension. (Allport and Postman 1947, p. 36)

Thus rumor helps one to reason and often provides a plausible explanation for confused and otherwise unexplainable ideas.

Public Relations or Publicity. The marketing activity designed to promote a favorable image of an individual or an organization rather than a specific product is known as public relations. Thus, although marketing's product is engineered to satisfy the needs of potential consumers, publicity as a product, must appeal to all of society. The rationale for public relations stems from the realization that not only customers, but many other segments of the public, influence the welfare of the organization. There is yet another distinction between marketing and public relations: In marketing the sponsor is identified and pays the medium for delivering the message. In the case of publicity, media space is usually not paid for, because the notice appears as editorial matter, and the sponsor's identity is not necessarily self-evident.

A popular belief is that public relations consists of correcting a false impression people have of an institution. However, according to sound marketing precepts, if an institution has a poor image, then the appropriate course of action is not to artificially change that image through promotion techniques, but to remove the causes of the negative image. The relationship between public relations and marketing is implied in the very definition of marketing, which states that marketers produce products designed to satisfy the needs and wants of their market. The role of public relations is to determine what image people have of the institution and to devise a program to remove the causes of that image, that is, to improve the institutional "product." Press releases on behalf of the client are merely tools of enhancement, not corrective devices. Therefore they do not in themselves make for good public relations. A PR person who sets out to change people's perceptions without taking the necessary steps to correct whatever lies behind those perceptions lacks integrity and violates the marketing concept. A favorable image is not sold with words but with performance.

Public Opinion. To the extent that public opinion is marketed, the price paid in the exchange might very well be the surrender of the individual's freedom to choose a *private* opinion. Lacking the time, patience, and perseverance to inform oneself intelligently about social issues, one absorbs an opinion preselected by others as public, and then sinks into a state of unthinking conformism:

> Stepan Arkadyevitch took in and read a liberal paper, not an extreme one, but one advocating the views held by the majority. And in spite of the fact that science, art, and politics had no special interest for him, he firmly held those views on all these subjects which were held by the majority and by his paper, and he only changed them when the majority changed them or, more strictly speaking, he did not change them, but they imperceptibly changed of themselves within him. Stepan Arkadyevitch had not chosen his political opinions or his views, these political opinions and views had come to him of themselves, . . . liberalism had become a habit of Stepan Arkadyevitch's and he liked his newspaper, as he did his cigar after dinner, for the slight fog it diffused in his brain. (Tolstoy, in Carlson 1975, p. 43)

Lobbying. Lobbying is a form of marketing conducted by an estimated 15,000 professionals who canvas legislators in the U.S. Capitol's corridors and lobbies (hence their title) on behalf of their clients. They are intermediaries between special interest groups and lawmakers and are concerned with social and political issues. The product offering is usually a strong position on an issue, in exchange for favors, political contributions, and the services of election or campaign workers. The lawmaking consumers of this product pay for their purchases with time spent attending to lobbyists, but more significantly they must sometimes trade off their own convictions as well as those of constituents who hold opposing views. Lobbyists include representatives of the National Association of Manufacturers, the U.S. Chamber of Commerce, trade and professional organizations (such as the American Medical Association, National Rifle Association, and American Petroleum Institute), labor unions, and the Business Round Table.

The lobbying process provides a valuable forum in the marketplace for ideas. Legislators rely on lobbyists to a great extent for information from their constituencies. Yet lobbying, like propaganda, is frequently thought to have a pejorative connotation, although that perception is altered somewhat when lobbying is seen as a two-way need-satisfying exchange, in which each side benefits from the activity.

Advocacy. An exchange transaction in which a highly credible source popularizes a concept and thereby generates widespread demand for it is known as advocacy. It is a marketing process in every way. For example, Sinclair Lewis's book *The Jungle* called attention to shoddy practices in the meat-packing industry; when the book joined the best-seller list, it became a mass medium. Its ideas quickly matured into a social issue that was resolved with the passage of the Meat Act of 1906. Purchasers of that issue paid the cash price for the book and a price of time spent in reading and discussing it. In turn, they promoted the issue in the form of public outcry to lawmakers, the ultimate customers who bought the idea in exchange for promise of reelection. A marketing view of the process is thus simply that of a distribution channel.

Pressure and advocacy groups are alike in that each is organized to foster some cause benefiting the special concerns of its members or of constituents that the group has been chosen to represent. They differ principally in the direction their respective efforts take. Advocacy groups offer advisory service downward and outward to consumers and others seeking advice. (In the history of English and German law, the advocate was a special kind of lawyer who advised other lawyers in the preparation of cases.) Pressure groups representing individuals or institutions set out to systematically cajole government to enact laws favoring their causes. Pressure groups are macro in nature because they seek to bring about social change, whereas advocacy is a micro-process in which ideas are transmitted to individuals.

The advocacy group may be seen as a "top-down" channel for ideas, as exemplified by Consumer Reports, the Center for Automobile Safety, the Association for Rating Charitable Organizations, and the Better Business Bureau, as well as groups providing advice for the elderly, apartment dwellers, and so on. On the other hand, pressure groups are a "bottom-up" channel in that they attempt to influence legislators on behalf of individuals or groups. Examples include the several well-known civil rights and feminist groups and lobbies sponsored by trade organizations. A prominent pressure group is the organization Common Cause, which has attracted a following of nearly a quarter million members. It is a citizens' action lobby organized to pressure politicians into taking action on various issues in the public interest (see Chapter 2).

There is yet another communication link of interest to the P&NP administrator—propaganda. This link warrants special attention.

THE SPECIAL CASE OF PROPAGANDA

Propaganda is a highly maligned and misunderstood activity that plays an important role in social marketing. The dictionary defines propaganda as idea dissemination, which is the same definition applied to social marketing in this book. However, Kotler and Andreasen (1987) suggest that there is a slight difference between the two: Social marketing is an attempt to achieve behavior change, whereas the respective goals of education and propaganda are to increase knowledge and mold opinions. I accept that distinction but point out that unless idea marketers succeed in increasing product knowledge and molding the opinions of would-be purchasers, the program will not sell—behavior change will not be achieved. Propaganda is thus a necessary but not sufficient prerequisite for social marketing. Moreover, since social marketing is largely idea marketing, the two may, for our purposes, be taken as synonymous.

Propagandizing is another form of human exchange amenable to a marketing perspective, but the term has taken on a pejorative connotation because it has come to be associated with the dissemination of self-serving points of view, particularly by governments. Yet propaganda is not by definition, a "bad" practice. Moreover, an evaluation of the use of propaganda depends on whose side the observer is on, as with Radio Free Europe, Voice of America, and Radio Liberty broadcasts. Recently, a student walking with me to the university parking lot remarked that all advertising was "just plain propaganda." However, I noticed that her vehicle bore a bumper sticker asking, "Did you hug your child today?" That, she told me, was not propaganda of course.

Propaganda is a marketing transaction because it is a process in which an idea is promoted and delivered and then "bought" by purchasers who pay for it with attention, support, risk, and such psychic factors as loss of freedom. But not every exchange is propaganda. In the strictest sense, an exchange cannot be considered propaganda unless it conforms to three conditions (see Lazarsfeld and Merton in Schramm and Roberts 1971, pp. 459–80):

1. Monopolization, or the absence of neutralizing counterpropaganda. If opposing views tend to cancel each other out, then exchange has not been effected. In this sense, the effort by Canada to rally popular support for its Third World development pro-

gram (see Chapter 21) cannot be called propaganda because opposing points of view are permitted to be heard. But ideas spread by the Hitler regime and the Ku Klux Klan, violently resisting opposition, surely fall under the propaganda heading. Interestingly, most commercial advertising must escape the propaganda rubric because of co-opting and opposing messages inevitably counteracting ad effectiveness. (In the parking lot chat cited earlier, the student's perception would, according to Lazarsfeld and Merton, be inaccurate, for who would counter the hug-your-child theme?) The absence of a counterargument, ipso facto renders the message propaganda. By the definition, government antismoking advertising is not propaganda since tobacco interests do engage in counterargument.

2. Canalization, or the channeling or redirecting of preexisting attitude and behavior rather than attempting to instill radical change. A nutrition campaign is propaganda because sound nutrition is entirely in harmony with interest in good health: It asks only for a redirecting of dietary habits.

3. Supplementation of mass media campaigns with interpersonal word-of-mouth promotion. In the Soviet Union, "Red corners," "reading huts," and "listening stations" where groups can converse are encouraged in order to achieve a "clinching effect" of mass-communicated messages. These facilitate the exchange of concepts, and justify the propaganda appellation.

In sum, the only form of P&NP marketing that may be called propaganda is marketing that has no opposition, is not too radical in nature, and employs both mass and personal media. By that definition, the ideas of free enterprise, "drive 55," and gun control movements are not propaganda. However, and contrary to conventional usage, "hug your child," "save energy," "don't litter," and "say no to drugs" are all propaganda (for a detailed discussion of propaganda see Benn 1984). The point here is that propaganda can be employed to promote socially useful programs as effectively as it has been used to spread hate.

The extent to which marketing theory has penetrated government propaganda worldwide can be seen in the following quotation from an article referring to a resolution adopted by the Mongolian People's Republic's Central Committee, "combining mass and individual forms of political education and propaganda, . . . ensuring a differentiated approach to different population strata and strictly observing the principles of openness and publicity." It is paradoxical that most marketing concepts have originated in the United States, but we lag far behind the Eastern Bloc in propaganda expertise. That reality is argued by several commentators in the February/March 1982 issue of the journal *Public Opinion*.

Disinformation. In a review of Anatoly Golitsyn's book, *New Lies for Old: The Communist Strategy of Deception and Disinformation*, Beichman (1984, p. 40) writes:

> There is a famous Minsk-Pinsk "disinformation" story. It seems that two Jewish merchants and business competitors, Muttel and Yussel, living in a small town in Czarist Russia, meet one morning at the local railroad platform, luggage in hand. Muttel asks Yussel, "So where are you traveling?" Yussel responds, "To Minsk." Angered by the reply, Muttel shouts: "You, Yussel, are telling me that you're going to Minsk so that I will think you're *really* going to Pinsk. But I know for a fact that you're going to Minsk, so why do you lie to me that you're going to Minsk?"

The story has many versions. There is even a philosophical riddle about how one can distinguish between a known habitual liar and a truthful person when the observer does not know which is which, but is permitted to ask one question about a bowl of poisoned soup on the table before them. The solution: Ask the question of either of the two men, pointing to the other one, "Would he say this soup is good?" If the response is yes, its maker is the liar. If the response is no, its maker is the truth-teller.

The point here concerns the interpretation of propaganda and the propagandist's knowledge about how his or her audience will interpret the propaganda message. It is a difficult task but a challenge propagandists must deal with. Disinformation is untrue information communicated as though true for the purpose of creating certain desired perceptions.

THE CONSUMER'S PLACE IN "PLACE"

Channel theorists are divided on the question of whether the ultimate consumer should be considered part of the distribution structure. Typically, the consumer appears at the lower end of channel diagrams as the recipient of the product, below all of the other members who ostensibly have performed their assigned functions in the marketing scenario. But the consumer is by no means an insignificant actor in that process. The adopter of an idea meets all the qualifications for channel membership: a party to the process, an independent entity, a performer of one or more marketing functions. By including the target consumer as an integral part of the channel structure, the marketer is alerted to the importance of considering consumer wants and needs. The social product must find a satisfied market; consumers' dissatisfaction with a social good implies that the product needs to be modified or portends early obsolescence, as in the case of the Susan B. Anthony one-dollar coin.

The central role of consumer acceptance in marketing raises the question of whether the consumer should be encouraged to participate in the planning process to any extent. In this era of consumer enlightenment, more individuals seem to be demanding that their voices be heard by the marketers of products they buy. Purveyors of ideas must also attach credence to consumer feedback, and in some cases, consumers of ideas should have input into the formulation and dissemination processes. Involvement can go a long way to build trust.

The Consumer in the Public Sector. There is one striking difference between the marketing done by public agencies and commercial and social marketing—it has to do with the marketer's awareness of who is to be served. The business person knows exactly which people and firms are being catered to, but the bureaucrat is not so certain (Sethi 1981). That point was driven home to me several years ago when I was speaking to a group of federal administrators. At the outset of the meeting, I was interested to learn what the attendees thought about marketing and the extent to which they saw their roles within the framework of a marketing philosophy. So an informal questionnaire was hastily prepared containing a few questions, one of which was: "List the constituent groups whose needs and wants your agency must satisfy."

Although the attendees had ample time to fill out the questionnaires, only eleven of about fifty in the group completed them. In attempting to explain the poor response, I recalled the adage, "Man despises what he doesn't know." Here was a captive audience of responsible and intelligent officials, but most of them would not participate in a simple exercise that was introduced as an informal, anonymous, "just-for-curiosity" survey. It can be assumed some were fearful of revealing their lack of understanding of the concept or of submitting anything in their own handwriting, or perhaps they were just reluctant to divulge information in general.

The ensuing discussion revealed still more—many were not sure what markets agencies actually serve. Do they primarily serve the general public, or must they cater to other "middlemen" in the channel such as congressional committees, lobbying pressure groups, and other federal agencies?

A moral dilemma exists in the mind of the public administrator who, according to one (admittedly incomplete) survey, considers the needs and wants of intermediary groups before those of the general public. Administrators cater to these middlemen because the degree to which these middlemen's needs and wants are satisfied determines the amount of support the administrators receive from the groups—support in terms of resources allocation and in terms of rapport between the government administrator and others with whom he or she must interact. The welfare and sometimes the very existence of the administrators' job may depend on these middlemen. So it is easy to understand why *their* needs often come before those of the general public.

In marketing, we say that the middlemen are the primary level of acceptance for the product. If the middleman doesn't buy the product, the ultimate consumer will never see it. In the commercial realm, the producer must consider the needs of the wholesaler as the primary level of acceptance. The manufacturer must please the wholesaler, who then must satisfy the retailer, and so on. Similarly, the government agency must perhaps consider the needs of its unique intermediaries before considering the welfare of the general public.

One difference here is that the manufacturer of commercial goods often conducts consumer research to ferret out and understand the needs and wants of the consuming public. This is usually not done by the public administrator, who instead looks "in-house" for guidance.

This raises a question: Would the public administrator perform more effectively if the consumers' needs were taken into account before the needs of other public groups? I believe the dilemma could be resolved if the planner was to identify not one, but several "products," one for each constituency, in addition to the principal or overall product going to the consumer, the general public. Consumer products differ from those designed for intermediaries, who have different needs from those of the general public and need different products to satisfy those needs. (Table 1.2 identifies channel members and the products to be offered to each in the case of the university, but may serve as a model for any P&NP situation.) Thus, the social service agency markets counseling to the consuming public, but to the congressional committee the agency markets the assurance that it is carrying out its mandate effectively and efficiently. It might also act as a vehicle for carrying out various functions, for providing information feedback, and for scapegoating, that is, accepting blame for mishaps in the system.

Still another product "sold" by the government agency is interagency support. The agency must engage in mutually beneficial activities. "Today you support me, tomorrow I'll support you." These realities are never spelled out; they are usually taken for granted. But one wonders. Suppose that an agency can demonstrate it is doing a good job of serving the general public. Should that fact alone not please other channel members and gain their respect and support? Can not the administrator's adoption of a consumer orientation be recognized by other agencies as sound strategy? Would such an approach not enhance the agency's image, impart to it an enviable position as an important link in the distribution channel? Is it not simply good public relations to have public respect?

In the last analysis, the moral dilemma thus posed is resolved by identifying the various channel members and the programs by which to cater to each member.

DESIGN AND ORGANIZATION OF THE CHANNEL

The structure of the channel itself might vary from that of a loosely knit group of separate entities to a highly cohesive network that might in many ways resemble a single organization. An idea channel may be designed by listing all organizations interested in the promotion of the idea, or having some capability useful to its marketing. These are then arranged hierarchically in the form of a flowchart to create the channel. A generalized channel of distribution for ideas is illustrated in Figure 10.1.

Channel designing encourages zero-based planning of the roles and functions of institutions participating in the program. It also suggests reappraisal of, and improvement in day-to-day operations of these institutions with respect to the objectives of the entire channel.

FIGURE 10.1   A General Channel of Distribution for Concepts

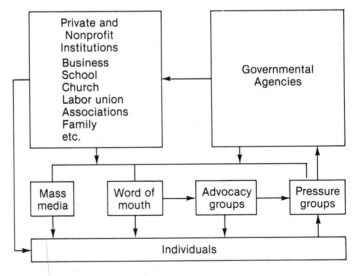

Source: Seymour H. Fine, *Marketing of Ideas and Social Issues.* (New York: Praeger Publishers, 1981) p. 116. Copyright © 1981 by Praeger Publishers. Reprinted with permission.

SUMMARY

Ideas and programs promulgated in the concept sector must be accessible to potential adopters at the time and place and in a manner that will facilitate adoption. To accomplish this, the marketer constructs a network of institutions, each of which performs certain marketing functions. These are the parties to the marketing process; each makes a contribution. A typical network for concept marketing includes the organization initiating the particular cause, community-based institutions, mass and personal media, pressure and advocacy groups, private firms, government, and finally the consumer.

Just as no ship can sail smoothly without a chief officer, the channel usually operates under a channel captain who is responsible for the smooth delivery of the concept from its source to those whose needs are to be satisfied in the transaction. The channel must be sufficiently "long," that is, must contain enough members, so that all tasks necessary for the successful execution of the total job will be performed. At the same time, it must not be too unwieldy. In the same way that conventional goods and services have greater utility when they are made readily accessible to their buyers, the availability of concepts at the "point of purchase" increases their chances of being adopted.

NOTE

Portions of this chapter were originally published in, or adapted from: (1) Seymour H. Fine, *Marketing of Ideas and Social Issues* (Praeger Publishers, New York, 1981). Copyright © 1981 by Praeger Publishers. Reprinted with permission. (2) Seymour H. Fine, "Social and Nonprofit Marketing: Some Trends and Issues," in *Advances in Nonprofit Marketing*, 2nd ed., ed. Russell Belk (Greenwich, CT: JAI Press, 1987), 77-98.

11

Segmenting the Health Care Market

JAGDISH N. SHETH
University of Southern California

There is a large body of literature on market segmentation but little of it deals with segmentation for social products, even though the theory applies to a service or a concept as much as a tangible product. The segmentation technique can be illustrated by an ideational product such as health care. Extrapolation to other types of product offerings is possible, although considerable thought is required to determine the most appropriate criteria and to identify plausible segments to cultivate.

Henry Ford pioneered the automobile market with the successful Model T car, which was mass-assembled at a very affordable price and was well built. It was a tremendous success. However, it came in only one color: black. Many customers praised Mr. Ford for building an excellent car and requested that he offer more colors. Mr. Ford is reputed to have responded, "Customers can have any choice of color as long as it is black!"

At about the same time, General Motors came along with another strategy: Offer customers what they want. GM offered a variety of cars, such as the Chevrolet, Pontiac, Oldsmobile, and Cadillac, which were targeted for different segments of the market based on affordability and prestige. Many experts have suggested that Ford Motor Company lost its leadership role because it chose the wrong strategy: It offered only one model in one color whereas market needs and wants were clearly not homogeneous.

Market segmentation refers to dividing the total market into segments consisting of customers with homogeneous needs/wants and resources. Once these segments are identified, it is up to the supplier to decide whether to cater to one segment or all of them. For example, General Motors opted to cater to all the segments through separate automobile divisions, but Rolls Royce decided to cater to a small, select segment of the market.

Segmenting the market becomes not only desirable, but necessary if the customers in a given industry have *diverse* needs or wants *or* if the resources of time and money are diverse. In other words, only when the market is truly homogeneous with respect to needs/wants and resources, can the marketer practice a universal philosophy comparable to the Model T strategy. Figure 11.1 summarizes this point.

THE IMPORTANCE OF SEGMENTATION IN HEALTH CARE

The market is becoming more and more segmented in the health care industry. This is happening because patient needs/wants are not homogeneous, and neither are their time and money resources.

Resource Diversity: Affordability. Affordability has become a critical issue in the health care delivery systems. Although some patients are able to afford better and more expensive medical services, many other patients find health care beyond their reach. This difference in affordability is further heightened by the erosion of employee fringe benefits offered by corporations and public service programs offered by the government.

Resource Diversity: Time. Patients are also becoming more diverse with respect to time. For example, with the increase in the number of dual wage earners in many families, it is no longer possible for working spouses to seek medical care during the traditional hours of nine to five,

MARKET NEEDS/WANTS

		Homogeneous	Diverse
MARKET RESOURCES	Homogeneous	Undifferentiated Marketing	Market Segmentation
	Diverse	Market Segmentation	Market Segmentation

FIGURE 11.1 The Need for Market Segmentation

Monday through Friday, opening and closing hours. Similarly, we are witnessing an explosive growth in the singles market. For example, nearly 24 percent of all American households are headed by single adults. The breakdown of the traditional family, which consisted of a breadwinner and a homemaker, is largely responsible for creating this diversity in the time resource. Single working parents experience considerable difficulty finding time to take care of the home and children.

A second factor responsible for generating greater time resource diversity among patients is the explosive growth of leisure activities and interests. The increase in choices available to consumers is reducing discretionary time available for health care services. It is an unfortunate fact of present-day life-styles that what the patient needs most (to take care of health) is often given lower priority than other less essential but more desirable activities.

Needs Diversity: Diseases. Patients are also suffering from a more diverse set of diseases than they did, say, two or three generations ago, although this is not so surprising. As the economic and social activities of the country become more diversified, one should expect a proliferation of diseases that are the side effects of more diverse occupations, life-styles, and living arrangements.

Needs Diversity: Psychosomatics. Society is also becoming more diverse with respect to psychological diseases and emotional disturbances. Again, this should not be surprising. As a society progresses beyond the hardships of economic survival and the struggle to obtain food, shelter, and clothing, it focuses more on interpersonal relationships as well as self-identity.

With the breakdown of social norms and values, the individual is required to cope with social relationships alone, without the support of family or community members. If the individual is not trained early in life to cope with interpersonal situations, it becomes more difficult to do so later on. This may help to explain the rising psychological problems experienced by teenagers and adolescents.

Society is not only offering more choices, it is also setting higher goals. Consequently, despite hard work and basic intelligence, many people seem to be more frustrated and unhappy, and emotionally disturbed. The increasing popularity of psychological counseling or psychiatric help in the work setting and in public service agencies, is one manifestation of this phenomenon.

Market segmentation as a strategic concept is likely to become more important in the health care industry as the health care market grows more diverse in its needs/wants and in its time and money resources.

BENEFITS OF HEALTH CARE SEGMENTATION

Segmenting the market can help health care practitioners in at least three ways.

Cost Efficiency through Target Marketing. Market segmentation encourages health care practitioners to use a rifle approach. Instead of trying to be everything to everyone, practitioners match their expertise and resources to a specific segment of the total health care market. For example, one may specialize in oncology, gastrointestinal illness, or heart disease and then target such expertise to the patients who need these specialized services instead of serving everyone for all diseases as well as routine physical examinations. Similarly, if a physician is located in a neighborhood containing many older people, it would make sense to target his or her expertise to the elderly market.

Identifying Neglected Segments. Often, we tend to neglect many smaller, highly unique market segments and cater instead to the mainstream market. Market segmentation enables the health care practitioner to identify these neglected segments and reorganize resources to satisfy their unique needs.

The best example of neglected segments are teenagers and immigrants. It is difficult to understand the lack of specialization in the teenage market. Many a teenager grudgingly continues with a pediatrician until adulthood.

Immigrants form another neglected segment. In addition to having cultural and linguistic problems, some immigrants carry or acquire diseases requiring special diagnosis and treatment. For example, immigrants from Asian countries may carry tropical diseases such as malaria, small pox, and jaundice.

Other specialty segments include the rural market, the in-home market, and the skilled-care market.

Keeping Customers Happy. Market segmentation also offers a means of maintaining customer satisfaction. Each customer feels his or her illness or problem is unique and wants personalized service. In particular, people resent the idea of being considered a "number" in a long line of patients.

Market segmentation, if properly implemented, differentiates services, facilities, and delivery systems. For example, if a special location or floor was dedicated to the disabled with specializing equipment and personnel, it might be more satisfying to both the disabled and to other patients. Similarly, non–life-threatening emergencies can be physically segmented from life-threatening emergencies to make both segments happy. Indeed, some experts have argued that it was the failure to segment these two emergencies that led to the growth of twenty-four-hour emergency centers in shopping malls and other locations throughout the nation.

METHODS OF SEGMENTING THE HEALTH CARE MARKET

There are two principal ways to segment the health care market: on the basis of patient characteristics and marketing practices. Each of these two categories can be subdivided as follows:

> Patient characteristics
> 1. Demographics
>   a. Age
>   b. Sex
>   c. Occupation
> 2. Psychographics
>   a. Values
>   b. Attitudes
> 3. Usage patterns
> Marketing practices
>   1. Competitive positioning
>   2. Specialization
>   3. Payment mode.

SEGMENTATION BASED ON PATIENT CHARACTERISTICS

Three types of patient characteristics are useful for segmenting the health care market: patient demographics, patient psychographics, and patient frequency of health care utilization.

Patient Demographics. Perhaps the two most relevant patient characteristics are age and affluence. Since the incidence and types of diseases tend to vary significantly by age of the patient, the health care market can be segmented according to age group (e.g., children, teenagers, adults, and senior citizens). As mentioned earlier, it is surprising that little has been done to segment the teenager market.

Affluence is an important factor because it is related to affordability. Even in countries with socialized medicine, such as Sweden and Denmark, private medical practice has always coexisted with socialized free health care services. It should therefore be possible to segment the market at least with respect to premium versus best value services. People who can afford it are likely to patronize premium health care services. This does not mean that best value services should be inferior in quality. It simply means that premium services will probably have better ambiance, modern equipment, more comfortable facilities, and the like. It also means perhaps more personalized health care. Health Maintenance Organizations (HMOs) would represent the best value offering, whereas the Mayo Clinic would offer premium service.

A third demographic characteristic that is likely to become more important in the coming years is occupation. A person's occupation often dictates his or her life-style and work style. Both are probably the most direct sources of types and incidences of diseases, including psychosomatic diseases. Typical occupational groupings are factory workers, office workers, athletes, students, farmers, mobile workers (truck drivers and airline crews), and those in hazardous jobs.

Patient Psychographics. The psychology of the patient is becoming important in shaping the utilization of health care services. People differ significantly in their attitudes toward modern health care. Therefore, it should be possible to segment the health care market accordingly. However, the psychographics concept is still relatively new and therefore, there is no standardized typology, as is the case with patient demographics.

One possible typology suggested here is based on people's attitudes toward different ways of caring for their illnesses. For example, some people believe in home remedies, others believe in self-medication, and still others may prefer nonpharmaceutical remedies such as chiropractic, acupuncture, or acupressure techniques. There are still others who believe in preventive methods such as physical fitness, vitamin intake, and even meditation as ways of preventing illnesses. Of course, the hypochondriacs make up a segment of their own!

In general, we can probably categorize patients into four psychographic types: skeptics, traditionals, hypochondriacs, and realists. The last group is likely to be the best informed and most appealing group of patients, because they will not hesitate to call the physician when necessary, nor will they abuse the health care system.

Frequency or Usage Patterns. Probably about 20 percent of patients contribute toward 80 percent of health care utilization. It is therefore possible to segment the market by the degree and type of health care utilization. For example, we can segment all patients into heavy, light, and infrequent users. Furthermore, the heavy segment can be divided by type of health care utilization, such as general practice (GP) versus specialist need. Fortunately, the health care industry has patient records, owing to the regulations governing its agencies, which contain the data needed to carry out such segmentation procedures.

MARKETING PRACTICES

It is also possible to segment the health care market on the basis of the marketing practices of providers. Three aspects of marketing practices are plausible bases for segmentation: competitive positioning, specialization, and payment method.

Competitive Positioning. The health care market can be segmented according to quality-price variations, as indicated in Figure 11.2.

The provider might select a group described in one of the boxes in the figure as a market segment and offer services in a manner consistent with that quality-price combination. For example, if the premium positioning segment is selected, the implication is that care will be given by the best physicians, nurses, and paramedics; that physical facilities will be well appointed; that support staff will be courteous and professional; and that follow-through services such as billings, reminders, and documentation will be handled efficiently. Clearly, this will be the highest priced facility in the marketplace. In general, most health care providers can easily be positioned into one of the cells of the matrix on the basis of their past and current practices.

Unfortunately, patients perceive most health care providers as either premium suppliers or cheap goods suppliers. This has created a

FIGURE 11.2 Positioning for Health Care Products

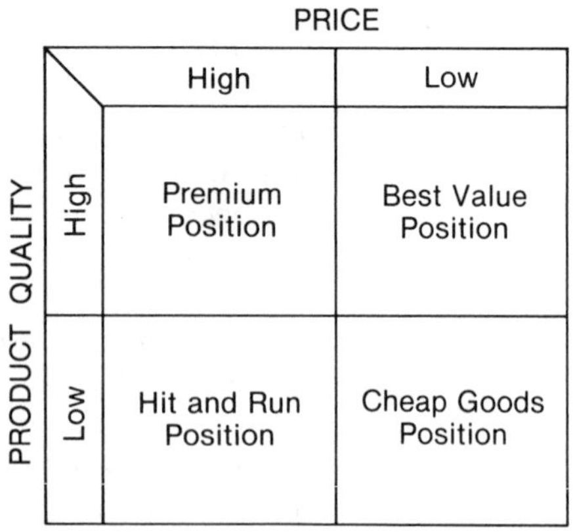

		PRICE	
		High	Low
PRODUCT QUALITY	High	Premium Position	Best Value Position
	Low	Hit and Run Position	Cheap Goods Position

void in the best value position, which is being filled by large retailers such as the HMOs.

Full Service versus Specialty. A second method of segmenting the health care market is based on the concept of fully integrated, one-stop health care centers. For example, Kaiser Permanente in California is a one-stop, full service "department store" where all health care services can be provided by the same organization and possibly under one roof. However, it is possible to specialize by certain diseases such as oncology, gynecology, heart diseases, or allergies.

Payment Plans. The health care provider can also segment the market by method of payment. For example, it may offer an in-house prepaid plan, limit the practice to certain group insurance plans, or provide services exclusively to one corporation or organization.

Undoubtedly payment plans will become more popular as a basis for segmenting the market as the affordability issue gains more attention in the health care field.

SUMMARY

Market segmentation is becoming more prevalent in the health care industry, no doubt because it is extremely useful to the health care practitioners. Segmentation may be based on three customer characteristics (demographics, psychographics, and usage patterns) or on three marketing practices (competitive positioning, full line versus specialty, and payment plans). These concepts apply to a wide variety of product offerings of public and nonprofit organizations.

12

Advertising in the Social Sector

DAVID L. RADOS
Vanderbilt University

To many administrators in the concept sector, marketing and advertising are synonymous. Actually, advertising is just one part of the promotion "P" in the marketing mix, along with personal selling, sales promotion, and public relations. Broadly speaking, it is the most important and most popular of them all. It also happens to be the most expensive.

Both the public and nonprofit (P&NP) manager are well advised to study the principles of campaign planning. They have bearing on budgeting and segmentation as well as advertising research.

Public and nonprofit organizations communicate with their clients in various ways. They may rely on speakers, public relations, meetings and public events, or publications; they may communicate face to face using what a business manager would call a salesperson; or they may use advertising.

All these communication tools, and others, have their place. For example, in fund-raising the standard way to ask for a large donation is through personal communication. But this can only be done when the prospective givers are few in number. Although some P&NPOs still rely on door-to-door solicitations, most organizations find this unsuitable for their fund-raising needs. To reach mass audiences, one uses advertising.

What distinguishes advertising from other forms of communication? (1) It reaches the masses, (2) it is an impersonal form of communication, (3) the sponsor is identified, and (4) the media used are paid.

A COMMUNICATIONS MODEL

Communication may be said to consist of seven elements: source, encoding, message, media, decoding, receiver, and feedback. To understand these elements is to understand advertising.

The source is the party sending the message. Whereas the source of an advertisement is identified in the ad, public relations (usually) masquerades as straight news from an unknown source. It is important to know how the audience feels about the source, because messages thought to come from biased sources often fall on deaf ears. The astute marketer assesses these perceptions and tries to adapt to them.

Encoding is the process of converting a message into symbols that will allow it to be transmitted. The form of messages aimed at a mass market should be as simple and direct as possible. One school of advertising practitioners insists that the advertiser find a *unique selling proposition* (USP) that promises users strong benefits from an idea, product, or service.

Messages are usually communicated via words and pictures. Those responsible for choosing the particular words and pictures face a difficult task because they are required to make numerous value judgments. For example, they must decide whether to use humorous words and pictures in ads warning people not to drink and drive. Should their messages present only one side of the argument or two sides? And is it acceptable to use symbols that provoke fear?

Media are the means by which the message is transmitted from the source to the audience. Like the symbols, the medium may be difficult to select to ensure that the message reaches a given audience.

Decoding is the process by which the recipient interprets the words and pictures and thus arrives at the meaning of the message.

Receiver refers to the audience, actual as well as intended, and direct (e.g., magazine subscribers) and indirect (I read my friend's copy).

Feedback is that part of the receiver's response to the messages that gets back to the source. Businesses have two sources of feedback, sales and market research. Nonprofit organizations can use the same two, although in somewhat different ways, as we shall see.

The marketer's central concern in communication is the receiver of the information, the customer or, in P&NP terms, the "client." The P&NP marketer must understand how clients behave—what motivates them, what they believe, and what they already know. A marketing plan must be built on the premise that the organization does not have a single, average client. The market must be divided into subgroups, each of which is to be considered separately—that is, they must be segmented.

SEGMENTATION

Segmentation is common in business, where marketers routinely design different marketing strategies for different segments of the audience. P&NPOs must do the same thing. As already noted, fund-raisers treat donors differently. They may communicate with one group in person and with another group through advertising. Like the astute politician, they must recognize that the public is not a homogeneous mass, and that appeals must be made to each of the segments in order to capture favor.

The advertiser, in particular, must have a clear idea of the target audience. Segments will respond differently to copy styles, layout, and artwork. A museum that wishes to increase its membership may recognize that it has two distinct segments to appeal to: those who are already members (or who have been members in the past), and those who have never been members. Copy written for the first group will assume the reader already knows the benefits of being a museum member and will concentrate on obtaining membership renewal. Copy written for the second group must explain why one should join the museum in the first place.

Segmentation also affects the choice of medium. Since it is easy to identify current museum members, the phone would be the natural channel to choose when soliciting a renewal. However, prospective members are more difficult to identify and phone solicitations are certain to reach a large number of people who are not interested. In any case, the telephone is probably too expensive to reach a large group, and mail might be better.

The importance of planning advertising campaigns around segments can be demonstrated by the antismoking campaigns. Which of the possible segments should the promotion seek to influence?

Nonsmokers
Teenage male smokers
Teenage female smokers
All adult smokers
Young adult smokers
Older adult smokers
Heavy smokers of any age
Groups at special risk, like pregnant women or women taking birth control pills.

Clearly, the messages and the media will differ, depending on which segments are chosen. For example, adults do not read teenage magazines or listen to radio stations that teenagers favor. Even if they did, messages appropriate for teenagers would not work with adults. By the same token, it is relatively easy to identify and communicate with pregnant women, but the messages best suited for them would differ markedly from those best suited for heavy smokers or nonsmokers.

HOW DOES ADVERTISING WORK?

Unfortunately, no one knows how advertising works. But there has been a great deal of speculation on the subject, all of which agrees on at least one point—that advertising must not be considered a panacea. One problem is that the word "work" can have many meanings. One ad may be said to work if the audience responds by donating time or money to a charity; while another may work if the audience merely becomes faintly aware of the service being advertised after several exposures.

It is clear that a great deal of advertising doesn't work in the sense that it does not produce sales, as in the case of a recent direct-mail campaign for alcohol prevention in which 93 percent of respondents admitted that they had read the letter but that their drinking behavior remained unchanged (McCarty et al. 1987). Most candidates for high public office make heavy use of advertising. In the typical campaign both candidates advertise but only one wins. The naive view would be that one candidate's advertising didn't "work."

Third, advertising is usually part of an overall marketing program, which means that other forces are influencing audience behavior at the same time. The contribution that advertising makes to the overall program is hard to pinpoint because in a team effort the contribution of team members may overlap. This also adds another dimension to the meaning of "work;" advertising can "work" but the program can fail, just as a goalie might perform magnificently but his team might still lose the championship cup.

THREE THEORIES OF ADVERTISING

Consider now three explanations of how advertising works.

Stimulus-Response Theory. One theory of advertising is that it stimulates audiences by putting repeated "pressure" on them. In general, this theory holds that the more advertising exposures the better. The central concern of the advertiser in this case is the amount spent on advertising.

In this view, the effect of advertising depends on the amount spent, as illustrated by the "S"-curve model. According to this model, at low levels of spending on advertising, returns to advertising investment increase as advertising increases, whereas at high advertising levels, returns to advertising decrease as advertising increases. Another common model based on returns assumes continuously decreasing sales returns: As advertising increases, sales increase too, but the size of the increase grows smaller and smaller. In this view, each successive dollar spent for advertising yields less than the one before.

Virtually all advertising practitioners believe in the stimulus-response theory of advertising, at least in part. One need only observe how much attention they pay to repetition in planning and evaluating advertising.

Active Learning Theory. Another school of thought is that (1) audiences look to advertising for information and (2) advertising conveys such information. The information may be nothing more than awareness about some person, object, or idea. The ad may make these things known, or it may persuade someone to adopt a new idea or plan to behave differently. This is perhaps the natural way to think about advertising, natural in the sense that many outside the field of advertising believe that advertising involves active learning. (Still others believe that it is the way advertising *should* work, which, of course, is quite a different thing.)

The idea behind this theory is that when people are exposed to information, they move through a series of stages from unawareness to action. This idea dates back to the 1920s and is known as AIDA, which stands for awareness-interest-desire-action. The current view is that the four-step process consists of awareness, comprehension, conviction, and action, but the principle is the same.

The active learning theory seems to hold when (1) decisions are extremely important to the client and (2) the differences between the alternatives under consideration are large—such as buying a personal computer or a car, choosing a mate, deciding where to go for an overseas vacation, and choosing living-room furniture. Marketers call such decisions *high-involvement* decisions.

Selecting a college probably fits these two criteria. Where to go to college is very important to most students, and colleges differ substantially on many dimensions. Hence most young people would be expected to go through the four stages from unawareness to a decision. Imagine, for example, a young San Diegan who loves computers and wants to study them in college. His or her first choice is MIT. One day a letter arrives from Carnegie Mellon University telling about its computer programs. The student has never heard of CMU and so is unmoved, but for the first time is aware of that institution. A friend later mentions that Carnegie has a strong computer program. Curiosity and interest are rekindled and the student decides to seek more information. Inquiries are made to CMU, which is then discussed with others deemed influential in the community. The student writes Carnegie for more material; and from all this he or she begins to form some ideas about the kind of school that Carnegie is and whether it is the place to go. As more knowledge is gained, it grows into conviction and a decision is made one way or the other.

Here we see two things. First, advertising in the form of letters and other materials from Carnegie is only one source of information among many that people draw on when making high-involvement decisions such as this. Second, the advertising worked in the sense that it informed the student of an alternative choice and elicited a response, whether or not it was the desired action. Advertising's role in such a marketing program is not to lead to action, but to generate awareness, disseminate knowledge, and perhaps help the young person to make a decision. It is too much to ask that advertising produce action where prospective freshmen are concerned. In high-involvement decisions, advertising takes prospects part of the way down the road of the AIDA model, toward action. It seldom produces action directly.

Low-Involvement Theory. Critics of the active learning theory of advertising believe that a great deal of consumer advertising is concerned with low-involvement decisions that do not require a large base of information.

According to this theory, the individual absorbs much advertising, perhaps most, while in a state of absent-mindedness. The individual is not paying much attention because (1) the product is not too important, and (2) the products in the brand category are all pretty much alike. Such low-involvement decisions deal with the commonplaces of everyday life—soap, beer, toothbrushes, car waxes, socks, selecting television shows and deciding what to eat and drink.

Political choices provide an example. Most elections offer voters two classes of choices: high-involvement races, where the outcome is important to the voter and the choice is crucial, and low-involvement races, where the voter sees little difference between candidates and does not care who wins. For many voters an example of the first is a presidential or gubernatorial election. In such elections the active voter has many sources of information: advertising by the candidate, advertising by the opponent', television news, newspapers and, most important of all, discussions with friends and fellows. In such a situation, one would expect advertising to play a minor role in influencing action—that is, in influencing how people vote. The evidence strongly points in this direction (see Jacobson 1975, pp. 769–793 and Agranoff 1976, pp. 67–80). In low-involvement races, however, the voter is passive and advertising has some opportunity to influence choice.

BUDGETING

Another important question is how much should be spent on advertising? Some P&NPOs have financial guidelines to follow; one rule is to keep on spending until it no longer pays, which seems to make sense but, alas, is difficult to follow in practice. Agencies having close links with their clients can study the relationship between advertising and the returns it brings and thereby determine what amount should be spent. For example, a P&NP magazine or a political fund raiser, both of whom use direct mail, should be able to find the most profitable level to spend on advertising after some experimenting.

Organizations seeking communications objectives or dealing with situations in which it is difficult to trace the link between advertising and effect, will have a much harder time. They can use one of four possible approaches, none of which will produce a "best" budget, however: (1) they can raise special funds for specific communications campaigns, as the Public Broadcasting System sometimes does; (2) they can spend what remains after all other activities have been funded; (3) they can employ the "task method," which means pricing each objective sought in the campaign and then basing the budget on the sum of the individual mini-budgets; or (4) they can assess their ratios of advertising to sales (or to budget).

Timing to Extend the Budget. Budgets can usually be stretched by judicious scheduling of media placement. The timing methods employed will take advantage of peoples' ability to remember messages for some time. One such technique is *phasing* or *pulsing*. Ads are placed often enough to make an impression on the audience, but at the same time are spaced far enough apart so as not to strain the budget. Early in the campaign, for example, ads might be scheduled frequently in order to overcome any "noise in the system" from competing messages. Later on, frequency may be reduced. The audience will barely notice the omissions because they will retain some information from the earlier copies. Thus, after, say, three consecutive months of magazine ads, readers will likely report having seen two or three additional appearances.

SETTING ADVERTISING OBJECTIVES

P&NPOs advertise to achieve broad program objectives, or marketing objectives, as well as advertising objectives. For example, the British Post Office is considering the idea of selling stamps as they are sold everywhere else in Europe, through other outlets, such as shops, hotels, railway stations, and the like ("Britain May Stamp on the Queue" 1987). If the Post Office goes that route, it will have to create a broad marketing program to make sure the plan succeeds. Advertising will play a role in that program, because when the new distribution channels are first established, the Post Office will need to inform potential stamp buyers they can now buy stamps without waiting in a long queue in the Post Office (an experience that is said to have "helped form the British character"). If the program does succeed, it will likely be because (1) stamps are in fact easier to buy through other outlets and (2) the advertising has helped communicate the message about the new plan. The point is that these two aspects of marketing work together. If new outlets are not advertised, fewer people will use them, and, of course, advertising the new outlets without making them available does not make sense.

In this case, the Post Office's advertising goal is not to get the new distribution channels successfully launched. Although this is a sound objective, it is not a sound advertising objective. Rather, it is a marketing objective, that is to say, a program objective. Advertising can help, however, by informing customers of the new stamp outlets and, perhaps, encouraging them to give the new outlets a try.

Once customers have tried the new outlets, however, there is little more that advertising can do. If the system is more convenient than the old one, customers will use it again and again; they will tell their friends, and the new channels will become established. If the new system works less well than the old system, it will languish and the Post Office will have failed in its efforts. In either case, advertising will have little effect on the level of use. Thus it is possible for advertising to meet its objectives while the overall marketing program may not.

This simple idea—that there are two levels of objectives, not one— should clear up some of the confusion regarding advertising objectives. At times, however, advertising may carry most of the burden of the entire marketing program, as in the case of magazine subscriptions and direct-mail fund-raising. Here the objective of advertising is to sell magazines or raise money. In other cases, such as advertising by hospitals, advertising plays only a limited role in the overall marketing program.

Broadly speaking, advertising can influence behavior or it can influence attitudes, opinions, or intentions. Of course the two are often related: A P&NPO advertises to change people's opinions and thereby encourage them to behave differently.

Behavioral Objectives. Some campaigns set out to do nothing more than change people's behavior. For example, a museum shop might wish to sell merchandise via a mail-order catalog, an environmental group might wish to raise funds, or a local blood bank might wish to solicit donors over the Christmas holidays. In all these cases, we can expect the response to follow closely on the heels of the advertising, and the link between the two will be easy to see. More important, because the decision that the client is asked to make is relatively simple, the advertising will precipitate the decision, which would (probably) not be made without the advertising. When marketing programs have such objectives, it makes sense to define the advertising objectives in terms of sales (action).

Communications Objectives. Some advertising makes no attempt to change people's behavior. Its sole purpose is to influence people's thinking. An example would be union advertising seeking to generate a favorable public opinion toward its legislative aims. Here, the objectives have to do with attitudes.

How, then, does an organization know if its advertising is accomplishing what it hopes to accomplish? One important way is to undertake marketing research, which is an important component of most professional advertising efforts. When the advertising objective is to modify behavior, it is usually easy to see how well the advertising has worked. It is often as simple as counting "sales"—which might be units of blood donated or membership renewals—and comparing the results of the campaign with some baseline measurement. When the objective is to influence how people think, the P&NPO must survey its intended audience and again compare the results of the survey with some baseline. However, this time the results are more tenuous; it is simpler to measure action than it is to measure thought.

Either way, the game of setting objectives can be overdone, as an advertising agency in Australia demonstrated when it proposed a campaign for a family-planning clinic (Rados and Gilmour 1981, p. 112). Women went to the clinic for medical examinations and for prescriptions for contraceptives. The clinic also performed vasectomies and conducted a lecture series. Basically, the clinic wanted to publicize its work and build up its clientele. The advertising agency proposed three sets of objectives, which are listed here to illustrate the absurdity of overkill:

1. Social objectives
   a. To reduce the incidence of unwanted pregnancies.
   b. To reduce the incidence of abortions.
   c. To provide alternative clinical opportunities for the early detection of psychological "sex problems," related to physiological problems and medical problems concerned with disease.
   d. To reduce the marriage failure rate associated with so-called shotgun weddings.
   e. To ease the strain on orphanages and associated institutions.
   f. To ease the national demand for food, power, housing, health care, and public service, by controlling the rate of population growth.

g. To ease the economic burden on large, low-income families.
2. Institutional objectives
   a. To promote the family planning clinic's services to those members of the public with potential problems, that is, an education and information campaign designed to promote public awareness of (i) the range, and (ii) the availability of services provided by the association through direct media.
   b. To educate the public through a media promotion of the "Orientation Program" and presentation of the facilities available to institutions, or through an arbitrary assembly of individuals.
   c. To promote the association to those institutions that are in a position to refer patients to the clinic.
3. Motivational objectives
   a. To provide an opportunity, through direct media advertising, for those people who have problems or who do not know how to identify a personal and possibly urgent need.
   b. To motivate these people to come forward and take advantage of the clinic's services.

No ad campaign can possibly accomplish so much. The social objectives also aim too high. No one can expect an advertising campaign in one city to ease the national demand for food, power, and housing, Furthermore, the objectives are not stated in a way that allows them to be measured. Finally, and perhaps most serious in a marketing program, they show no clear grasp of clients' attitudes toward the clinic, and thus rest on a weak foundation. That is, the objectives, particularly the social objectives, assume that a little bit of birth control will cure a wide variety of society's ills. When the campaign is over, it will not be possible to say whether it has indeed educated the public or motivated people to come to the clinic.

The last point is particularly important: When the campaign is over, will we be able to measure the extent to which the campaign succeeded? In a poorly conceived advertising campaign this question is not raised until the campaign is completed, by which time it is too late. A professional campaign devotes considerable thought to setting objectives and tries to make sure that objectives can be assessed when the campaign is over.

THE IMPORTANCE OF RESEARCH

Marketing research serves three broad managerial interests. First, it describes how things are—how many people say they have been to an opera in the past two years, the size of the average gift given to a university, what proportion of recruits for the army come from homes with below-average incomes, and so on. These are all verifiable, at least in principle. Second, it describes states of mind, which, of course, are not verifiable, even in principle. This includes such things as how many people believe that stamp collectors make money from their collections, how many are aware of a new law requiring residents to curb their pets, and to what degree people believe the latest health warnings broadcast by the surgeon general. Third, research can be used to develop beneficial objectives. For example, "to increase peoples' knowledge about the hours and location of the blood donation center" is a vague objective. A better one is "to increase the proportion of people who know about the blood center and its hours from its current level of 3 percent of the target population to 6 percent." This is a more specific objective, and the campaign's success can be measured against a clear standard. But knowing what donors currently believe about operating hours implies that research will be conducted before the ads are run.

Research is also used to pretest the effectiveness of planned advertising. If an organization is simply going to run some quick public service advertisements on the radio and hope for the best, then one need not bother much with pretesting. But if a labor union plans to spend two or three million dollars on a campaign, it must find out which ads work and why before it starts.

Finally, research can help evaluate the campaign. Did the symphony manage to increase the proportion of the house sold by 20 percent, as it had planned to do? More important, did the increase come from advertising or from other sources? Did the blood donation center succeed in increasing awareness from 3 to 6 percent? Which targets were most receptive to the message? Another example of the benefits of advertising research conducted by a concept-sector organization comes from the experience of a labor union.

In 1975, faced with continuing decline in its membership, the International Ladies' Garment Workers' Union (ILG) began a union label campaign featuring a song beginning, "Look for the union label." The campaign appeared to be enormously successful. Editorials and feature stories appeared in many newspapers, and the ILG received many letters commenting on the campaign. Several entertainers performed "take-offs" of the campaign or of its song. For example, the comedienne Carol Burnett did a spoof on television, ending with her clothes being torn off as the cast members, singing the union song, looked for the union label. U.S. garment manufacturers praised the campaign.

But these happy events are little more than anecdotal. How was the campaign's effectiveness measured? And what, in the first place, were the campaign's objectives? The union followed the best practice in assessing the effectiveness of the campaign. Before the campaign started it surveyed some twelve hundred respondents by telephone to get baseline figures on such things as what proportion of the respondents were aware of the ILG, and of the union label, and what proportion agreed with such statements as "The ILG is one of the best unions." Then in each successive year it repeated the survey with another twelve hundred respondents. This careful research design enabled the ILG to track its progress over time. Thus it had clear evidence of the impact of the campaign on its communications objectives (Rados 1981, pp. 446–460).

PUBLIC SERVICE ANNOUNCEMENTS

One aspect of advertising that is particularly appropriate to P&NPs is the public service announcement, the PSA. PSAs are announcements promoting the activities of P&NPOs for which no charge is made. Because the airwaves are owned by the public, radio and television stations must periodically ask the Federal Communications Commission (FCC) to renew their licenses. In justifying the renewals, stations must establish that they serve the public interest, and one of the ways they do that is to demonstrate that they run PSAs and that they plan to continue running them during the next licensing period. In applying for license renewals, stations in effect agree to devote a certain percentage of their time to PSAs.

But broadcasters have a great deal of flexibility. They determine the percentage of time to be devoted to PSAs. They decide the frequency with which a PSA will run and when it will run. If it chooses, a station may count a five- or ten-second announcement as a PSA. It may even count the two-second ID (station identification). The station may run some PSAs after 11 A.M. or before 7 P.M. If it chooses, it may work off its commitment to the FCC by running most of its PSAs during the summer, when audiences are small and thus will not have to run any during the pre-Christmas season when time is valuable. And it may arbitrarily refuse all PSAs of a certain type, for example, those seeking to raise funds or those dealing with such controversial issues as abortion. Local charities might be forced to give way to PSAs of such national organizations as the Advertising Council. A station may prepare a PSA for a P&NPO by writing a script, filming a spokesman in the studio, or taking a film crew into the field; but it can also refuse to do any of these things. Sometimes, preference is given to PSAs for an organization that also runs paid advertising, or for one likely to buy space in the future.

All this flexibility is available to broadcast media, but at least broadcast media must run some PSAs. Not so with print media, which are not licensed and need not justify themselves to any public body, and hence are not under any obligation to run PSAs. If they run PSAs at all, they run them as a moral obligation, and always "at the convenience of the publisher." (For more on this, see the discussion on the Fairness Doctrine in Chapter 2.)

The persons responsible for deciding which PSAs will run are usually called public service directors. They usually base their decisions on four criteria:

1. The PSAs must be technically right—the right length for example, and of broadcast quality. A PSA made in poor light in the church basement with a hand-held camera is not going to pass muster. PSAs must arrive early enough to be scheduled properly and they must come from a bona fide organization.
2. The PSAs must avoid controversy for the public service director, for the station manager, for the station, and, most important, for the owner.
3. The PSAs must be of interest to the station's audience. The station's profits come from selling advertising time, and the value of time depends on the size and quality of its audience. A PSA that does not appeal to its audience is a poor PSA. This explains why public service directors are so interested in PSAs with local interest. Local interest means more audience appeal.

In addition, those who work with P&NPOs find the experience personally satisfying. One can expect the public service director to have a sense of commitment and to be altruistic.

What does this imply for the P&NP marketer? All stations and all print media differ. Each has its own audience, its own technical requirements, its own touchy subjects, its own commercial clients. And the interests of public service directors differ from station to station. This means that the social marketer must visit the station in person and talk to the public service director. That is the best way to break through the clamor for attention in which the public service director resides, and it is the only way to learn how the P&NP must adapt its PSAs to the station's requirements. If a radio station requires that all PSAs on cassettes be accompanied by a written script and one organization does not have a script, its PSAs will not even be reviewed. If a television station runs only fifteen- and thirty-second PSAs, a sixty has a slim chance of ever being run.

There are three rules to follow here: (1) tailor the offerings to the specific audience; (2) never rely on the mail or other impersonal ways to request air time—do it in person; and (3) PSAs must be combined with other media. That is what Michael Stringer accomplished in a recent Ohio campaign against armed robbery. Director of the Ohio Governor's

Office of Criminal Justice Services, Stringer included television and radio PSAs along with billboards and posters. As he explained, "According to a recent citizen-attitude survey, over 60 percent of the public has strong opinions on criminal justice, but only 10 percent of those polled said they based their opinions on factual knowledge. Our challenge is to get people more information and increase their understanding (of the criminal justice system)" (Lehrman 1986, p. 11).

SUMMARY

As with most other marketing decisions by P&NPOs, advertising decisions are rooted in an understanding of clients and how they behave. One cannot hope to select advertising messages, media, or even advertising objectives, without such an understanding. This focus on the client is what gives the marketer a unique brand of expertise in the organization.

Beginning with a communications model, the marketer must relate marketing concepts to mass media planning. These concepts include segmentation, advertising's role in the marketing mix, budgeting, the importance of objectives and research, and PSAs. Advertising is not the most powerful way to communicate a message, often not as powerful as face-to-face techniques. And there are many traps that can spoil the attempts of P&NPOs to mount effective advertising campaigns. But to reach mass audiences with standardized messages it cannot be surpassed. Used with discrimination, it definitely has a place in the communications tool kit of the social marketer.

13

The Starving Baby Appeal

SEYMOUR H. FINE

Rutgers, The State University of New Jersey

As marketers well know, every advertising campaign should have a strong theme. The theme is the message. This is where creativity, nay, genius, enters the scene.

In a broad sense, most themes can be divided into two classes, sad or glad. Sad themes are those associated with fear, guilt, pity, and criticism. Glad themes are those connected with patriotism, security, self-esteem, the good life, sex, love, and companionship. Each type of theme has its own style of presentation. For example, humor is often used to convey happy themes, as illustrated by a campaign promoting condom use to check Thailand's population growth. Social marketer Mechai Viravaidya has, since 1970, engaged in such flamboyant activities as handing out free condoms to police in a "cops and rubbers" campaign and staging exhibitions like condom blowing contests and demonstrating that a condom can hold water. Plastic key rings containing condoms and inscribed, "In case of emergency, break glass," are distributed to all members of Parliament. The result: a dramatic decrease in Thailand's population growth rate (Landy 1985). But many advertising appeals use pity to convey their themes. These comprise the subject of this chapter.

Because many public and nonprofit organizations promote ideas and programs designed to ameliorate human suffering, some of their promotion themes have depicted people in a miserable condition. This type of presentation—which may show malnourished children with distended stomachs, bodies of drunken drivers being thrown through demolished windshields, and the well-known American Indian with tears on his face riding a horse through garbage and telling people not to litter—is designed to arouse empathy. The same effect may be sought by showing not the victims, but the perpetrators of wretchedness, such as sinister-looking prowlers burglarizing homes.

Sometimes referred to as the *starving baby appeal*, this approach has been effective in some campaigns. Even its critics acknowledge that this may be the only way to elicit emergency support in a crisis. The blind, disabled, or impoverished street beggar always dressed in tatters is a common sight in most parts of the world.

During the 1985 Ethiopian famine emergency, two pity ads in the New York Times brought three-quarters of a million dollars in contributions to the Save the Children Fund. They depicted an emaciated-looking child over the caption, "Whether she lives or dies, depends on what you do next." Admitting that such themes have serious drawbacks if used steadily, the agency commented that the resulting success "defies almost every rule of nonprofit new donor acquisition" ("Famine in Ethiopia" 1985, p. 44).

The pity appeal works because many people, when they observe suffering, tend to count their blessings, feel good, and respond charitably. Some marketers argue that if we see an improvement in poverty, we tend to want to give less to charitable causes. They claim that people are unwilling to give too much for fear that the poor will become equal with their benefactors, who will then not be able to feel superior. People are better off primarily because some members of society are worse off, a psychological reality that cannot go unnoticed by the social marketer in planning advertising platforms.

At the same time, some criticize the starving baby syndrome for being too negative: "The practice assaults human dignity, reducing the victim to an object of pity and placing emphasis on the physical manifestations of hunger—thereby highlighting its symptoms but ignoring its causes. It also peddles, perhaps unintentionally, a view of the world that is out of date, out of touch with reality, arrogantly conceived and potentially dangerous" (Hollon 1983, p. 968).

Moreover, a British agency responsible for promoting a drive against drunk driving proved that ads using calm, rational explanations were more effective than the gruesome depictions ("Tell Them Not To" 1988). In contrast, fire insurance companies in Ohio that employed TV campaigns showing photographs of badly burned children received numerous complaints (Philip D. Cooper, personal communication). Similarly, advertisements that depict the peoples of developing countries as helpless and dependent may elicit an unfavorable response. Such a portrayal completely overlooks the rich culture, traditions, and creativity among developing societies.

A principal criticism of the starving baby syndrome is that its short-term advertising objectives are only effective for emergency aid and fail to pay court to many potential long-term donors, who find the presentation distasteful. It does little to instill self-esteem, self-help, and human dignity, and merely prolongs the state of misery. It rarely touches on the fundamental causes of the problem; pity puts out fires without removing combustible materials. This is paradoxical because the sum of all the short-term contributions to a cause might add up to a larger amount of money than a one-time expenditure used wisely to ameliorate the problem once and for all. The welfare system provides an example: It has been argued that the totality of welfare funds could be used for programs to help people to lift themselves up by their bootstraps, so that they would no longer require assistance.

This point also applies to the overall image of organizations, particularly those becoming more independent because they have established profit-making ventures. As the executive director of an urban development agency has noted: "You can use the sad story of a depressed neighborhood for only so long. People get bored with it. And nothing impresses people more than earning money" (Williams 1982, Part II, p. 17).

Closely related to pity is the *guilt* appeal, a flagrant example being that employed by the television evangelist, Oral Roberts, who threatened that unless he collected sufficient monies for missionary work, God would "call me home." According to Victoria Sackett, an editor of *Public Opinion* magazine, "From here it was a short step to the National Lampoon . . . to appeal to us in heart-rending black and white with a 'Petey' look-alike (the dog with the circle around his eye from 'Our Gang'). A gun was held to his adorably cocked head above this message: 'Buy our magazine, or we'll shoot the dog.' . . . This is a routine that will work only once" (1987, p. 19).

ALTERNATIVES

The question is, to what extent should the starving baby approach be replaced by more positive, dignified, and rational appeals in social cause marketing? Many have already employed the "healthy baby" theme. For example, the Save the Children Federation has printed ads showing Paul Newman and his wife, Joanne Woodward, as a happy family complete with a fox terrier and photographs of seven smiling children whom they have sponsored for the past sixteen years. Similarly, the American Cancer Society has shown nonsmokers jogging healthfully in the park, and the Israeli government's successful fund-raising campaigns for agricultural development emphasize its accomplishments in reclaiming desert lands, now planted with lush greenery. Still other social marketers, perhaps unsure of which appeal is best, have struck a compromise with photos of both the sick and the healthy in a before-and-after format. A

Christian Children's Fund ad, for example, shows a picture of a sickly child alongside a healthy one, with the caption, "Look what an incredible difference my sponsorship has made in this little boy's life." The healthy baby appeal focuses on the solution to the problem, rather than the problem itself. It is a positive, more rational approach that plays on consumers' zest for life, and produces happy, not sad advertising.

There is no shortage of illustrations supporting the shift in philosophy in social advertising. The American Cancer Society's fund-raising copy can cite frightening mortality statistics but instead chooses the theme, "Today's Woman Has a Will of Her Own." That campaign capitalized on the individuality and independence of women with a positive message: "Many women prefer to handle things themselves . . . and to make their own decisions. After you have remembered those close to you (in your will), we ask you to remember the American Cancer Society." Not a negative thought anywhere.

One wonders whether the tear-faced Indian brought cleaner streets than the earlier "Give a Hoot, Don't Pollute" campaign. In that television commercial, Woodsy the Owl sang approval of the cleanup job by a group of happy, playing children.

Still another example comes from research on organ donations (McIntyre 1983), which has demonstrated that promotion themes emphasizing the health of the would-be donor tend to be more acceptable than purely informative messages, and certainly more than those of the "You have nothing to fear" or "Signing up for organ donation does not violate religious precepts" variety.

The same philosophy applies in commercial marketing. Consider the home computer advertisement showing a woebegone youngster standing at a blackboard with simple addition problems undone. The headline reads: "Because if he stumbles he may never catch up." We are expected to believe that academic progress is impossible without a computer. A wise competitor instead chose to show two smiling children seated before the computer, which is referred to in the caption as "a friendly teacher."

TOWARD A MODEL

Social marketing is sorely in need of a model that would help the promotion strategist find the appropriate message appeal. Such a model would suggest when it is best to employ a factual appeal, and when to use pity, fun, shock, or healthy appeals, and so on. It is a complex matter. Some situations call for two different appeals in tandem. In others, one theme might be appropriate at the outset of the campaign and another later on, as a private university in serious financial trouble discovered several years ago. The trustees built their fund-raising program around a frank admission of the gravity of the situation—"Can the community afford to see us drown?" After several months of running this appeal—which produced substantial bequests—the trustees decided to change to a happier theme: "Thank you; you saved us; look at what you've accomplished." Promotion and publicity emphasized a bustling atmosphere, depicting contented students, athletic and social events, and filled classrooms. After the change, contribution activity decreased somewhat but later continued at a reasonably satisfactory level.

A Two-Step Model. This example suggests that charity appeals would do well using a two-step campaign: a pity theme for emergency relief, followed by a rational theme to obtain long-term goals. Such an approach would be equally effective in altruistic advertising in general and in the social sector in particular.

Some work has been done toward developing a model along these lines (Patti and Murphy 1983), in an empirical test of ads on behalf of the United Ostomy Association, a national nonprofit organization concerned with the problems of (mostly cancer) patients who have lost part or all of their intestines or urinary tracts. As a result, many of these patients wear a device that helps them to function. Some 100,000 ostomy operations are performed every year. The organization's goals are to inform people about the importance of early diagnosis of cancer and about the apparatus, and to increase membership. Three types of mass media appeals were considered—shock, factual, and fun. Sample ads were created to illustrate these three appeals, and all were subjected to elaborate copytesting procedures. In test results, the fun ad ranked first in overall effectiveness, the factual ad second, and the shock ad last.

However, the tests revealed that each type of appeal was valuable in its own right in certain areas: The fun ad scored highest on respondent desire for additional information and intention to join the organization. The factual ad proved most effective in providing information. Of the three, the shock ad ranked highest credence.

Consequently, the two-step model—or perhaps a multistep model—may have considerable merit. A combination of themes might prove more effective than any single one.

SUMMARY

Whether social causes and P&NP programs promoted through the use of pity appeals alone can generate lasting support is open to question. Although this approach has often been successful in short-term fund-raising campaigns, it does not build a following of committed patrons. What themes will ensure that a given promotion objective is achieved? This question has not yet been answered in social marketing. More research is needed to develop a theme selection model that can be used as a guide for this purpose. At present, the tendency is to rely on happy themes.

NOTE

An earlier version of this chapter appeared in Seymour H. Fine, "Social and Nonprofit Marketing: Some Trends and Issues," in *Advances in Nonprofit Marketing*, 2nd ed., ed. Russell Belk (Greenwich, CT: JAI Press, 1987), 71–98. Reprinted with permission.

14

Fund-Raising

SEYMOUR H. FINE

Rutgers, The State University of New Jersey

In most marketing transactions, a buyer pays a price to a seller for certain goods. Public goods, those marketed by government agencies, are paid for primarily by taxation. However, some 5 percent of the American economy, the nonprofit sector, is financed by voluntary contributions. People pay these resources whether or not they consume what they are paying for, and they do so by choice, not by necessity. These resources are amassed largely through the efforts of fund-raising planners. (For an excellent compendium of statistics on philanthropy, see Weber 1988.)

Government agencies also engage in fund-raising activity, although to a lesser extent. This category includes the phonathon campaigns of state universities; sales at the gift shop in the Smithsonian Institution, whose profits accrue to an agency of the U.S. government; and such international campaigns as the food programs of India and Ethiopia and the Jewish National Fund of Israel. When we contribute to social and fraternal activities of police benevolent associations, fire and ambulance groups, "Friends of the Library," county zoos, and town playgrounds, we are supporting municipal services (see Hawkins 1986, p. 57).

Fund-raising is one special type of social marketing, one of the most vital and yet one that is too often seen in a negative light. Few individuals relish the prospect of soliciting contributions. At the giving end, many are uncertain whether and how much to give, and how to select the most deserving charities. Tax deductibility is another important issue.

FUND-RAISING TECHNIQUES

Periodical indexes are filled with titles that refer to successful case studies and offer the development director a wealth of ideas. This section contains several examples of creative techniques gleaned from such listings.

Fun. The Friends of the Alexander Hamilton Memorial Library in Waynesboro, Pennsylvania, needed three thousand dollars to supplement the library's reduced budget. A list of potential "jailees" was drawn up to include elected officials, local businesspeople, and school teachers. Flyers were posted, a local radio station publicized the event, and the local newspaper printed the top ten "most wanted" list on its front page every other day. For every $50 raised, the "convict" would spend fifteen minutes in jail. Over five thousand dollars was raised, the community was informed of the library and its needs, and the library won a John Cotton Dana Library Public Relations Award ("Jail-A-Thon" 1985).

Select Treatment. The Jewish National Fund of South Africa wished to plant a forest as a monument to the fifty-three young South African Jews who were killed defending the people and land of Israel. A motorcycle messenger hand-delivered a promotional package to twenty-five selected "key" individuals while other potential sponsors were contacted by telephone. More than $134,000 was raised ("Potted Trees" 1984).

Civic Pride. The Nature Conservancy is a preservation group, working to conserve mountain areas, marshlands, prairies, and other threatened environments throughout the United States, Latin America, and the Caribbean. A regionalized and personalized direct mail campaign was undertaken in which donors were asked to support conservation projects in their own locales (Hoffman 1986).

Factual Appeal. To alleviate serious funding distress, KCET, a public television station in Los Angeles, instituted a series of pledge breaks—spot announcements designed to be "simple, straightforward and sincere appeals that contain facts." Examples: "KCET, Your Vacation from Ordinary TV" and "Light Up KCET for the Holidays." The spots were reinforced with newspaper and television ads as well as scripted celebrity tapes. In the first year of the campaign, pledges rose from $699,000 to $1,120,000 ("Providing Public Television's Tools" 1986).

Mega-event. The well-publicized Hands Across America campaign to combat hunger and homelessness was staged by the organization USA for Africa, which succeeded in obtaining support from Citicorp/Citibank, New York, and the Coca-Cola Co., Atlanta. The bank contributed more than $3 million to the event. Six million consumers and corporate representatives linked hands from Los Angeles to New York and contributed funds for the cause. Additional funds came from merchandise bearing the "Hands" logo, and EMI America Records released an album with "Hands" on one side and "World" on the other (Forkan 1986).

Contest. A program called View from the Torch used a unique contest format to support the restoration of the Statue of Liberty. Lists were printed containing clues leading treasure hunters to certain cultural and social events, and to some tangible aspect of each event, that is, the "treasure." Participants submitted their answers and the winners were drawn from the correct responses. There were twenty prizes in all, donated by hotels, airlines, and other companies ("Checking Out the View" 1986).

Sex. Thirty-three bachelors donated dates to raise money for the March of Dimes. Dinner in New York and a weekend on an island were two of the many kinds of dates for which women were invited to bid. The bids started at $100 and were expected to rise up somewhere in the thousands. The event was scheduled to be held on a specified date in a major hotel in the suburbs of New York City. The scheme provided tax deductions for both the male participants, who paid for the dates, and the women, who bid for them (Kathy Valle, personal communication).

Sweepstakes. The American Lung Association (ALS) has conducted tests with various forms of fund-raising sweepstakes. By offering entry gifts such as bumper stickers and Christmas seals, it increased the campaign response. As for sweepstakes prizes, it was found that the greater the utilitarian value, the more people were attracted to the sweepstakes. Sweepstakes have become a major source of funds for the ALS, raising more than $7 million in 1985 (Roel 1985).

UNBUNDLING AND ESTABLISHING BUSINESS VENTURES

A more commercially oriented approach that is also making headway throughout the social sector is one in which the organization spins off, or "unbundles" certain existing departments (such as the cardiovascular clinic of a hospital) and turns them into separate profit-making enterprises. Or an agency might venture forth into a new activity in order to earn income—for example, a hospital might open a motel nearby. The practice seems to be growing in popularity. It originated with the recent cutbacks in government support for social programs; increases in fuel, labor, and other operating expenses; and shrinking private donations. During the first Reagan administration, nonprofit organizations lost $13.5 billion in decreased federal grants and faced another estimated loss of $12 billion each year as a result of the Treasury Department's proposed restrictions on tax benefits to charitable contributors (Teltsch 1987). Those staggering figures dramatize the plight of thousands of nonprofit organizations throughout the country, many of which were in financial trouble even before the budget cuts. In order to cope, agency administrators faced three choices: cut costs, look for new fund-raising sources, or earn money through profit-making ventures. Many turned to the profit-making strategy, which in the past had been generally frowned upon.

Commercialization in the nonprofit sector probably dates back to 1874, when the Metropolitan Museum of Art began selling prints of art masterpieces. Subsequently, however, the trend was slow to develop. For one thing, most nonprofit organizations are not financially or business-oriented, and for years have accepted deficits as a fact of life, always hoping for assistance from the government or from private donors. Then, too, many organizations feared that such activities would cancel their tax-exempt status. Only recently has the unbundling move accelerated, as has the spread of marketing to the nonprofit sector.

Some Examples

A number of examples can be cited to illustrate how nonprofit organizations have implemented unbundling programs. These might serve to tempt other institutions to test their ingenuity in business ventures.

Museum gift shops are now commonplace. Lesser known are enterprises such as the gift bar, in existence at the New York City Ballet. The organization grosses about $125,000 per year, netting almost half of that because the shop is staffed by volunteers. Sales are made only in the half hour prior to curtain time and during intermissions. Starting out only with a line of posters, the gift bar now merchandises about two hundred items.

Possessing a few thousand Currier and Ives lithographs, the Museum of the City of New York is involved in a venture with a publisher, Abbeville Press, to produce and market Currier and Ives books. For a few years, Abbeville funded the effort by a fee to the museum, but now itself enjoys a handsome profit on the line, which includes a large expensive volume, a popular-priced paperback, and a calendar series.

When the New York Museum of Modern Art recently doubled its size by building a new wing, it financed the addition in an unusual manner. A builder purchased from the museum the air rights required to erect a forty-four story condominium building. The transaction yielded $17 million tax-free dollars to the museum.

Richard Steckel, former director of the Children's Museum of Denver, says "Nonprofits are businesses and must think exactly like businesses." When Mr. Steckel arrived at the Children's Museum in 1977, three federal grants had just expired. To earn revenue quickly, the museum started charging for exhibits, opened a gift shop, and created a line of childrens' publications. It also developed a mascot: a cuddly creature called NUZZ, which led to toys, fruit punch, and frozen fruit juice bars. The museum recently completed a $13 million expansion and is now 95 percent self-sufficient (Calonius et al. 1987).

The Delancey Street Foundation in San Francisco is one of the nation's most successful treatment centers for ex-addicts, alcoholics, convicts, and prostitutes. Since its founding in 1973, it has operated under the philosophy that it must engage in profit-making enterprises and not rely exclusively on grants and doles (Williams, Part II, 1982).

Contraceptive producers are keeping a watchful eye on marketing activities of the Planned Parenthood Federation of America, which has begun promoting condoms under its own brand name. Originally made to sell at its clinics, the group plans to place its products with retail drug stores. In a similar move, the American Red Cross has test-marketed a first-aid kit. Both ventures seem quite logical when one thinks of the well-established business of cookie sales by the Girl Scouts—one of the more classic examples of a tie-in of a tangible product with the cause of a social organization.

The Bank Street College of Education in New York City is earning several hundred thousand dollars each year marketing computer software. The school established royalty arrangements with Broderbund Software and Scholastics, Inc., to perform the publishing and marketing functions, respectively.

The Pikes Peak Mental Health Center in Colorado Springs leases a portion of its land to Wendy's, the fast-food franchise. The plan for the joint venture includes an option under which the center might ultimately own the business outright. But that is only one of several real estate innovations it has under way. Taking full advantage of tax code provisions to increase cash flow, it finances the purchase of properties, which it rents out to other organizations.

The main mission of the Bronx Frontier Development is to create park areas within the slums of the South Bronx in New York City. To raise funds, the organization produces and markets topsoil by composting garbage from a local produce market and sells the output to residents in suburban Westchester County. Williams notes sardonically, this is a form of "the underclass returning to the upper class a different form of the 'crap' it's been taking for generations" (Part I, 1982, p. 20).

Finally, Michael Bernick (1984) described several nonprofit organizations in the San Francisco Bay area that have gone into profit-making businesses in order to become financially independent and to create jobs as well. One of these is the Spanish-speaking Unity Council, a San Francisco–based organization that provides housing and job training. After analyzing numerous options, they chose to buy a Thrifty Rent-A-Car franchise using a $400,000 government grant. In the first two years, they had losses of $20,000 and $60,000. The third year they grossed $2 million and currently expect their profits to continue.

The Chinatown Resources Development Center launched a janitorial service hiring Asian immigrants with poor skills in English. It soon generated $20,000 per month in revenues, employing twenty persons and providing significant income for the organization.

Implementation

These unbundling cases were found in recent periodicals and newspapers, which, understandably, are more likely to report successes than failures. Lest an unrealistic picture be painted, it should be emphasized that only 10 to 15 percent of such ventures achieve any degree of profitability. It is interesting that the success rate for new products in the commercial realm is about the same—about 10 percent. Moreover, nonprofit enterprises fail for much the same reasons that ordinary businesses do: misreading consumer needs and wants, poor timing, mismanagement, poor choice of consultants, underestimating the competition, and failing to assess and take into account the organization's strengths and weaknesses.

Although these are reasonable speculations, they do not suggest how to plan and implement a business enterprise. Far more useful would be a marketing plan, such as that suggested in Chapter 1.

Ordinarily, agencies cannot go it alone. Unless individuals with solid entrepreneurial experience can be found among administrative or staff personnel, the organization is well-advised to seek assistance from outside. A number of firms specializing in earned-income business formation in the social sector include New Ventures and Museum Quality Services, Inc. in New York City; Fine Marketing Associates in Glen Rock, New Jersey; and Peter C. Brown in Minneapolis-St. Paul, Minnesota. The agency might also inquire at a nearby university. Faculty with research interests in the social sector are often willing to help. But it is important that the individual's competence be thoroughly investigated; free or low-cost but ineffective counsel can become expensive in the long run.

The trustee of the nonprofit organization can play an important part in implementing the business enterprise. Trustees are valuable sources of expertise in accounting, law, marketing, and finance, and most are eager to advise agency administrators and staff. (Of course, this presupposes that trustees support the idea of going commercial. If too many board members oppose it, the venture warrants careful rethinking.) Advice should also be sought from other influential people in the community, who should be invited to sit on advisory committees, which are especially important in planning the operation and guiding it through those difficult early periods.

Some Caveats

Before plunging into a commercial venture, the nonprofit agency must be aware that several pitfalls exist even beyond the high risk of failure ordinarily associated with a new business undertaking. One danger is that the new venture might meet with strong opposition from the for-profit firms it will be competing with (see Chapter 2). Another is that it might endanger its tax-exempt status. The IRS grants tax exemption when the income-producing venture is substantially related to the main purpose of the agency. But if a 501(3)(C) corporation grosses more than $1,000 per year from unrelated operations, it is required to file a Form 990-T and to pay taxes on that income. The requirements are set forth in an IRS publication, "Tax on Unrelated Business Income of Exempt Organizations." The purpose is to establish a degree of competitive parity between nonprofit agencies and commercial firms.

The threat of taxation does not deter many agencies from venturing forth into worthwhile income-producing activities, regardless of the tax burden. In 1982, a total of $24.6 million was paid by nonprofit organizations in federal taxes for business income unrelated to the agencies' principal purposes (Solomon 1984). Even where the extracurricular business is somewhat related, some organizations pay the resulting taxes just to be on the safe side. For example, when the public broadcasting station WETA in Washington, D.C., unbundled an income-producing unit called WETACOM, offering video production and teleconferencing services, it paid taxes on all profits derived from the subsidiary. At this writing, the "publicized threat of additional legislation has already doubled voluntary payments of the unrelated business income tax" ("Why the Rush?" 1988).

In many cases it is questionable whether the nonprofit organization should cross over into the profit-making domain. Skloot (1983) argues that only a small fraction of agencies should even try. However, I am more optimistic, in the spirit of the adage, "Behold the turtle, he never progresses unless he sticks his neck out." Moreover, public and nonprofit organizations (P&NPOs) "create business for others. Book and print stores near museums, for example, benefit from the excitement and crowds generated by big exhibitions. Many flower stores would not exist but for nearby hospitals" ("Why the Rush?" 1988).

RECIPROCAL BENEFITS FROM SOCIAL MARKETING

Strategies for corporate giving have changed over the years, and corporations are looking for new ways and places to give (see Avery Hunt 1986). Two successful approaches devised in recent years—in-kind philanthropy and cause-related marketing—rely on commercial firms to assist in promoting P&NPOs and their causes. This has proved beneficial to the firms themselves.

In-kind Philanthropy

It is not uncommon for a firm to be called upon to contribute in-kind goods and services to P&NPOs. Advertising agencies in particular, are in a unique position to contribute in this way, and to benefit as well. By donating talent to create social ads, the agency gains an opportunity to display its work publicly. The audience is likely to include at least a few prospective corporate clients who will take note of the agency credited in the fine print. How better to advertise advertising! No wonder the practice is so widespread.

In fact, the entire advertising industry, through its American Association of Advertising Agencies (4 A's) recently adopted the cause of drug use prevention by embarking on a collaborative "war on drugs" campaign. Announcing the multimedia public service program to the 1986 annual meeting of the 4 A's, its chairman, Louis Hagopian, explained the purpose was to enhance "advertising's accountability in America" (Brown 1986).

Phoenix House, a drug treatment facility, asked an ad agency for marketing assistance and received a unique program by way of response—the agency, Wunderman, Ricotta and Kline, Inc.—agreed to train Phoenix House residents in the art of direct marketing (Hanley 1984). As a result, this NPO now conducts sophisticated and successful mail campaigns as part of its fund-raising efforts.

World Vision, a Christian relief organization, and the Russ Reid agency, which specializes in fund-raising, combined efforts to raise money for starving Africans, organizing the first live broadcast to originate from Ethiopia. The program consisted of live footage from an Ethiopian refugee camp, performances by celebrities and musicians, and interviews with politicians. An estimated 150,000 calls with pledges were received ("Telethon" 1985). In another example, "After the Minneapolis agency, Clarity Coverdale Rueff, offered to develop a pro bona ad campaign for a local YMCA, the national YMCA organization asked the agency to handle its advertising, too. Since then, CCR's commercial billings have increased fivefold" (Miller and Williams 1986, p. 58).

The other side of the coin is described by Stern (1986, p. 44):

> On one hand, as an agency develops a large roster of paying clients, devoting its time to PSA accounts becomes less viable economically. On the other, the better known an agency becomes for PSA's, the more the requests pour in, and it often feels a responsibility to accept them. Confesses Elaine Silverstein, executive vice president of Beber Silverstein & Partners Advertising in Miami, "A direct mail piece for the American Jewish Committee got us our first paying client, and we always feel that if we don't continue to pay back the community, something terrible might happen to us."

Quite apart from advertising professionals, virtually all businesses are called upon to donate goods and services to organizations, most notably on the occasions of church bazaars, grand openings, and emergency fund-raising events. P&NPOs make up an industry in which "free-loading" is not only respectable, but often mutually beneficial. For example, The Murtis H. Taylor Service Center, a halfway house for mental patients, wanted to put its patient and accounting records on computer but its staff lacked the expertise. Through the United Way's loaned executive program, help was obtained from an electric company executive who contributed three hours each week for six months, until the center succeeded in getting "on-line" (Alexander 1985).

A great many companies promote voluntarism in order to increase their visibility. The insurance industry alone has contributed nearly half a million hours each year to community projects: "Both the private and public sectors have much to gain by promoting voluntarism and community service. If these deeds can also serve as marketing tools, they are also defensible as contributors to company profits" (Walker 1987, p. 35).

The types of possible joint ventures are endless and provide unlimited opportunities for stretching one's creativity: "Members Only, the New York-based sportswear chain, has announced that it will donate its entire $6 million advertising budget to an anti-drug campaign featuring, among others, Yankees manager Lou Piniella and New Jersey Nets basketball star Buck Williams. The catch: Piniella and Williams appear in the advertisements wearing—what else—Members Only jackets" (Miller and Williams 1986, p. 58).

The Corporate Special Projects Fund in New York is a group of major New York corporations that give approximately $300,000 every year to projects in the areas of hunger, the homeless, youth employment, and housing. By combining efforts and using a nonprofit foundation to administer the fund, these firms support social service projects they might not otherwise be able to afford.

Burger King invests $4 million a year into highly focused programs to help students, teachers, and schools. Much of this goes to scholarships for its teen work force in an effort to reduce the high turnover rate among those workers. One program is tied to length of employment and another to school performance and community involvement.

The volunteer chairman of the finance committee for the Atlanta Ballet collared personnel from his own construction company in Atlanta as well as others among the building, architecture, and design professions through a "Hard Hats for the Symphony" campaign. Each $250 donor received a symbolic hard hat and the industry-wide scheme gained support from a large number of small- and medium-size businesses (Hunt 1986).

Cause-Related Marketing

In the late 1980s, cause-related marketing has become increasingly popular. The term itself seems to have originated in the American Express Corporation, which used it to describe a number of activities the firm had undertaken in order to benefit both itself and an assortment of social causes. The concept is being hailed or criticized (depending upon the source) as a new form of marketing that brings the activities of the public and private sectors closer together.

Cause-related marketing refers to programs that are mutually beneficial to a private firm and a selected social or charitable cause. An effort that provides support to a cause but is not beneficial to the firm does not satisfy this definition. American Express, for example, promoted what it called Project Hometown America; each time a new American Express card was issued or an existing one used, a specified dollar amount was earmarked for a fund providing support for a variety of grassroots social programs throughout the country. While raising $4 million for the social programs, American Express reported only marginal increases in card usage and applications; the scheme was judged a failure. The focus on tangible benefit to the business in this definition distinguishes cause-related marketing from the general philanthropic activities of a firm (Krentler 1988).

The Miller Brewing Company, for example, encourages its distributors to participate in three- to six-mile races with 1,500–4,000 participants. A percentage of the entry fee and proceeds from T-shirts, souvenirs, and food sales are donated to United Cerebral Palsy's area affiliates (Ball 1984).

The Dallas Symphony Orchestra funded a European concert tour through a novel fund-raising effort sponsored by American Airlines. At the time, the airline was introducing service between Dallas and London and offered to donate $5 to the orchestra for every passenger flying the new route. In six months $100,000 was raised for the symphony and the London-Dallas service established. This was not a first for American. In 1983, the airline helped the Fort Worth symphony orchestra by underwriting a concert tour of China. American Airlines donated $3 for every flight made in the frequent flyers program. This effort raised half of the $150,000 needed for the tour ("Music" 1985). Clearly, the firm enjoyed more satisfactory results than did American Express.

KRBE-FM sponsored a Toys for Tots drive in conjunction with Foley's department store in Houston. The station distributed 1,400 movie passes asking theater-goers to donate toys in return. It held a Christmas party at First's, the town's newest nightclub, where it also asked attendees to contribute toys. KRBE-FM disc jockeys kept listeners updated with a running total of contributions and for each 1,000 toys contributed a light was added to a christmas tree. The toys collected were distributed by the Salvation Army to needy children, KRBE-FM attracted many new listeners, and Foley's department store received free publicity by cosponsoring the event ("Airwaves" 1985).

A yearly golf tournament is sponsored by Manufacturers Hanover for the benefit of local hospitals. The best-known event in the tournament is one in which local individuals pay substantial amounts for the privilege of playing with the pro-golfers. This event raised $1.5 million in 1985 (Hill 1986).

General Foods Corporation donated five cents to the Muscular Dystrophy Association for each of its promotional coupons redeemed by consumers. More than 500 million coupons were distributed in newspapers and direct mail, and promotion was supported on the telethon and network television. The donation was limited to $1 million by General Foods.

Lever Brothers Company contributed $5 to the March of Dimes for every consumer who sent in five proof-of-purchase seals from its ALL detergent. Kimberly-Clark supported the American Heart Association with store coupons and a mail-in coupon. The consumer had the option of donating $.25 or $1.25 to the heart association and in return received cash, coupons, or a good health tips booklet. The National Easter Seal Society asked manufacturers to participate by distributing coupons in an Easter Seal "Coupon Savings" book. Each participating brand donated $50,000. The book was offered through the Carol Wright mailing operation for a $2 donation to the Easter Seal Society. Bristol-Myers supported United Cerebral Palsy with store coupons plus a sweepstakes for the consumer.

Advocating cause-related marketing to public relations practitioners, Goldblatt (1985) described it as an all-win situation. Everyone benefits—the public relations professional, the charity, and the corporate entity. Furthermore, "The longer groups work together, the greater understanding both will have."

> A local Washington, DC shopping center enhanced its public image by giving a portion of the proceeds from its Santa Claus photo booth to UNICEF. The program was so successful that many celebrities attended, and local and network-news crews covered the "Help Santa Help the World's Children" opening day. UNICEF was selected primarily because of its good image with children and because of its ability to attract positive media attention for the shopping center. UNICEF raised thousands of dollars, and the center received measurable public visibility by introducing a spirit of love and caring into a traditionally commercial setting. . . .
>
> Leo Schargorodski, executive director of the National Capital Area March of Dimes, suggests that the charity organizers try to establish a "right of first refusal" agreement with a major corporate sponsor. He cites his chapter's relationship with the Southland Corporation (owners of the 7-Eleven chain) as an example. "We give them the type of visibility they cannot pay for, and we offer them the opportunity to review each proposal first and become part of those events that most benefit their marketing programs," says Schargorodski. "They assist us with printing and staff support, and Southland's corporate logo appears on event flyers and brochures and in public-service announcements." He does caution charities to be careful not to approach more than one corporate competitor at a time, even if it takes weeks for the proposal to be reviewed. Most corporations will not, for obvious reasons, support a charity already supported by a major competitor. (Goldblatt 1985, p. 16)

Affinity cards are another type of reciprocal fund-raising device. Under this arrangement, some social cause receives a small percentage of every credit card transaction recorded by an agency. To illustrate, Augusta College raised funds through a credit card plan offered by Bankers First Federal Savings and Loan of Augusta. The card was adopted by the college's alumni association, and bears the college name and logo. The bank pays a percentage of the annual fee to the organization for each new card issued. Members can also make donations through an automatic charging arrangement. The college expects to raise $64,000 through the Augusta College Alumni Card ("Marketing Briefs" 1987). In 1988 affinity cards accounted for some 6 percent of the 205 million credit cards in use in the United States (Gould 1988).

Advocacy advertising is similar to cause-related marketing in that a business usually "adopts" and supports a nonprofit organization. In the former, the firm assumes responsibility for promoting a favorite social cause independent of any organization. Thus in recent years, United Technologies, a Connecticut-based producer of aircraft engines and other industrial products, conducted a massive campaign promoting crime prevention. And Peter Grace, Chairman of the W. R. Grace Company, campaigned for (via full-page ads in major newspapers) a decrease in the capital gains tax. Although advocacy advertising is a way of disseminating ideas and hence can be considered social marketing, it is conducted by commercial firms and is thus outside the scope of this book.

SUMMARY

Many excellent books cover the subject of fund-raising, as do numerous articles in periodicals and newspapers. The publication, *Fund-Raising Management* is a byword in the nonprofit field. Among the fund-raising techniques being tested by nonprofit organizations, unbundling, or spinning off commercial ventures, is becoming increasingly popular. Many corporations are eager to support the causes of the social sector, especially where benefits are reciprocal. There are countless possibilities in the area of interactive schemes for agencies' development officers to explore. Two that have been particularly successful are in-kind philanthropy and such cause-related practices as affinity cards.

15

Analyzing Marketing Performance

CHARLES W. LAMB, JR.
Texas Christian University

JOHN L. CROMPTON
Texas A&M University

The feathers in the consultant's cap are always at least somewhat ruffled when a client inquires about the evaluation of marketing efforts or the assessment of marketing programs, for there are not many effective ways to assess and evaluate them. But for many reasons, analyze we must. There are at least a few techniques that can help agency administrators analyze the problems and prospects of marketing performance. Managers have at their disposal certain evaluation procedures, which can be used for specific programs, in addition to the marketing audit, which can provide a comprehensive profile of the organization's total marketing effort and a basis for developing and revising its marketing plan.

Experience has shown that marketing plans do not always work exactly as expected. Sometimes performance exceeds expectations and sometimes it falls short. The final step in the marketing planning process is to evaluate the organization's marketing performance. Evaluation addresses the question, "Where are we now in relation to where we wanted to be at this time?" The purpose of evaluation is to maximize the probability that the organization will achieve both short- and long-term objectives. The process has two components—program evaluation and the marketing audit.

Program evaluation entails making periodic assessments of specific programs or services. It monitors the extent to which individual programs are being implemented in the desired manner and whether specified milestones and objectives are being achieved. The overall goal of evaluation is to discover and, if necessary, act upon deviations from anticipated happenings and recognize unanticipated weaknesses, threats, or opportunities in specific programs.

The marketing audit, on the other hand, focuses on evaluation of the total set of agency programs: An audit is "a comprehensive, systematic, independent, and periodic examination of an organization's marketing environment, objectives, strategies, and activities with a view of determining problem areas and opportunities and recommending a plan of action to improve the organization's strategic marketing performance" (Kotler and Andreasen 1987, p. 638). Although the evaluation and the audit both look to the past for guidelines for the future, audits focus on the entire organization whereas evaluations are concerned with specific programs. Furthermore, audits are much more comprehensive and are therefore performed less frequently, perhaps every five years.

PROGRAM EVALUATION

Effectiveness and Efficiency

In general, public and nonprofit organizations evaluate programs on the basis of their effectiveness or efficiency. Effectiveness has to do with end results and the impact of a marketing effort on a clientele. The central question here is "Does the program offer the benefits that it was intended to deliver to clients?" Efficiency characterizes the relationship between inputs and outputs and reflects the amount of effort, expense, or waste involved in the marketing process. To assess efficiency, one asks, "Is the program being delivered in the least costly way?"

The first step in evaluation is to define what should be measured. Too much emphasis is often placed on evaluating the efficiency of a program, to the neglect of its impact. The average citizen evaluates P&NPOs on the basis of results. People want their garbage collected on time and without mess. They want good schools, minimal losses from fire, and political leadership of high integrity. The local citizen is more interested in crime rate statistics than the dollars spent on police services, miles covered patroling, or arrests made.

Because efficiency and effectiveness are measured by different criteria, programs may rate high on one and low on the other. For example, streets may be kept extraordinarily clean, but the street-cleaning program may require an inordinate allocation of resources to achieve its results. In contrast, social workers may process large numbers of clients, but the processing may be performed hastily and with little attention to clients' circumstances. Efficiency is frequently the main evaluation criterion because effectiveness is more difficult to measure. However, it can only be judged by its relationship to effectiveness.

Measuring Effectiveness

From the client's standpoint, measuring effectiveness is tantamount to finding out if the audience concerned is satisfied with the benefits of the program. Client satisfaction can be measured in four ways: (1) unsolicited client response, (2) observation, (3) one-dimensional surveys, and (4) two-dimensional saliency surveys.

The unsolicited client response technique is the least rigorous of the four, as it only requires a mechanism that will enable clients to report their level of satisfaction if they so desire. Suggestion or comment boxes are commonly used. This approach has two limitations. First, neither positive nor negative comments can be generalized for all groups, since the views of those who comment may be very different from the views of those who do not. Second, the absence of a large number of complaints cannot be interpreted as a high degree of satisfaction because as long as the service does not deteriorate below some minimal satisfaction level, many people may not make an effort to complain.

The observation approach is somewhat more representative because it entails direct observation and interaction with clients. A manager may visit a park, library, or neighborhood and talk to participants or residents about their likes, dislikes, and suggestions for improving the program. The technique allows a manager to seek input from anyone he or she chooses, but again there is no guarantee that the respondents represent all the relevant groups in the audience.

The one-dimensional survey asks individuals to assess the quality of a particular program on a scale ranging from very good to very poor. This approach is not likely to provide useful results. As long as their level of satisfaction is within some adequate range, most respondents will answer positively. A high percentage of favorable evaluations or satisfied responses does not necessarily reflect a high level of satisfaction; it merely reflects a lack of dissatisfaction. Indeed, it has been shown that a program's clients almost always report high satisfaction levels and provide favorable evaluations, even for programs that are not effective (Scheirer 1978, p. 55). Only if a program becomes excessively bad are individuals likely to respond negatively to generalized questions.

Two-dimensional saliency is another survey method, but it measures satisfaction differently. First, it identifies the constituents of "satisfaction." Respondents are then asked to evaluate each perceived benefit on a scale (1 to 7, for example) ranging from extremely satisfactory to extremely unsatisfactory (Table 15.la).

This information alone is of limited value because it gives no indication of the relative importance clients attach to each of the program's benefits. For example, if the items shown in Dimension (a) of Table 15.1 measure sociability and prestige benefits derived from a program, both may receive a score of 4 on a seven-point scale (neither satisfactory nor unsatisfactory). However, sociability may be an important benefit to clients, whereas prestige may be of little interest.

This problem is corrected by the second series of questions, which are designed to rate the salient benefit attributes sought by clients. These measures are most useful for determining whether more effort should be given to improving certain attributes of the program.

If clients rate sociability and prestige benefits 7 and 2, respectively, on this importance scale, then the previous satisfaction score of 4 for the prestige benefit may be considered adequate because a score of 2 shows clients consider it to be unimportant. Thus it is of little concern that the program is not facilitating this benefit particularly well. In contrast, sociability is rated extremely important (a score of 7), so the agency should be greatly concerned if the program is not producing this benefit. Unless the program is restructured in some way to increase its potential for encouraging interaction with others, client support is likely to diminish.

Measuring Efficiency

As already mentioned, efficiency describes the relationship between outputs (products) and inputs (resources)—specifically, it denotes the degree to which the organization produces the product as inexpensively as possible. By regularly measuring various aspects of efficiency, the manager should have a picture of how delivery efficiency is changing over time for individual product offerings. (This section was adapted from Hatry et al. 1977, pp. 223–243.)

The most common efficiency measures are output–input ratios, which use work load accomplished as the measure of output. Examples of outputs are tons of refuse collected, miles of street repaired, acres of grass mowed, number of park trees trimmed, and number of complaints or requests handled. These outputs are related to the input resources used in producing them in terms of dollars or employee hours. Thus they can be expressed as ratios such as "the number of tons collected per dollar or per employee hour" (if dollars are used they should be adjusted annually to reflect real dollar costs and not inflated dollar costs). The employee hour measure produces major insights regarding personnel productivity. Dollar costs represent all inputs and thus make it possible

TABLE 15.1 A Two-Dimensional Survey Approach to Measuring Satisfaction

Dimension (a)

	Extremely Unsatisfactory	Very Unsatisfactory	Slightly Unsatisfactory	Neither Unsatisfactory nor Satisfactory	Slightly Satisfactory	Very Satisfactory	Extremely Satisfactory
Opportunity to interact with others in this program is	1	2	3	④	5	6	7
Discussion generated among my friends by my participation in this program is	1	2	3	④	5	6	7

Dimension (b)

	Extremely Unimportant	Very Unimportant	Slightly Unimportant	Neither Unimportant nor Important	Slightly Important	Very Important	Extremely Important
Opportunity to interact with others in this program is	1	2	3	4	5	6	⑦
Discussion generated among my friends by my participation in this program is	1	②	3	4	5	6	7

Source: Reprinted with permission from John L. Crompton and Charles W. Lamb, *Marketing Government and Social Services* (New York: John Wiley & Sons, 1986), p. 15. Copyright © 1986 by John Wiley & Sons, Inc.

to consider the efficiency with which all resources are being used, not just personnel.

The major weakness in the output–input method is that an improvement in the ratio of work accomplished per unit of input may be attributed to an improvement in efficiency when in fact, it may more accurately reflect deterioration in the level of service offered. To rectify this problem, a second and more sophisticated type of measure has been suggested. This method adopts output–input ratio measures using effectiveness data as the measure of output. This type of measure assesses the proportion of households, citizens, or clients satisfied with the service per dollar or per employee hour. It combines the conventional number-of-persons-served rules with a measure of the percentage of citizens satisfied with the service. This measure ensures that gains in efficiency are not taking place at the expense of effectiveness.

When efficiency measures concentrate on one dimension of a service, personnel tend to interpret this imbalance as a signal of management priority and concentrate on the activities measured. For example, if police officers are evaluated on traffic ticketing or vice arrests, efficiency in these areas will increase. Similarly,

> If welfare workers are assessed on their error rate, the error rate will go down because workers pay more attention to it. If teachers are assessed or even remotely evaluated on the proportion of their charges who pass year-end examinations, more will pass because teachers will "teach the test." This is neither surprising nor in itself deplorable, but simply highly probable. (Lipsky 1980, p. 166)

Clearly, whatever efficiency measures are selected should reflect those benefits that the organization's public perceive as the most important. Otherwise, personnel could receive the wrong message, as did the employment counselors who, when assessed in terms of successful placement ratios, concentrated on easy-to-place clients at the expense of more difficult cases (Blau 1964, pp. 36–56).

Three other problems may emerge when P&NPOs undertake to measure efficiency. First, there is some danger of encouraging excessive concern with current performance at the expense of future performance. If too much emphasis is placed on current efficiency, efforts aimed at improving future performance may be neglected. This may result in much higher expenditures in future years to rectify problems, because the cost of decay is invariably greater than that required to provide timely maintenance.

Second, changes in results obtained from efficiency measures must be interpreted carefully: "Substantial increases or decreases in the incoming workload can by themselves significantly affect efficiency values. The type of service offered may change. In addition, differing external characteristics of neighborhoods (such as the terrain or resident population) make it difficult to compare various facilities or different units of workers in different areas" (Hatry et al. 1977, p. 239).

Third, concern for efficiency can become self-defeating. Local governments, for example, have been known to carry out such detailed efficiency measurements, that they cannot pass their own tests of cost-effectiveness.

Utilization of Evaluation Research

Evaluation should be an integral part of an organization's marketing planning system, but for several reasons it is often ignored by decision-makers. First, P&NPOs usually function in a political environment that forces them to consider other factors beyond research evidence. At times negative evaluations have been ignored because withdrawal or modification of the program would have had an adverse effect on the clienteles served, other support groups, and the organization's prestige (Rocheleau and Mackesey 1981, p. 187). At other times, the issues and goals pursued and measured by evaluations are often not the issues or goals in which program managers are interested, and so the findings are ignored. In addition, many evaluations fail to suggest how the service might be improved. Consequently, the evaluation results are greeted with indifference or hostility.

Still other administrators practice "pseudomanagement" (Nigro and Nigro 1980, p. 256). They do not support unambiguous statements of objectives or seek tangible evidence of an offering's success or failure. Their attitude stems either from inertia and lack of genuine commitment, or from the notion that vagueness gives them more room to maneuver.

Attitudes of the Players in the Scenario

The ideal program evaluation involves three characters: (1) a top executive who supports and uses the results of evaluations to make important decisions, (2) a program manager who encourages and supports the evaluation of his or her program, and (3) an evaluator whose insightful recommendations produce "slam bang" changes in the efficiency and effectiveness of the program.

Actual program evaluations are often quite different: (1) many top executives distrust or ignore evaluations done by anyone else, (2) some program managers use subversive tactics to thwart, mislead, and discredit evaluations and evaluators, and (3) many evaluators are concerned with survival and advocating personal agendas and have little time for unbiased, independent assessment.

This characterization may seem cynical, but unfortunately, it is not far off the mark. The underlying reasons behind program evaluation strongly influence the attitudes of all personnel toward the process. In turn, their attitudes create either a sympathetic or an unsympathetic internal climate in which evaluations are conducted and, therefore, influence the usefulness of the results that will emerge from the evaluations.

THE MARKETING AUDIT

The marketing audit is "an attempt to describe the current marketing situation, to speculate about the relevant future and to analyze the organization's marketing performance and potential" (Mokwa 1981, p. 272). It puts into practice Abraham Lincoln's advice: "If we could first know where we are, and whither we are tending, we could better judge what to do and how to do it." The marketing audit uses past experience to anticipate changes in the environments and search for new potential market opportunities while minimizing risk.

The marketing audit has four characteristics. It must be comprehensive, systematic, independent, and periodic (see Kotler and Clarke 1987, p. 203):

> *Comprehensive.* The marketing audit covers all the major marketing issues facing an organization and not just trouble spots.
>
> *Systematic.* The marketing audit involves an orderly sequence of diagnostic steps covering the organization's marketing environment, internal marketing system, and specific marketing activities. The diagnosis is followed by a corrective action plan involving both short-run and long-run proposals to improve overall marketing effectiveness.
>
> *Independent.* The marketing audit is normally conducted by an inside or outside party who is sufficiently independent to have top management's confidence and the needed objectivity.
>
> *Periodic.* The marketing audit should be carried out on a regular schedule instead of only in a crisis. The organization that is seemingly successful, as well as one that is in deep trouble, can benefit greatly from such an audit.

Although the primary purpose of the audit is to develop a comprehensive profile of the organization's total marketing effort and to provide a basis for developing and revising the marketing plan, it is also an excellent mechanism for improving communications and raising the level of marketing consciousness within the organization. That is, it is a useful vehicle for marketing the philosophy and techniques of marketing.

The Marketing Audit Process

Marketing audits may be requested by governing boards, government bodies, funding agencies, or by the organization's managers. Before undertaking a marketing audit, the organization must take three important steps (Mokwa 1981, p. 272): (1) determine the scope of the audit; (2) delineate the methods by which data are to be collected; and (3) select an auditor.

As with any other information-gathering process, the first attempt at performing an organization-wide marketing audit is likely to be more costly in effort and resources than subsequent efforts. And it is important to keep in mind the futility of collecting detailed and refined information unless the organization is able to use it. Finally, the level of detail may vary considerably.

Although no single format is appropriate for all organizations, the major topics normally addressed in an audit are shown in Table 15.2.

Data Collection. Data are compiled for analysis and evaluation from three main sources: internal interviews, external interviews, and secondary documentary sources.

Internal interviews with key individuals in the organization seek to draw on their knowledge of all aspects of the organization's operations, competencies, and constraints. They should be supplemented by a series of extended interviews with key members of the organization's external clientele, such as elected officials, suppliers, competitors, and clients.

In addition, the audit should tap all secondary sources of data available in files or in literature that pertains to the issues of interest. Secondary sources do not provide reliable information on which to base evaluations unless they have been identified with this intent in mind. If evaluation capability is not deliberately built into the administrative machinery, then data retrieval becomes a more complicated affair.

Together these three sources of information offer a broad-based approach for assessing an organization's current marketing operations. Again, the number of sources consulted and the amount of data collected will depend on the scope of the audit to which the organization is committed. Smaller organizations, for example, may use only one or two sources.

TABLE 15.2   Marketing Audits Covered by Major Topics

I. Orientation
II. Marketing planning
  A. External environment
    1. Social
    2. Demographic
    3. Economic
    4. Political, legal, and financial
    5. Competition
    6. Technology
    7. Ecology
  B. Needs assessments
  C. Objectives and mission
  D. Marketing planning and evaluation
III. Target market strategies
  A. Target markets
  B. Other clientele
IV. Distribution decisions
  A. The equity issue
  B. Strategic distribution decisions
V. Program strategies
  A. Program management
  B. New program development
  C. Diffusion of new services
  D. Program retrenchment
VI. Pricing strategies
  A. Pricing objectives and policies
  B. Establishing a price
VII. Promotion strategies
  A. Strategic promotion decisions
  B. Advertising and publicity
  C. Personal selling
  D. Incentives

Who Should Conduct the Audit?

Ideally, a marketing audit should be an independent, objective appraisal and review, and should be conducted by experts not affiliated with the organization. Employees, volunteers, managers, and board members are often biased about how the organization is being, and should be, run. They tend to lack the objectivity of a trained external expert. Furthermore, personnel and volunteers may not be as open and candid with their own colleagues as they would be with outsiders. Self-audits are less likely to reveal "sacred cows" since it is difficult for individuals to objectively critique decisions that they themselves or their close colleagues have made or influenced. A third party, with whom people can talk openly without feeling any threat toward their position in the organization, can report insights that might not be offered as candidly as someone from within the organization.

Criteria of Audit Success

According to Kotler and Andreasen (1987, p. 643), an effective marketing audit is one that is

> *Comprehensive* (Have all the key dimensions of the organization's marketing program been investigated?)
> *Objective* (To what extent have the evaluations been quantified? Based on valid internal or external secondary data? If subjective, replicated or cross-checked with other observers? If original research, based on a valid, reliable research methodology?)
> *Timely* (Was the examination based on up-to-date inputs and information?)
> *Useful* (Was the report delivered in time to meet management decisionmaking needs? Were the recommendations relevant, affordable, and otherwise feasible?)
> *Well-communicated* (Was the final report simply and clearly written? Prefaced by an executive summary? Illustrated with forceful, necessary graphics? Concise and understandable? Supplemented by necessary documentation and appendixes?)

Postaudit Tasks

After the audit, three tasks remain. First, after the data have been assembled, their usefulness will depend on the auditor's skill in interpreting and presenting them so that the decisionmakers can quickly grasp the major points. The presentation should address results of the appraisal in each of the seven areas of marketing operations (Table 15.2) and from these points evaluate the overall performance of marketing operations. The audit should provide a profile that identifies not only existing weaknesses and inhibiting factors, but also the organization's strengths and new opportunities. Recommendations must be judged and ranked so that those likely to contribute most to improving marketing performance are implemented first.

The second task is to ensure that the purpose of the audit is clearly understood. It is unlikely to produce suggestions requiring radical changes in the way the organization operates. Any radical changes in direction that do emerge from the auditing process will probably be concerned with defining the agency's mission, formulating objectives to guide its future actions, developing strategy, and implementing an action plan. The final postaudit task is to put someone in charge of implementing the recommendations. We are all familiar with reports that have been prepared, presented, applauded, and filed away to gather dust. The person made accountable should be committed to the project and have the political clout and leverage to make things happen. (For more details on how to conduct marketing audits in government and social service agencies, see Crompton and Lamb 1986. Marketing audits in arts organizations are discussed in Horowitz 1978, pp. 81–85; and health care in Berkowitz and Flexner 1978, pp. 55–56.)

SUMMARY

Evaluation is the final stage in marketing planning. It answers the question, "Where are we now in relation to where we said we wanted to be in our objectives?" Its purpose is to review and evaluate current marketing activities. Given the pressures confronting P&NPOs for alternative use of their resources, it is unlikely that sufficient resources will be made available to generate perfect information. Although incomplete information may be misleading, it is better than none at all. The task of evaluation is to provide the best possible information at the time when it is needed.

Now that program evaluation has been a mandatory requirement of most federal programs since the mid-1960s, interest in it has trickled down to state and local government, social service agencies, and other nonprofit organizations. Consequently, they are putting more emphasis on increasing accountability and prioritizing projects in their reduction and termination decisions. The scope of a program evaluation depends on its importance to the organization's mission and the resources it consumes.

Evaluation is an essential management tool. It not only measures the results of marketing efforts but also helps managers identify appropriate program objectives, supports their basic decisions, and helps them implement difficult decisions by providing an empirical rationale.

PART THREE

Applications

16

The Case of Health Care

JOHN R. DEATS
New York University Medical Center

The health industry accounts for more than 10 percent of the gross national product of the United States. Although its member organizations provide a wide variety of services, from surgical procedures to emergency treatment, they also bear the awesome responsibility of disseminating information about health maintenance and the prevention of illness and accident. Because their product mix is largely ideational in nature, health organizations in the public and nonprofit sectors have enthusiastically begun to adopt social marketing techniques. The trend has already produced a fraternity of productive practitioners as well as a distinct branch of the marketing professional association with its own growing literature. How the health care industry was subjected to competition and then converted from societal orientation to business perspective can be illustrated by its experience with Diagnostic Related Groups (DRGs).

For many years, doctors, hospitals, and those of us involved in health care administration thought that we had as little to do with marketing as Lee Iococca did with the Statue of Liberty. However, the federal government has changed the relationship forever. Hospitals in the United States and New York's Liberty Island will never be the same.

The dawn of this new age had its origins in a study that attempted to categorize some 456 illnesses by intensity, duration of care, and average cost. The system originated at Yale University, was tested in New Jersey and elsewhere, and was implemented as the DRG (Diagnostic Related Group) system of reimbursement by the federal government and applied to the payment for illnesses covered under Medicare.

The impact, however, was more far-reaching, more dramatic, and more important than first imagined. This perspective on health care reimbursement turned on its head a system that had always paid for hospitalization on a "cost plus" basis. The new payment system shifted the burden of efficiency from the rate setter (the insurance company) to the care provider (hospitals). Although the initial impact affected only one program (Medicare), its implementation caused a new word to enter the health care vernacular. That word was "competition."

Although the DRG system was devised on the East Coast, the health care marketing revolution has by and large moved from west to east and from south to north. The challenge became the delivery of health care at a price—a better price—than the competition offered, or the development of a niche that would differentiate one facility from another, regardless of price. In this metamorphosis, hospitals had a difficult time shedding the role of compassionate care-giver for the new perspective of businessman, marketer, *and* compassionate care-giver.

Whatever the cause, competition has become a part of business as usual in hospitals and medical centers. Some institutions have adopted a straightforward advertising approach to marketing products, services, and expertise. A cottage industry of publications is being supported by health care providers anxious to learn the "latest" in techniques with which to smite the competition. (For more details on health care marketing, see Novelli 1984.)

There is an efficacy in this approach, and there are incumbent problems with it as well. Advertising in the mass media is efficient when you need to quickly establish an identity, when introducing a particular product or sometimes, when important competitors are advertising. Marketing is a much broader concept of which mass media advertising is but one element.

There are three basic elements, it is said, to every marketing opportunity: time, talent, and money. When time is short, the other two elements become proportionately more significant. The same applies to either of the other elements. Advertising is a shortcut in achieving levels of recognition and understanding not available through other means— given the unavailability of increased time or enhanced talent. The downside, of course, is that an institution sacrifices an amount of credibility available from the same exposure in a nonpaid capacity, in the same medium. That is, the sponsor of the message is trading control for credence. Sometimes it is worth it.

If, however, the institution has the luxury of time and possesses sufficient talent, there is a more effective manner of securing recognition and approval. That tact is called marketing public relations and it consists of research, planning, strategy, tactics, and ultimately, evaluation.

One is not superior to the other. The endeavors are equally laudatory. It is a choice of weapons, not a mutually exclusive decision among conflicting theories. Advertising is a seductress. The price paid for this certainty is a relatively reduced level of believability and a budget usually significantly larger than other approaches. The benefits reaped are attractive: In an unambiguous message, the institution is represented precisely to a specific audience selected in a time frame of choice. Marketing public relations is powerful—but control is sacrificed in order to avail the institution of the force of third-party endorsement. The choice is yours. But, one does not preclude the other. Take the case of New York University Medical Center.

A CASE STUDY: THE IMAGE DEVELOPMENT CAMPAIGN

Why We Started. The marketing public relations program at NYU Medical Center started in 1981. In response to perceptions by the external Relations Committee of the Medical Center's Board of Trustees, a market study was commissioned to determine consumer attitudes about NYU Medical Center among the prime target audiences in the metropolitan region. The sample was defined as individuals in the metropolitan area with incomes exceeding $50,000 per year—the income level determined to represent the community leadership group most immediately important to the institution.

The qualitative study determined that the medical center had three problems: Most of the target audience did not know it existed; those who did, confused it with other local medical institutions with similar names; the remainder thought that this private institution was a subordinate part of its better-known public affiliate, Bellevue Hospital.

A parallel study was conducted among faculty, administrators, employees, and medical school students within the institution. The study revealed skepticism about whether the "medical center" entity added to the accomplishment of their professional mission. Most believed that it was an unnecessary complication.

Our early objectives were to make members of the target audience aware of the medical center; differentiate NYU from the other major teaching hospitals/medical schools in the region; and increase employee morale and understanding of the medical center as a positive factor.

Our Plan. A practical analysis of the institution's place in the milieu of health care delivery systems in the region pointed to a simple problem: New York University Medical Center is a name bordering on the generic in a locale where everything has "New York" in its title and where nearly every office or medical practice staffed by two or more professionals calls itself a medical center.

The first step we took was to change the center's name—from New York University Medical Center to NYU Medical Center. Virtually overnight, the news media stopped misidentifying the medical center. Prior to the change, nearly half of the media mentions erred in naming the institution. Second, we established "excellence" as our communications theme. We analyzed programs in the education, research and clinical care for examples of unique achievement to demonstrate this excellence. Third, we retained professional public relations counsel to market these stories to selected writers and broadcasters. Fourth, we modified our program of exterior signing. Prior to the initiation of the program, the NYU campus was contiguous with that of Bellevue Hospital and totally indistinguishable from that institution. Last, we revised, refocused, and made more professional the various internally produced publications and at the same time initiated new publications specifically aimed at particular audiences within the medical center.

Did It Do Any Good? Although we are dealing with attitudes and opinions subject to infinite variables, there is clear evidence attesting to progress. For example, a 1983 follow-up study among the same target audience showed that NYU Medical Center had become the best-known medical center in the region in a test of unaided recall. The news media published twice as many NYU mentions as that of any other medical institution in the metropolitan region. Within its field, virtually every public relations professional organization and medical public affairs and marketing association cited the NYU program as the best of its kind.

Where We Are Today. In late 1986 we conducted another follow-up study to determine our standing in the marketplace, adding a "product" element to the ongoing "awareness and regard" study. Among the findings, we determined that NYU was still the medical institution most frequently mentioned first by our target public; but the difference in awareness levels among the top six medical centers in the metropolitan region was negligible. More important, NYU was the consistent leader in the hospital of choice selected by members of the target audience for a variety of intensive medical diagnostic and surgical procedures. Whereas other institutions had achieved our level in the competition for consumer awareness, NYU still appeared to have a plurality in the category of "enhanced regard."

As a footnote, just days after the completion of the study, a major teaching hospital embarked on a paid advertising campaign to achieve the image-enhancement goals previously described for NYU Medical Center. Data analyzed thus far indicate that, short-term, awareness goals have been achieved and a consumer perception has been developed with respect to "quality of care." Although it remains to be seen whether a ninety-day campaign will have the lasting value of an ongoing marketing public relations program, it is apparent that in itself the $3 million effort is neither cost-effective nor substantial enough to propel the institution into the first rank of metropolitan biomedical teaching/research/patient care facilities and sustain that perception.

THE COMPETITION

Competition in the delivery of health care is a relatively new activity in the New York metropolitan market. The trend in the marketing of health care has generally moved from west to east, and New York still trails most of the country in the execution of programs to promote facilities and programs. However, a Madison Avenue perspective coupled with an immediate need for increased revenue is propelling the Empire State into the fray.

The $3 Million Campaign. One institution has sought to capture the attention and commitment of the public by a series of print, television, and radio advertisements promoting the hospital's image without regard to specific services. The tag line in each message promotes a physician referral telephone number. The designated number received more than four hundred calls a week, although the number of actual appointments kept and hospitals admissions are not known. The campaign continues periodically to date.

The Art of Medicine. A campaign conducted on the Op Ed pages of the *New York Times* focused on anecdotes of patients and physicians successfully embodying the copy line, "The art of medicine, the love of humanity." Again, hospital admission numbers are not known, but the awareness level in this case increased by 60 percent, to 16 percent, during the campaign. Budgeted at less than $500,000 per year, this campaign continued for two years.

Physician Referral Lines. Two New York City institutions have used physician referral to increase census (the hospital's "occupancy rate"). The lesser-known of these two hospitals has experimented with several marketing managers, at least two advertising agencies, and a variety of approaches. Both budget and results are undetermined. The other institution, which hired a marketing vice-president from the pharmaceutical industry and organized its effort around research and the delivery of product, has created a demand for in-hospital doctors that approaches the $3 million campaign in effectiveness. This hospital, however, accomplished similar response rates at significantly less than a third of the cost.

Urgi-Center Promotions. A hospital emergency room in another institution with a limited catchment area is ripe for promotion. For a modest budget, this institution promoted its fast and efficient service to target consumers who do not like to wait in line. Although too early to evaluate completely, early returns indicate a successful promotion based on limited resources, limited expectations, and limited exposure (buses, subways, and neighborhood print media).

WHAT DO WE DO NEXT?

Marketing communications at NYU is budgeted at considerably less than 1 percent of the institutional budget of $450 million per year. In order to maintain our leadership position in the hearts and minds of the target audience, we chose to emphasize a variety of communications vehicles emphasizing third-party endorsement and, in other cases, selected promotional publications and activities produced by the medical center to focus attention on the best in biomedical research, education, and patient care available at the institution.

As the competition's approach to communication with the marketplace changed, we added to existing communications activities and developed certain innovative approaches in order to secure and expand our share of the market. Some of the activities are uniquely available in New York City. However, the underlying communications techniques are valid in virtually any marketplace, regardless of size or geography.

Our approach was to use the communications opportunities available in the nonpaid sector, sustaining the communications theme of "excellence" throughout and performing at a level that would make possible the maintenance and expansion of the institution's share of market.

Programs with the News Media. An original thrust of the Image Development Campaign, the effort continues with New York metropolitan media. NYU remains the most accessible of metropolitan medical institutions to the metropolitan news media. Day or night, weekend or holiday, there is a person willing to help writers and broadcasters complete a story, whether or not it directly involves this medical center. Coupled with the ongoing effort of public relations counsel in placing specific stories, NYU has maintained its dominance in the region: We average almost fifty print and broadcast placements per week.

However, we have added a national dimension to the media program. In conjunction with the Associated Press News Feature Service, ten feature stories are released each month bearing the NYU byline quoting medical physician and health care professionals on issues of medical concern. The program was initiated to solve a need by the wire service to provide information on health to its fifteen hundred daily newspaper subscribers and a desire on our part to extend the visibility of the medical center to a national audience. Approaching its second anniversary, the service is published in all fifty states on a weekly basis in an average of 250 newspapers. The information is both helpful to readers and satisfies institutional marketing communications objectives.

Targeted Publications. A four-color magazine evolved from a publication written for, and read by alumni of the medical school. The magazine was recognized as the best in its class by several national organizations and the internally produced material consistently supported the communications theme of excellence, regardless of content or intent.

The Health Letter. A hybrid designed to bridge the gap between the control afforded by paid advertising and the credibility offered by information published (supported) by an unbiased third party, the "NYU Medical Center Health Letter" was launched in January 1987 as a self-sustaining vehicle that would showcase the best in important, pragmatic and interesting biomedical information forthcoming from this institution. In its first months, the publication met all its editorial and financial goals and, as this is being written, is about to be marketed nationally as a co-venture with a consortium of newsletter publishers. The competition is formidable: Harvard, the Mayo Clinic, the University of California at Berkeley, and Tufts University. However, our research indicates that there is a niche still available to NYU for a clearly written, pragmatic, unbiased medical communication to a lay audience, especially the seventeen million people in the New York metropolitan region.

SUMMARY

Marketing communications is subtly grounded in knowledge, research and, in equal measure, instinct. The tools available to practitioners are no mystery; neither are the methods of implementation. The successful programs blend opportunity with consensus, problems with probabilities and diligence with good luck.

The situation among biomedical academic institutions in New York was not very different from that of competitors in the banking industry, the insurance industry, and the retail industry. Neither was the response. Those institutions with the most immediate need took the most direct approach: advertising. Those institutions in the strongest positions used the momentum of public acceptance to sustain their rank in the marketplace.

Doing well by doing good is a unique opportunity available to those of us in the health sector. It is an activity only a fortunate few of us are able to experience. In all, the frustrations are well worth the effort.

17

The Case of Planned Parenthood's Campaign against Unintended Teen Pregnancy and Childbearing

DOUGLAS GOULD
Planned Parenthood Federation of America

In 1987 a British film, "Wish You Were Here," appeared in U.S. movie thea-ters. It portrayed the lively zany story of a rebellious teenage girl and con-tained a full complement of fun, adventure, and, above all, sex, none of which was very new to American movies. What was new, at least to most audiences was the showing of a condom during one of several scenes of in-timately detailed lovemaking. Until that time, because sexy scenes had al-ways been favorite ingredients in cinema productions and television as well, organizations such as the Planned Parenthood Federation of America (PPFA) argued vociferously that such scenes should include birth control practices. If youngsters must be exposed to sex, then why exclude methods of protection against pregnancy and disease? The issue became a major controversy and was resolved primarily as a result of the epidemic of ac-quired immune deficiency syndrome (AIDS), which precipitated revolution-ary acceptance of the idea that condoms should be promoted. Even beyond the AIDS consideration, teen pregnancy has received enormous but well-de-served publicity. (For an analysis from the social marketing perspective, see Marsiglio 1985.)

BACKGROUND

Since its inception in 1916, Planned Parenthood—the nation's oldest and largest voluntary family planning organization—has been committed to the eradication of unintended pregnancy, particularly among teenagers. Through its national network of 786 family planning centers and 183 affiliates in forty-seven states and the District of Columbia, the Planned Parenthood Federation of America has provided medical, counseling, and educational services to an ever-increasing number of sexually active teens. PPFA's educational programs reach millions through schools, community groups, churches, and the popular media. These programs provide critical information about contraception, abortion, reproductive health, and responsibility. Policymakers, too, hear from Planned Parenthood activists in an effort to keep the government out of people's private decisionmaking about whether or when to bear children. These efforts have led us in recent years to expand our litigation, public advocacy, and lobbying programs, which, in close cooperation with our direct service program, give Planned Parenthood a unique perspective and authoritative voice in matters of national policy.

Planned Parenthood has always faced powerful opponents. Our founder, Margaret Sanger was jailed in 1916 in her campaign to legalize the practice of birth control in the United States. More recently, far-right extremists, with the support of the White House and many in the U.S. Congress, have worked to eliminate or restrict the right of women to choose abortion and have tried to end U.S. government support for family planning programs at home and abroad.

Because of Planned Parenthood's prominent role, it has been the focus of a series of attacks, including harassing government audits; repeated attempts to withdraw federal, state, and local government support for its programs; and regulatory measures that have attempted to make it more difficult for PPFA to serve its clients here and overseas. But PPFA has discovered that vigorous opposition can help build support among policymakers, the donor community, and the general public. After ten years of grueling battles stemming from the political growth of the far right, PPFA has more than doubled the size of its caseload, income, and donor base; and has expanded its capacity to face new challenges in the courts, Congress, and the marketplace of ideas.

PPFA benefits from almost universal name recognition. Our research shows that for every ten people who have a favorable impression of us, only one dislikes us. More than 90 percent of Americans support the basic principles that we articulate, and the vast majority respect PPFA for taking a tough stand on the issue of abortion. Most, too, understand that Planned Parenthood is dedicated to providing family planning services and education about human reproduction and sexuality in order to reduce the need for abortion. So Planned Parenthood is well positioned to move ahead with its efforts to eradicate teen pregnancy.

TEENAGE PREGNANCY AS A NATIONAL TRAGEDY

Here are some statistics to indicate the severity of the problems surrounding teen pregnancy in the United States in the 1980s:

- Each year in the United States more than 1.1 million teenage girls become pregnant, more than 80 percent of them unintentionally.
- Eighty percent of boys and 70 percent of girls will have experienced sexual intercourse by age nineteen—a two-thirds increase since 1970.
- Although more adolescents are practicing contraception (70 percent in 1979 compared with 50 percent in 1971), the number of pregnancies to teenagers is not declining, because teens are inconsistent in their use of contraception and often choose less effective methods of birth control.
- Fifty percent of teen pregnancies occur within the first six months of initiating sexual intercourse. The median delay between teenagers initiating intercourse and obtaining a medically prescribed method of contraception is almost a year. Only 14 percent come to family planning clinics *before* they initiate sexual intercourse.
- Teenage pregnancy is one of the leading causes of welfare dependency in the United States. Families headed by young mothers are more likely to be below the poverty line.
- The death rate for adolescent women under sixteen years of age from complications of pregnancy and birth is 2.5 times the rate among women aged twenty to twenty-four.
- Most teens choose abortion when an untimely pregnancy occurs, with teens accounting for more than one-third of all abortions performed in the United States.

IN THE PUBLIC EYE

Obviously, the teenage pregnancy problem has always been with us to some extent, but it has gained attention as the numbers have grown and the resolution of the crisis has shifted away from the hushed-up shotgun marriage of the 1950s to increasingly common single parenthood and abortion. Fewer than 5 percent of girls who choose to carry their pregnancies to term will give their babies up for adoption, once a common practice.

Sexual practices have changed, too, as have sexual images emanating from rock music, advertising, and television, which have bombarded teens with pro-intercourse messages. Teens also learn from example. There are a total of three million unintended pregnancies each year in the United States, half of which end in abortion, and teens account for only one-third of them. So, in a way, teens are mirroring the poor contraceptive practices of the rest of society.

Although this issue was first identified as a national problem by Planned Parenthood's Alan Guttmacher Institute (AGI) with the publication in 1976 of its study "Eleven Million Teenagers," public concern (but not programmatic action) faded somewhat until the early 1980s. Then, increased interest was prompted by the growing magnitude and complexity of public welfare dependency. AGI, too, had taken another look at the problem.

In an effort to better understand the problem and its possible solutions, AGI undertook a massive comparative analysis of teenage pregnancy in the United States and other industrialized nations. Shockingly, the study revealed that American teens experienced far greater rates of teenage pregnancy and childbearing than did their European cousins, twice as high as Great Britain (our nearest competitor in this dubious game) and ten times as high as the Netherlands! More surprising was the revelation that teens in those countries initiated sexual intercourse at about the same age as U.S. teens, and they had similar sexual practices—the same frequency and number of partners.

The difference, it seems, is that teens in other industrialized nations use contraceptives far more effectively than teens do here. On further analysis, those other societies were found to share a consensus about sexuality that is not found in the United States—that sex is a normal part of life, but that sex without contraception is foolish. This message is echoed from all quarters; it is taught in schools, preached in churches, discussed openly in the media (which accept contraceptive advertising), and emphasized at home. This is not to say that parents in these countries are totally comfortable about teen sexual activity. But they are comfortable enough to talk about sex and birth control. And, if they don't, youngsters will learn about this from other responsible institutions. But in the United States, double messages are the norm. While the media reverberates with hypersexuality, contraception is virtually never discussed. It is not advertised in the electronic media, and it is often condemned by religious leaders as sinful. Schools that offer some sexuality education programs are often afraid to teach about contraceptives and their availability, thereby conveying the message that contraception is taboo.

PLANNED PARENTHOOD'S RESPONSE

A broadly based study group within Planned Parenthood sifted through the data about the problem and the various proposed solutions and devised a program strategy, approved by the Planned Parenthood membership at its 1984 annual meeting. The strategy included the following measures:

> Making sex education, including information about birth control, universally available, in grades K–12 in public and private schools.
>
> Changing society's attitudes about sexuality to increase communication between couples and between parents and children. This means eliminating television's ban of contraception from the airwaves, in both advertising and entertainment offerings.
>
> Increasing male responsibility in contraceptive practices and the postponement of sexual activity.
>
> Improving access to free- or low-cost family planning services to teens without requiring parental consent, and improving contraceptive practices among young people.
>
> Keeping abortion available without restrictions and advocating for the reinstatement of public funding for abortion for those dependent on Medicaid for their health care.
>
> Working to strengthen the American family by advocating for greater educational and economic opportunities—a chance for a quality education, meaningful work opportunities, and safe neighborhoods.

THE MARKETPLACE OF IDEAS

Most of what we seek entails changing attitudes and motivating people to change their behavior. This is essentially the social marketing of ideas, but, in our situation, we also need to persuade key policymakers in government and the electronic media to take actions that could dramatically alter the social and institutional climate affecting teens.

By the mid-1980s, PPFA already had the clinical service component of its program in place, but family planners needed new money to serve more teens with free- or low-cost services. Funds were also needed for experimental programs to test new ways of reaching and serving sexually active teenagers. We also needed to increase public awareness and action through the media. We hoped that the media could help us create the consensus, accepted by our European neighbors, that we must stop teenage pregnancy, not teenage sex. In 1985, PPFA commissioned Louis Harris and Associates to conduct a national public opinion survey of attitudes on reproductive health issues with specific attention paid to assessing the level of public support for the solutions Planned Parenthood was proposing. We also wanted to discover avenues of approach that might prompt greater parent-child communication about sex and birth control; ways to motivate people to pressure government and media policymakers; and the level of receptivity of the public to the pro-punishment, antiprevention arguments made by our opponents.

The poll results were published amid much media fanfare; they were covered by virtually all major U.S. media outlets in January 1986. We found that

Eighty-four percent of Americans consider teenage pregnancy a serious problem in the United States. The consensus among adults is that parents should encourage open communication within the family about sex and birth control to help alleviate the problem of teen pregnancy.

Although 76 percent of parents say that an adult has talked with their children about sex, only one-third say that birth control was part of the discussion.

Only 18 percent of adults felt that teen pregnancy would decrease by reducing access to information and contraceptive services to teens. This reflected narrow support for the policy of the Reagan administration and its right-wing supporters. Sixty-eight percent of Americans think that television gives an exaggerated picture of people making love, and majorities or strong pluralities think that television fails to deal at all with pregnancy and the consequences of sex (45 percent), family planning to prevent pregnancy (68 percent), and information about sexually transmitted diseases (63 percent).

More important, there is a mandate for television to deal more realistically with the subjects of sex and birth control. Nearly 80 percent of adults think that television should present messages about birth control as part of its programming.

Eighty-five percent support sex education in the public schools, but slightly over half have the mistaken impression that sex education is already available in public schools.

A surprising two-to-one majority of adults (67 percent) favor requiring public schools to establish links with family planning clinics, so that teenagers can learn about contraceptives and obtain them.

The poll documented extraordinary public support for the programs of Planned Parenthood. American adults understood the problem and endorsed the solutions we were advocating. The question then was how to motivate them to act.

KEY AUDIENCES

Parents. The poll data showed that parents were worried about the teen pregnancy problem, and they were trying to improve communication at home about sexuality. Sadly, we also found that the conversations about sex were often a "one-shot" approach, initiated at an age when many teens were already sexually active, and, as mentioned earlier, usually did not include birth control among the topics covered. Parents need to be motivated, and they need the communications skills to do the job.

Working with Doubleday & Company, PPFA published a book in 1986 entitled *How to Talk with Your Child about Sexuality.* It was launched with a national media tour, which included appearances by PPFA President Faye Wattleton on all the major national talk shows and on major TV and radio programs in eight of the nation's largest cities. A video version of the book is planned for the home video market. In the spring of 1988, a revised version, with a new chapter on talking with children about AIDS, was published. An inexpensive brochure, highlighting the critical facts and carrying the same title, was also published and distributed in mass quantities.

Planned Parenthood affiliates have stepped up their local community-based educational programs for parents, offering hands-on training for parents in both the facts and the communications skills needed to convey those facts to youngsters.

The PPFA national office, in conjunction with its advertising agency, Public Media Center, developed a broad-based advertising campaign. Included was a series of magazine ads for placement in national media and local media by our affiliates. These were designed to sensitize parents to the need to talk with their teens and to persuade them to try. The ads, which offered parents a copy of our brochure, had provocative headlines: "If They're Old Enough to Get Pregnant, They're Old Enough Not to"; "When I Found My Daughter's Birth Control Pills, I Hit the Ceiling"; "Kids Deserve a Better Teacher than Experience"; "If Your 15-Year-Old Daughter (Son) Asked You about Birth Control, What Would You Say?" A full-page newspaper ad was also developed, with the headline "Sex Education for Parents."

Television ads, now running throughout the country in paid and public service time slots, feature intensive closeups of parents talking about the need to talk to their kids about sex and a son who comically reflects on his father's discomfort at talking with him about birth control.

A national campaign will soon be launched to recruit parents to work as advocates *for* information and against ignorance. We will pull together a star-studded national panel of famous parents to spearhead this organizing effort. Lobbying for sex education, which includes concrete information about AIDS prevention and contraception, and against the policies of the three television networks, will become major activities of the "parents campaign." Recruitment will be through direct mail and affiliate grass roots organizing throughout the country.

Teenagers. Planned Parenthood's message to teens is one of responsibility. Teens who are engaging in sexual activity without contraceptives are taking unnecessary risks: "Do not succumb to pressure from your friends to have sex."

It is a common misperception that American teenagers are fully aware of all the methods of birth control, but deliberately avoid using them. Adults think of teens as being more sexually sophisticated than they really are.

To determine how much young people do know about birth control, in 1986 Planned Parenthood again commissioned a national opinion survey, conducted by Louis Harris and Associates, this time of teens. Planned Parenthood's first national random sample of teens, aged thirteen to seventeen, was conducted through personal interviews in the homes of one thousand youngsters. The findings revealed that most teens were likely to become sexually active before reaching their eighteenth birthday, but that only a third of them consistently used contraceptives. A vast number were ignorant about how contraceptives worked, many exaggerated the side effects of contraceptives, and many did not understand that contraceptives could be obtained in drugstores or from physicians and clinics without their parents' permission. Backing this up with a series of focus groups conducted in Arkansas, Pennsylvania, and Washington, D.C., we tested the acceptability of a variety of different messages with teens. Generally, we found that they wanted more factual, unvarnished information about the various methods of birth control. They rejected admonitions of abstinence. They seemed to respond well to advertisements that featured girls and boys—not adults—talking about their personal experiences. And they could not in any way handle humorous approaches to discussing anything sexual. Sex is serious business.

This led us to develop a series of informational print ads for high school newspapers, now being placed around the country. Some ads dealt with the most dangerous myths teens harbor about sex and carried headlines such as "FAMOUS LAST WORDS: 'BUT YOU CAN'T GET PREGNANT DOING IT STANDING UP' ", and "THE ONLY PREGNANCY TEST YOU CAN TAKE WITH A PENCIL." Two other ads dealt directly with contraceptives and where to obtain them: "3 WAYS TO KEEP FROM GETTING PREGNANT YOU CAN GET AT ANY DRUGSTORE OR PLANNED PARENTHOOD," and "SHOULD I TAKE THE PILL?"

These print ads are supported by television and radio spots, which feature an older brother and sister talking about advising younger siblings to be smart and use birth control, and a teen talking to her peers about specific over-the-counter birth control methods and how they work. Our research also indicated that very often teens are swept away by the moment and, therefore, do not use contraception. They do not prepare for the possibility that they may engage in sex, and they often do not have the language they need to fend off sexual pressures. A series of print, television, and radio ads was created to project this information. They all carry the headline, "HE SAID IF I DIDN'T DO IT HE WOULDN'T LOVE ME ANYMORE." In these, the copy tries to help teens to learn the difference between sex and love and to question the love of someone who would force you to do something you think is wrong.

Finally, some ads were created for teenage boys to tell them, subtly, about how they would feel if they impregnated a girl. The headline we used was, "AND THEN I GOT THAT AWFUL PHONE CALL." The ads feature good-looking young men talking about their experience, directly to the teen reader.

All of these efforts are backed up by Planned Parenthood's extensive array of educational and clinical service programs for teens nationwide, through which we work to actually provide the contraceptive supplies and information teens need in a medically supervised environment.

Government Officials. Because of the enormity of the problem, we cannot hope to find the means to solve it without the cooperation of all levels of government. We need their money to fund the educational, clinical, and in some cases, job-training programs for teens at risk. Too often, however, government officials have been cowed by the small but noisy anti–family planning and anti–sex education minority. To mobilize our side in the debate to urge government officials to act, we have developed a national grass roots organizing effort with our affiliates and state offices. Fifteen states have been targeted for legislative mandates to require sex education in all schools, grades K–12, and two were achieved in 1987. In addition, we have been trying to persuade the federal government to act.

An ad containing coupons addressed to public officials, with the headline "WHY A MILLION TEENS WILL GET PREGNANT THIS YEAR," sets forth our case for a new national initiative to prevent teen pregnancy. PPFA has been working to persuade other groups to join in a national "campaign" to combat teen pregnancy, to work in concert to achieve our legislative goals, but to date this has been less successful than we had hoped.

Network Executives. Each major television network, according to our tracking studies, beams out approximately 55,000 sexual messages annually in daytime and prime-time programming. Yet, until 1987, contraception was never mentioned. All three television networks still ban ads for contraceptive products, but we sense they are on the verge of breaking this barrier.

PPFA representatives began negotiating with censors at the three networks in 1985, urging them to change their advertising and entertainment policies. They voiced considerable objections to this suggestion, saying that "contraception is too controversial." They expressed a belief that contraceptive ads would encourage young viewers to initiate sexual activity (ignoring the possibility that their titillating programs might do just that) and that people would be confused by information about contraceptive products and, as a result, become pregnant. Network TV, of course, does not feel that the latter possibility applies to any other products.

Although our 1985 poll revealed that the public *wanted* messages about birth control on television, the networks claim that we did not ask the "right questions," and that if we did, we would see that people objected to some messages being televised. So Planned Parenthood rose to the challenge and commissioned Louis Harris and Associates to conduct still another public opinion survey, this time focusing on the public's attitudes about contraceptive advertising and the portrayal of sex on television.

We found that the public well understood the link between teenagers' sexuality and the powerful medium's messages. We found, too, that Americans would find contraceptive ads more acceptable than ads for beer, wine, and feminine hygiene sprays. Even cigarette advertising, which the networks fought to retain when the federal government banned it from the airwaves, was far less acceptable than ads for contraceptives.

In the winter of 1986, PPFA initiated a hard-hitting campaign, placing ads in major U.S. cities and in national publications, calling on the public to write to the network presidents complaining about their policies. The headlines read: "THEY DID IT 20,000 TIMES ON TELEVISION LAST YEAR, HOW COME NOBODY GOT PREGNANT?" and "WHEN J.R. TOOK MANDY FOR A LITTLE ROLL IN THE HAY WHICH ONE HAD THE CONDOM?" A few of the print ads are reproduced as Figures 17.1 through 17.4.

The provocative nature of the ads generated tremendous national publicity and enabled us to place PPFA's president on numerous national television programs. More than one hundred print stories appeared on

FIGURE 17.1

"Then I got that awful phone call."

"SHE'D NEVER CALLED ME BEFORE. We'd just been together a couple of times.

So she tells me she's pregnant.

I mean, I didn't know what to say. There's just this silence on the phone until she asks if I died.

She sounds like she's burnt out on crying and you don't know what to do. It's like you're a blank.

The worst part is I wake up in the morning and it just rushes at me. Quit school. Get married. Run away from it. I don't know.

I didn't know then and I don't know now.

All I know is all the ways it shouldn't have happened. All those easy ways. But it's a little too late for that, I guess. Too late this lifetime, for me."

Nobody has all the answers about sex. But keep in mind that a million teen girls get pregnant every year. Which means a million guys don't hear the end of it. Here's your choice. You can take responsibility when it's easy or you can wait until it's impossible. Don't make a big mistake. Buy a condom. You can get them at any drugstore or from your local Planned Parenthood. If you need help or information, call us. That's what we're here for.

Planned Parenthood®
Federation of America

810 Seventh Avenue,
New York, NY 10019

FIGURE 17.2

FAMOUS LAST WORDS:

"But you can't get pregnant doing it standing up!"

There's a lot of dangerous information about sex. Dangerous because it's just plain wrong.

If you don't know the facts, you can get into extremely serious trouble. How many of these mistakes have you heard others make?

"YOU CAN'T GET PREGNANT DOING IT STANDING UP."

Gravity has nothing to do with getting pregnant. The millions of sperm in each ejaculation can live for two or three days inside of you. Jumping up and down won't stop them. Doing it standing up won't faze them. It takes just one sperm to get you pregnant.

"YOU CAN'T GET PREGNANT WHEN YOU'RE BLEEDING."

Oh, yes you can. Some girls can have bleeding when they ovulate—the most fertile time—and think it's their period. Think of bleeding as the start of a cycle, not the end of one. Because few girls have periods like clockwork, calculating the actual low points in your fertility cycle is the most difficult birth control method there is. Even when you do it right, it's the one that's most likely to go wrong.

"DOUCHING WITH SODA POP REALLY WORKS."

If it did, you can bet the companies who make the stuff would be selling it for a lot more than they do! The fact is, douching

with any kind of soda pop is not only useless, it's extremely dangerous. Douching with anything is no substitute for the simple, effective birth control methods you can buy at any drugstore without a prescription. We wish there was an easy way to prevent pregnancy "after the fact," but there isn't.

"YOU CAN'T GET PREGNANT THE FIRST TIME."

It's all the same to eggs and sperm. They're ready the first time, every time, even if you're not. It's not a matter of "luck." It's just a fact of life. If you have sex and don't use an effective method of birth control, you are going to get pregnant. If you don't want it to happen, you have to do something to stop it from happening.

This year, a million teenage girls will get pregnant because they didn't know how not to. Or because they "thought" they knew, but really didn't.

Getting pregnant is easy. You don't have to be smart. You don't have to be popular. You don't have to be anything except mistaken. Just once, about one thing.

Nobody's born knowing the facts of life. Everybody has to learn them. And the best way to learn is by asking people you're absolutely sure know the answer. Like your parents. Or your teacher. Or the people at Planned Parenthood. We're listed in the phone book. We can help. That's what we're here for.

 Planned Parenthood®
Federation of America

810 Seventh Avenue,
New York, NY 10019

FIGURE 17.3

"He said if I didn't do it, he wouldn't love me anymore."

"AND YOU KNOW WHAT? I GOT angry. It was such a trashy thing to say. Like I was so desperate for him I'd jump off a cliff or something.

We didn't have any birth control. I started out saying it was just the wrong time.

Then I started thinking it was the wrong guy.

After he said that, he put on this big act about it. If he really cared, he'd have let it drop. He'd have given me time.

I mean, you don't have to be the brain of the world to know you don't have sex without protection.

And you sure don't make a baby with a guy who thinks he can threaten you."

Nobody should pressure anybody to have sex. Especially if you feel you're not ready. Or prepared. It's a fact of life that if you have sex without safe, effective birth control, you're going to get pregnant. Who should be responsible for birth control? It can be you, it can be him, even better when it's both. If you need information or just someone to talk to, call your nearest Planned Parenthood. We can help. That's what we're here for.

 **Planned Parenthood®**
Federation of America

810 Seventh Avenue
New York, NY 10019

FIGURE 17.4

They did it 20,000 times on television last year.

*T*eenage pregnancy in the U.S. has reached epidemic proportions, shattering hundreds of thousands of lives and costing taxpayers $16 billion per year. Instead of helping to solve this problem, the TV networks have virtually banned any mention of birth control in programs and advertising. We need to turn this policy around. You can help.

I. On television, sex is good, contraception is taboo.

There's a lot of sex on television. We all know that. What most people don't realize is that while the networks have been hyping sex, they've banned all mention of birth control in advertising, and censor information about it in programming. (It is permitted in the news.) Millions of dollars in sexually alluring ads are okay. Ads for vaginal sprays and hemorrhoidal products are okay. So are the ads which use nudity here and there to sell products. And characters like J.R. Ewing have been seducing women a few times an hour for eight years.

In 1978, researchers counted 20,000 sexual scenes on prime-time network television (which does not even include soap operas), with nary a mention of consequences or protection. It's even higher today. The only sexual mystery left seems to be how all these people keep doing it without contraception while nobody gets pregnant.

With all that worry-free hot action on television, it's no wonder American youngsters are having sex earlier and more often. *And* getting pregnant. Kids watch an average of four hours every day. That's more time than they spend in school or doing anything else in life, except sleeping. That's four hours per day inside a world where no one ever says "no," where sex is loose and often violent, and where sexual responsibility is as out-of-date as hula-hoops. Today's TV message is this: "GO FOR IT *NOW*. GO FOR IT AGAIN. AND DON'T WORRY ABOUT ANYTHING."

How come nobody got pregnant?

But there is plenty to worry about. The teen pregnancy rate in this country is now the highest of any country in the industrialized world. In the U.S. more than a million teens get pregnant every year. The consequences are tragic: high rates of school drop-outs, broken families, welfare and abortion. Who pays the tab? You do. About $16 billion yearly.

Of course television is *not* the only cause. When it comes to sex, there's a terrible breakdown of communications between parents and kids. There's also an appalling lack of timely, comprehensive sex education in schools. So kids are learning about sex the hard way—by experience. But television is making matters worse. Both because of what's on TV, and because of what is not.

II. Censorship by the Networks

The television industry is very sensitive about people telling them what they cannot broadcast. But the TV industry itself feels free to censor content.

Last year, the American College of Obstetricians and Gynecologists (ACOG)—a most prestigious physicians organization—prepared an ad campaign to educate kids about how to prevent pregnancy. They wanted to use print media, radio, and television. The brochure for the campaign said this: (1) Kids *can* resist peer pressure. They can take the option of postponing sex until they're ready. (2) The pill *is* a safe contraceptive for young women. And (3) sexually active young *men* should also be responsible—use condoms. These were useful statements.

The TV commercials ACOG prepared were even milder. All they suggested was that *unintended pregnancy* can interfere with career goals for women, and they offered to send the brochure. But, amazingly, the network execs said the ads were too "controversial," because they made mention of the word "contraceptives." These are the same networks which routinely show thousands of murders, rapes and acts of kinky sex. And 94% of the sexual encounters in soap operas are among people not married to each other. Are *those* presentations non-controversial? Do *those* represent some kind of higher moral value?

Finally, after long negotiations, the three networks agreed to let the spots run. But only after the dreaded "C-word" –"contraception"–was censored. Instead, the networks substituted this dynamic phrase: "There are many ways to prevent unintended pregnancy."

As for network policies censoring "birth control" within programs? No change. As for the rejection of commercials for contraceptive products like condoms, foams, the pill? No change. As for the reduction of irresponsible sexual imagery? No change. As for a sense of balance between sexual hype and realistic useful information? No change.

III. Blaming the public tastes

Network executives argue that they've a responsibility to uphold high standards of public taste. The mention of birth control (except in the news) would somehow violate that. Is that true? Does the public really want uneducated pregnant teenagers? And a tax bill for $16 billion?

A recent Louis Harris Poll showed exactly what the public wants. Most Americans believe that television portrays an unrealistic and irresponsible view of sex. And 78% would like to see messages about contraception on TV. A similar percentage wants more sex education in schools. So it's not the public which resists more responsible sexual imagery. It's the television executives who resist it. Why? Maybe it's just a creative problem for them. We think they can solve it. Right now they don't even mention birth control when it's exactly appropriate. Why can't J.R. ask his latest conquest if she is prepared? Why can't she ask him? The screenwriters can work it out.

The television industry once said the public couldn't handle images of people wearing seatbelts, and they figured that one out. The case of birth control should be simpler than seatbelts, since 90% of adults already accept its use. It's mainly teenagers who don't.

IV. What you can do

Television executives keep trying to avoid their own responsibility, telling us that TV imagery has nothing to do with shaping teens' attitudes, that television doesn't influence them. But this is ridiculous. Television is the most powerful medium ever invented to influence mass behavior. It's on that basis that the networks sell their advertising.

Television influences all of us every day. And it is a major influence on teenagers about sexuality and responsibility. It may now be a more important influence than school, parents, or even peers. The problem is that television is putting out an unbalanced view which is causing *more* problems for teenagers and society. The situation has got to change.

It's time we turn to the small number of men who control this medium and tell them they have a responsibility to the public beyond entertainment, titillation, pushing products and making money.

They need to know you are out there, and that you are concerned. It will make a tremendous difference. Use the coupons. Write letters and make phone calls. And join Planned Parenthood's efforts in your area.

Thank you.

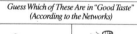

Guess Which of These Are in "Good Taste" (According to the Networks)

The tv network execs have decided that all advertisements for contraceptive products are in "bad taste" and they have banned them. Vaginal sprays, hemorrhoidal products, tampons are all in "good taste," according to them. So are toilet paper ads, underwear ads and nudity in everything from soap and cosmetic ads to beer ads. As for network drama and comedy programs which emphasize sexual doings? "Good taste." But mentioning "contraception" or "birth control" within programming (except news) is censored. ✒ The networks have not yet got the message. Our country is suffering a major problem of teen pregnancy, and television network policy is making it worse. Hyping sexuality while censoring information about responsibility is giving a terrible double message. ✒ The networks need to hear from you. Now. Please use the coupons above, write letters, phone. Your response can turn things around.

Planned Parenthood®
Federation of America, Inc.

the issue around the nation. We arranged dozens of TV and radio debates with reluctant network representatives, with our spokespeople always encouraging viewers and listeners to call or write the networks to complain if they agreed with our position. We supported this campaign with an affiliate-based national media event entitled the "Planned Parenthood Sweeps," wherein our affiliates monitored local television programming in their communities and reported, through press conferences, the number of sexual messages that appeared on their local TV stations. At the same time, they reported a dearth of information on TV about birth control and sexual responsibility.

Finally, working with a number of affiliates, we continue to create local forums on the subject of sex in the media that generate still more community interest regarding the problem of teenage pregnancy and the role played by the media. Numerous PPFA spokespersons have appeared on platforms around the country, speaking out on this issue and holding local press conferences. Direct mail letters, which include postcards now addressed to the owners of the three networks, are currently being distributed to PPFA's national donor base. This should help to maintain the public pressure on the networks to change their policies.

Progress has been made. In the first half of 1987, the networks decided to loosen the shackles on their screenwriters, and, on a dozen occasions, allowed contraception to be discussed in entertainment segments. Although these small numbers in no way mirror the thousands of references to sexual intercourse on the tube, it is progress, which Planned Parenthood applauds.

ORGANIZATIONAL CONFLICTS PROMPTED BY THE CAMPAIGN

Although the campaign to date has prompted few internal conflicts, healthy debates continue to rage over truly substantive issues. These came about as PPFA attempted to increase the organization's visibility around the teen pregnancy issue and result from philosophical differences inherent in any advocacy group. Running a campaign forces previously submerged differences to come to the fore, as the leaders attempt to rally constituent groups.

In our case, they arose around the issue of advocating for free- or low-cost services for teens; medical/legal requirements for medical services that seem to inhibit teens' access to contraceptive care; and the competition between advocacy and service for limited money. A broader external conflict of interest occurs in that the messages that are most effective in reaching and educating teens are the same messages most likely to infuriate their parents. All of these conflicts are discussed below.

FREE OR LOW-COST SERVICES TO TEENS

Planned Parenthood has always been divided on the subject of whether providing family planning services to teens free of charge makes it more or less likely that teens will use the service effectively. Complicating the search for an answer to this are some service providers' discomfort with teen sexuality, the fear that giving them contraceptives might encourage them to become sexually active, the need for funds to pay clinic bills, and the apparent affluence of some of our clients. The question has been raised, "Should we give free services to a teen who drives to the clinic in a BMW?" Far from representing the typical Planned Parenthood client, who is more often from a low-income group, the teen from an affluent home, who may have little or no disposable income, raises tough questions about our priorities.

On the one hand, some service providers feel their chief goal is to encourage the sexually active teen to use contraceptives as soon as possible, regardless of their resources. They believe financial considerations must take a backseat to service, and they act accordingly. On the other side, we find providers who believe that people are more effective managers of their fertility—that they value the service more—if they pay for it. They think teens who refuse to use their money to pay for birth control, but who spend money on cigarettes or records, should learn a lesson about priorities.

The unanswered question is whether teens ever actually value health care enough to pay for it. Teens tell us that cost is the second most important factor in determining whether they will use contraceptives, and they suggest that making contraceptives free will lead more teens to take the necessary precautions. The issue is far from being resolved, and PPFA plans to conduct further research to answer this critical question.

MEDICAL/LEGAL PROTECTION VERSUS SERVING TEENS

Another barrier to serving teens, quantified for the first time in our teen poll, was girls' fears of the pelvic exam. Never a pleasant experience, a pelvic exam is required in our clinics and is the "community standard" of care before the prescription of birth control pills, as well as other birth control methods. For many young women, the pelvic exam represents a "right of passage" into adult sexuality, and we suspect that it keeps a number of sexually active teens from seeking contraceptives. But we just aren't sure.

There would be no question of the advisability of a pelvic exam if there was agreement about its medical necessity. Although all sexually active women are advised to have a pelvic exam to rule out sexually transmitted diseases and cervical cancer, high-risk teen clients can be easily screened out using a simple health questionnaire. Furthermore, there is no reason to withhold the contraceptive method until the exam takes place.

The conflict arises over lawyers' concerns that bucking the community standard of care is fraught with danger. It could prompt lawsuits or a public outcry about the quality of service, despite the fact that the data do not justify the pelvic exam for all teens seeking the pill.

This, too, will be evaluated through a series of "action research" projects in 1988. We will attempt to see if removing the hurdle of the pelvic exam in the early stage of oral contraceptive use increases the volume of clients in a few of our centers. If it can be demonstrated that it does, we will consider moving aggressively to change this practice, not just for Planned Parenthood, but, through our advocacy efforts, for the entire reproductive health field.

ADVOCACY VERSUS SERVICE

Planned Parenthood has always engaged in a mix of advocacy and direct services programs for people in need of reproductive health care. PPFA's affiliates provide direct services to hundreds of thousands of teens. Its national headquarters seeks to lead the national organization's advocacy efforts through lobbying and public education. But these efforts are in competition for limited dollars. In trying to rally support for PPFA's campaign to prevent unintended teen pregnancy, there were cries that we should spend our money on trying to reach out and serve teens, not change their attitudes or behavior.

Service is a concrete entity. Attitudinal change is more abstract, and therefore its constituency is harder to build. It also takes longer. One is never sure that any progress is being made.

Conflicts aside, PPFA's affiliates support the national headquarter's public education efforts on the teenage pregnancy issue and feel that it improves the climate for their work locally.

CONFLICT IN THE COMMUNITY

Conflict is part of the culture of our organization because of the nature of our issues and the intensity of our opponents' wrath. Planned Parenthood has learned to cope with it. However, we have a natural tendency to try to avoid any new conflicts if we can predict where they might arise. Planned Parenthood's values were put to the test as we developed and mounted this campaign.

The public messages most likely to persuade sexually active teens to use birth control are those most likely to engender the discomfort of their parents. Their parents are important to us, too. We want them to be better communicators with their youngsters, and we want them to support our work in advocating changes in government and media policies.

Teens tell us that they want services that are free, available for the asking, and confidential—so that their parents will never find out. We must assure teens that contraceptives are, indeed, free, accessible and confidential, but these messages may jeopardize the good will of the community toward Planned Parenthood. We recognize, nevertheless, that our priority is serving the teens who were at greatest risk of curtailing their futures through unintended pregnancy. Taking tough positions that are correct has been our forte, and PPFA's board backed this aggressive campaign 100 percent.

THE NEXT WAVE

The AIDS crisis has brought home, in painful terms, the fact that the ultimate barrier we confront is Americans' acute discomfort with sexuality. Despite extraordinary media attention to the AIDS problem and the general awareness of society as to its causes, little in the way of behavioral change has taken place outside the gay community.

While everyone glibly acknowledges the importance of using condoms during sexual intercourse, social marketers have yet to consider the complexities involved in achieving this end. First, a person must be honest enough to admit that he or she is likely to have sexual intercourse, and, secondly, he or she must travel to the store and search for the condom, and perhaps even ask the salesperson for assistance, despite embarrassment. Then the condom must be carried around or stored in a handy place. Finally, in the heat of passion, one must pause, open the package and put it on. There are a lot of opportunities for error here, which are only exacerbated by our discomfort with our own sexuality.

We find the same difficulties with contraceptive use. It requires forethought and determination to be an effective contraceptive user, but too often we hear from clients that sex "just happened." Often, it "just happens" for a year or more. Somehow, even in our sex-saturated society, people deny that they are sexual and that they are likely to engage in sexual relationships. This clearly must change.

THE SEXUAL LITERACY CAMPAIGN

Planned Parenthood currently is designing a long-term, overarching campaign aimed at making Americans "sexually literate." It is our belief that if people are armed with facts about their feelings and how their bodies work, they can be more open and achieve healthier lives. Better communication about sex within couples can only enrich their unions, and we know from our research that better communication between parents and children can improve a youngster's likelihood of making a safe passage through a stormy adolescence.

The first phase of this effort will sensitize the public to the need for "sexual literacy." Then we plan a massive educational effort through schools, churches, other community organizations, and all possible media to bring people the facts and inspire them to improve their own communication skills in this arena. While we are just beginning to explore the range of messages and tone of such an effort, we suspect that humor might be effective with adults and might help us break more easily through our national "hangup" about sexuality.

SUMMARY

The Planned Parenthood Federation of America provides a benchmark against which other causes in the nonprofit sector might measure the applicability of marketing to their programs. In particular, the PPFA has demonstrated how in-depth research and surveys can translate into a meaningful strategy for the social marketing of ideas, which in this case have to do with a highly sensitive and controversial subject—human sexuality and teen pregnancies.

When the PPFA undertook a massive comparative analysis of teenage pregnancy in the United States and industrialized nations, the results indicated a dire need for greater parent–child communication about sex and birth control in the United States, whose inhabitants seem far more inhibited about openly discussing sexuality and contraception than those in the other nations surveyed. Using marketing's basic methods, the PPFA launched a nationwide campaign to provide the much-needed information—through the publication of a book, a national media tour, a video version of the book, brochures distributed in mass quantities, printed ads, and an extensive array of educational and clinical service programs for teens.

The PPFA's campaign has hit hard in an effort to educate the public about teen pregnancy, despite criticism from some quarters, not to mention the enormous difficulty of changing public attitudes. The PPFA's dedication to this effort is reflected in its current project: It is designing a long-term campaign to help all Americans, adults and adolescents alike, become "sexually literate."

18

Marketing Self-Help Groups
The Case of a Social and Personal Growth Organization for Singles

MARVIN BERKOWITZ
Fairfield University

The marketing of a social organization consists of both social (idea) marketing and the marketing of services. The prospective joiner of an organization intends not only to purchase the services offered by the group, but also to "buy" the idea itself that the group has value and is an acceptable entity with which to become associated. Even if the main product offering is a leisure time service, it is by and large an ideational product that is being sought. Moreover, the nature of the research to be conducted is quite the same for services and ideas. The same demographic and psychographic data need to be gathered for strategic planning purposes. This is known as attitude research, an example of which can be found in a study of one of the most successful self-help groups in the country—a singles group.

Organizations of single persons, self-help innovations of the 1970s, are rapidly becoming important institutional vehicles for significant numbers of never-married, divorced, and widowed persons to socialize while pursuing a broad range of common interests and needs. The personal services now offered by these mutual-aid groups include educational, cultural, health/fitness, entertainment, family support, career and financial, and personal growth programs. This study discusses how consumer surveys of one of the nation's largest singles organizations were used to design and implement strategies in the marketing mix that have helped the organization remain successful in a highly competitive and vulnerable service area.

The purpose of this chapter is to discuss the development of a marketing orientation in a rather unique organization, self-help groups—those providing for mutual assistance among adult single persons to meet and socialize, that is, "singles groups." These organizations supply a variety of social, educational, cultural, health/fitness, entertainment, and personal growth services that broadly fit within a self-help framework.

The research literature on marketing of social ideas and practices in general is extremely limited (e.g., Andreasen 1982; Barach 1984; Fine 1980; Hensel and Dubinsky 1985) and even less has been reported on the generation of such intangibles by self-help groups like the one studied. This research gap exists despite the fact that voluntary organizations for mutual assistance—both for profit and nonprofit—are rapidly increasing and providing vehicles through which an expanding segment of American society spends its time, money, and energies. One self-help group of single parents, Parents without Partners (PWP), for example, has over 100,000 members in fifty states.

The elderly, blacks, Hispanics, single persons, and a variety of other special-interest minorities are now being recognized by marketers as segments with significant buying power and distinct needs that are not being adequately met (Bartos 1982; Hirschman 1987). Organizations championing the needs of these special populations or attempting to attract them as loyal customers must tackle a host of problems that are still not fully understood. Marketing-oriented thinking can lead such organizations to search for meaningful and defensible positions by helping them establish their mission, market coverage, idea dissemination techniques, and service portfolio.

BACKGROUND OF SELF-HELP GROUPS

Self-help groups are relatively small voluntary structures established to provide mutual aid and accomplish special tasks. Mutual-aid groups and private voluntary associations (PVOs) are essentially the same types of social organizations. Members in such groups typically share similar experiences and have certain problems or interests in common. The initiators and members of self-help groups believe that all members can benefit from mutual assistance in the form of information, services, material help, and emotional support or campaigns to encourage communities to provide such assistance. Self-help groups emphasize face-to-face social interaction through group discussions or one-on-one sharing in solving individual and organizational problems. They assume that members are or can become personally responsible. Frequently self-help groups are cause-oriented and believe that through consciousness-raising and by championing certain ideologies, values, or social agendas members may attain an enhanced sense of "self" and achieve personal growth (Katz and Bender 1976). This is the grist of social marketing.

Self-help groups include many types of voluntary organizations with various types and degrees of problems or interests, professional involvement, and influence on the life style of its participants. Groups such as Alcoholics Anonymous, Narcotics Anonymous, Gay Rights Activists, National Organization of Women, Weight Watchers, and various indigenous agricultural cooperatives deal with fundamental long-term and often life-determining issues. There are also a number of affiliated groups whose membership is composed of relatives and friends of those who have a serious concern or problem, such as Adult Children of Alcoholic Parents, Alanon, Parents of Gays, and Parent-Teacher Associations. A third classification of highly involved self-help organizations includes life-transition groups formed to deal with a particular crisis that people have experienced. One such group is Parents of Perinatal Death, Recovery, Inc. (the first peer self-help psychotherapy group).

Self-help movements in the United States date back to colonial days. They were the means by which citizens participated in democratic politics and contributed to community welfare. In the late 1800s, self-help groups were primarily concerned with social action and thus focused on mobilizing resources to this end or directly attacking social problems related to homeless children, the poor, the mentally ill, and the like. In the early 1900s, a variety of neighborhood- and community-based movements initiated by outsiders with moral concerns, such as settlement houses, provided social services and led to the development of social work as a profession. In 1909, the National Association for the Advancement of Colored People was established; in 1911, the National Urban League. In the 1920s, the labor and union movement set off a chain of events that culminated in the formation of voluntary action groups aimed at furthering political, economic and other interests of special groups such as the blacks, aged, blind, welfare mothers, ex-offenders, low-income tenants, American Indians, women, homosexuals, and other needy minorities. The YM and YWCAs, the Boy and Girl Scouts, the PTA, the 4H Clubs, the United Way and other full-blown special interest groups active today all have their roots in this movement.

RISE OF SINGLES GROUPS

The idea of promoting an organization that encourages individuals to follow their hobbies, socialize, and establish friendships and relationships is as old as society itself. However, singles groups are an American phenomenon of the post–World War II period, which has witnessed an erosion of the nuclear and extended family. Ministering to the concerns of adult singles as a group is an especially novel concept in a couple-oriented society, in which churches have taken a lead in sponsoring self-help organizations for singles.

There have always been matchmakers. But singles groups, health clubs, singles vacations at resorts, personal ads in newspapers, bachelor directories, and special nights that supermarkets designate for single shoppers are all recent innovations. These new services emerged in the late 1960s and 1970s as a result of several social trends. During the 1970s, the number of singles eighteen or older in the United States who had never married, were separated, divorced, or widowed, rose from forty to fifty-nine million, or some 46 percent. Three-quarters of this growth was accounted for by the children born in the post–Korean War boom, who were reaching college age, and the increase in the graying older population as people lived longer and wives survived their husbands. The remaining quarter of the singles boom stems from the increased acceptability of divorce, and the tendency among young people to delay first marriages in order to further their education and establish a career. That, in turn, left young people with a smaller pool of potential mates once out of school.

Newly divorced and widowed people also had difficulty locating compatible companions. Moreover, with the increased numbers of male homosexuals, there were fewer eligible men. Another factor affecting the number of unattached men was that divorced men remarry more quickly. In addition, there were few convenient places to meet men, since it was still not quite acceptable for women to go to bars alone. And many women in service employment such as secretaries and teachers, found themselves with fewer work and professional contacts. Divorced men had to search harder, too, even though there were more working women to woo. By and large, men couldn't depend on friends to introduce them to a new pool of prospective mates because so many were divorced themselves. Increasing alienation in the general society, due to suburbanization, and to the substitution of TV and video watching for going out, also reduced the opportunities to meet people in traditional private entertainment settings. These factors all led to the birth of singles groups.

THE STUDY

Considerable insight into self-help groups has been gained from a study of the usage and attitudes of the participants of the Westport Unitarian

Singles Group (WUSG), one of the nation's most successful self-help singles organizations. The data from the study provide a basis for modeling consumption and evaluation in mutual and singles groups.

The WUSG had a modest beginning in 1975, with about a dozen recently divorced members of the Unitarian Church of Westport, Connecticut. By 1986, the group had a membership of about four thousand and a program of over fifty activities a month. It attracts upward of fifty thousand singles who live within a seventy-five mile radius of its center, and has an annual budget of some $500,000.

Methodology. Two systematic surveys were conducted in 1982–83 and 1984–85 to examine the need for self-help services. In addition, about one hundred singles were interviewed in depth, and several experienced observers studied the singles scene. The 1982–83 survey included 1,108 responses from people who came to the group's most popular program, its weeknight discussions on topics of interest to singles, followed by socials. It is at these meetings that participants usually have their first contact with the organization. The data were collected by structured self-administered questionnaires during three evenings devoted to a discussion of self-evaluation and improvement of the organization. Each survey took about twenty minutes to complete and was monitored by designated individuals. Some 246 responses (22 percent) were from "newcomers" who were attending functions for the first time; the newcomers were asked, primarily for demographic information, as well as details of their goals and expectations. About eight hundred of the respondents were members of the organization who paid annual dues of $20 and received a 50 percent discount on activity charges and a monthly newsletter announcing activities.

The 1984–85 research was based on self-administered responses to a survey of some five hundred attendees at the discussion group evenings. It focused more on gauging satisfaction with the group's activities and on programmatic and organizational innovations desired. This work was performed as a result of changes in the demographic makeup of the organization's participants.

RESEARCH FINDINGS

Characteristics of Services to Singles. The basic characteristics of the social products offered by mutual-aid singles organizations are presented in Table 18.1, using a classification system proposed by Lovelock (1983). Results show that singles groups offer largely high-contact services in the way of social and educational activities. They also provide a forum in

TABLE 18.1   Characteristics of Services Offered by Singles Groups

Object of service	Mainly to the person or the consumer or his/her children and to other persons in a similar situation. Services also delivered to the organization providing the service.
Discrete or continuous	Discrete customer/provider relationship on a per activity basis. Annual membership in organization ensures some continuity in terms of information flow from provider.
Role of physical goods service	Consumer consumes a perishable service, and utilizes some physical facilities—buildings, chairs, sports equipment, etc.—in doing so.
Role and extent of personal service	Personally delivered services are the central component in the service package or dominate others in importance. Services are intangible and heterogeneous.
Breadth of benefit package	Consumption experience usually involves delivery of several different services on each occasion—e.g., social and cultural.
Timing and duration of benefits	Benefits are received during the service delivery plus over a long-term period following service delivery.
Nature of consumer provider interaction	Production and consumption are inseparable. Personal presence required throughout delivery of many services; consumer may be a provider of services him/herself.
Length of consumer provider relationship	Interaction for many consumers is limited to a single trial—i.e., such services are not acceptable to everyone and switching occurs between different providers. For a given provider, there is a high turnover of customers with period of relationship typically under six months.
Payment for services	Payment usually on a per activity basis. Annual membership is not required for participation.

which people can create or alter ideas, attitudes, and behavior toward themselves and toward singles organizations per se (e.g., "It's quite okay to be single").

In a society where couples predominate, but singles are rapidly increasing, advocacy of the singles' life style is a significant function. Religious organizations that sponsor singles groups may also be hoping to revitalize dormant members or to gain new ones. Church-sponsored singles groups may be seen as community outreach efforts that bring many people into the church who are not of the same faith. However, as a strategy to build church membership, singles groups are likely to be ineffective. In the group intensively studied, only 3 percent of the participants were Unitarians; 30 percent said religion was unimportant; and 47 percent rarely, if ever, attended religious services.

MAJOR STRATEGY CONSIDERATIONS

Consumer Psychographics. A number of strategic considerations in designing and operating a mutual-aid singles organization emerging from these studies are summarized in Table 18.2. One of the most critical yet most difficult steps is to formulate a consumer-based service philosophy. The usual product market objective of establishing loyal long-term customers does not always apply in mutual-aid groups since the primary goal of these groups is to help individuals meet the specific goals that brought them to the group. In the case of singles groups, where being single is an acute or transitional state to some members, this may mean "marrying off" many of their participants. Without the continual influx of new participants, such mutual-aid organizations would cease to grow and remain vital. This is but one example of how social marketing strategy often differs from marketing strategy in general.

As a result of this difference, a goal of the research was to assess attitudes about being single and explore motivations for coming to the singles organization. The areas in which the organization's 1982–83 consumers wanted to make big changes in their lives ranged from finding new jobs and help with child care to improving intimate relationships. Most respondents said they were managing their practical lives as a single adequately. Information sharing was not a major concern. It was in the more personal aspects of their lives—achieving better relationships and friendships, and handling emotional stresses—that singles of all age groups wanted to see an improvement. And 90 percent said they would like to be married.

Most singles said they came to the group searching for companionship and love, not just casual sex. More recent data in the aftermath of the AIDS scare emphasize this. Particular issues varied by sex and age; twice as many men, for example, were concerned with making a new male friend as women were with making female friends. Those aged thirty-five and younger expressed a greater urge for attachment than persons over thirty-five. One-quarter reported that a very important reason for participation was to escape "the blues" and just get out of the house. This motivational analysis confirmed that the organization's primary mission should be in facilitating and improving personal relationships

TABLE 18.2 Major Strategy Considerations in Designing and Operating an Organization for Single Persons

Decision	Considerations
Facility location	Many activities geographically segmented to be near major centers where consumers live. For example, in 1983 the group expanded to a new meeting center in Westchester County; in 1984 it incorporated a declining singles group about twenty-five miles from its headquarters and began meeting there.
Facility choice design	Facility choice must meet psychological needs of the customer with regard to safety, security, cleanliness, crowding, appropriateness, and atmosphere in order to achieve desired production effects. Church and school locations selected when possible to enhance nonthreatening image and defuse negative sexual associations of the swinging single. These "atmospheric" elements provide favorable "proper" image of singles activities to children of participants. Consideration also is given to the cost of meeting spaces.
Service design	Personal services designed around consumer wants and needs, also around the interests of volunteers who lead specific activities—e.g., investment seminars, personal emotional growth, folk singing, volleyball, tennis, classical music, coping with their children, vacation trips. Customers are prone to pursuing fads. Product life cycles vary in length from very short (days) to years.
Scheduling	Activity schedules determined in part by customer preferences, in part by the availability and size of meeting locations, and availability of activity leaders. The environment (community and sponsoring organizations) influence scheduling to the extent they impose their own standards on whether alcohol may be served, timing of activities and types of activities that do not have externalities for them—e.g., neighbors complain about loud music late in the evening and call the police. Weather and season are important influences.
Production planning	Orders for services cannot be stored in the main—i.e., they are perishable. Some backlogging is possible for participation at special seminars—e.g., workshops for those newly single. However smoothing production is not possible. Bottlenecks and blockages occur frequently in that more singles want to participate in a particular activity than space limitations permit.
Worker skills and performance	Direct work force comprises a major part of the service—e.g., as discussion group leaders—and so must be able to interact well with customers. Staff vary in background, socioeconomic levels, and competency. Hence it is difficult to standardize output. Cannot depend on training and continuity of work force over an extended time period.

TABLE 18.2 (continued)

Decision	Considerations
Quality control	Quality standards are highly variable and subjectively determined by different customers—what one consumer thinks superior, others frequently rate as poor. Problem is that poor services cannot be returned. Consumers are highly demanding with many options if service levels do not meet their standards, and simply may be lost as future consumers.
Time standards	The nonstandardization (heterogeneity) of time standards reflects the high variablity in the specifications for services and how they are performed. Service times are tightly set for some activities, and loosely for others. In many cases customers set their own standards of what's appropriate for them by coming and going as they choose.
Wage payment	Only one full-time paid worker (a secretary) for organization with $500,000 budget. Particular services like police security guards are paid by time-based system.
Capacity and service planning	To avoid losing activity fees (sales), facility locations are selected to match projected peak demand levels when possible. Space limitations or fire safety rules can impose limits on attendance and revenue. Capacity planning also depends on willingness of customers to make available their own homes for parties and social events—space is often severely restricted here. Forecasting is largely short term.
Production	Most activities involve simultaneous production and consumption. Consumer is in intimate contact with producer—often the consumer is the producer him/herself or party to the production. How much one benefits from services may depend on how much one is able to share oneself.
Promotional mechanisms	Word-of-mouth advertising through friends, family, professional therapists, etc., is the main mechanism by which singles learn about the organization. The organization's monthly newsletter (direct mail) gives information about activities and schedules. Space in local media is purchased to announce the group's program. The group has a communications director who prepares public relations articles for the media and arranges for radio and television coverage to enhance its image and keep the group in the public eye.
Pricing	The overall organizational goal is maximum use of services rather than profit maximization. Consequently, cost-oriented pricing strategies basically used. For major activities, costs applied are full costs including a measure of projected overhead. Overheads are assigned in proportion to the level of revenue generated by activities. For minor activities, marginal costs are often used. Consideration is usually given to prices of competitive or substitute services and to the likely impact on demand/draw.

TABLE 18.2 (continued)

Decision	Considerations
Mechanisms to cope with fluctuating demand	Demand peaks during the warmer months and drops to a minimum in the dead of winter. Price incentives or promotions are not used to induce demand during slow periods. Only occasionally are consumers turned away: crowding is more common. Reservations are used for some activities. A rationing plan (odd-even) was imposed to limit demand due to space constraints in 1983 and almost caused the demise of the group by antagonizing consumers.
Research orientation	Periodic surveys of consumer needs and satisfaction with the organization are conducted.
Mechanisms for controlling supply	Have customers do more for themselves e.g., more "pot luck" dinners than prepared buffets. Reduce service frequency and quality—e.g., lower the quality of wine served, reduce contact of leadership with membership, place restrictions on use of services.
Organizational structure	Some difficult problems arise for singles groups typically sponsored by a nonprofit parent body such as a church or community organization. For example, a major continuing concern is to maintain a satisfactory working relationship with its parent organization. The group acts largely in an autonomous fashion, essentially paying a rental fee for use of facilities, yet formally is a committee of the church. The group frequently wonders whether to seek formal independent status or remain under the wing of the church. Control battles were common during 1981–84 as the singles group sought greater use of the church, and the church sought to establish its formal authority and limit wear and tear on its physical facilities. Negotiations over a three-year period and a change of leadership in both organizations led to a compromise.

for both newly single persons in transition and persons for whom singleness is a long-term life-style (Table 18.3).

Occasionally the leadership tried to test out other goals, for example, to encourage consumers to become involved in socially conscious activities beyond their own selves. These moves brought favorable community attention to the group but failed to motivate members to participate. Thus the group's primary mission became almost totally devoid of any religious or ethical component, which created considerable concern and misgivings among members of the organization's church parent body.

Activities. Further insight into what might be an effective promotional strategy was derived from consumer perceptions of the appropriate fo-

TABLE 18.3 Areas Where Singles Want to Make Big Changes in Their Lives, 1982 (percent)

Area	Men	Women
Intimate relationships	49	61
Emotional aspects of single life	30	29
Money	30	33
Housing	25	15
Things to do in free time	22	18
Same-sex friends	20	9
Children's behavior	12	8
Care and activities for children	10	7
Education	9	9

Source: 1982 Survey of Participants, Westport Unitarian Singles Group. Sample size: 1,108.

cus of the group—that is, whether it should emphasize support and enrichment programs, or be a place for people to meet potential partners. This is the standard marketing approach adapted for the service organization (see Lovelock 1984). Attribute ratings of these two benefit objectives were about equal (mean scores of 3.8 out of 5.0 for support and 3.6 out of 5.0 for a meeting place).

The helping process in this organization consisted of group discussions about what being a single person meant. It was assumed that the helping process also operated outside of regular group functions, as individuals called on one another for emotional and practical support. The group's sponsors believed that social and recreational activities contributed to the therapeutic process by increasing the probability of members' participation in the group and offering ways to fill the void in members' lives left by a separation, divorce, or death of a spouse. Workshops in personal growth techniques to increase self-esteem and practical functioning were regular components of the group's program. There was no antagonism or antithetical disposition in the singles group to for-profit professional activities for singles, and referral to such services was made available to members.

Data on participation levels in the group's unique variety of programs also provided guidelines on what activities to emphasize in future programs. The most popular activities were dances and parties in members' homes (about 35–40 percent participated in these). Sports were next in importance, with 5–10 percent participation, followed by cultural activities with 1–5 percent participation (see Table 18.4).

Competition. The 1982–83 findings also revealed how much competition the organization was experiencing from other singles groups. About 30

TABLE 18.4 Participation Rates at Singles Organizations' Functions, 1982

Function	Percent
Discussion groups	100
Dances	38
Socials in members' homes	35
Tennis	7
Camping	6
Racketball/volleyball	6
Skiing or hiking	5
Music events	5
Literature/other cultural programs	5
Life transition workshops	3

Source: 1982 Survey of Participants, Westport Unitarian Singles Group. Sample size: 1,108.

percent of the sample belonged to at least one other of the area's hundred or so singles groups, but most of these were relatively close to members' homes. In contrast, they traveled up to seventy-five miles each way to get to the center in Westport. Suburban but not too rural and within an hour's ride to Manhattan, Fairfield County is the home of many of America's most glamorous corporations and their employees. The "Gold Coast," as it is known, is one of America's most affluent areas—the average family income is roughly 50 percent higher than in the entire state of Connecticut or the United States. The "mystique" or favorable image created by the group's location in upscale Westport encouraged people to participate in the organization. Two other significant reasons why this group became dominant in the singles market in the New York metropolitan area were the organization's large critical mass of new and different faces, and its unique high-quality program. The group's program became known primarily by word of mouth but the media were also used to disseminate information, and the group advertised selectively.

MARKET SEGMENTATION

Participation was analyzed along standard demographic and life-style dimensions. To illustrate, WUSG singles differ greatly in terms of their values, attitudes, available time, financial flexibility, and emotional energy depending on the stage in their life cycles. Bachelors (24 percent of the group in 1982) had the most options for participation. Next came formerly marrieds without children (14 percent), then parents whose children had left the roost, and weekend parents (32 percent). Heads of households with school-age children under eighteen (30 percent) have the most responsibility, the lowest flexibility, and lowest participation levels. It was apparent that most women had the burden of raising children: 53 percent of the women thirty-five and older, and 18 percent under thirty-five—44 percent of the women overall—were heads of households with school-age children. Well over 75 percent of the fathers in their forties and fifties were "empty nesters" (Table 18.5).

These and similar data not only identified those members of the singles market most attracted to the group, but also made it easier to organize the program to suit the identified market segments. For example, the age profile of persons attending various activities indicated a need to structure discussion evenings so that those under thirty-five could meet separately. Two-thirds of these younger singles were bachelors or never marrieds and had different interests from older divorced persons. Some other lines of segmentation were based on marital status, place of residence, and special interests/hobbies.

CHURCH AFFILIATION AND ORGANIZATIONAL IMAGE

The respectability associated with church functions makes it easy for single parents to tell their kids where they're going without telling them precisely why. The church offers an especially safe, nonthreatening atmosphere to women. The beauty and warmth of the particular Unitarian Church building in Westport and its calm spiritual feeling, without the visible trappings of most churches, also were viewed as positive atmospheric elements promoting the group. (The favorable affects of atmospheric cues on consumers have been reported by Kotler 1973.) On the other hand, roughly 66 percent of the respondents said they would come to the singles group and become members even if it were not located in a church or affiliated with one. This response indicated that the success of the group was more closely allied with the characteristics of the organization's participants and their expectations than the characteristics of its meeting place. As a result, the group decided to establish satellite units outside Fairfield County in order to (a) minimize travel time for its consumers and (b) be responsive to pressure from its parent sponsoring organization to reduce physical wear and tear on the church, and to shift to other sites late evening and noisy activities such as dances, which nearby residents were complaining about. The organization subsequently established a successful satellite in a Unitarian Church in Westchester County (thirty miles away from the Westport headquarters), and later absorbed a failing organization of older singles in Stamford, Con-

TABLE 18.5 Stages in Life Cycles of Participants (percent)

Stage		Key Characteristics
Bachelors (24)		
Under 35		
Men	64	Most free time, options, mobility. Career oriented, rela-
Women	50	tively low incomes. Into sports, travel, experimenting.
35 & over		
Men	17	
Women	11	
Separated/divorced/widowed		
(without children; 14)		
Under 35		
Men	19	Similar to bachelors in mobility and finances. Likely to
Women	24	be in transition. Susceptible to a rush from more expe-
35 & over		rienced singles. Emotional & practical burdens of start-
Men	13	ing over.
Women	8	
Single parents (62):		
With school-age children (30)		
Under 35		
Men	5	Jobs, the kids, and the house impose peak demands on
Women	18	time, money, and emotional energy, especially for those
35 & over		with kids under 12. Arrangements for children and costs
Men	14	of baby-sitting may be problems.
Women	53	
Without children or weekend		
parents (32)		
Under 35		
Men	14	*Empty Nesters:* Relative freedom except for college bills,
Women	8	alimony, etc. Travel, recreation, and the self become re-
35 & over		newed interests.
Men	56	
Women	28	*Weekend Parents:* More flexibility for socializing than
		custodial parents but added responsibilities make rela-
		tionships difficult to create.

Source: 1982 Survey of Participants, Westport Unitarian Singles Group. Sample size: 1,108.

necticut (some twenty miles away). It also began to use hotels and other commercial sites. Schools were used only for weekend conferences and large meetings because they did not permit alcohol on the premises, an important icebreaker in social settings.

A CHANGING SOCIAL AND COMPETITIVE ENVIRONMENT

The 1984–85 study revealed changes in the consumer base and a decline in satisfaction with the group's programs as the organization and its service offerings matured. Overall it was apparent that the group's phenomenal growth in the early 1980s had peaked and changes were necessary. Between 1982 and 1984, the organization's audience had aged by an average of two years or more. The group was no longer quite as appealing to persons in their thirties and early forties. As an early warning sign of trouble, the organization was not attracting quite as many newly divorced or separated persons. Newcomers would try out the group's program one time but not become repeat customers. It was just possible that the group was succeeding too well at its mission of connecting recent divorcees. On the other hand, established singles kept coming back. In 1982, 50 percent of the participants had been coming to the organization for more than six months, whereas 64 percent were satisfied repeat customers for more than six months in 1984. Once a group of people in transition from marriage, the organization was becoming predominantly one of established singles. It appeared that the vast untouched reservoir of ex-divorcees and never-marrieds who were attracted to the organization when it first began in 1975 had been absorbed or gone elsewhere. With increased competition from an expanding number of singles groups, the organization faced the prospects of a declining share of the replacement market for those newly in transition to singleness, as well as a smaller share of the mature market of established singles.

BUILDING CONTINUITY

Selling participants of singles groups the idea that they themselves will be better off by becoming communicators of the concept to others is a fundamental basis of self-help groups and other organizations managed by volunteers. Roughly 15 percent of the membership in the singles group studied were involved at any one time in helping to run the organization. These more highly involved participants became role models for new members and for bolstering support in the community. Encouraging the most competent of the highly involved members to become committed leaders in self-help singles groups is a most perplexing problem (as noted for other social marketing situations; see, e.g., Bloom and Novelli 1981). Many are single parents, stretched thin, and do not have the necessary time and stability in their own lives to extend to others; child care may be a major constraint. Turnover of leadership is a way of life in the self-help singles organization, with periods of involvement of one to two years being typical. This in effect reduces the danger that singles groups will become rigid, undemocratic, and unresponsive. However, many groups collapse when leaders become involved in long-term love relationships, or marry and leave the organization. Consequently, staffing its leadership positions with people who are gifted at recruiting workers for the many operational functions and future leadership roles is the most critical concern.

Singles groups have been characterized as unique contemporary mutual-aid organizations. Acceptance of the marketing concept—that the organization should come to grips with its participants' stated needs—proved a key ingredient in the performance of the singles organization studied. Although attendance dropped sharply on a few occasions when the group presumed that participants were a captive body and would follow the leadership's direction, members and other participants sought out alternative activities to obtain the benefits they desired.

Discussions with leaders of other singles organizations suggest that they have experienced many of the problems and solutions discussed here, as have mutual-aid groups in general. What made the WUSG unique was its large size and rapid growth, and its relationship with the parent sponsoring body. It had the unusual good fortune to attract a rather sophisticated membership that was willing to become highly involved in setting and implementing the group's agenda. This is the basic requirement for a successful mutual-aid organization.

The nature of the services provided—they were intangible, heterogeneous, and perishable and production and consumption were difficult to separate—created repeated problems for the organization studied. Singles organizations provide somewhat unique offerings compared with other service or social marketers on account of the nature and breadth of their service mix. To illustrate, many traditional firms that manufacture and sell tangible products attempt to motivate purchases by associating the acquisition of affection and affiliation with consumption. However, this is distinctly different from marketing opportunities for emotional support, and building self-esteem or love directly. The services for the special singles market studied involve high risk purchases: There is no certainty whatever that a recently widowed woman will quickly overcome her loss, or meet the new man of her dreams. This is one reason why an emotional support function is such a critical component of singles organizations. Uniform quality is especially difficult to achieve in services offered by volunteers in mutual-aid groups since it is not possible to control the willingness and ability to satisfy member needs, particularly when members themselves participate in the production process. Recruiting, training, and maintaining good staff is a fundamental problem in singles organizations since participation in the group and its social advocacy agenda usually ceases when a consumer makes a good interpersonal connection and forms an intimate love relationship. The individual then no longer needs the group. Maintaining management continuity is extremely difficult.

SUMMARY

This study has shown that a great number of factors—some specific to services for single adults, some specific to self-help groups, some specific to the particular organization examined—determine the type of marketing and management that will successfully promote the organization's goals. The variety of problems encountered by the WUSG frequently required specialized solutions and strategies that differed from those that were effective in product-based consumer marketing or in services marketing per se. Pricing, facility choice, and selection and payment of staff all differ markedly.

The evidence shows that singles groups that do not follow marketing approaches are especially vulnerable to fierce competition from other singles organizations—many of which are for-profit institutions, not burdened by a continually changing staff and leadership, and frequent problems with parent bodies. In the case studied, when adaptive marketing approaches were applied consistently, considerable success was achieved.

The realities of present-day American family life are such that (1) 33 percent of first marriages end in divorce (marriages are now lasting fewer years, and if current trends keep up, 50 percent of today's first marriages are likely to fail); (2) 85 percent of divorced people remarry, usually within three years of the divorce (men remarry sooner than women); (3) 59 percent of second marriages also end in divorce; (4) few adults live with their parents or other relatives if they can afford to live independently; (5) the age at which couples first marry continues to rise as young adults put off their decisions until after college or career formation; (6) more women are choosing careers over motherhood (when they do have children, they tend to have fewer of them, which makes divorce easier). In short, social trends indicate further marital instability, growth in the number of families headed by one parent, and continued geographical separation of singles and their relatives. Midlife singles will continue to have a need for warm, helping institutions espousing emotional and practical support.

Empirical and conceptual research on marketing self-help groups and their programs is extremely limited. It would be interesting to examine the extent to which the findings here typify similar organizations and institutional settings. This is a rich area for a variety of future studies.

19

The Marketing of Political Candidates
Current Tactics and Future Strategies

CLARKE L. CAYWOOD
University of Wisconsin–Madison

GENE R. LACZNIAK
Marquette University

Alexander Haig, Jr., a 1988 presidential hopeful, remarked, concerning campaign politics: "I have learned the secret of life—it's in marketing" (1986). The emergence of marketing in nonbusiness organizations, so well documented in recent writings, is accented by its ascendancy in politics (Laczniak and Caywood 1987; "Four More Years" 1985; Mauser 1983; Rothschild 1978). Any campaign manager interested in applying orthodox marketing principles to his or her craft will find the use of marketing techniques in the political sphere particularly instructive.

The area of modern campaign management that introduced marketing tools into the political process was probably public relations (PR). In the early 1950s, PR professionals began to manage various political campaigns, including the much-discussed California election that launched the political career of Richard Nixon (Kelly 1956). Twenty years later, the "selling of the presidency" received wide public attention in the popular book on the 1968 Nixon campaign by a young journalist, Joe McGinnis (1969). But even in that first twenty-year period, marketing had not really reached its full potential in national or local campaigns. Now, despite an additional two decades, the capabilities of marketing as a political campaign management strategy have still not been realized.

In the past few years, marketing academics and practitioners have become interested in applying marketing concepts and tools to political campaigns. Researchers, including Caywood and Preston (1989), Newton and Sheth (1985), Caywood (1985), Merritt (1984), Rust, Baja, and Haley (1984), Mauser (1983), Rothschild (1978) and others, have analyzed the applicability of various communications, advertising, and marketing concepts to political marketing. They have analyzed political marketing from the standpoint of information processing, consumer behavior, law, ethics, and voter choice; however, a unified theory about political marketing does not exist.

At the pragmatic level of actual campaign management, marketing techniques are widely used. As one political expert has noted, "Today choosing policy advisors is insignificant compared to lining up the right pollster, media advisor, direct mail operator, fund-raiser and make-up artist" (Sorenson 1984). There are a number of books on how to run a campaign as well as numerous chronicles of campaign anecdotes (see Trafton 1984; Napolitan 1972; Goldenberg and Traugott 1984; Parkinson 1970; Kelley 1956). However, none of these manuals is grounded in a thorough knowledge of marketing theory and strategic management.

The fact that marketing theory has not made a greater contribution to political campaigns is understandable. The typical focus of academic marketing research is business. The diffusion of marketing knowledge into nonbusiness sectors, including nonprofit organizations, is recent enough that only some use has been made of marketing strategies. The diffusion of insights from one field to another often begins with tactical knowledge, which is more convenient and understandable than the more complex and challenging strategic approaches. Many large businesses are still attempting to integrate the insights of strategic management theory into their operations (Aaker 1984; Henderson 1983; Ansoff 1957).

THE ECONOMIC DIMENSIONS OF POLITICAL MARKETING

Although political marketing is still evolving, it is "big business," and significant economic stakes are involved. Expenditures for congressional campaigns in 1985 and 1986 alone were in the neighborhood of $480 million, an increase of 20 percent over the previous record (Gaunt 1987). Recent U.S. Senate races consumed a record $211 million. This included the Zschau versus Cranston race in California in which each candidate spent in excess of $11 million. Every Senate candidate spent *at least* $1.3 million in 1986. Actual marketing expenditures at all political levels are unknown, but printing costs for brochures, campaign buttons, consultants, outdoor advertising, and all other forms of promotion would certainly add up to billions of dollars.

In addition, traditional business marketers have become increasingly involved with politics through the rise of the political action committee (PAC) (Sabato 1984). The PAC is the main avenue corporations can use to influence the political process, and thus has called for a higher degree of management in campaigns. Corporations and related business, labor, and professional organizations, reportedly contributed $132.2 million through PACs, or 28 percent of total contributions to congressional political campaigns in the 1986 elections (Gaunt 1987).

In general, such increased financial and volunteer support by business executives for sundry political candidates would suggest that marketing knowledge will continue to trickle into the political campaign arena at an increasing rate. It is useful, therefore, to examine the marketing tools and concepts that have already been adapted to politics and those that may be used more and more in the future. The objective of this chapter is to explore where tactical and strategic elements of marketing have contributed to modern political campaign management to date and to speculate about the elements of marketing that have not been fully utilized.

CURRENT APPLICATIONS OF MARKETING IN POLITICAL CAMPAIGNING

What kinds of marketing techniques are used most often in current political campaigns? Some of the more common methods used are as follows:

Advertising
Survey research
Publicity
Focus groups
Direct mail
Telemarketing
Sales promotions.

In general, the integrated application of marketing and related techniques to political campaigns has been relatively minor, although individual techniques have been used skillfully. For example, although some tools of marketing research have been employed (e.g., survey research), the strategic connections between research, candidate development, and subsequent voter cultivation have not been as effective as possible. In addition, political consultants using marketing have not fully understood the value of exploratory research methods (e.g., focus groups, elite interviewing) in developing ongoing research programs for longer-term strategic decisionmaking in the campaign and beyond.

Nonetheless, candidates, political consultants, and occasional bona fide marketing managers with corporate backgrounds have successfully employed some marketing methods in politics. Marketing elements such as advertising, direct mail, publicity, and sales promotion are currently used in political campaigns throughout the United States.

ADVERTISING

Media advertising techniques, including both electronic and print, are commonplace and have been well integrated into political campaigns for some time. Early use of print, outdoor, and eventually radio and television advertising as applied to politics have been well documented (e.g., Jamieson 1984; Diamond and Bates 1984). Significantly, some advertising agencies have been reluctant to work with political campaigns. Advertising legend David Ogilvy (1983) has criticized television commercials for candidates in presidential elections as flagrantly dishonest (1983). And John O'Toole (1981), chairman of Foote, Cone and Belding, has been somewhat critical of the inherently misleading nature of such advertising. Other academic and journalistic researchers have shown that television is particularly vulnerable to criticism (Laczniak and Caywood 1987; Spero 1980).

On the other hand, the business of political advertising is well accepted and is a significant economic force in advertising. Rothschild (1987, p. 765) notes that if one extrapolates the compressed two-month $40 million expenditures for the presidential election in 1984, it would translate into a $240 million campaign—which would be greater than the expenditures for all but five national brand name products.

Madison Avenue's involvement, although substantial, is perhaps not as great as that of smaller "main street" advertising agencies in local and state campaigns. Also, since most mass media offer the campaign committee itself traditional agency discounts of 15 percent, an agency may be of no obvious economic benefit to some campaign managers. However, most state candidates for federal or state office opt for a local agency. In addition, federal rules require broadcast media to offer available radio and television time to candidates at the lowest commercial rates. This has encouraged the use of mass media. Thus, advertising plays a visible and arguably influential role in modern politics (Laczniak and Caywood 1987). Rothschild (1987, p. 745) notes that the intensity of political advertising signals one objective: "When a short message of little substance is repeated that often, it is clear that the goal is not to inform, but rather to persuade." However, advertising may have a more significant role for voter information than traditional news coverage because it provides a shorthand mechanism for diffusing potentially salient information (Clarke and Evans 1983).

If politics has failed to recognize the full value of advertising—which, *is* indeed, used profusely—it may be because political advisers see advertising as an isolated element of the campaign rather than an integrated component of promotional strategy.

SURVEY RESEARCH

Polling, or survey research, has also been used in politics for many years. The technique has been refined in recent times as political advisers have become more aware of appropriate social science methods (Mauser 1983; Honomichl 1984). Some years ago, pollsters proposed that surveys of voter intention for presidential candidate Hubert H. Humphrey should be administered in the second weeks of September, October, and November (Napolitan 1972), forgetting that the third survey of voter opinion would be unnecessary since the election would have been held the prior week. Things have improved since then.

In recent years the concept of a "bus," that is, appended questions, to a scheduled opinion survey has been offered to political managers. In addition, a number of national firms, including Market Opinion Research and Lance Terrance and Associates, have offered to conduct multiple wave panel studies for candidates. Although the complexity of the research used in political campaigns has increased, many of the questions asked in such polls elicit essentially descriptive information. Attitude, opinion, and behavioral intention questions regarding public issues, voting preferences, and candidate name recognition are the most typical ones. Contributing to the melange of political surveys are periodic reports from Gallup, Yankelovich, Harris, and others, as well as the national networks and even local media.

Although the quality of research has improved (for instance, sample size and statistical error range are now routinely reported), voters and candidates are often confronted with widely disparate statistics on how one candidate is doing over another. This stems partly from the different questions being asked, the different ways that the same questions are asked, the timing of the survey, the variation in sample composition, and a host of other factors. In addition, each candidate will selectively report his or her commissioned research. Other more objective sources may report conflicting results.

In a recent Wisconsin race, various polls showed the challenger supported by either 50 percent or 41 percent and the incumbent supported by either 29 percent or 48 percent. The challenger and eventual victor, obviously seizing on the most optimistic numbers, was "elated" according to his aide ("Poll" 1986). Although conflicting information is not unusual even in more traditional marketing areas (e.g., comparative advertising), political opinion polls are often used as campaign cannon fodder rather than as dispassionate sources of information for decision-making. For example, in an Ohio gubernatorial race in 1982, a survey question about the opposition candidate's sexual activities became the subject of an advertising rebuttal on television ("Candidate Tells" 1982). Again, political campaign managers may use a tool of marketing, but the chaotic decision environment during a political campaign distorts the value of the tool in making substantive, issue-focused decisions.

PUBLICITY

Publicity, which gives candidates free coverage in the press, is an element of both public relations and marketing (Kotler and Mindak 1978). It is found to be necessary in most political campaigns. Owing to the public nature and potential impact of election campaigns, they are more or less inherently newsworthy. Major campaigns, such as those for statewide or federal offices, would not normally be able to afford to communicate the amount of information necessary to create general awareness of the candidate's position on major issues without publicity or the so-called free media.

In one campaign for a statewide office in Wisconsin, a candidate conducted a "fly-in" to each of the state's seven major television markets with advance notice to the press concerning an airport announcement of his candidacy and platform. Media representatives not present at the event were sent preproduced taped spots of the announcement. The estimated cost of the news coverage for this tactic was greater than the budget for all paid broadcast media during the entire campaign. Throughout the campaign, this particular candidate continued to successfully use free media with a series of so-called workdays. The candidate worked for part of a day in various jobs around the state, including an assembly line, road crew, drycleaners, and so on. He continued to receive an amazing amount of publicity for these somewhat trival activities. Attempts to connect serious economic policy issues to the jobs were not used by the media as much as the unusual photo opportunity of a politician working at something meaningful.

Free media can also have a negative effect. Despite the old campaign cliché, I don't care what they say about me as long as they spell my name right," the press coverage the *Miami Herald* gave Gary Hart in 1987 was damaging, and certainly was not part of his campaign plan ("Hart Campaign" 1987). Since a newsworthy story can be favorable as well as unfavorable to the candidate, publicity must be managed as carefully as possible.

However, publicity is only one aspect of public relations. Marketers must recognize that public relations is a two-way form of communications (Cutlip, Center, and Broom 1986) if they are to avoid severe errors in campaign management. For example, a clear understanding of the role of the press under the First Amendment is necessary to avoid conflict. Some negative commentary from the press should be expected. Campaign managers should look at these instances as an opportunity to provide an appropriate rebuttal. Thus, the reinforcement of positive messages or the rebuttal of contradictory messages from the press must be integrated into a fully strategic marketing plan.

FOCUS GROUPS

Another tool of marketing that political campaign consultants have discovered is the focus group (Patton 1980). Such groups are regularly used by commercial marketing and advertising firms to systematically gather information from small samples of likely product users or service clients. The technique is thought to be more time-efficient and as cost-effective as collecting information through in-depth interviews (Calder 1977).

How do campaigns utilize the popular focus group? Starting with a sample of seven to twelve individuals (e.g., voters from a certain ward or first-time voters), two or three hours of structured group discussion may eventually pinpoint key questions or other discussion points thought to be particular strengths or weaknesses of a candidate. For example, during one 1986 gubernatorial campaign, a small advertising agency was commissioned to conduct regional focus groups for a candidate. Proposed video and audio tapes about the candidate were reviewed by campaign leaders to identify promotional message themes and speech ideas, and to confirm that this information reflected the themes developed from other qualitative and quantitative research. However, such exploratory research methods were not extended to more valid follow-up activities such as voter opinion surveys and platform refinement. Again, a tool of marketing was used, but not in the context of a more pervasive marketing plan. This is a common failing of political marketers, who often overlook the benefits of combining research with other marketing devices.

DIRECT MAIL

Perhaps the most visible application of purely tactical marketing methods to politics is direct mail. This practice has grown so rapidly that a separate division has been created within the Direct Marketing and Mail Association to handle it. Candidate committees and PACs have used direct mail primarily for fund-raising. One irony of the current process—at least for presidential campaigns—is that the candidate can spend $100,000 to send out a direct mail to voters, get back only $90,000 in small contributions, and then have the government match it with $90,000—which means a net gain of $80,000 rather than a loss of $10,000 (O'Leary 1987).

A statewide campaign or congressional election may send as many as five separate mailings to names on a past donors list. Improved computer capability, direct mail software, job shops specializing in the generation of voter lists, and past contributor lists have made direct mail the fastest-growing promotional area of political marketing. One political consultant has reported that 1988 presidential contender and television evangelist Pat Robertson had "a donor list which numbered about 2.5 million. . . . In comparison, Ronald Reagan went into the 1980 race with only a 200,000 donor file, while Bush, Baker, Kemp and Dole have substantially smaller files, all of which are in the 30,000 to 75,000 donor range" (O'Leary 1987, p. 24). Today political consulting newsletters boast that management software such as D-Base has been adapted to political campaigns and made it possible to manage lists containing a million names (Below, Tobe, and Associates 1987).

Many of the professional elements of commercial direct mail have been adopted in politics. Personal salutations, individualized names in the body of the letter, targeted inserts to various lists, prepaid return mail envelopes, and other elements have all been utilized. However, as with other marketing techniques, the procurement of the more sophisticated aspects of direct mail generally has not reached politics. For example, research testing of copy and response rate management, as well as key dimensions of commercial direct mail management programs, have not usually been fully implemented. Advanced direct mail research and testing programs like *Direct Test* (available from Foote, Cone and Belding and Direct Marketing Systems of Chicago) have not yet been used in political campaigns. Such software makes it possible to systematically cull names according to the level and timing of previous donations. At present, candidate egos may enter into decisions to leave nonproductive names on the lists, usually based on dubious arguments having to do with the value of "getting-out-the-vote." Because of the hurried nature of the campaign process, "list management" during most preelection periods is much more slipshod than the improved techniques of the more efficient commercial, direct mail, organizations. In addition, a case can be made that direct mail techniques may have also become overused in political marketing. The vast number of local, state, and national candidates—both conservative and liberal—has created a storm of often unwelcome mail for the general public.

In addition, ethical and legal issues emanating from direct mail abuse have given the tactic a bad name. For example, an election watchdog committee in California reported that outside envelopes would carry messages like "court summons," "official document," "county sheriffs' office," and "important Social Security information" to encourage recipients to open the envelope (Fair Campaign Practices Commission 1982).

TELEMARKETING

Political campaigns have also been using telemarketing for a wide range of activities. Not only are survey and opinion polls often conducted by telephone (Honomichl 1984), but a host of other activities—including initial voter identification, get-out-the-vote drives, and ticket sales for political events—are being orchestrated over the telephone.

Unlike commercial marketers, political campaigners generally use volunteers to implement their telemarketing programs rather than professional telephone operators. These volunteers often use home phones rather than more expensive "telephone banks." Some say that this has reduced the efficiency of such efforts. One political consultant developed a comprehensive organizational scheme to recruit, train, and use volunteers in telephone-based campaigns. Armed with job descriptions, training manuals, and task simulations, most political campaign managers are developing an army of inexpensive telephone volunteers to "reach out and touch someone"—hopefully someone who would vote for, or contribute to their candidate's cause. On election day, only the voters who express support for the candidate are called to remind them to vote.

Although telemarketing is now widely used, the political application of telephone technology could be expanded if it was hooked up to computer screens and terminals, computer-generated dialing, professional scripting of prerecorded messages, and leveraged response rates. Fortunately, it takes only a short time to learn new methods in this area and political marketers have been quick to integrate them into their overall marketing strategy.

SALES PROMOTION

Campaigns for political office have also used buttons, posters, yard signs, banners, hats, bumper stickers, matchbooks, and other such devices associated with sales promotion. Although some state laws regulate the value of any item given away in a campaign, to safeguard against bribery, campaign collectibles (for example, the button) were traditionally de rigeur in politics. Also, although there is no empirical evidence that items such as replica wooden nickels or glassware figures of donkeys and elephants create the desired results, campaigns continue to purchase an amazing variety of items for the purpose of fund-raising and hopefully stimulating voter name recognition. Several catalogues specialize in providing sundry doorknob hangers, emery boards, matchbooks, pens, combs, rulers, bookmarks, sun visors, feathered headbands, fans, and buttons in all shapes and colors.

Again, the practice should be part of a comprehensive marketing strategy. Campaign colors and the script utilized in printing the candidate's name on placards are too often the product of long strategy sessions in otherwise issueless campaigns. Nonetheless, a certain amount of sales promotion is part of the tradition and is to be expected, even as expenditures drop as a percentage of the total spent on advertising (Royko 1984).

SELECTED STRATEGIC AREAS OF MARKETING APPLICABLE TO POLITICAL CAMPAIGNING

Just because campaigners apply marketing tools does not necessarily mean that they fully understand the marketing function. To illustrate the potential for coordinated marketing practice, one must consider the strategic dimensions of marketing that have *not* been as widely adopted by political campaign professionals, notably,

> Promotional strategy
> Improved marketing research
> Personal selling and
>   sales management
> Segmentation and target
>   marketing

The next section provides a basic agenda for campaign managers and marketing consultants who might wish to apply their knowledge and skills in the political campaign setting. On the other hand, the strategic approach, while uniformly praised, is not always rewarded, even in the business world. As Gale Haymen (creator of the successful Georgio scent) has noted, "When I created the Georgio scent, everyone asked where was my marketing study, my demographic plan? I told them to forget all that. I know what I want by my nose" (*Elle* 1986). Still, in most cases, comprehensive planning produces better results than serendipity. Thus, the following paragraphs suggest several areas of marketing from which political strategists could fruitfully borrow.

PROMOTIONAL STRATEGY

In general, one of the greatest failings of those who try to apply marketing communications theory to political campaigns is that they neglect to formulate a well-coordinated promotional strategy. Each element of marketing communications—including publicity, advertising, sales promotion, personal selling and re-seller support (Rothschild 1987; Engel, Warshaw, and Kinnear 1987)—needs to be used in an integrated fashion. Utilized independently, the component elements may succeed, but will lack the synergistic effect they would have if used in conjunction with each other.

For example, a hypothetical political campaign that uses television spots (advertising); direct mail, billboards, posters, and buttons (sales promotion); door-to-door vote solicitation by the candidate and telemarketing volunteers (personal selling); publicity and press conferences (public relations); plus party leadership training and endorsements (reseller support) has incorporated all the critical elements of a strategic marketing communications plan. However, if these elements are not systematically coordinated in terms of timing, message development, reinforcement, audience analysis, involvement level, audience reach/overlap, and other factors, then the communications program may have little synergistic value. The most common pitfall here is not specifying the global communications objective to which each aspect of the communications campaign should contribute.

Where a political campaign is driven by the actions of the opponent, the outcome is often disastrous. For instance, the campaign leaders may decide that they need to respond to the competitor's radio ads with radio ads of their own. Although such immediate response tactics may be both tempting and *sometimes* useful (the increased direct mail and opportunistic public visibility of other Democratic challengers after the

Gary Hart–Donna Rice debacle comes to mind), such knee-jerk responses may undermine the major communication themes that a well-conceived campaign should strive to present and reinforce.

Ideally, a campaign should integrate all elements of the promotional mix—including direct mail, telemarketing, advertising, and publicity—in an objective manner. Perhaps it is the hurried nature of political campaigns, limited budgets, and the temptation to respond to the opposition candidate that prevent campaigners from fully planning and coordinating their overall marketing communication efforts. Indeed, isolated tactics may be counterproductive. As a general principle, budgets for each dimension of promotion should be based on the nature of its contribution to the communications objectives of the campaign.

IMPROVED MARKETING RESEARCH

In the scientific approach to management, decisions are based on solid research, where possible. In the business world, this ideal is not always attained as time pressures force managers to base decisions on less complete information than they would like. This is especially true in the "hip-shooting" context of a political campaign. Nevertheless, most political campaigns do use some research in formulating their strategy. What is done in the political marketplace varies widely in methodology, objectives, utility level, time frame, and expenditures. Like other marketing tactics, political campaigns have latched onto the most obvious tools—opinion polls, for instance—and have overlooked other options appropriate to a systematic ongoing and formative research program.

Although the validity of public opinion polling for political candidates has improved with the increased usage of voter panels, scientific sampling, and the reporting of confidence statistics, the polls are often not well integrated into a structured research program. Even focus groups are sometimes used without any concern for strategic orientation and may concentrate on such narrow issues as the candidates's physical appearance or a single platform item.

In general, corporate marketing researchers seem to recognize the value of programmatic research. They know that different problems call for different types of solutions—exploratory, descriptive or "cause and effect" designs. Similarly, statistical methods must be matched to the stage of research and the questions being investigated.

For example, a political campaign might begin with in-depth interviews, focus groups, or secondary research with voters to gain a *qualitative* understanding of the key variables involved in a forthcoming election. From a preliminary understanding of how voters view the issues, the candidate's campaign style, and other factors, researchers can then develop a more descriptive and *quantitative* research effort. Such second-stage investigation might involve mail or telephone surveys or personal interviews. The point of such research would be to measure the intensity of individual attitudes and the relative importance of opinions that have bearing on the campaign, and to see how differences break down demographically among voter segments.

The next level of research could extend such descriptive research longitudinally or attempt to establish "cause and effect" via laboratory research. Such efforts would be intended to take descriptive research to a plateau of (qualified) prediction. By subjecting such longitudinal information to statistical analysis, researchers can help campaign managers better understand the shifting motivations of voters and the dynamics of a particular election. Ongoing research, that is, longitudinal studies, offers the obvious advantage of overcoming sometimes misleading pictures generated by taking a poll only at one point in time. As political researchers have discovered, voters come to a decision as the election nears and a series of opinion polls of the same group of voters permits the decisionmakers to both follow voter shifts and anticipate trends (McCombs 1972). Another advantage of using laboratory studies is that they help one isolate specific variables without the intrusion of other uncontrollable factors that might affect voters. For example, laboratory methods are ideal to study specific questions such as whether a particular TV spot evokes too much anxiety in voters because of its hard-hitting message or whether a candidate's smile appears "sneaky" on a proposed campaign poster. Although such approaches have been more commonly used in academic and commercial research, their wide-scale application to campaign decisionmaking may only be a matter of time. At present, however, except for national elections, widely accepted scientific methods such as pretesting, alternative sampling schemes, and multivariate statistics have not typically been adopted by campaign professionals. Thus, even in research, marketing tools remain tactical in their purpose and isolated from broader strategic considerations.

PERSONAL SELLING AND SALES MANAGEMENT

The notion of "selling" a political candidate has strong negative connotations. When McGinnis published his controversial book, *The Selling of the President*, 1968, many social commentators recoiled at the idea that politicians could be packaged and sold like laundry soap (Jamieson 1984). However, certain aspects of personal selling and sales management theory can contribute insight into the political scene.

Sales management can be considered a means of organizing interpersonal communications so that customers will be encouraged to use a sponsor's products or services. Clearly the activities of a political candidate expressed in euphemisms such as "pressing the flesh, "kissing babies," "working the crowds," "ringing doorbells," "door-to-door canvassing," and other personal appearances qualify as interpersonal persuasion. Only in their case, the seller seeks to procure a voter rather than to sell a product or service. Although many politicians have a great deal of experience in the inherent activities of personal selling, they can still benefit from a deeper understanding of how corporations orchestrate personal selling.

First, just as a sales representative cultivates a purchasing agent over time, it is useful for the politician to conceive of the campaign process as a multiple-step model that involves systematically developing and harvesting the votes of the public (Xerox 1983). Some of the critical steps to take would be to *qualify voters* (via voter eligibility and shaping partisan affiliation), to *generate awareness* by personal appearances, and *to enact a particular platform* in exchange for the vote. On the other hand, related elements of the traditional model such as "listening to objections" and "post-sales service" have applicability in the sense that politicians should design mechanisms for soliciting ongoing feedback from their constituency.

Other dimensions of personal selling such as *benefit selling* may also be useful. This involves matching voter concerns with campaign issues. Some presidential candidates have been particularly effective in influencing votes and raising funds when addressing trade associations on issues of special concern to their members. Obviously, it helps if the candidate's platform offers some remedies for the legislative needs of the group being addressed. At present, business firms are putting considerable effort into developing sophisticated scripted or "canned" sales presentations and applying artificial intelligence software to personal selling (Teleconference 1985; Collins 1985). Political volunteers are trained to use scripted telephone messages in voter identification. For face-to-face and door-to-door meetings, both volunteers and candidates may follow scripts that will help them convey their message more efficiently and effectively. Advanced levels of computer-aided learning and software may be used to refine presentations as is being done in sales.

In general, the sales management concepts of planning and control, so central to many business firms, seem unevenly applied in politics. While well-worn campaign anecdotes tell of the ingenious one-page plans devised by President Jimmy Carter's advisers, more elaborate plans used by other candidates seem to quickly fall out of use in the heat of a political campaign. Historically, there has been a strong tendency to rely mainly on summative or postelection analysis of the campaign.

Formative or ongoing evaluations are still largely intuitive. Campaigns, to the extent that they use marketing planning, are most likely to emphasize the scheduling of the day-to-day activities of the campaign and the presentation of media spots.

Some of the more complex models of sales management may also have a great deal to contribute to political campaigning. For example, the well-known (in academic marketing) Churchill, Ford, and Walker model (1985) based on motivation and satisfaction theory probably could be adopted to campaign worker selection, training, and job assignment. Also, although some campaigns have used voter identification efforts (i.e., "walking lists") to target partisan neighborhoods for canvassing, certain sales management techniques are better able to incorporate additional factors such as voting frequency, opinion leadership level of the voter, need for transportation to the polls, and other items. Sales management theory can be mined for new perspectives on how interpersonal communications frameworks may help people manage political campaigns more efficiently.

SEGMENTATION AND TARGET MARKETING

A powerful concept in the application of strategic marketing to political campaigns is "segmentation" and the subsequent selection of the target market and candidate positioning. Since political campaign managers have tended to rely on somewhat roughshod methods of identifying priority blocks of voters (i.e., target markets), the full force of strategic segmentation has not yet been introduced to politics.

Segmentation, as applied to politics, consists of dividing the market of voters into distinct groups that might require separate marketing "mixes." For example, the mix might be varied by message content (e.g., issues of aging versus welfare policy) or message channel (e.g., television ads versus print ads), or even the candidate's qualifications (emphasis on experience or image or accomplishments). In addition, the voters' *perceptions* of the candidate will contribute to the ideal positioning strategy.

In an early attempt to apply segmentation theory to politics, a state Republican political party, under the guidance of an engineering professor, developed a classification system to segment voting districts according to past voting behavior. The computer program identified areas by the degree of past votes for Republicans versus Democrats as well as turnout levels. Candidates were directed not to spend door-to-door time or even media dollars in areas that were clearly Democratic. Similarly, Republican candidates were instructed to spend minimal time in Republican strongholds on the assumption that the candidates should appeal to swing voters for maximum benefit.

In addition, politicians often rely on partisan mailing lists of delegates, party contributors, or persons qualified by telephone as probable party voters. Although some states require voter registration, others do not, so some campaigns may be able to use direct mail in order to contact straight party-line voters. Since most national election voters are becoming more "independent," however, the full value of such party-based segmentation cannot be utilized as effectively as in the past.

Today, a more useful basis for segmentation is voters' positions on popular public issues. For example, a candidate may use public opinion surveys to determine which issues to emphasize, such as economic issues over environmental issues or other public policy subjects. Even though some degree of market segmentation is reflected in such examples, the full market segmentation sequence of (1) segmentation, (2) targeting, and (3) positioning are not yet typically used.

In the initial step, *segmentation* voters are divided into distinct groups according to certain descriptive and behavioral variables such as geographic, demographic, psychographic, and behavioral traits. Each variable may require a different approach. For example, an older voter can be reached though different media channels than a younger voter; a first-time voter may need different information than an experienced voter, and an unemployed person may be reached with a uniquely different message than a two-income family. Often multiple variables can be used. A candidate for Congress might design a message dealing, say, with Social Security or health care specifically for females, over sixty, who are Democrats and regular voters. Here four different bases have been utilized in the targeting effort.

In one statewide primary election, voter areas were initially segmented into "highly partisan" versus "nonpartisan" versus "independent" voter strongholds. Campaign expenditures were then allocated only to areas with significant numbers of independent voters in high turnout districts. In this case, target areas were chosen on the basis of nonparty affiliation and voting behavior.

The second step, after segmentation of voters, is to *target priority segments*. Given the limited resources in many political campaigns, the management team must select the most efficient (i.e., least cost per expected vote) and most effective (i.e., consistent with the goal of election success) segments. For example, while the state party may target young voters through an information campaign designed to teach them how to vote and why to vote for a particular party, a specific candidate may not be able to afford to target the same group. Instead, the candidate may spend greater resources on "getting the vote" of high turnout, senior citizens, and merely reinforce the state party effort directed toward young voters with a few selected appearances at party-organized events. Campaigns that do not have a well-conceptualized segmentation and targeting plan may be whipsawed from one likely segment to another, depending upon random requests, opportunities, and pressures. Since time and other resources are in short supply in the normal three-month campaign, a qualitative and quantitative ranking of priority voter segments is absolutely necessary.

The third step of a fully developed segmentation scheme is *positioning*. Positioning means describing the candidate's image and/or actions in relation to those of other candidates. So-called survey run-offs or straw votes pitting one candidate against another may be a crude form of positioning. However, a fully developed analysis of segmentation variables to predict election outcomes is seldom used. If, for example, the voter correctly or incorrectly sees the role of the (ineffectual) lieutenant governor as an important member of the executive management team, that candidate may well (exploitatively) foster the belief that campaign support from various lobbying groups will influence the governor's issue agenda. Or if voters associate a particular candidate with an issue position in a favorable way, the candidate may well adopt that position, or at least examine how the positive association can be continued in the public's mind. Using marketing research techniques such as perceptual mapping (see Green and Tull 1978), strategists can analyze the candidate's *perceived* experience, the candidate's *perceived* ability to solve problems, and even how the public *thinks* it sees the candidate on specific issues. Positioning then becomes a matter of adjusting campaign themes toward the critical views of the voters while sustaining a positive perception among existing supporters. Needless to say, such shifting of positions in order to strike a responsive chord among voters raises some major ethical questions, which are discussed later in the chapter.

In general, more and more campaigns in the future will use segmented mailing lists and narrowcast cable and radio media with varying messages and format as an intensive form of target marketing. For example, lists of subscribers to popular scientific publications may receive letters from the candidate addressing science policy issues. Such special audience letters might suggest a Machiavellian opportunity to tell voters mostly what they want to hear. However, the public nature of elections will also likely force a candidate to formulate educated stands on a wide variety of complex issues in order to appeal to several targeted voter segments.

In the future, it will be necessary for political strategists to begin campaigns by identifying voter segments more precisely (on the basis of marketing research). Such new marketing strategies will include the coordinated use of marketing tactics such as direct mail, narrowcasting, and the promotion of multiple themes that are designed to reach targeted, priority voters. Finally, future strategies will include the fine tuning of the candidate's image along with a program to match issues and voter opinions. Perceptions about where the candidate stands on an issue have become as important as where the candidate actually stands on the issue. Indeed, for the good of his or her long-term brand loyalty, the candidate might endeavor to match his actual positions with voters' perceptions of his positions.

THINKING STRATEGICALLY IN POLITICAL CAMPAIGNS

In the last analysis, campaign managers must find out what they can do to utilize the strategic aspects of marketing rather than simply apply tactical tools. Before they can do so, they must be aware that strategy orientation should drive the political campaign rather than be appended after the fact. As Machiavelli pointed out long ago: "Men who have any great undertaking in mind must first make all necessary preparations for it, so that, when an opportunity arises, they may be ready to put it in execution according to their design."

Most traditional campaign management texts offer particular interpretations of what constitutes a strategy. Trafton (1984) advises candidates that "solid strategy" means that the candidate must (1) know your message, (2) know the issues, (3) know the voters, and (4) know the limits of your resources. Another handbook suggests that having a "theory" of campaigns means understanding the realities of the current race and knowing that "probabilities of success" are components of a strategic approach to campaigning (Goldenberg and Traugott 1984).

The marketing approach to strategy development is more comprehensive and cost-effective than these bromides. Given the influx of modern marketing tools, a strategic marketing framework is well suited to incorporate the range of marketing tactics into a comprehensive, targeted, and systematic approach. In essence, marketing strategy consists of two elements: (a) decisions concerning what products will be produced for what markets and (b) the articulation and development of *sustainable competitive advantages* that will allow products to succeed in those markets. (For a general discussion of such issues, see Aaker 1984 or Mauser 1983.)

It is imperative to realize that in the context of a political campaign, the product is a given—it is the candidate and the ideas that she or he stand for. The market is also somewhat constrained in that it is circumscribed by the voter constituency being focused on in the campaign, whether it be a district, regional, statewide, or national election. Thus strategic political marketing translates into the development of sustainable competitive advantages which the candidate can then communicate and implement through traditional marketing tools and frameworks.

COMPETITIVE ANALYSIS

One such marketing framework would involve *competitive analysis* (Aaker 1984; Henderson 1983; Ansoff 1957). To implement this approach, political candidates must analyze, via marketing research, not only their own strengths and weaknesses but those of their political opponents. These would include such dimensions as name recognition, physical appearance, expertise on the issues, perceived credibility, expected level of financial support, charisma, and related factors. In the traditional business setting, competitive analysis has little meaning except in the context of a particular marketplace. In the case of a political candidate, the marketplace would be the voter constituency that needs to be cultivated. Thus the strengths and weaknesses of a particular candidate and his or her opponents only have pragmatic meaning in relation to the stated preferences of the voter constituency (i.e., consumers) at question. For example, the perception of a candidate as a "conservative" may be an advantage or a disadvantage, depending on the particular voter constituency involved. Even a factor such as "experience," which would normally be considered a positive trait, might be a liability in a political environment where public opinion seems to want a sweeping away of the old guard. Thus, a competitive analysis of the candidate and his or her competition that is matched to the appropriate voter group should occur early in any political campaign.

Other subtleties need to be considered in competitive analysis. In a business organization, firms are constantly concerned about the sources of materials and the relative power of the organization with respect to its suppliers. In a political context, such suppliers would translate to the sources of funds likely to underwrite the political campaign as well as the relative level of support from significant party officials who are in a position to lend legitimacy to a particular campaign undertaking. A thorough analysis should clearly enumerate both the number and intensity of sustainable competitive advantages inherent in a particular candidate. For example, all other things equal, the incumbent will have an edge over the nonincumbent with respect to the sustainable advantage of "name recognition." Conversely, the newcomer will be forced to expend resources in order to generate name recognition, as illustrated by the expensive and remarkable campaign of Louis Lehrman when he ran for governor of New York in 1982; Lehrman was relatively unknown at the outset of his campaign but succeeded in almost defeating Governor Mario Cuomo in part because of the vast amounts spent on advertising.

As a rule, the sustainable competitive advantage of one candidate forces the deficient candidate to cover the existing "advantage gap" with a commitment of resources. Sometimes a competitive advantage may be so strong that it is not only sustainable but insurmountable. Consider the case of a powerful incumbent, such as recently retired House Speaker Tip O'Neil, who had been elected to multiple terms in Congress. Such an individual may be virtually unassailable in his or her own district and may function as a king maker when he endorses other politicians. This situation is not unlike the case of the so-called cash cow product in a business where the dependable profits of the successful product are siphoned off in order to support more tenuous, though promising, ventures (Hedley 1977). In other words, the sustainable competition advantage of some politicians in the marketplace is so strong that their endorsement can create advantages for other less powerful candidates.

The strategic marketing approach also suggests that each of these advantages should be included in a *statement of objectives* that will drive the other tactical decisions made in the campaign. For instance, the strategic competitive advantage of candidate A might be that he is an experienced legislator who has a deep and abiding concern for environmental issues. Or, the sustainable competitive advantages of candidate B might be that she is (a) an unabashed liberal, (b) who has spent a long time cultivating party favor and commitment and (c) has made the reduction of defense spending the central platform of her campaign. Whatever the case, the main concern at this objective setting stage is to ensure that later marketing decisions such as the form of the advertising campaign, the type of personal appearances made, the brochure utilized in direct mail marketing, the campaign placards, the press releases, and so on, will reflect these consistent and research-based campaign visions.

This is not to say that all voters should be targeted in the same fashion. *Market segmentation* is obviously an integral part of the strategy approach to marketing. For example, it is commonplace to divide voters into the "favorable," "unfavorable," and "undecided." It is easiest to design marketing communication messages for those who are already committed to the candidate—which is the equivalent of preaching to the converted. However, competitive analysis may also reveal that the voter profile of the "unfavorables" overlaps with the platform of the candidate. This is an opportunity for strategic exploitation. For instance, suppose candidate X is a traditional conservative Republican with little appeal to the blue-collar, mostly Democratic, middle class. However, as a conservative candidate, X is a pro-family and pro-school player—two themes with particular appeal to this Democrat/union constituency.

Thus, it seems logical that this symmetry should be considered and possibly be utilized as a major campaign theme.

In general, however, the ability to capitalize upon identified segments can only be successful if a candidate is able to communicate a perceived relative advantage over other alternative candidate choices. The number of relative strategic advantages and the degree to which they match various voter segments will establish the ability of a given candidate to retain favorable voters, influence a proportion of the undecided voter group, and persuade some smaller proportion of those initially not in favor. Where relative differences among candidates are small or the significant advantages of any candidate compared with another candidate are minimal, such campaigns will attract a large number of candidates at the primary stage.

Figure 19.1 attempts to capture the notion of sustainable comparative advantage and link it to a contingency framework of campaign strategy. The typology presented there is loosely based on the work of Achrol and Apple (1983) and Miles and Snow (1978). In this particular typology, the sustainable competitive advantages identified in political candidates are categorized according to their *quantity* and *quality*. A particular political candidate may have several quantitative advantages over the other candidates in the race or may have only one or two. Similarly, the assessed quality of those competitive advantages might be characterized as *marginal* or *substantial*.

This broad array of characterizations can be juxtaposed to create the range of possibilities shown in the matrix illustrated in Figure 19.1.

FIGURE 19.1 A Contingency Framework for Relating Sustainable Competitive Advantages to Campaign Strategy

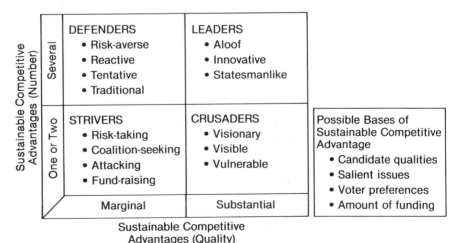

Needless to say, political candidates with *several* and *substantial* sustainable competitive advantages are in the best position. These candidates could be designated *leaders* because they have much going for them. In the course of a political campaign and strategy development, they can often afford to be aloof, as George Bush was in 1987–88, or they can dare to be innovative and seek path-breaking political solutions. Because they hold a substantial edge, they also have the flexibility to remain statesmanlike in the face of controversy and to generally ignore the charges or specific queries of the competition that are put to them. Ronald Reagan, in the 1984 election, held this enviable position as did President Dwight Eisenhower in 1956.

The next category of political candidates—*crusaders*—hold a sustainable competitive advantage over the field, although the number of these advantages is few. To the extent that they can build a campaign around their sustainable advantage, such a campaign may well be focused and visionary since it is based upon this single or at most dual competitive advantage. Thus, as the crusader candidate builds a campaign theme around these selected issues, the candidate is likely to gain high visibility because of his or her association with specific policy positions. However, such candidates are also extremely vulnerable to a changing external environment, particularly one that shifts voter concerns away from the issues where this candidate holds superiority. For example, one candidate may be more experienced in foreign affairs than all other potential candidates. This becomes his or her singular strategic advantage. Nevertheless, if the domestic economy is in a state of turmoil and voter constituencies are concerned with domestic economic performance, this competitive advantage would be canceled out. Thus, crusader candidates are likely to pin their futures on the one or two issues where they hold clear advantages. They are truly crusaders because they will become strongly identified with a point of view embodied in their sustainable competitive advantage. Pat Robertson, the religious broadcaster and candidate for president in 1988, held this position. Representative Jack Kemp, because of his association with conservative supply-side economics, might fall into this category. Some would contend that Rev. Jesse Jackson, because he is a black and a social activist, could also be in it.

In contrast to crusaders, there seems to be a category of politicians who have several sustainable competitive advantages, but they would be classified as marginal. In our scheme such politicians are categorized as *defenders*. In some cases, they might have a "lead"—as defined by an opinion poll—over the field of other potential candidates, but such a lead is likely to be extremely shaky. Most of the time the campaign of such a candidate would be rather risky and tentative. Marketing strategies would probably be rather traditional so as not to upset the status quo.

Campaigns of defenders tend to consist of a series of reactions to what other candidates are doing because the candidates and/or their managers fear they will lose their (at best) tenuous competitive advantages. A number of the Democrats in the 1988 presidential sweepstakes, including Richard Gephardt, Paul Simon, and Bruce Babbit, fit this description—members of the so-called seven dwarfs.

Needless to say, *strivers* are in the most difficult position. This category of political candidates would include those who have only one or two sustainable competitive advantages that are of a marginal nature. These candidates would necessarily be taking a risk because they are probably behind in the polls. They would also be seeking a coalition because they need endorsements from the help of significant others who can play a part in the campaign. They probably would be tempted to attack other political candidates on their shortcomings because their own accomplishments are limited. Finally, they would be more desperate to raising funds and might gamble that the shear magnitude of their expenditures might overcome other potential political liabilities. "Pete" DuPont, another candidate who hoped to qualify for the GOP ticket in 1988, seemed to qualify as a striver.

Admittedly, the ideas presented in the above paragraphs are highly speculative, but it illustrates how a marketing-based method of analysis can be used to identify campaign themes. That is to say, political campaigns should be driven by clearly defined objectives that are rooted in sustainable competitive advantages. The wisdom or folly of the more tactical aspects of marketing—such as advertising campaigns, political rallies, sales promotion, and managed publicity—are only valuable in the context of strategically developed issues and themes.

ETHICS AND THE MARKETING OF POLITICAL CANDIDATES

Any discussion of the marketing of political candidates would be incomplete without some formal mention of the topic of ethics. Legions of social critics and newspaper editorialists have rightly questioned the ongoing application of marketing techniques to political campaigns. Many have questioned whether (a) political marketing pressures candidates to substitute image and style for substantive campaign issues, (b) political marketing has accentuated the trend toward negative campaigning (i.e., practice of denigrating one's opponent rather than specifying one's beliefs), (c) political marketing has made voters skeptical and has contributed to increasingly lower voter turnout, and (d) political marketing techniques lend themselves to, and sometimes pressure candidates to adopt emotional and single-issue positions since these are more easily managed in a mass communications campaign. Our purpose here is not to comment on the merits of these charges (see Laczniak and Caywood 1987). Rather, it is merely to emphasize a prevailing feeling that there are substantial ethical questions to consider when marketing tools and techniques are adapted to political campaigns. We believe that political marketing enables candidates to exercise their right to free speech and that it is protected under the First Amendment (Caywood and Preston 1989). As the U.S. Supreme Court noted in its famous *Mills v. Alabama* (1966) decision, "Whatever differences may exist about the interpretations of the First Amendment, there is practically universal agreement that a major purpose of that amendment was to protect the free discussion of governmental affairs. This, of course, includes discussion of candidates . . . and all such matters relating to political processes."

Thus, from the judicial standpoint, political marketing is sacrosanct at present. But the marketing of political candidates also raises ethical questions that citizens, academic researchers, and policy analysts interested in social issues must ponder. Clearly, some aspects of political marketing are arguably deceptive, misleading, or unfair. Presumably, such promotional techniques will influence a particular group of voters in selecting a particular candidate. In the business sector, remedies are available when marketing abuses occur. For instance, what marketers can or cannot say about a can of hair spray, a package of gum, or other consumer products is strictly regulated by agencies of the government such as the Federal Trade Commission, the Food and Drug Administration, the Department of the Treasury, the Securities and Exchange Commission, and so forth. In contrast, the rules of political campaigning remain almost devoid of constraints. There are numerous protections to minimize the probability of a consumer purchasing a defective vegetable slicer or other consumer product. Yet there are no restrictions on a category of advertising that could lead a voter to choose an incompetent senator (or other politician), who could serve up to six years in office without review.

There are some voluntary efforts afoot. The American Association of Advertising Agencies has produced a "code of fair campaign practices," which they ask candidates for political office to sign. In it, candidates promise to refrain from the harshest kinds of mud slinging, racial and ethnic stereotyping, and various voter manipulation schemes. Nevertheless, the strictures remain totally voluntary. In general, ethical controls on political marketing practices emanate from the personal values of the candidates themselves and seem inadequate to prevent future abuses. It appears that some voluntary effective mechanisms short of government regulation must be found. As the search unfolds, the marketing of political candidates seems destined to create much public discussion and a few spectacular cases of questionable behavior, and will remain ripe for serious research and debate.

SUMMARY

The numerous articles and books on political marketing indicate that marketers are going to become more and more involved in political campaigns. The opportunity to contribute to the democratic election process would seem a naturally important application of the discipline of marketing. In the end however, its ethical and strategically correct application should be the foremost concern of marketing scholars and practitioners.

20

Promoting Calgary through the Olympics
The Mega-Event as a Strategy for Community Development

J. R. BRENT RITCHIE
University of Calgary

In the marketing model the Promotion P subsumes advertising, personal selling, public relations, and sales promotion, which, in turn, takes in contests, coupons, demonstrations, and the staging of special events, such as the XV Olympic Winter Games held in the city of Calgary early in 1988. Few marketing efforts in either the social or the commercial realm can compare with that city's achievement, which took 20 years to plan and had the co-operation of some 9,000 volunteers.

A well-conceived event not only enhances an institution's image, but can be a great deal of fun to plan and execute. When we speak of special events for social marketing, we generally mean joyous events. Whether a flea market or carnival, and whatever purposes they serve, these events produce an esprit de corps among the planners in their organizations and administrations. The staging of the Olympic Games by Calgary and a Sunday picnic for contributors to a local charity are based on a similar philosophy and social marketing principles, even though they differ in format and magnitude.

The use of marketing to enhance the economic development of cities and towns has been a well-established practice for many years. Indeed, it is unusual today to find a municipality of any size that does not include among its agencies some form of Economic Development Authority whose primary role is to promote the city/town, so as to attract industry and generate new employment. Because this type of marketing activity is frequently carried out by a body in the public sector, it is sometimes called nonprofit marketing. However, because of the very commercial nature of the activities and the expectation of long-term economic gain for the communities involved, this type of marketing is clearly not "social marketing," except in the broadest sense of the term.

This chapter deals with a particular form of marketing activity that is geared toward enhancing the well-being of the community across a broad range of dimensions. These dimensions certainly include economic health, but also encompass social development, cultural growth, and even political strength. As such, the activity would appear to qualify as social marketing in the truest sense.

The type of activity in question is that of community promotion and development by means of a specific long-term strategy, namely the "mega-event," or community "mega-attraction." The example discussed here is the City of Calgary's hosting of the Olympic Winter Games.

MEGA-EVENTS AND ATTRACTIONS

Although the present example focuses on a specific event, the broader goal of the discussion is to examine the hosting of mega-events and attractions as a general strategy for the marketing of a community with a view to its long-term development. With this in mind, it may be useful to provide additional background information concerning earlier work and previous thinking related to the planning, development, and marketing of mega-events and attractions.

First, it is important to clearly define and understand the nature of both mega-events and attractions. A definition and classification of "Hallmark Events" has been proposed elsewhere, (Ritchie 1984) but there is some debate as to the most appropriate terminology (and there are some differences in meaning). Even so it is desirable to move toward a merging of the concepts of hallmark events and mega-events. A hallmark/mega-event has been defined as follows: "A major one time or recurring event of limited duration which serves to enhance the awareness, appeal and profitability of a tourism destination in the short and/or long term. Such events rely for their success on uniqueness, status or timely significance to create interest and attract attention" (Ritchie and Hu 1987, p. 20).

This general definition takes in seven major categories (see Table 20.1). Readers will note that to date the definition has focused primarily on dimensions related to the enhancement of tourism. This simply reflects the fact that thus far such events have been conceived within the context of tourism development. In the case of the Olympic Winter Games in Calgary, however, tourism was only one important dimension. The vision of Calgary's civic leaders was much broader. For this reason it

TABLE 20.1 Classification of Hallmark/Mega-Events

Classification	Examples and Locations
World fairs/expositions	Expo '67, Montreal Knoxville '82 New Orleans '84 Expo '86, Vancouver
Unique carnivals and festivals	Mardi Gras, New Orleans Quebec Winter Carnival, Quebec City Oktoberfest, Munich Stampede, Calgary
Major sports events	Summer Olympic, Los Angeles 1984 Winter Olympic, Calgary 1988 World Cup Soccer, Spain 1982 Marathons, Boston Grand Prix Racing, Monza
Significant cultural and religious events	Oberammergau, Germany Papal Coronation, Rome Royal Wedding, London
Historical milestones	Los Angeles Bicentennial 500th Anniversary of the Discovery of America (1492–1992)
Classical commercial and agricultural events	Wine Purchasing, France Royal Winter Fair, Toronto Floriade '82, Amsterdam
Major political personage events	Presidential inaugurations Funerals of heads of state/Tito (Yugoslavia), Brezhnev (Russia) Papal visits Major political conventions
Major entertainment events	Woodstock Band Aide Concerts

seems appropriate to examine the impact of such mega-events in an overall development setting.

In contrast to mega-events, mega-attractions have received relatively little formal attention in the literature. Nevertheless a definition of mega-attractions has been proposed:

Major attractions, which because of their significance, size or location, attract substantial attention to a region thereby providing a focal point for the enhancement of tourism development. This enhancement may take several forms such as the provision of a well defined image through symbols associated with the event, or support for the development of tourism infrastructure, thereby serving as a catalyst for accelerated tourism development. (Ritchie and Hu 1987, p. 22)

Similarly, an initial classification has been proposed for mega-events (see Table 20.2). It contains eight categories of mega-attractions.

TABLE 20.2 Classification of Mega-Attractions

Classification	Examples and Locations
Symbolic architecture and structures	Eiffel Tower, Paris Pyramids, Egypt Taj Mahal, India Statue of Liberty, New York Parthenon, Greece
Historic sites	Terra Cotta Army, Xi'an, People's Republic of China Macchu Picchu, Peru Stonehenge, Great Britain
Commercial	Champs Elysses, Les Halles, Paris West Edmonton Mall, Canada Hong Kong
Natural wonders	Grand Canyon, United States Valley of the Dinosaurs, Alberta, Canada
Wildlife areas	National Parks, Kenya Banff, Jasper National Parks, Canada
Religious centers	Vatican, Rome Jerusalem Mecca
Sculpture and art collections	Louvre, Paris Prado, Madrid
World capitals	Moscow, Washington, London, Paris, Rome
Climate, natural beauty	Greek Islands California Hawaii

UNDERSTANDING THE IMPACT OF MEGA-EVENTS/ ATTRACTIONS

Defining the Impacts

As Table 20.3 shows, a mega-event/attraction can have at least six major types of impact on the host region.

Economic impacts have received the greatest attention from those concerned with evaluating the costs and benefits of mega-events/attractions (see, e.g., Della Bitta et al. 1977; Ritchie and Beliveau 1974). Indeed, it is often only the economic impacts that are considered, and then usually the positive ones, such as the increased revenues and employment created by the event/attraction. Although these impacts are important, an honest assessment of the value of a particular event/attraction must also include estimates of the negative impacts, such as commodity price increases and real estate speculation.

Tourism and commercial impacts are also generally recognized as important outcomes resulting from mega-events/attractions, and here again it is commonly assumed that these impacts are primarily positive in nature. Little effort has been made to assess their significance owing to the difficulty of measuring them.

A third category is made up of *physical impacts*. The positive elements of such impacts usually relate to the new facilities constructed as a result of the event/attraction, as well as the improvements made to local infrastructures, which might not have been politically or financially feasible without the event. On the negative side, the development of certain events/attractions may cause environmental damage. Some concern is also being expressed about the uncontrolled overcrowding of facilities connected with such events/attractions and the resulting threat to public safety.

Although the other three categories of potential impacts have received much less formal attention, their importance have been underestimated. The *psychological impacts*, while generally assumed to lead to favorable outcomes, are poorly understood. A similar situation exists in the case of *sociocultural impacts*, despite the view that the primary role of many mega-events is to promote social interactions by drawing on the traditions, values, and interests of local residents. On the negative side, it has been noted (Jafari 1982) that overzealous attempts at commercialization may in fact destroy the sociocultural values and traditions that planners hoped to develop. The final category of effects, the *political impacts*, has been ignored in most previous attempts to assess the significance of mega-events/attractions. The more acceptable effects of this

TABLE 20.3 Types of Impact of Mega-Events/Attractions

Impact	Positive Manifestations	Negative Manifestations
Economic	Increased expenditures	Price increases due to event/attraction
	Creation of employment	Real estate speculation
Tourism/commercial	Increased awareness of the region as a travel/tourism destination	Acquisition of a poor reputation as a result of inadequate facilities or improper practices
	Increased knowledge about the potential for investment and commercial activity in the region	Negative reactions from existing enterprises due to the possibility of new competition for local manpower and government assistance
Physical	Construction of new facilities	Environmental damage
	Improvement of local infrastructure	Overcrowding
Sociocultural	Increase in permanent level of local interest and participation in type of activity associated with event/attraction	Commercialization of activities
	Strengthening of regional traditions and values	Modification of nature of event/activity/attraction to accommodate tourism
Psychological	Increased local pride and community spirit	Tendency toward defensive attitudes concerning host regions
	Increased awareness of nonlocal perceptions	High possibility of misunderstanding, and thus varying degrees of host/visitor hostility
Political	Enhanced international recognition of region and its values	Economic exploitation of local population to satisfy ambitions of political elite
	Propagation of political values held by government and/or population	Distortion of true nature of event/attraction to reflect values of political system

type may be defined as macro-level impacts. This refers to the short- and long-term enhancement of the image of a tourist region that may result from an event such as the Olympic Games or an attraction of political significance such as the seat of the United Nations. The less acceptable effects are those that further the ends of a small elite that is pursuing its own interests in the name of community development or of a nation that is using the attraction for political purposes.

Measuring the Impacts

Once some agreement has been reached on the impacts that are important, one must decide how to measure and monitor these impacts over time—which is a particularly difficult task. An attempt has already been made to identify the variables that should be measured for each of the six impacts outlined above. An attempt has been also made to highlight some of the problems that can arise in collecting such data. (For further details, see Ritchie 1984.)

CALGARY AND THE OLYMPIC WINTER GAMES

The three Canadian cities that are best known in international circles are Montreal, Toronto, and Vancouver. Each has a population well in excess of one million. All three are considered attractive in social, cultural, and economic terms and have grown substantially over the years.

Canada's "second tier" of thriving cities is made up of Quebec City, Ottawa, Winnipeg, Edmonton, and Calgary, whose populations range from 500,000 to 1,000,000. Of this group, Calgary is the only one that was not internationally known until recently. This prominence is in part the result of the success of the Calgary Stampede and the city's proximity to Banff and the Canadian Rockies, both of which have created a substantial tourism industry. The engine driving Calgary's growth (from a city of just over 200,000 in the early 1960s to over 650,000 in 1988) has been the petroleum industry. With the dramatic increase in oil prices in 1973, Calgary quickly became the fourth leading business center in Canada as major oil companies concentrated their head offices in the city. In less than fifteen years, the city was transformed from a western prairie city to a modern metropolitan center having the character of a Houston or a Dallas.

Despite this rapid transformation, Calgary remained, at least until the late 1970s, a somewhat one-dimensional and relatively unknown Canadian city. Frustrated by this reality, community leaders were constantly searching for ways to draw attention to the fact that Calgary was now a dynamic center ready to join the mainstream of national and international activity of all types. From the outset, they were struck by the fact that Montreal was by far the best-known Canadian city, even though Toronto was larger and more economically dynamic. Although a number of factors may account for this situation, one notable difference is that Montreal hosted the highly successful Expo '67 and the more recent 1976 Olympic Summer Games. In contrast, Toronto has never hosted an international exposition or an Olympic Games.

Calgary (or more precisely the neighboring Banff region) had considered making an Olympic bid in the late 1960s, with the idea of holding the athletic events in the Banff National Park at existing ski areas. However, opposition from environmental protection groups squelched these earlier efforts. The renewed efforts of the late 1970s pushed, for the first time, the idea of holding the games in a larger metropolitan location rather than the traditional smaller mountain community setting typified by such previous sites as Lake Placid (New York), Innsbruck (Austria), and Cortina D'Ampezzo (Italy). Indeed, the idea was to use the Olympics (perhaps for the first time) to instigate a whole range of community developments, rather than simply the development of a winter resort area. Once the games were formally awarded to Calgary in the fall of 1981, a long-term process of designing, transforming, and upgrading was set in motion.

MEGA-EVENTS/ATTRACTIONS AS VEHICLES FOR COMMUNITY MARKETING

In traditional marketing terms, the marketing role of mega-events/attractions would appear to relate more directly to promoting the host region than to developing a product. Promotion in this case had three major objectives:

1. *To increase awareness and knowledge of Calgary.* The city was expected to become better known as a result of
   a. the generally high international profile of the event itself,
   b. the spillover effect from the advertising carried out by "official" corporate sponsors of the event,
   c. print media coverage in both the sports and nonsports area, and most important,
   d. the television reporting leading up to the event and the intensive coverage during the sixteen days of the event (more than

two billion persons watched some part of the games coverage).

2. *To "legitimize" Calgary* as a significant, recognizable international destination, not simply in terms of size or economics. Rather, community leaders hoped to develop a certain "mystique," which appears to attach itself to regions that have hosted the Olympics, as is evoked in endless film clips when the name of the city is repeated over and over in numerous settings. Associated with this is an enhanced appeal to potential visitors who, when in the general vicinity, tend to make a special effort to visit the site "where the Olympics were held." This appeal arises from the fact that visitors returning home are able to mention a location that their peers and friends recognize. In brief, the site becomes a legitimate destination.

3. *To create real or imagined symbols*, which become permanent statements and which instantaneously bring to mind a multitude of stored information. The Eiffel Tower, built for the 1896 World Exposition in Paris, has come to symbolize all that is Paris. The Statue of Liberty is immediately associated with New York and America. The Acropolis is Athens. The Coliseum is Rome and its past. Similarly, on a less grand scale, the 1962 World's Fair Space Needle has become one of the symbols associated with Seattle. It is in this tradition that the Olympic flame atop the Calgary Tower, the distinctive architecture of the Olympic Saddledome, and the jagged profile of the Canadian Rockies now symbolize Calgary to the rest of the world.

From the perspective of "product development," the Olympics have provided a mechanism to accelerate and enhance the total infrastructure of the city, in both quantitative and qualitative terms. Some of these infrastructure developments have put Calgary "on the map" in the minds of individuals and firms looking for attractive locations in which to live and work. Following are the most notable of these infrastructure enhancements:

1. *First-class sporting facilities*. At the present time, Calgary possesses some of the finest high-performance and recreational sports facilities in the world. As a result, Calgary has virtually become the permanent national center for the training and development of Olympic winter athletes in Canada. In addition, it has become one of a few leading centers in competitive winter sports in North America.

2. *Enhanced tourism facilities*. Looking to the period following the games, a number of the venues were designed and built with a

view to contributing to the appeal of Calgary as a tourism destination. Most notable among these facilities is Canada Olympic Park. During the main summer tourism season, this multimillion dollar complex serves as a major attraction to visitors, many of whom have little direct interest in winter sports as such.

3. *Dramatically upgraded cultural facilities and programs.* Perhaps the greatest criticism of Calgary by "Easterners" was the lack of cultural ambience. The Olympics changed everything. The four-week Olympic Arts Festival that preceded the games brought to Calgary an unprecedented number of high-quality performers and artists. More important in the longer term is the fact that the city is now increasingly being included in the circuit of cultural performances, largely as a result of the multitude of personal contacts engendered by the hosting of the games.

Another significant contribution to the cultural growth of Calgary has been the construction (in time for the games) of a world-class Center for the Performing Arts and a nearby central city park (the Olympic Plaza). Although it might be argued that such facilities would have been built in any case, the fact remains that the Olympics served to substantially accelerate the development of what are often viewed as "luxury" facilities.

Other Effects

A More Diversified Economy. As already mentioned, the dramatic growth of Calgary since 1960 was driven by the petroleum industry. Although more time will be required to assess the full impact of the Olympics, the games seem to have helped to diversify the city's economy. In addition to the direct long-term enhancement of the tourism industry, there is some evidence of increased manufacturing, particularly of sports equipment and clothing. In addition, some "high-tech" firms have been drawn to Calgary by the high quality of life in this location.

A Legacy of Social Cohesion. One of the most distinctive characteristics of the Calgary Games was the extent to which the event involved and depended on volunteers. More than 9,000 residents of the city contributed uncounted hours to the staging of the games. Consequently, the costs of hosting the event were drastically reduced and the games realized a $40 million profit. A more indirect, but equally important outcome, was the groundswell of community support and enthusiasm for the games, as a large percentage of households participated in the preparations. This high level of support served to overcome any minor opposition that may have arisen in relation to an event of this magnitude and minimized the inevitable mistakes that occur at such times.

Enhanced National Visibility and Political Clout. In a country as large as Canada, one in which the majority of the population is concentrated in the eastern third of the land mass, it is not surprising that little is known about a western city such as Calgary. The 1988 Olympics substantially changed at least the lack of awareness. The cross-Canada Olympic Torch Run had a particularly important role in this regard. More than 7,000 Canadians across the country participated in what became a daily reinforcement of national unity. Among Canadians, Calgary has achieved recognition and acceptance as a leading force in contributing to the national destiny.

MEASURING THE SUCCESS OF THE MARKETING EFFORT

Some preliminary evidence of the impact of the XVth Olympic Winter Games on the host community is now available from three sources. First, two (to date) economic impact assessments have been completed by the Alberta Government (Nicholls 1982; DPA Group 1985). Second, annual surveys concerning the games have been conducted since 1983. These surveys, identified as the OLYMPULSE Monitor, are designed to measure local, national, and international views concerning a wide range of economic, social, and cultural issues related to the hosting of the XV Olympic Winter Games (Ritchie and Aitken 1984, 1985; Ritchie and Lyons 1987). Third, efforts have been made to assess the degree to which the many volunteers involved in the games derived satisfaction from the experience. Of particular concern was the impact on the social fabric of the city and its implications for future large-scale undertakings that might benefit from volunteer input.

Economic Impacts

The final tally will probably reveal that total expenditures related to the games were close to $1 billion, and were divided almost equally between capital investments and facilities, on one hand, and operating expenses related to the event itself, on the other. Earlier formal estimates available at this time indicate total expenditures of $559 million and $812 million in 1981 and 1984, respectively. A more detailed comparison of the economic impacts, as reported in 1982 and in 1985, is given in Table 20.4.

TABLE 20.4 Economic Impact of the XV Olympic Winter Games (millions of U.S. dollars)

Area of Estimated Economic Impact	Nicholls (1982)	DPA (1985)
Direct capital expenditures	239.0	528.4
Direct operating expenditures	146.0	194.1
Subtotal direct expenditures	385.0	722.5
Olympic endowments/contributions	174.0	90.0
Total expenditures	559.0	812.5
Income		
Estimated total, direct and indirect income impact	233.4	449.0
Employment		
Person-year (before/during/after games)	4,500.0	18,500.0
Consumer Price Index (January)	94.6	120.2

Note: Inflation during 1981–1984 averaged 27.1 percent.

Although the absolute values reported should be treated with some caution, some tentative conclusions can be drawn from the data in Table 20.4:

1. Total direct capital expenditures rose by some 87 percent in nominal terms between 1981 and 1984. This increase appears to reflect a qualitative and quantitative upgrading of facilities being provided for the games. This was possibly due in large part to the success of the organizing committee in securing additional revenues beyond those anticipated in 1981. The most notable increase was that related to the television contract, which at US $309 million was substantially higher than expected by most observers.

2. Total estimated direct operating expenditures have not risen significantly when inflation is taken into account.

3. The estimated income and employment impact have risen dramatically. The former has risen by 92 percent (nominal $) while the latter has increased fourfold. Although these increases need to be analyzed further, one suspects that methodological differences account for the sharp changes in these estimates.

Research Results

OLYMPULSE Monitor (resident). The Calgary OLYMPULSE Monitor normally contained about twenty-five questions each time it was administered. Of this total, about one-half were the same for each wave, with the remainder being adapted to explore current issues related to the games. In order to give some idea of the issues addressed by OYMPULSE, selected data related to recurring questions from versions I, II and III, IV and V of the Monitor are given in Table 20.5. For example, it can be seen

TABLE 20.5 Selected Responses to Questions from the Calgary Olympulse Monitor, 1983–87 (percent)

Issue/Item	Olympulse				
	I	*II*	*III*	*IV*	*VA*
Support for games (yes)	85.0	87.6	86.6	85.6	88.0
Expect to attend (yes)	87.9	84.6	84.8	78.4	56.0
High level of interest	73.5	78.3	72.2	73.2	75.0
Appropriateness of Speed of Development					
Too slow	48.6	31.9	15.2	9.2	N/M
Too fast	4.3	1.6	1.0	0.0	N/M
About right	34.5	34.0	54.8	56.1	N/M
Uncertain	12.5	32.4	29.1	34.7	N/M
Expect to Attend					
Alpine skiing	53.0	46.4	39.5	35.5	N/M
Hockey	23.5	32.6	31.4	42.6	N/M
Luge	3.8	8.6	12.4	17.2	N/M
Good/Excellent Performance Rating of Organization					
Federal government	12.7	8.6	22.7	30.7	N/M
Provincial government	28.5	35.7	40.4	53.4	N/M
City of Calgary	67.2	72.7	70.2	81.5	N/M
Organizing committee	61.4	67.3	65.5	63.3	54.0
Awareness of Previous/ Future Games Sites					
Lake Placid (1980)	37.2	49.4	40.0	26.2	32.0
Sarajevo (1984)	12.7	88.1	62.9	41.4	46.0
Calgary (1988)	86.3	93.1	98.6	96.3	N/M
Albertville (1992)	N/M	N/M	N/M	N/M	2.0

N/M = not measured.

that resident support for the games has remained at a consistently high level across the five measures. Expectation of attendance also remained consistently high until 1987, at which point a restricted supply of tickets acted to constrain anticipated attendance. Conversely, resident views concerning the appropriateness of the speed of development of Olympic facilities showed a marked positive increase over the period covered by the surveys. Whereas nearly 50 percent were critical in 1983, only 9 percent remained so as of 1986.

National OLYMPULSE. In 1987, the first national survey concerning the Calgary Olympics was conducted among 1,500 Canadians. Space does not permit the presentation of all the findings, but it should be noted that support for the games was nearly as high across the country (84 percent) as in Calgary itself (88 percent; see Table 20.6).

International OLYMPULSE. Because the enhancement of international awareness was a primary motive for hosting the 1988 Winter Olympics, the degree to which the games actually increased awareness and knowledge of Calgary will be a major determinant of the success of the event from a tourism perspective. In an attempt to measure the nature and extent of this input, a modest, low-cost project was initiated in 1986 in

TABLE 20.6 National Olympulse: Canadian Support for the Hosting of the 1988 Olympic Winter Games in Calgary (percent)

	Yes	*No*	*Don't Know, Not Stated*
All Respondents			
(*n* = 1,486)	84	7	9
Location			
British Columbia (*n* = 171)	90	4	6
Prairies (*n* = 238)	86	11	4
Ontario (*n* = 553)	84	9	7
Quebec (*n* = 338)	78	5	17
Atlantic (*n* = 137)	89	4	7

twenty centers in North America and Europe. Many academic colleagues graciously agreed to participate in the project. Data from the project are currently being analyzed and some of the first baseline results are summarized in Table 20.7.

Volunteer Reactions

The 9,000 volunteers enlisted (from the 22,000 applicants) assisted in a broad range of tasks that had to be done by the host city. Before the event could be perceived as a success by local inhabitants, it was essential that the "Olympic Experience" be positively viewed by this highly active and involved group of citizens. To assess their views in this regard, a survey of the volunteers was conducted in November 1987. The survey measured the reasons for volunteering, the degree of satisfaction with the volunteer experience to date, the degree of confidence in the success of the games, and demographics. Volunteers were also asked for suggestions for improving the volunteer program. Selected data are presented in Table 20.8.

Of particular interest to the present discussion were the reasons given for volunteering and the aspects of the experience that volunteers

TABLE 20.7 Initial Measures of Awareness of Calgary and Nine Other Canadian Cities in Europe and the United States, 1986 (percent)

| | Percentage of Aware Respondents | | | | | |
| | United States (10 centers) | | | Europe (10 centers) | | |
City	Without Prompt	With Prompt	Total	Without Prompt	With Prompt	Total
Montreal	66.3	32.0	98.3	58.0	38.0	96.0
Toronto	47.8	48.8	96.6	46.6	44.4	91.2
Vancouver	38.0	51.9	89.9	34.3	51.2	85.5
Quebec	46.8	41.4	88.2	41.4	41.9	83.3
Winnipeg	9.6	66.9	76.5	8.2	41.6	49.8
Ottawa	9.9	64.8	74.7	28.9	58.6	87.5
Calgary	19.5	52.9	72.4	10.1	38.2	48.3
Edmonton	12.3	53.2	65.5	5.3	33.3	38.6
Halifax	2.4	41.1	43.6	2.8	40.8	43.6
Regina	1.1	24.0	25.1	1.0	14.3	15.3

TABLE 20.8 Survey of Olympic Volunteers, Selected Results

	Percentage of Responses
Reason for Volunteering	
Excitement of the games	40.5
Interest in sports	15.9
For work experience	15.9
Something to do	13.3
To be part of a unique experience	15.4
To be part of group/group effort required	12.8
To do something for Calgary	9.2
To meet people	8.7
Enjoy public work	8.2
Asked to join	3.1
To meet the athletes	0.5
Total	143.6[a]
Aspects Enjoyed Most	
Meeting people	59.3
Participation in games	18.7
Education	14.8
Enthusiasm/spirit	14.3
Experience	7.1
Training programs	6.6
Opportunity to attend events	6.6
Part of a large, unique event	5.5
Satisfaction of seeing success so close	3.8
Meeting athletes	3.3
Great treatment by OCO	1.1
Total	141.2[a]

[a]Totals more than 100 percent owing to multiple mentions.

enjoyed the most. As shown in Table 20.8, "the excitement of the games" was the reason given most often for volunteering (40.5 percent of the cases). This was followed by an "interest in sports," and "for work experience," both mentioned by 15.9 percent of cases. When volunteers were asked what they had enjoyed most, "the opportunity to meet people" was cited most frequently (59.3 percent).

Perhaps not surprisingly, the vast majority of volunteers, 98.5 percent, were confident that the XV Olympic Winter Games would be a success. More than 78.3 percent, said that they were "very confident" of success.

SUMMARY

The hosting of a mega-event such as the Olympics may not be viewed as marketing in the traditional sense. This said, there is probably not a resident of the city of Calgary who does not believe that the underlying goal of the hosting of the 1988 Winter Games was to raise the level of national and international awareness of the city, and enhance its long-term growth and development in economic, social, cultural, and political terms. There was a broad consensus among community leaders that the hosting of such a mega-event would greatly enhance awareness and knowledge concerning Calgary around the world and thus thrust the city into the mainstream of international activity.

The short-term results show that substantial progress toward this goal has been made both within the city itself and across the country. It is too early to determine whether the games will provide sufficient impetus to achieve some of the city's longer-term goals. Although there are certainly some positive indicators, the final results will not be evident for several years. Additional assessments in the period immediately following the event may in fact be misleading, as they will undoubtedly indicate increased levels of awareness in the short run. What is not clear is how the increased levels of awareness will translate into continued community growth and development.

Also of concern is the reality of awareness decay. Similar data gathered in relation to previous game sites show clearly that awareness levels fall off rapidly once the games are over. If Calgary or any other city attempting to use a mega-event for community marketing wishes to ensure long-term effects, it must be prepared to view this activity as only one component of a longer-term marketing strategy. Specifically, the community must identify a continuing stream of events, attractions, and activities that build upon accumulated strengths, contribute to an ongoing spirit of enthusiasm and innovation, and reinforce one another in a consistent and logical manner. In this way, it is entirely possible that the city and its surrounding regions can achieve a clearly defined positioning and a recognition for excellence in selected spheres of activity that are critical to the long-term well-being and growth of the community. If the approach succeeds, then the use of mega-events as a component of the overall community marketing strategy must be judged viable.

21

Canada Seeks Support for a Cause

STANLEY J. SHAPIRO
Simon Fraser University

The question of whether the process of promoting a government program is social marketing is best analyzed through case studies of past efforts along these lines. A particularly interesting case is the Canadian government's program of assistance to developing nations, operated by the Canadian International Development Agency (CIDA). The approach and the processes the Canadians have used to promote support for the program provide insight into how the marketing process takes place within a bureaucracy.

Marketing is generally considered—with obvious justification—a business activity that must be carried out by profit-oriented firms. However, much of the marketing literature of the past twenty years has focused on two other dimensions of marketing: (1) the contribution that marketing, viewed in a macro sense as society's provisioning technology, can make to Third World economic development; and (2) how the tools of the corporate marketing manager can and should be used by organizations that are not profit-oriented. Discussions of marketing and economic development appear with some degree of regularity. A review article by Wood and Vitell (1986) contains a fairly detailed but by no means all-inclusive reference list of 125 different items. The literature on the related areas of social, public, and nonprofit marketing is even more voluminous. Recent books in this burgeoning area of interest, such as those by Fine (1981), Lovelock and Weinberg (1984), and Kotler and Andreasen (1987), cite hundreds of relevant sources. Useful discussions are to be found not only in the "mainstream" marketing literature but also in publications directed toward those administering state-owned enterprises, hospitals, libraries, universities, and performing arts organizations.

A detailed analysis of either body of literature—that dealing with marketing and economic development or with nonprofit and social marketing—falls outside the scope of this essay. However, certain aspects of that literature are relevant to the analysis that follows and deserve at least brief mention.

The basic idea behind both social and nonprofit marketing is easily expressed. It is possible to broaden the concept of marketing to include much more than meeting consumer needs at a profit. Many other kinds of organizations must operate within a framework of uncontrollable elements. Such organizations could effectively use the same marketing research techniques that business employs. There are, in all cases, nonprofit equivalents to commercial marketing's four P's, although the exact form that Product, Price, Promotion, or Place might take would be somewhat different. Target markets can be selected and appropriate marketing programs put together by all kinds of organizations (Kotler and Levy 1969). This approach to broadening the marketing concept by discovering new areas of application gained widespread acceptance within a brief period.

Also requiring mention, however, is the growing realization close to two decades after the concept was first popularized, that differences do exist between social and commercial marketing. For example, Bloom and Novelli (1981) have identified a number of differences between social and commercial marketing that make the former activity an especially difficult task. The nature and scope of these differences is outlined in Table 21.1. Also worth noting is a key article by Rothschild (1979), which focuses on the problems social marketing must overcome when fashioning an effective marketing communications program:

> Problems more prevalent in non-business cases include the intangibility of non-business products, the non-monetary price of purchase, the extreme lack of frequency of purchase, the lack of behavioral reinforcers, the need to market to an entire but heterogeneous society/market and the extreme levels of involvement varying from very low to very high. Because of these factors, the transference of marketing principles from the business to the non-business sector is far more complex than originally had been thought. (p. 12)

Attempts have been made to use social marketing to facilitate economic and social development. A modest body of literature demonstrates how a social marketing approach—most often in the areas of birth control, preventive medicine, and oral rehydration—can contribute to Third World social development. Dholakia (1984), for example, advocates the design of family planning–oriented social marketing plans compatible with both individual and collective welfare. Duhaime et al. (1985) argue that social marketing provides would-be Third World change agents with both an approach and a set of tools that will increase their likelihood of success.

TABLE 21.1 What's Different about Social Marketing?

1. Market analysis differences
   A. Social marketers usually have
   Less good secondary data available about their consumers.
   B. Social marketers have more difficulty
   Obtaining valid and reliable measures of key factors.
   Determining how important each such factor is in affecting consumer behavior.
   Getting consumer research studies funded, approved and completed.

2. Market segmentation differences
   A. Social marketers
   Frequently do not have accurate behavior to use in identifying segments.
   Face pressure against segmentation that leads to the ignoring of certain groups.
   Often have target segments consisting of the most negatively disposed consumers.

3. Product strategy differences
   A. Social marketers have
   Less flexibility in shaping their products or offerings.
   More difficulty in formulating product concepts.
   More difficulty selecting and implementing long-term positioning strategies.

4. Pricing strategy differences
   A. The development of a pricing strategy primarily involves trying to reduce the monetary, psychic, energy, and time costs of consumers.
   B. Social marketers
   Can encounter real difficulties in measuring their prices.
   Tend to have less control over consumer costs.

5. Place strategy differences
   A. Social marketers have more difficulty utilizing and controlling desired intermediaries.

6. Promotional strategy differences
   A. Social marketers usually
   Find paid advertising impossible to use.
   Must communicate relatively large amounts of complex information.
   B. Social marketers often
   Face pressure not to use certain types of appeals in their messages.
   Have difficulty conducting meaningful pretests of alternate appeals.

7. Organizational design differences
   A. Social marketers must function in organizations
   Where marketing activities are poorly understood, weakly appreciated, and improperly located.
   Where plans (if any are developed) are treated as records rather than as action documents.

(continued)

TABLE 21.1 What's Different about Social Marketing? (continued)

8. Evaluation differences
   A. Social marketers often find it difficult
      Even to establish effectiveness measures.
      To estimate marketing's contribution to the achievement of these objectives.

Source: Reprinted from the *Journal of Marketing*, published by the American Marketing Association. Paul N. Bloom and William Novelli, "Problems and Challenges of Social Marketing," *Journal of Marketing* 45 (Spring 1981): 79–88.

Another dimension of social marketing that may be relevant to marketing and economic development is explored in this essay. That dimension is exemplified by Canada's Third World development and assistance program.

CANADA'S OFFICIAL DEVELOPMENT ASSISTANCE PROGRAM

As approved by Parliament, the official development assistance (ODA) program is one of the main instruments with which Canada advances the goal of international social justice.[1] The assistance program seeks to support the efforts of developing countries in fostering economic and social programs, placing emphasis on poorer developing countries and the needy within developing countries. These objectives are pursued through official bilateral (government-to-government) channels, multilateral development institutions, and support of the development activities of nongovernmental organizations and the private sector.

Development has been defined as a process by which societies change so that they are able to meet the basic needs of their populations, in a way that is sustainable in the long term and is based largely on indigenous resources and values. Canada's official development assistance (ODA) program has made important contributions in this regard, representing the Canadian tradition of generosity and support for long-term development projects. In 1984–85 Canada allocated $2.1 billion (Canadian) to international cooperation (0.49 percent of the gross national product), which placed Canada among the principal donors of the Development Assistance Committee of the Organization for Economic Cooperation and Development.

The Canadian International Development Agency is responsible for implementing a large part of the Canadian development cooperation program, managing about 75 percent of the total ODA budget. The agency's goal is to support the efforts of the peoples and countries of the Third World to achieve self-sustaining social and economic development. CIDA focuses its efforts on the poorest countries and pays special attention to three crucial aspects of development, where the needs are immense: agriculture (including fisheries and forestry), energy, and human resource development. Assistance is provided through four main channels:

1. Bilateral (government-to-government) programs, which use about 40 percent of CIDA's budget to finance more than a thousand projects in over ninety developing countries. Aid is used for, among other things, infrastructure projects, rural and agricultural development, food aid, lines of credit, and technical assistance. In 1984–85, about one-quarter of bilateral assistance consisted of food aid to countries afflicted by drought, famine, and food deficits.
2. Multilateral programs, which support the development efforts of some eighty-five international organizations, including United Nations agencies, development banks, humanitarian institutions and other international groups seeking solutions to the problems of world development.
3. Special programs, which support and encourage the initiatives of Canadian institutions and voluntary groups playing an active role in international development.
4. The business cooperation program, which supports the initiatives of Canadian businesses interested in participating in development efforts. This program has been warmly received by the Canadian business community.

CIDA draws upon all sectors of the Canadian economy in implementing the aid program, bringing together numerous individual resources to provide a better contribution to international development. The remaining 25 percent of Canada's ODA is administered by other government departments and agencies. The Department of Finance, for example, provides Canada's contribution to the International Bank for Reconstruction and Development (IBRD) and its concessional funding arm, the International Development Association. Canada contributed $207.7 million to these institutions in 1984–85.

The International Development Research Center (IDRC) supports the efforts of developing countries to build up their own research capabilities, particularly in the areas of agriculture, farming, forestry, fisheries, energy, health, and education. IDRC provided $84.6 million toward these efforts in 1984–85.

The Department of External Affairs contributes to the regular budgets and voluntary funds of several multilateral organizations, such as the World Health Organization and the Food and Agriculture Organization. Canada Post and National Health and Welfare also provide support to international agencies active in development. Together, these sources provided $50.5 million in 1984–85.

The Petro-Canada International Assistance Corporation (PCIAC) was established in 1981 to assist developing countries in reducing their dependence on imported oil by using Canadian technology and expertise for oil and gas exploration. In 1984–85, PCIAC disbursed $53.2 million on development projects.

Provincial governments are also involved in international development, contributing $9.7 million in 1984–85 to assist in the work of nongovernmental organizations (NGOs).

CIDA'S PUBLIC AFFAIRS PROGRAM

How CIDA works to obtain the degree of public assistance required to sustain a $2 billion a year Canadian commitment to development assistance can best be seen by focusing on the activities of CIDA's Public Affairs Branch (PAB).

Personal interviews with PAB staff and documents suggest that PAB had a clearly defined sense of its mandate by 1984–85 and 1985–86. The following extract from the 1984–85 Public Affairs Branch Work Plan reveals that those responsible clearly understood both PAB's intended role and objectives:

> Under the direction of the Minister of External Affairs and President, the mandate of the Public Affairs Branch (PAB) is (1) to promote the policies of the Government of Canada in relation to international development and cooperation, and (2) to make known the objectives, programs and projects of the Agency to the Canadian public.
>
> The mandate's two parts are not equal. Priority is given to the first part. To promote means to publicize and explain policies in such a way as to strengthen public acceptance and support. The second part of the mandate is separate, but not distinct. It supports the first. We disseminate information not only to fulfil an obligation of public accountability, but also to raise public awareness of development issues and Canada's role, and thereby to strengthen public support for Canada's development program and objectives. (Public Affairs Branch Work Plan, 1984–85)

Its primary objective was to help CIDA and the government increase public support for international development. Like so many other government programs, CIDA included a significant marketing component, without referring to it by that rubric.

Special surveys conducted by Decima Research in July 1985 and January 1986, during the height of Canada's African famine relief campaign, revealed the impact on Canadian attitudes of this widely publicized crisis. As might be expected, the African crisis led to a marked increase in Canadian willingness to have its government use Canadian resources for Third World assistance. Attitudes at that time are revealed in the following extract from the press release issued after the completion of the second of the two surveys:

> Ottawa:—Results of a recent nationwide survey conducted by Decima Research indicate very clearly that Canadians have lost none of their enthusiasm for the task of helping alleviate the problems caused by the drought and famine in Africa.

> *Concern about World Hunger Remains High*

> Only one Canadian in five thinks Canada spends too much money assisting poor countries around the world, while 47 percent say the right amount and 32 percent say not enough. Most people feel Canada is among the world's more generous nations in terms of our aid efforts and would prefer to continue in that role, rather than be either "a world leader," or "among the less generous nations."

> Three out of four (75 percent) say that while they are concerned about restraining government spending, they don't think we should reduce Canada's foreign aid contribution. Two thirds (67 percent) believe Canada's aid has been very or somewhat effective at resolving the problems of poorer countries.

> While three out of four people (77 percent) "often wonder if we shouldn't help people here in Canada, rather than people living in other countries," most (68 percent) also feel that "when Canadians give more to help relieve hunger in other countries, they don't necessarily give less to help the needy in Canada." (Decima Research Press Release, February 13, 1984)

It was also made clear, however, that most Canadians were thinking primarily in terms of humanitarian aid rather than the CIDA focus on long-term development assistance.

The Public Affairs Branch is itself aware, and striving to make all of CIDA conscious, of the context in which public opinion regarding development is being formed. CIDA uses a variety of approaches in its efforts to influence public opinion. However, the use of paid advertising is considered inappropriate.

The Public Affairs Branch Work Plan for 1984–85 spells out in considerable detail the message to be used in CIDA's attempts to generate an increased degree of public support for Canada's development efforts. The relevant section is reproduced here in its entirety from Public Affairs Branch Work Plan, 1984–85.

Stimulating stronger public support for Canada's development policies and activities involves reaching the public with a message which contains many elements (or points we want to put across) and three essential components:

1. Information
2. Education
3. Persuasion

Although some elements of the message will contain more of one component than of another, no element is complete unless it contains all three components. The elements of the message should be chosen with a view to:

1. Linking CIDA and development with Canadians' concerns, values and interests, both domestic and foreign.
2. Demonstrating that the benefits to developing countries are real, and that they justify the costs.
3. Showing that development benefits Canadians, both directly and indirectly, in both the short and long term.
4. Proving that development is a necessary Canadian and international priority.
5. Demonstrating that CIDA is a proficient and efficient organization.
6. Raising the level of public understanding of interdependence, development issues and Canada's role.

Those purposes suggest that the message should contain the following elements:

1. Development works.
2. Development benefits Canada.
3. The Third World is not aid-dependent; assistance is only one of many factors in its progress.
4. The developing world has changed dramatically in our lifetime.
5. Development tries to accelerate the stages of change which all countries experience.
6. Development is more complex, costly and urgent than before.
7. Canada's development effort is national, not just the government's or CIDA's.
8. Comparisons between ordinary life in Canada and in a developing country.
9. Development is not just us helping them, but all helping each other to create a more stable, just, hopeful and secure global society.

Those familiar with commercial marketing are certain to notice the obvious parallels between this presentation of the message PAB wishes to communicate and the discussion of the "copy platform" found in a corporate or brand marketing plan.

Other aspects of PAB thinking also have commercial parallels. One finds, for example, a marked similarity between conventional target market thinking and CIDA's efforts to reach the unconverted. "Since increased support is the goal, we should give a higher priority to the unconverted (to groups likely to include a cross-section of opinion on aid) and a subordinate priority to reaching people who are already aware and supportive of international development." There is, therefore, one very important difference between target marketing as practiced by groups such as CIDA and that of corporate marketing departments. One finds in a private sector target market those groups most favorably disposed and, consequently, most likely to purchase the good or service being offered. Social marketing's target groups are very often made up primarily of those indifferent, or even hostile, to the product offering.

ESSENTIALS OF A SOCIAL MARKETING APPROACH

Philip Kotler, the chief proponent of "broadened marketing," has defined and discussed social marketing in a number of different but closely related ways. In Kotler's seminal article with Levy (1969), the emphasis is on recognizing that all sorts of organizations serve markets whose needs must be met. This could best be done, it is argued, by using, with appropriate modification, tools and concepts long employed by commercial marketers.

Kotler's article with Zaltman (1971), published some two and one-half years later, focuses more specifically on social marketing. Kotler and Zaltman argued that all forms of marketing, not just commercial transactions, require a mutually beneficial exchange relationship. Marketing management occurs when people become conscious of an opportunity to gain from a more careful planning of exchange relationships. "Although planned social change is not often viewed from the client's point of view, it involves very much an exchange relationship between client and change agent" (p. 4). That exchange might involve, for example, what the volunteer pays in time or the blood donor in blood for the sense of social satisfaction received from aiding the elderly or giving blood.

Another key distinction is that between "social advertising" and "social marketing." Wiebe (1951) maintains that one of the major determinants of the success or failure of social advertising campaigns is the relative ease with which the recipients of the social advertising message can act in a manner consistent with the desires of the initiator of that campaign. Kotler and Zaltman then argue that a social marketing approach is far more likely to bring about the desired action or behavior change than is a social advertising or even a social communications approach. They also maintain that a distinguishing feature of social marketing is the fact that an integrated marketing effort makes it easy for members of the target market to do something (pp. 7–12).

The distinction made between social advertising and social marketing is mentioned again, close to a decade later, by Fox and Kotler (1980) in their assessment of the first ten years of the marketing of social causes. They call attention to a gradual evolution from social advertising through social communication to social marketing. What social communication means is made quite clear:

> Social communicators make greater use of personal selling and editorial support in addition to mass advertising. Thus, the family planning campaign in India utilizes a network of agents, including doctors, dentists and bankers, to "talk up" family planning to people with whom they come in contact. Events such as "Family Planning Day" and family planning fairs together with buttons, signs, and other media get across the message. (p. 25)

Social marketing is then presented as a broader scale of effort to effect social change. This is done by adding four elements that are missing from a pure social communications approach: sophisticated marketing research, a commitment to making necessary modifications in the product offering, the use of incentives, and facilitation, all of which make it easier for the target market to act in a manner consistent with the desires of the social marketer (pp. 25–26). Much of the remainder of the Fox and Kotler article focuses on the degree of success achieved by various social marketing programs in getting people to *do something*.

Also deserving of mention is an article by Andreasen (1982) focusing on the difference between the real and the apparent in many allegedly marketing-oreinted nonprofit organizations:

> While they believe they are marketing oriented, these organizations actually have a product oriented approach. They start with their own organizations and services, determine how they want to market them, and then turn to customer analysis to achieve their goals. Despite their protestations to the contrary, they do not begin the process with consumers. The distinction is subtle but important. (p. 105)

> These marketers start with what they wish others to know about their organizations and only later think about customer needs and wants. This is very different from a modern marketing orientation, which espouses the opposite approach. Institutions shouldn't ignore their own goals, preferences, strengths and weaknesses. Nevertheless, these concerns should not outweigh consumers' interests. (p. 106)

Andreasen builds on the above to make an exceedingly important distinction. The truly marketing-oriented nonprofit will demonstrate a willingness to modify the product in light of the findings of consumer-oriented research. Any organization that considers its product offering as inherently desirable or otherwise fixed and immutable is not, Andreasen maintains, marketing oriented.

This brief review of the themes in social marketing literature suggests a number of dimensions that can be employed in determining whether the Public Affairs Branch of CIDA has, without realizing it, engaged in social marketing. That any such action would have been unconscious, unknowing, and intuitive was made clear in personal interviews with PAB administrators. Those individuals most immediately concerned had no prior exposure to marketing in any of its manifestations. Indeed, they had not even heard of the term "social marketing" until just a few weeks before I called them. However, the possibility remains that, like Molière's hero who had been speaking prose all his life without knowing it, the Public Affairs Branch of CIDA had practiced social marketing without being aware of that fact.

DOES CIDA USE A SOCIAL MARKETING APPROACH?

The Public Affairs Branch of CIDA obviously utilizes some of the same approaches and techniques employed by social marketers. We find, for example, social marketing's concern with creating and maintaining favorable attitudes shared by PAB. There is also mention of the development messages that PAB wishes to get across, of the target market it wishes to reach (more of the uncommitted and especially the private sector), of the role of the media as informational channels of distribution, of the need for a variety of closely coordinated programs focused on target markets and of the use of surveys to track public opinion.

But whether the PAB is actually engaged in social marketing is not an easy question to answer. Indeed, the appropriate response to that question appears to depend on how three more specific questions, each dealing with a different aspect of PAB activities, were answered. Is the CIDA product offering a given or a marketing variable? Does an identifiable exchange relationship exist? Is the target market for the PAB program being asked to do something?

1. *Is the CIDA product offering a given and hence the PAB program a form of social communications?* The CIDA product offering is subject to change but not by the agency itself and certainly not by its PAB. That branch lacks the authority to modify its own mandate and CIDA's overall mission is determined by others. The Public Affairs Branch mandate includes (a) promoting the policies of the Government of Canada in relation to international development and cooperation, and (b) making known the objectives, programs, and projects of the agency to the Canadian public. The first of these tasks, promoting Government of Canada policies, receives priority. Since CIDA is a governmental agency, changes in its product offering take place within a broader political context. Ultimately, the prime minister and his cabinet determine both CIDA's objectives and the degree of financial support official development assistance will receive in light of all the other claims on limited government resources. The prime minister's office and the cabinet are the units that have the authority to change the CIDA product offering—either the total amount of funding provided or the purposes for which the global allocation will be used.

2. *Is an exchange relationship and/or a payment an essential characteristic of the program being promoted?* An exchange relationship exists but it is of a relatively passive nature. The consumer costs involved are subsumed within a much larger overall tax bill. The Canadian population makes a collective tax payment to a government that considers development assistance to be but one of many legitimate expenditures. That same government, at approximately four-year intervals, asks the electorate for a legitimizing vote that will renew its mandate. Those who support Canada's efforts at Third World development are expected, in return for a generous development appropriation, to vote for the incumbent government. But development outlays account for just over 2 percent of all federal government expenditures and about 3 percent of all tax payments. And when the Canadian electorate casts its votes, the attitude of the three major parties toward development assistance is far less important than many other issues.

3. *Is the Public Affairs Branch of CIDA encouraging its market to do anything about the Third World development policies of the federal government? If not, can what PAB does be called social marketing?* Kotler and Levy's seminal article focused on the role of social marketing in getting message recipients to do something. One finds the same emphasis in Fox and Kotler's work close to a decade later. Social marketing programs are evaluated by these authors primarily in terms of their effect on behavior. The Public Affairs Branch, by contrast, has no real interest in having its target market do anything. PAB definitely does not wish to encourage those receiving its attitude-oriented messages to lobby on behalf of a greater Canadian financial commitment to Third World development. Encouraging such action would be entirely inappropriate behavior by an agency of the Canadian government. Rather, PAB's objective is to create favorable attitudes toward development assistance, attitudes that will be expressed whenever the public's views on this matter are solicited—either nationally or locally.

But does changing an attitude or, alternately, adhering more tenaciously to a previously held position involve "doing something"? Professor Gary Mauser of Simon Fraser University has argued that changing attitudes (racism or patriotism) should be seen as getting people to do something, since changing attitudes would implicate a large number of behavioral correlates and not just a single "action"—such as buying a product or voting. Why not include the full panoply of behaviors associated with a given change in attitude? By decreasing the legitimacy of "racism" within a society, a large number of behaviors would be expected to change toward a particular social group. Wouldn't you admit that the goal of antiracism efforts "is to get people to do things?" But if attitude change is action enough, does not conventional social marketing wisdom require a degree of modification?

SUMMARY

Are PAB efforts to gain Canadian support for official development assistance best characterized as social marketing or social communication? This is a difficult question to answer as a great deal depends on one's unit of analysis. From a PAB or even a CIDA perspective, a social communications approach is being used. Various forms of public relations and publicity are being utilized along with public participation via nongovernmental organizations. CIDA is not free to change its product offering, those reached are not encouraged to do anything, and there is no direct exchange between the agency and its target market.

Within a broader governmental context, however, efforts to maintain a high level of Canadian support for official development assistance can be characterized as social marketing. The prime minister and his cabinet can and have changed development objectives and allocations. The payment by the citizenry of taxes to support a $2 billion foreign aid program can be viewed as part of an exchange. A decision by those supportive of such a program to vote in favor of reelecting the government in power can be viewed as the desired action or behavior.

NOTE

The author wishes to thank Professors Gary Mauser of Simon Fraser University and Chuck Weinberg of the University of British Columbia for their helpful comments on earlier drafts of this essay.

1. This section is drawn from the Canadian International Development Agency's 1984–1985 Annual Report, pp. 6, 9, and 10.

22

A Generic Social Marketing Plan

SEYMOUR H. FINE
Rutgers, The State University of New Jersey

The Third World is made up of vast regions inhabited by large numbers of individuals who are plagued with dire problems such as exploding populations, severe malnutrition, poor sanitation, and illiteracy. These problems are of direct concern to government agencies of the United States, and of the United Nations, all of whom are ever on the alert for, and often eager to adopt, innovative methods for disseminating public awareness programs. Thus, it is not surprising that social marketing has found a receptive audience among these institutions. Social marketing appears to be at least as well accepted in developing countries as in the United States. Scholars and practitioners from far-off lands speak of social marketing with familiarity surpassing that prevailing in much of the United States. For example, they speak of globalization of ad campaigns in order to reduce costs to individual countries. This is a notion one finds in commercial marketing by multinational corporations, but rarely if ever, in social marketing. However, social marketers might find such campaigns an effective way of solving many social problems throughout the world. (For examples of some efforts in this direction, see Brieger, Ramakrishna, and Adeniyi 1986–87; Rule 1987; Manoff 1987; Webb et al. 1988; and Belk 1988.)

A MARKETING PLAN FOR THE PROBLEM OF FOOD SAFETY

One widespread problem still far from being under control is that of disease stemming from food spoilage and poor hygiene. A new approach to food safety is needed if the countries of the world, particularly those in the Third World, are to ameliorate this problem. One promising idea is that of a generic marketing plan for the dissemination of food safety "products," namely, interventions designed to decrease the incidence of food contamination and to relieve its ill effects.

The plan is an adaptation of the 7P's model introduced in Chapter 1 and the marketing plan suggested there. Those concepts are translated here into strategies for dealing with other problems unique to developing countries. Although the plan is illustrated in terms of food safety, it can easily be extended to any other product; only minor modifications would be needed to apply it to any idea, product, or service. It is termed "generic" because it was designed to be used by any member country of the World Health Organization (WHO) and can thus be tailored to their particular situations.

As noted in Chapter 1, a marketing plan begins with the statement of a goal and then proceeds to deal with the questions posed by the 7P's model:

1. Who is the *producer*, the source of the promotional message?
2. Who makes up the market of potential *purchasers* we are to address, and what needs and wants do these people have?
3. What *product*(s) can we design specifically to help fill those needs?
4. What *price*(s) must our consumers sacrifice in order to purchase our product?
5. How can we *promote* (communicate with) our market?
6. Which parties (institutions) will participate in the process of making the product available at the best *place* and time (best for the purchaser)?
7. What *probing* will be necessary to evaluate our campaign and to obtain feedback from our audiences?

In the remainder of this chapter, these seven questions are translated into a strategy to attain a specific goal: improved food safety.

GOAL OF THE PROGRAM

The central goal is to significantly ameliorate the disastrous effects of food contamination in developing countries as quickly as humanly possible. The immediate objective is to make people everywhere acutely aware of the dangers of food contamination and to tell them how to prevent it.

THE MARKETER

Having enunciated the goals, the next step is to identify the marketer. Who is to draw up the blueprint by which the goal is to be attained and who will execute the plan? A campaign needs overall direction, and it was suggested that the World Health Organization is the logical choice to carry out the leadership function, as it has for many years.

This role must be filled by an organization perceived as neutral, credible, and broad in scope. Other groups may have axes to grind. For example, educators would probably promote the school as the best forum for health education, advertising agencies would argue in favor of mass media, statisticians would push for empirical research, cultural anthropologists would stress the value of in-depth interviews, and sociologists would emphasize community organization. All are important, but none of these entities is equipped to integrate and coordinate the complete process.

The government, too, has its shortcomings as a possible leader of the food safety program; the government is not always perceived as a trustworthy source of information, and bureaucrats have been known to concentrate on issues of "turf" and nest-feathering. There is also the question of whether the private sector in general, and the food industry in particular, can be expected to function with complete objectivity.

Consequently, no one special-interest group is as qualified to serve as marketer for the food safety product as the WHO. Each is too preoccupied with its own concerns to effectively lead the overall campaign. However, each has a significant contribution to make as a participant and can act as catalyst. Full responsibility for direction and control no doubt falls upon an existing department within the WHO, which can be assigned budget and staffing to implement and execute a marketing plan.

THE PURCHASERS

Depending on the discipline one is studying, the group of individuals to be served by a social movement is known by such names as audience, constituency, or public; in marketing we call it a *market* of consumers.

Usually, there is not one market but several. Therefore an overall effort aimed at a heterogeneous audience will usually have little effect on the largest portion of that audience, and will merely waste precious resources. One must partition the market (on the basis of some criterion) into homogeneous subgroups, and then custom-design a campaign to suit the characteristics of each group. That is what is meant by *market segmentation*. Properly executed, segmentation is perhaps the most important step in the marketing process, because it renders the program more efficient. The choice of the segmentation criterion is crucial and must be made early on. One can segment on the basis of geography, socioeconomic level, familiarity with food safety, or any of the standard demographic or psychographic variables (Fine 1981). But segment we must, or we are not doing our marketing homework.

It would appear that the principal market for food safety is the poor, particularly within the Third World. Because poor people suffer from inadequate supplies of food, they are the ones most likely to eat food that is spoiled. Therefore at first glance, it seems that education programs should first be developed for this audience. But creative segmentation planning might dictate differently: Perhaps it would be prudent to first appeal to the middle class, whose customs and mores are often emulated by the poor. Every relevant target segment must be considered.

The tourist market is an example. It needs to be addressed not only for its own benefit, but also as a means of stimulating travel to places suffering from adverse reputations regarding food safety. A case in point is Mexico, where visitors are usually cautioned against drinking the water or eating leafy vegetables.

Ordinarily, segmentation is accomplished by elaborate, quantitative consumer research. However, for the marketing plan described here, it may suffice to identify the few target groups in an intuitive manner by questioning appropriate field personnel. For social marketing in development, there is good reason to rely on informal qualitative data; empirical data are too expensive, take too long to generate, and may contain no fewer errors than qualitative information. Social research in the Third World is often a matter of "educated guess, go back and ask them, ad hoc, anecdotal, process evaluation, action research," and so on.

The segments are specified and listed (e.g., rural farmers, the urban poor, students, factory workers)—three or four segments are enough. Experience has shown that if more than just a few segments are identified, the plan will be unmanageable and overly expensive because a separate strategy must be designed to suit the needs of each segment.

Some final thoughts about Third World purchasers: A strategy for effecting behavioral change must include some means of making the change a *wanted* commodity. For example, all people want good health. But how can we spread information about the relationship between food safety and health in such a way as to make people demand food safety information? The change agent must identify local symbolic metaphors, language, and markers and must compose messages in that language. We need to know who talks to whom, who are the gatekeepers.

Moreover, the consumer must possess (a) the knowledge and ability to make the change; (b) the desire to upset old habits necessitated by the change (change must occur within the acceptable social norms and customs); and (c) authority (permission) to make the change. Social marketing needs to begin with a presentation of data that depict the severity of the problem. This must be done succinctly. A presentation that is too long merely distracts the reader (or listener) from the message.

THE PRODUCT

The product in the campaign is the idea that people should adopt certain measures to avoid eating contaminated foods. What measures? Some are listed in Table 22.1. The social marketer prepares a list of them, a "product mix," and then assigns a brand name/campaign slogan, such as "Safe Food Means Better Health." Recall from Chapter 1 what marketers have learned from psycholinguistics, that people remember a product better if it is called by a name that easily rolls off the tongue.

TABLE 22.1 Practices That Prevent or Curtail Contamination of Foods in Poor Rural Ecosystems

Activity	Practice
Weaning foods	Breast feed exclusively for months Cook foods thoroughly; minimize interval between cooking and feeding Feed supplements in clean containers Feed by cup or spoon Prepare foods just before needed Protect foods from insects
Feeding children	Wash hands before feeding Avoid contact with feces before feeding
Handling water	Use safe water supply Treat unsafe water Boil water for drinking Store water for drinking in separate container
Defecation and disposal	Use latrine or toilet Wash hands after defecation Wash hands after contact with human or animal feces

Source: Mata (1987)

Another point to be made in connection with product management concerns accessorizing. The marketer might package the product with "accessory products" such as sound nutrition, breast-feeding, pure water, and immunization. In commercial marketing, one would be encouraged to purchase a handbag, for example, along with a pair of shoes.

THE PRICE

Strategic market planning must consider "social prices," payments to be made by consumers quite apart from monetary fees. These include such sacrifices as time, effort, and change in life-style. What "prices" do individuals pay when "buying" the idea of food safety? They pay in the time and the trouble it takes to learn how to recognize defective food, how to exercise preventive measures. They also pay in the tribulation involved in unlearning prior eating habits, such as eating with the hands; and they must often relinquish some perceived pleasure in the taste of familiar foods that might have to be replaced.

As for discarding spoiled food, in some cultures and in some religions it is considered a *sin* to throw food away, to waste food. In any case, there must surely be a price of *guilt* to be paid by the consumer who discards contaminated food bought with scarce money, or grown with precious labor.

Other social prices, perhaps characteristic of a particular group, should be identified by the social marketer who is familiar with each local situation. One needs to know what changes in life-style or habit will be imposed upon the purchaser of the idea of food safety. Change in time-honored habits is a high social price to pay for adopting an idea, especially when gratification is not immediately apparent. The social marketer tries to "reduce" these prices by skillfully designing the message in the promotion campaign. Taking social price into account renders the exchange more fair, more palatable. It is helpful to prepare a chart listing the parties to the food safety process (Table 22.2), the benefits each obtains from "buying" the food safety product, and the "price" each pays for that product.

PROMOTION

At the heart of the marketing plan is its communication component. The campaign should be based on a multimedia, multimethod, multiap-

TABLE 22.2 Members of a Distribution Channel for Food Safety

World Health Organization (as "Channel Captain")
UNICEF, FAO
Public health service
Higher education
Mass media
Professional associations
Anthropologists, sociologists
Food producers (name brand and local)
Personal communication channels (rumor, gossip)
Opinion leaders
Community organizations
Food wholesalers
Supermarket
Local food shop
Street vendor
Church
School
Local police
Urban dwellers
Advocacy groups
Rural dwellers
Tourists

proach strategy. One cannot repeat the message too often when seeking a change in behavior. And the message is at the heart of the communication; message design is an art. Although it may be true that "a picture is worth a thousand words," it is perhaps still more difficult to communicate with words than with pictures. The following is suggested as a guide—a list of three standards by which messages may be evaluated.

1. Brevity. A message should be brief. According to theory, human short-term memory can only absorb about five "chunks" (i.e., individual bits) of information.
2. Appeal. A message should appeal to positive emotions like fun, happiness, and good health, rather than sickness, fear, dire consequences, and misery. A success story is a good message (see Chapter 13).
3. Honesty. If a chemical is added to a packaged food to prolong its shelf life, that is a positive attribute and should be promoted as such. Instead, many Western producers have created a myth that all additives are bad. They are selling fear, which is a negative appeal (Kaferstein and Sims 1987).

As for media, the social marketer must become familiar with a solid mix of print and broadcast media, posters, picture-story books, the cinema, shadow plays, puppet shows, street hawkers, bulletins, exhibitions, lottery tickets, telephone, electricity and water bills, and so on.

The campaign deserves national status and all-out support. Food safety must become a byword in every home, workplace, and street corner. The campaign must reach every part of the system.

Budget and Schedule. The coordinator of the campaign creates a schedule of all media expenses for a period of one year such that its total remains well within the prescribed budget. One thus avoids both the perils of overspending and possible inadequacies stemming from underspending. Resources should be focused only on those strategies that are most likely to be carried out and that are affordable. For example, local villagers should be trained to produce printed materials in their own countries and in their own language, and these materials should be about problems they perceive as their own. The communication must be designed in, by, and for their own culture. A few years ago, a poster was created by one of the African governments as part of a program to emphasize that the housefly carries disease. The poster featured a picture of a fly, greatly enlarged behind a magnifying glass, with appropriate copy, headline, and so forth. The campaign did not succeed in its mission and an effort to determine the reason led a villager to comment, "They don't mean us because our houseflies are not so big."

PLACE: THE CHANNEL OF DISTRIBUTION

Experience has shown that no one agency, nor for that matter, any single sector can cope with the problem of illness from tainted food. A collaborative venture is needed in which expertise and resources of several entities are contributed and integrated under the direction of the WHO. Such a system of institutions, operating in close collaboration is what marketers call a *distribution channel* for a given product.

For the food safety product, the channel should consist of the organizations and individuals who are involved in the marketing process, primarily in the communication chain. Table 22.2 is a partial list of members of the channel for the food safety product.

The table lists the WHO as leader or "channel captain" of the system. The channel captain assigns roles and functions to the various members of this network, coordinates and controls their activities, and commends them for successes. Inevitably, it then takes the blame for any failures! Each member of the channel is made keenly aware of its responsibilities and contributions to the process. In any particular situation, a WHO representative or a local health official identifies the channel members and assigns them functions. That individual should record such assignments and note what functions each is expected to perform, thereby facilitating control and tracking of the progress of the operation. The procedure also reveals potential redundancies and omissions.

Private Sector Firms in the Channel. It is good business in any country, developing or otherwise, for large corporations to become involved in public education programs, especially where those programs concern the very product lines produced by the companies. Food is an excellent case in point. Social marketing is hardly a new experience to American industry; for many years, firms have conducted educative programs for social causes.

Larger producers, with a brand image to protect, try to maintain hygienic standards in the factory. They are more likely than smaller firms to have quality control experts on staff, and to operate in-plant training programs for cleanliness in food handling. For example, it is crucial to wash one's hands after using the toilet in a food plant, yet this practice is no doubt ignored in some local facilities for lack of proper education.

An important communicator in the channel for the food safety message is the opinion leader. Opinion leaders are trusted individuals to whom people go for advice on some subject. In a multinational food factory in Venezuela, it was found that many workers trained in food hygiene carried their new knowledge back to the home community. "If it is healthy to do so-and-so in the factory, then why not also at home?" The fact that someone holds an important job in a factory gives credence to the information this individual communicates.

Food producers should be especially aware of the fact that more food is sold to healthy people than to the sick or the dying. Educative campaigns must be undertaken toward food producers themselves, driving home this message. For it is in their long-term—yes, profit-motivated, selfish—interest to participate actively in food safety dissemination programs and they are clearly doing just that. As James Buchanan Duke, founder of the Duke Endowment, once commented when explaining his concern for expansion of health facilities, "People ought to be healthy. If they ain't healthy they can't work, and if they don't work they ain't healthy. And if they can't work there ain't any profit in them" (Lipset 1986, p. 12).

Retail food establishments constitute a prominent forum for the exchange of nutrition information. They are in an ideal position to convey ideas about sound nutrition and, in the long run, to benefit themselves, for nutritionally educated consumers must be healthier and hence better customers. Of course, they will be better customers not for packaged snacks, "junk foods," but for more wholesome items such as vegetables, fruit, bulk grains, unseasoned nuts, fish, and other basic foods. The information would be conveyed via word-of-mouth channels between staff and customers, posters, in-store loudspeaker announcements, and mass media. If by promoting the idea of sound nutrition, a merchant was to lose sales in the snack department, the loss should be offset by increased interest in healthier food items. At the same time, the store would be creating goodwill among a sizable health food segment that would otherwise have to search for specialty shops outside the community. At the higher rungs of the food distribution channel, wholesalers and producers have responded to such a shift in demand by themselves introducing more nutritious product lines.

In the United States, the social marketing channel frequently includes the Advertising Council, which is an organization of creative advertisers and advertising agency people who donate their time and talent, mostly without charge, to the promotion of social causes. The only expense incurred by the government or nonprofit agency involved is the cost of production. This is a classic example of private sector firms' demonstrating altruism while attaining some modicum of publicity for themselves. The concept is becoming globalized, as counterparts of the U.S. Ad Council are now appearing in other Western countries.

Public Health officials are obviously key elements in the channel. The American Food and Drug Administration (FDA) assists Third World countries in testing and training programs aimed at improving food safety. Its International Affairs Staff oversees visits to the FDA by hundreds of government officials from all over the world (Farley 1986).

The greatest challenge for the WHO is how to harness the most valuable resources each element of the channel is prepared to contribute to this crusade—financial support from government, technical and research expertise from industry, regulatory assistance from local law-enforcement agencies, and communication assistance from other community-based organizations.

For an illustration from the United States, consider the case of aflatoxin control, a joint ongoing cooperative effort between the U.S. Department of Agriculture, the Food and Drug Administration, a consortium of food manufacturers and an industry analytic laboratory. The problem is now well under control (Feldberg 1986).

Although governments purchase scientific and other expertise from the private sector, business will undoubtedly contribute such services free of charge when it can be convinced that it is in its best interests to do so. A strategy for any exchange transaction must be examined in terms of who is to win and who is to lose. The change agent must identify the psychological, political, and anthropological value of the program to each party involved in the process.

PROBING FOR EVALUATION AND FEEDBACK

Attitudinal and behavioral changes occur slowly and are difficult to measure. What tools are available in the form of social research, surveys, and so on, are fraught with error—response error, nonresponse error, and measurement error. When change does come about, it is often difficult to trace the change to any particular program. Many factors extraneous to the planned effort may either reinforce or subvert that effort. For these reasons scarce resources are better invested in careful planning and meticulous execution than in evaluative research.

Programs need not begin on a grandiose scale. Following the marketing concept, dissemination programs could be test-marketed in just one country or one region, before "rolling out" a major project. Before one commits large sums of resources and energies, one should pilot-test an effort within a circumscribed segment that is typical enough so that the results will be widely applicable. If the test market can show positive gains, then further support is warranted. Finally, test marketing provides an opportunity to enlist various community organizations in the channel to participate in the planning process.

IMPLEMENTATION

To implement social marketing for food safety one needs a task force under the direction of an individual experienced in social mobilization and at least somewhat informed about the food safety problem. The need of effective and qualified leadership cannot be overemphasized. Moreover, that person must maintain liaison with WHO officials already involved in worldwide food safety.[1] The task force organizes, directs, and evaluates the program both internationally and locally. At the local level, it supervises the creation of entities like itself within the various regions where the problem is known to exist. It is there that operational planning is to take place. The task force communicates to the regions an outline of a "model plan" like the one presented here, which they can use as a guide in creating their own plans, where they will take local factors into account. These regional plans should then be submitted to the task force for review, possible amendment, and final approval. A major role of the task force is to obtain, control, and allocate funds to the regions for assistance in financing food safety programs.

SUMMARY

Virtually any well-conceived plan is likely to be more effective than a hit-and-miss approach to problem solving. Such a plan can be constructed by social marketers to deal with the worldwide dilemma of food spoilage and to ameliorate its harmful effects.

The plan cannot work, however, without the collaboration of various sectors in any given economy—for example, government, business, education, the church, and law enforcement agencies. A project relying on the sponsorship of a single entity will have a narrow perspective. True synergy derives from an open system in which inputs from a variety of points of view enrich the program. Overall leadership should be the responsibility of an arm of the United Nations like the WHO, as a neutral and trusted entity with experience in such programs.

NOTE

1. At the time of this writing, two such individuals at the World Health Organization are Dr. H. S. Dhillon, associate director (health education), Division of Public Information and Education for Health, and Dr. Fritz Kaferstein, chief, Food Safety Unit, Division of Environmental Health.

23

Marketing Third World Social Change

GERSON DA CUNHA
United Nations Children's Fund

It would be interesting to speculate why programs for social change have been so wary of opening their front doors to marketing methods. On occasion, a backdoor has swung ajar, but the trysts have gone badly, until quite recently. It was not till the late 1970s, perhaps the early 1980s, that social marketing became respectable enough to saunter about in the noonday of places like Indonesia, Brazil, Egypt, Honduras, and the Gambia.

In practice, social change and marketing are both about modifying group behavior, the one in a community, the other in a market. In either case, the quarry is an elusive, tricky target. Both must deal with resistance to change and with competition for attention and/or clientele. Both need clear, strong distribution channels for ideas and products. Both require a price to be paid by those benefited, or canvassed. Neither could afford a once-only trial. Both seek long-term conversions and enduring results through sustained effort. Profit is the goal for both, social in one case, commercial in the other. Small wonder that social marketing concepts and methods have worked so well in social programs when properly used. The wonder is that they are not yet routinely applied.

Things may be somewhat different in environments like the United States and the major centers of Western Europe. Here, social marketing is not an infrequent approach in social causes like the fight against smoking or drug abuse and in the public and nonprofit sectors to promote orchestras, museums, the use of seat belts, and so on. But the major "market segment" for social marketing is surely the Third World, where the real challenges lie because the issues deal with life and death and the scale is vast.

SOCIAL CHANGE: THE OPPORTUNITIES FOR MARKETING

There is a bull market in development projects that cannot be denied. A few traditional donors may well have pared support in some project areas. But then, they seem stronger in others. New donors have appeared. A look at the development support budgets, bilateral and multilateral, of the United States, Canada, Italy, the Scandinavian countries (especially Finland), Saudi Arabia, and Japan would be instructive. Developing countries have never dug deeper into their own resources for investment in themselves.

A higher pile of resources in the kitty could safely be expected to spark, as it has, some busier work plans for international agencies, professional consultancies, and Third World development institutions. The feature worth noting at this stage of the argument is the stepped-up demand for professional involvement in social change programs. (Curiously, even if resources were tighter, the demand could only grow more pressing with the accent on doing more with less, for greater impact and effectiveness). As one looks down a lengthening roster of projects, one expects that sheer statistical probability would yield more instances of properly conceived and managed social marketing initiatives. But, no, it does not.

One would also have thought the time ripe for supplying a decades-old lack in social change projects: a viable conceptual framework for planning and implementing them. Social marketing should have been a candidate for testing and speculating in this context, but it is not.

There are, of course, important differences between social change and marketing, as we shall see, apart from those of scale. But the similarities are sufficiently striking for the hypothesis embedded in the term "social marketing" to be defensible. We may be staring here at a signpost pointing toward a holistic model of attitude and behavioral change. Potentially, such a model would save the endless starting from square one that goes on conceptually and methodologically in projects for social change and hence the waste of spirit, time, resources, and opportunity; the decisionmaking by whim; or irrelevant discipline (pediatricians choosing target groups and media), and so on.

Certainly, the framework would not provide yet another policy-and-procedure "how to," nor act as a matrix that one would apply robotlike everywhere. It would serve instead like the rules of warfare and navigation. No general or pilot ever flouts them, maintaining that each battle or journey is one of its kind. The rules are used, as those of marketing could be, to save resources and spark creativity. All of which must lead us to ask what marketing is, anyway.

MEETING THE UNMET NEED

At the risk of proposing the umpteenth explanation of the term in a book like this one, marketing is a process that, in essence, identifies an unmet consumer need and satisfies it at a profit. Typically, this is done with commercial products and services amid competition. Social research and commercial and production technologies are involved in market segmentation, target group selection, pricing, distribution, selling and promotion. So much for the often-held view that marketing amounts to little more than the use of mass media. Since it is based on consumer wants and desires, it starts with an assiduous study of human needs and ends with devising means of satisfying them best. Marketing does not ask questions already sure of the answers, as happens all too often in social programs ("A nutrition problem? Well, let us tell them about the balanced diet.") This is the crucial, people-centered, community-based characteristic of marketing and hence its social relevance. Marketing usually does not advise until and unless it conducts research.

Marketing, then, "is a neutral methodology and social marketing is its adaptation to social imperatives" (Manoff 1987, p. 7). Almost more important than the methodology itself is the set of underlying ideas, which, as we shall see, can animate much more than a marketplace. The ideas are worth a fairly close look because of their congruence with, and relevance in, projects for social change.

First among these is the primacy of the consumer in all marketing decisions. Running a very close second is the concern with modifying, or creating new, behavior—not just with spreading product awareness, or even with purchase intentions. The consumer must buy a particular brand and usually, keep buying it, in the teeth of other options. Around this core, marketing clusters a way of analyzing a situation; making a product; and pricing, distributing, and promoting it. This is always seen to be happening in a free-choice arena.

At the very least, therefore, the product must be acceptably formulated. For instance, just any soap will not do merely because it happens to be a lump of sodium stereate. Its composition and form must offer the properties that the target consumer is known through research to favor. These must at least match and probably surpass the performance of other brands, in the consumer's estimation, and do it at a competitive price.

DEMAND: THE LIFEBLOOD OF MARKETING

When the marketing process comes up with the right mix of brand performance, competitive appeal, and price, there is a good chance of the brand generating demand. That is, consumers in sufficient number will want it and patronize it faithfully, having made a price-performance decision in its favor. This decision is the heart of marketing, and demand the lifeblood. The words "price," "performance," and "decision" therefore deserve a moment's reflection.

The brand's price should be as low as possible after trade-offs among consumer considerations, production costs, competitive action, and shareholder requirements. But price demanded is inseparable from "benefit" obtained by the consumer. Therefore the brand benefit must not only be real and verifiable, it must justify the brand's price. This almost always necessitates "adding value" to the benefit in the consumer's eyes. For instance, Brand X Biscuits may have an intrinsic food value, which makes for a logical enough offer. But consider how the brand's appeal would heighten if Pele, the great soccer player, were to avow his faith in it. In marketing, logic is not all—as it often is not in human decisions. Would that the typical slide sets and flipcharts of "development communications" bore witness to this truth!

So marketing communications are not so much a matter of scientific verities and infrangible reasoning as of persuasive presentation. The first stresses the process leading up to a desired conclusion, the second stresses the conclusion itself (not, "Brand X Biscuits are good because . . ." but, "They are good—Pele eats them!").

ADVERTISING AND PROMOTION

Marketing communications, as a term, is another way of saying advertising. Indispensable in creating demand, advertising is commercial mass persuasion. It is normally handled by advertising agencies, which therefore make a business of knowing the consumer best. The advertising plan identifies who shall be addressed with what messages, through which channels in pursuance of the marketing objectives. It is advertising that creates demand for ice-cream among the Eskimo and for instant coffee in such sanctuaries of real coffee as Brazil and South India.

Advertising is probably the centerpiece of what is called "promotion" in marketing. But there are other promotional tools that may become primary, depending on the situation: special price offers, merchandising, salesman and dealer incentive schemes, and the like.

Product distribution can often pose the main marketing challenge, in which case transport, or dealer and sales management become top-priority topics.

It should now be fairly plain how much more is involved in the marketing process than just haranguing the end consumer. Although the consumer is certainly the touchstone of all decisions, consumer behavior will stay unaltered unless the whole chain is supportive—from, say, in-house quality controllers and sales staff through to retailers and opinion-formers in the community. It is taken for granted that they will do so only in the purest self-interest. The marketing sciences (and budget) must provide the incentives.

It is also a decision in self-interest that moves the consumer in the ruthless democracy of the grocery store. Everything—product, price, promotion and the rest—exists to influence that decision.

UNREALITY IN THE REAL WORLD

All of this is a world away from the philosophies and methods of programs for social change. In this sphere of harsh reality, a peculiar unreality is everywhere. For instance, and to exaggerate only slightly, change in health practices is considered the ineluctable consequence of planting a health service in the community. When the intervention grows a mite more sophisticated, new behavior is seen to be a function of community "awareness," or of appropriate "education," which together generate community "participation." These beliefs contain lethal doses of half-truths. They are the equivalent of a marketer believing that a good product merely needs to be stocked in a shop to sell itself profitably, or that advertising of the brand is all that really deserves attention, never mind making a good product and distributing it well.

Although they may certainly constitute a program component, straightforward information, or teaching, by themselves, rarely cause lasting changes in behavior. Knowledge is a poor predictor of practice. It is possible for 90 percent of mothers in a Bangladesh community to play back correctly Seven Points to Remember about Oral Rehydration Salts—and for only 8 percent of them actually to use the salts. To be sure, there is more to it than just information/education; for example, the salts must be available. But even if no other factors were involved, it is naive to believe, as so many program staff still do, that informing and educating people is more than half the battle of transforming their behavior. This may be little or nothing of the battle because it ignores the whole subject of human resistance to change and the slightly aging but vigorous theories of cognitive dissonance. Human beings tend to block out information that conflicts with existing behavior, such as the cigarette smoker's refusal to identify with lung cancer statistics. Information/education that is resisted does not work.

And yet, how many millions of project dollars go into manuals, leaflets, radio programs, features and posters every month, all owing much more allegiance to a textbook than to a community's barriers and perceptions. How much more is poured into "education"—which too often turns out to be efforts that treat target audiences as if they were captive, attentive, and compliant classrooms, and message content as if it were a syllabus. They never are, of course.

IGNORED: THE PRICE-PERFORMANCE DECISION

All too seldom is any thought given to fashioning a "product" for a target group and any effort made to go beyond a list of facts as strategy to motivation of demand. Does "Breast is Best," for instance, and its detailing of the virtues of breastmilk, really do enough? Is it the best formulation to foster acceptance by a mother? Perhaps she admits the thought already, and the "product" here must serve quite different needs and difficulties (see the case study at the end of this chapter).

In growth monitoring and promotion (GMP) for child health, the "product" marketed could never be the growth chart, or the scales themselves. It must be "healthy growth." Airlines never advertise the air ticket, or their sales offices, though both are essential to travel. Instead they sell the Taj Mahal and the dreams of international travel. Only if the perceived value of healthy growth, in a mother's eyes, is higher than the perceived cost of monthly weighing will she participate in a GMP program for her child.

Water and sanitation programs cannot merely emphasize well, pumps, and latrines. What products will prompt and sustain proper utilization of it all? A service is not correctly used simply because it is there. A creative confection of fact is necessary, of the kind that transfigures lumps of sodium stereate into desirable (and desired) tablets of soap. Otherwise the right price-performance decision will not get taken in use of latrines, or garbage disposal.

Breast-feeding is not free. A mother pays an enormous performance price in a dozen different ways, from dealing with sore nipples and a sometimes disgruntled husband to coping with deep-seated feelings of inadequacy transferred to her perception of breastmilk quality. Unless the "social price" of such behavior is recognized, not enough will go into enhancing the value of the benefit.

More seriously, a medically correct but socially costly practice may be enthroned as the project goal, when "cheaper" behavior, more easily practiced, is available and could mean a more successful program. For instance, we may propose the boiling of water to a mother, when all that is feasible (and should therefore be the project goal) is covering domestic water receptacles.

OTHER DEADLY SINS OF BAD PLANNING

One of the most tragic of spectacles in social intervention is waste, especially when it is avoidable and honestly caused. An example is a program that seems to be using all channels to say everything to everybody. This is usually evidence of poor target group identification and lack of systematic analysis, both second nature in a marketing person. He or she asks instinctively and establishes, whose behavior(s) must change, how, and to what end. He or she then sees what must be said to whom, through what media. In the absence of this framework, other sins get committed. There is nothing, for instance, to prevent irrational stop-go activities—that suddenly do stop forever, well before enough good has been done.

Lack of target group focus leads to trouble in many areas, not the least of which is message design. An episode related by a Bahraini doctor will help make a series of relevant points. A student nurse was retailing the nutritional benefits of breast-feeding to a woman who had just delivered her first child, a son. The young mother listened politely but took in little. An older nurse now came over. "My child," she said to the mother, "breast-feeding will keep your son devoted to you all his life." Instantly, the woman was attentive, now drinking in the details purveyed by the younger nurse.

The story illustrates the importance of a design that respects message expression as much as message content and that responds creatively to target group needs, perceptions and culture. In marketing, the importance of message expression and form is carried to million dollar points of exaggeration. It is too little, or wrongly observed in programs for social change; yet it is message expression that is the ailing spot in message design, because there is never a shortage of expertise on technically correct content.

There are in fact, experts who will insist on transmitting a whole filigree of related messages, without any of which the story would be "incomplete," or "misleading." And so one gets that hopeless dispersal of message, the twelve (or ten, or twenty-five) health points broadcast as thirty-second radio spots over three months. This is the lack of concentration that rules out adequate repetition, cost effective reinforcement, and, ultimately, easy acceptance. This is the illusion of communications.

DISTRIBUTION AND COMPETITION NEGLECTED

Frequently neglected in social programs, but always planned for by the social marketer, is the issue of distribution. Poor manning of, let us say, health and family planning centers is viewed with ritual concern, but less than panic by program managers. But the centers redistribute their "product" and push its "sales." Leaving them to their own devices however briefly is as absurd as manufacturing a product and advertising it, while allowing the shops to go unstocked. Panic is in order. But it is so infrequent that distribution is often to be blamed for failure in development programs.

Competition, very obvious in the marketplace, is too easily disregarded in the behavioral change transaction. Yet it is very much a factor. It is present as the other options that are available to the housewife whom we would, for instance, like to see at the immunization post. She may indeed succumb to the most intense competition of all, the inertial drag of the past that causes her to do nothing. Or, her resolve may evaporate in the heat of competing domestic demands. Competition, then, complicates adoption of recommended behavior. It adds to performance cost. Its reality emphasizes once again the importance of enhancing the appeal of, and facilitating, recommended practices.

There are other sins that marketing could never risk committing because it would court disaster: failures to monitor and evaluate, to innovate and build up critical mass, to use cutting-edge tactics and launch a product range on the back of a success, and so forth.

A HAZY BOTTOM LINE VERSUS A PROVEN FRAMEWORK

This is perhaps the point to be grasped. Errors in marketing show up unmistakably as a fearful bloodletting—declining market share, financial losses, and so on. The marketplace is a Roman circus teaching unforgettable lessons. Theory, shoddy thinking and planning, false theories, and irrelevancies get put to the sword of profit and loss. This is how the experimental and empirical framework of marketing experience grows and toughens.

It is different in the fields of social intervention. The resident culture here is pioneering and investment in change. It is gentle with failure, even if failures were simple to identify and their causes easy to pinpoint, which they are not. Hence error may be compounded, not checked. Here is an area of hazy bottom lines and an abounding lack of widely accepted indicators. Here then, is also the need for a steely conceptual framework that will guide us past waste and lack of experience. The programs grow more numerous, the failures must be corrected, the successes raise expectations, the donors of development resources demand greater accountability.

SOCIAL MARKETING: A UNIFYING FRAMEWORK

Social marketing could be such a framework. For one thing, it is quintessentially a methodology that responds to human need and desires. It is social marketing that forms when all the considerations of product and price, competition and distribution, promotion, cost, and profit condense and come correctly together—not, this time, in the market for soft drinks but in the life-and-death arena, say, of child survival, or AIDS. There is evidence that it works. There is even a certain illogicality in rejecting it as a resource. When we do, we push aside something born in the exacting and costly wedlock of science and the marketplace. We reach instead for a novice-crafted tool. Often, it starts being fashioned when a project is approved, yet previous experience is eschewed. Social marketing could provide at least as effective a preparation of, and reflex in, program technicians as economics, medicine, anthropology, and journalism, those hallowed disciplines of development.

Of course, social marketing is no magic wand. It is in fact far more complex and exacting than commercial marketing. It is usually proposing new and demanding behavior in unpleasant fields, flying in the face of peer group resistance. There is little consumer pleasure, or verifiable success, to imprint a particular practice and make it behavior—that is to say, better hygiene does not rapidly reward one, like a headache pill, fizzy drink, or electronic gadget. To be successful, social marketing must win far greater battles: It cannot be satisfied with 4 or 5 percent shifts in market share that are the triumphs of the consumer goods field. Social marketing aims at 100 percent conversion to its propositions.

Greater, then, the reason for employing the methodologies that marketing has validated. If nothing else, marketing systems provide social action with a simple checklist for analysis and planning that ensures greater rigor of method and thought. Implementing social marketing approaches guards against the ad-hocism and bright ideas so often sanctified as strategy.

SOME SUCCESSES

Elsewhere, there will be better examples. But, to provide a brief sketch in the interests of good order, a social marketing approach used in the Indonesian Nutrition Education and Behavior Change Project yielded good results, if on small scale. Using volunteer health workers, specially designed training materials, focus group research, and mass media, the project showed improvement in the nutrition status of target children through the use of communication/education alone. There was no "feeding" component in the project. Domestically available foodstuffs were made full use of and the communication/education cost was kept low.

In Egypt, a diarrhoea management social marketing program used mass media systematically for the first time. This alone increased the use of oral rehydration salts from 1 percent to nearly 70 percent of the diarrhoea episodes in the researched region, and in less than two years time. In Brazil, a professionally approached effort in breast-feeding promotion quickly yielded changes on a national scale. In Colombia and Turkey, the action to immunize children acquired national momentum, attracting resources from the armed forces and religious establishment, increasing coverage many times over.

PROBLEMS OF THE FUTURE

Oddly enough, there are those who regard social marketing as the devil's own work, or at least something slightly ignoble. It is supposed to cause a "vertical" imposition of rigid ideas, evolved with no consultation of the community. Or, it operates at an unfair "subliminal" level.

The "subliminal" phenomenon has been debunked too often to be taken seriously. As for the rest, clearly the messenger is being mistaken for the message. Because marketing traffics mostly in products and services often considered trivial, the process becomes colored in some eyes with the same candy stripes. But it is social marketing that places the individual and the community at the center of its world. It is much more observant of local culture and individual perceptions than what often passes for "education" and certainly than conventional medical prescription.

There is little that is arcane about the process. On its heart there is carved, if anything, a fairly simple thought: The community must be credited with common sense and the individual with the freedom to choose. They will decide. If our inputs into their decisionmaking are wrong, the decision will act against them and the project we are supporting.

THE NATIONAL BREAST-FEEDING PROGRAM: BRAZIL

A project that attempted to apply social marketing ideas and methods in a real-life situation is the national breast-feeding program in Brazil.

The Nature and Scope of the Program

The origins of this breast-feeding program go back, as they do pretty much everywhere, to the missionary but scattered work of a few doctors and health administrators. In Brazil, this was happening noticeably in the mid to late 1970s. The efforts found a direction and measure of cohesion when the Brazilian Ministry of Health, with the collaboration of UNICEF, resolved to take up the issue.

From early on, the action was seen as an intervention, which, with knowledge and experience, would systematize into a wider, better-based program, which in time would become a routine in Brazil's infrastructures. That is, the program components were meant to phase into the normal public health, legal surveillance, or educational systems of the country and its communications environment. So the activities had a starting point. But they were planned to endure because, of course, there will always be new Brazilian babies and mothers needing support to breast-feed them.

The goal is to save as many children, wherever they are in Brazil, as soon as possible, from the mortal perils of premature termination of breast-feeding. From the start, therefore, the scope of the program was national. This was greatly daring in a country not much smaller than all of Western Europe and, even without the Amazon forests, nearly twice the size of India. Its population accounts for a third of all Latin America: 130 million souls.

The program plan emphasized urban areas because the decline in breast-feeding is much more an affliction of the towns and cities, where two-thirds of Brazil lives anyway. It also emphasized the lowest income groups, because it is here that bottle-feeding does its worst, the mischief being compounded by insalubrious environments, inadequate medical services and nutrition, lack of clean water and health education, and so on. This means that the program's target group numbered some 70 million people.

The expansive scale of it all underlined the need for a central plan, but also for highly decentralized implementation. As will be seen, not only were four ministries involved, but numerous state secretariats as well, in various sectors of twenty states. Also, four major government health agencies and at least two nongovernmental institutions, one of which was the Catholic church, became closely concerned.

Problem Analysis and Program Goals

The goal of the Brazilian Health Ministry's program was to improve the nutritional status of children below one year of age. This is directly associated with the nutritional status of the pregnant woman, exclusive breast-feeding of the child for an adequate period, and appropriate supplementary feeding. So, the specific program objectives were to increase the prevalence and duration of exclusive breast-feeding (the latter for at least four to six months) and educate vulnerable groups on how the mother and the child should be fed.

Figure 23.1 depicts a hypothesis of how various forces act among various institutions and groups to frustrate breast-feeding. Action that would make those forces supportive of breast-feeding would, therefore, constitute the elements of an action program. A precis of research findings by target group follows, along with the program objectives they led to. (The numbering matches the numbering of the boxes in Figure 23.1.)

1. *The doctor.* His attitude and advice were, in the main, unhelpful—a result of faulty educational preparation, the activities of the makers of breastmilk substitutes and a lack of breastmilk promotion. He was immensely influential on the mother, the family/community, the health system, the hospital, and industry. Therefore, the program attempted to "educate" the doctor and professional bodies, involve them in specific aspects of the program, and modify medical curricula suitably.

2. *The health services.* These systems and the training of health personnel had left the mother and the personnel themselves very poorly informed on maternal lactation. The network provided an ideal medium to educate and train the mother. So the program was designed to transform the health system into a better informational/motivational vehicle to the mother.

3. *The hospital.* Hospital and obstetrical practices, which could do much to affect lactation physiology and set the mother off well or badly on the road to subsequent breast-feeding, were doing virtually nothing. They negated the wishes of the mother who arrived there, on the whole, correctly disposed. Therefore, the program aimed to move all decisionmaking and implementing groups to set up in maternity hospitals and wards the attitudes and systems that foster breast-feeding (including the right obstetrical approaches and "rooming-in").

4 and 5. *Industry.* This area needed to be looked at in two ways—as the sector making breastmilk substitutes and as industry in general. The former negatively influenced the doctor, health services, hospital, and community (through publicity, distribution

FIGURE 23.1 Principal Target Groups and Forces Acting against Breast-feeding.

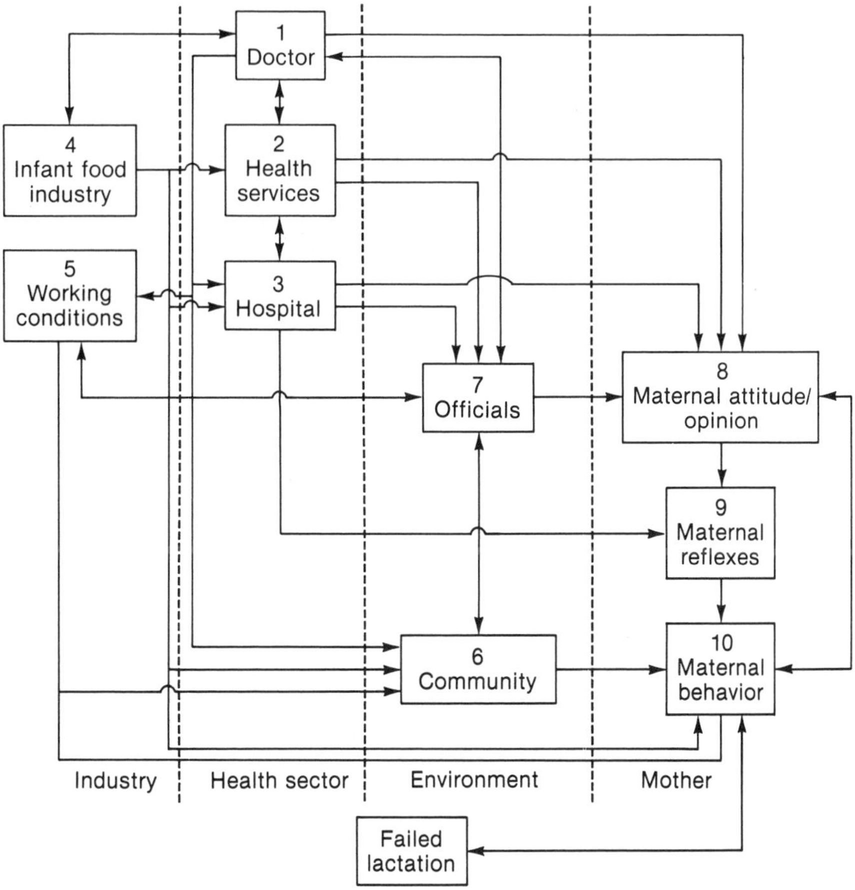

Source: Gerson da Cunha, UNICEF, Brasilia

of milk samples, etc.). Industry, by and large, failed to provide the working mother with what she needed to nurse her baby (leave rules, job security, creches, etc.), despite helpful provisions in the law of the land. Therefore, the program tried to work with government and industry to stop all undesirable marketing/promotional practices, and institute the right facilities for working mothers (adopt/enforce the UNICEF/WHO Code, institute suitable legislative/executive action).

6. *Community.* Here, prime importance devolved on the family, especially the father, older women, and neighborhood/other opinion-formers. This group was as important as prenatal instruction, which few mothers got anyway. The program built in action to mobilize the community in support of the mother in breast-feeding.

7. *Official groups.* The right policy, decisions, and funding were crucial for anything to happen at all. Of major importance was, of course, the health sector at central, state, and municipal levels. Therefore, the program envisaged widely spreading awareness of the problem and its causes, advocating what needs to be done over the short term and long term by official groups.

8, 9, and 10. *The mother.* The pregnant and nursing mother's information level and mental set, her self-confidence, and the way she was "processed" by the health and hospital system—all of this combined against her wishes and physiology. The doctor, the law, the community, and the environment did not help her. She would have been far from passive if she knew what was happening to hurt her child—and what she needed to do in response. So a key component in the program was the effort to motivate and reassure the mother and train her to breast-feed correctly.

The main components of the program were therefore

a. an educational and motivational campaign directed at mothers as the primary target group, and fathers, medical/health professionals, opinion formers in the community, and decisionmakers in government

b. suitable modification of maternity hospital systems and practices in health centers dealing with pregnant women

c. provision of facilities for pregnant and nursing mothers (especially those employed) within the community and where they work

d. fostering the drafting and observance of appropriate legislation, or a code of practice for manufacturers of breastmilk substitutes

e. association of the right action with the campaign to improve nutrition of the pregnant mother and weaning child.

Probably the most important feature of the program was that it was comprehensive—it tackled all the major actionable causes of the problem. Each cause could be determining, each interacted with others. Therefore, all had to be addressed systematically.

Program Implementation and Strategies

Earlier on, UNICEF created an audiovisual on breast-feeding for the National Food and Nutrition Institute, the program's coordinating agency. It posed the problem, its consequences, and causes and advocated a multisectoral approach to its solution. The production was aimed at decisionmaking levels in government and meant not to educate but to trigger a program. A screening to the ministers of health and social welfare resulted in a decision to launch the program.

Mass Media "Launch." The program was launched by a national campaign over TV, radio, and in the press. It lasted forty-five days, using time/space in media held by government. No campaign of this type had ever received such intensive support. The notional value of the campaign was well over US$3 million. It was used over nearly 100 TV stations, reaching 13.5 million households and 600 radio stations, covering some 20 million homes. Press advertisements and messages on lottery tickets, telephone/electricity/water bills, and bank statements all over the country helped sensitize and alert the public and the government—which was, of course, the main objective of the launch. All over Brazil it touched off thinking and action that prepared the ground for further program strategies.

Program Coordination and Management. The Health Ministry created a National Working Group to promote and coordinate the program. The group comprised nominees of various ministries, NGOs, professional bodies, and national institutions, in several concerned sectors. State governments and territories formed similar groups to run and coordinate their own programs.

Doctors and Health Professionals. The Brazilian Pediatric Society involved its 14,000 members in Brazil (and 28,000 colleagues in Latin America) through mailings. A slide set for doctors was reproduced, seminars, lectures, conferences, and contacts with mass media were undertaken at the national and state level. The Brazilian Nutrition Society supported the program nationally and, through international contacts, abroad. Eight states introduced breast-feeding into medical curricula.

Health Services. All states undertook training programs for health workers. More than forty workshops were held in twenty-three of Brazil's twenty-six states within a year of the program's start. Over 100,000 health workers attended training events lasting ten to fifteen hours. An evaluation of the training showed good results.

The Hospital. Rooming-in began progressively to arrive in government/private hospitals and the vast majority of the country's states now enjoy the amenity. In Recife, only two of the city's eight main maternity hospitals had rooming-in facilities before the program. Now all of them do. New government norms for construction/operation of health services specify rooming-in.

Breastmilk Substitutes. The leading manufacturer committed itself to observance of the WHO/UNICEF Code governing marketing of these products and set up a group to investigate/check infringement.

The Working Woman. Existing laws were studied and surveys conducted. Preliminary findings suggested the need for greater awareness among women of what the laws provide. One state showed that industry can be encouraged to observe the law more closely. A monitoring group was set up centrally.

The Community. The ministry funded the creation of mothers' and community groups to instruct nursing mothers. State-level organizations and university students participated actively. In eight states, 160 mothers' groups operated with La Leche League involvement. A bimonthly bulletin supported this activity. Some 20,000 volunteers in the Brazilian mass education movement were exposed to orientation. More than twenty voluntary organizations participated in the program through the state-level working groups. The Catholic and other denominational churches actively supported the program, especially in the South and Recife, in the Northeast.

The Communications Factor

Communications were a key aspect of the program's strategy and implementation. Communications were involved in all of the program's main components. Their task was, of course, to inform and educate. What is perhaps more important, they needed to help motivate attitudinal and behavioral changes among defined groups and to create a new public perception of breast-feeding. In a word, communications had to promote breast-feeding.

The Target Groups. The primary target was all Brazilian mothers in the lower socioeconomic strata (from a family income of about three minimum salaries down). But other important target groups, as well as the communications tasks involved, from 1 to 10 above, are listed in Figure 23.1.

The Message. The National Working Group believed from the start that program communications should, if possible, develop around a central basic theme, so that resources might be maximized through all activities and material being mutually reinforcing. But around what theme?

From early in the program, the working group consulted with a leading Brazilian advertising agency. This type of skill, it was thought, needed to be associated as early as possible with program thinking. Through the agency, small-sample, qualitative research was commissioned to generate and interpret leads on a mother's attitudes and motivations in breast-feeding. Apart from helping message design, it was felt that the study might also inform design of the larger quantitative benchmark study then in preparation.

The method selected was the in-depth, unstructured interview lasting between one and four hours each. The investigator asked no questions, but merely sought clarifications and unobtrusively helped the interview along. The sample comprised thirty mothers with children from four to ten months of age. Family income averaged 3.5 minimum salaries and less. Half the sample consisted of women who worked outside the home. The main conclusions were these:

1. All the women had a basically positive attitude toward breast-feeding and doing so for extended periods of time. Even those who had not breast-fed had a near perfect "image" of the practice.
2. Mothers lacked information and reassurance on breast-feeding. This used to come from the family and community; for a variety of reasons, it no longer does.
3. Initial difficulties with breast-feeding seemed to originate from two types of problems: psychological problems (feelings of inadequacy, rejection by the child, family, or husband, etc.); and problems arising from a lack of information about the practice of breast-feeding resulting in ideas of weak milk, lack of milk, problems of technique.
4. A mother's insecurity was increased by the normal difficulties encountered during breast-feeding. They confirmed her feelings of inadequacy and stirred up both guilt and anxiety. She now badly needed the reassurance and support that the traditional society once provided.
5. She sought this support from her doctor or health center—and did not get it. In the end, because he really had no solution, the doctor prescribed bottle-feeding. So social dynamics were reinforced by medical authority.
6. To be effective, a program should consistently provide information, helpful thoughts (like suggesting that it is suction at the

nipple that is the basis for successful breast-feeding), and reassurance (which passes on the idea that virtually all mothers can breast-feed, that there is no such thing as weak milk, etc.).

7. Therefore, campaigns that extol the romance of breast-feeding and simply say, for instance, that breastmilk is "love, nutrition, and protection" could indeed be counterproductive. They would continuously dismay a mother afflicted with the normal little problems of breast-feeding. The idealized presentation would confirm her own sense of inadequacy. By increasing her anxiety, it would help inhibit her all-important lactation reflexes, which, in the end, are psychosomatic.

These basic ideas were applied to all aspects of the communications task and all materials, from flipcharts to TV and radio commercials. The advertising agency working on the mass media proposal, CBBA Publicidade, Sao Paulo, came up with two approaches that, in their view, deserved pretesting. The two themes were "Breast-feeding—Every Mother Can! Stay with It!" and "Breast-feeding—the Six Months Worth a Lifetime!" A group discussion method, with a sample of fifty carefully selected target group mothers, was used for the pretest. The end judgment was that a combination of both themes would work better than either one on its own. Interestingly, the pretest discussions bore out the validity of the earlier, qualitative research: the need to demystify breast-feeding.

The TV/radio commercials, of thirty seconds each, presented the realities of breast-feeding, but through the testimonials of leading TV and film personalities, such as the captain of Brazil's World Cup soccer team. These personages, while candidly admitting difficulties ("I wasn't sure I could" and "Look, I was a bit jealous of my own son"), urged mothers to persist, as they themselves had done. The payoff was always "Breast-feeding—the Six Months Worth a Lifetime."

One interesting outcome of the pretest was the use of billboards. "We've reached a point," said a mother in one group discussion, "when we feel shy to breast-feed in public. Why don't you put up a big poster, out on the streets, showing a bare-breasted woman breast-feeding? It would give us all heart."

The Channels of Communications. The scale and nature of the problem in Brazil required the use of face-to-face as well as mass communications. The classic task for interpersonal contact is in training and informing health professionals and auxiliaries, also, in helping these cadres address mothers in various situations in the health center and hospital. Such contact also comes into its own in the mother-to-mother type dialogue visualized by the La Leche League technique.

This contact, so important in behavioral change, was the bedrock in a sense, on which the communications plan to the Brazil Breast-feeding Program was founded. Hence, the importance of the channels provided by the health services and by the women's and church organizations, the volunteer and semiofficial groups, above all by the mothers' breast-feeding groups with which the program began increasingly to work. But these highly specific and intensive personal communications needed, and got, the "umbrella" and facilitation that mass media provide, not just as journalism but also as advertising of breast-feeding.

The decision to use mass media was taken despite the high cost of time/space and of the professional skills required to create appropriate material. The National Working Group saw the obvious virtues of the enormous speed, reach, and low cost-per-contact of the mass media. They also appreciated that TV and radio were the only direct route to the target mother, who was otherwise encircled by barriers of bias, misinformation, and ignorance. They could reliably deliver a repetitive, high-frequency message—something essential in the attitudinal and behavior modifications intended by the program.

The problem of high cost was partially solved when CBBA Publicidade declared itself disposed to work at virtually no cost to the program (the firm was declared "Agency of the Year" in 1983 by the Brazilian Advertising Association). Rede Globo, the country's main TV/radio network, offered free time. Both offers were good for a two-year program. These offers were, of course, sought. They did not suddenly materialize. The audiovisual was a valuable instrument in mobilizing this type of support. It is worth noting that in the cities, say, of Sao Paulo and Rio de Janeiro, radio covers over 80 percent and 70 percent, respectively, of our target groups; in Recife, 60 percent. TV covers between 50 and 60 percent of the group in these cities. Rede Globo, the network that first aired the program's spots, attracts some 75 percent of evening prime time audiences, when 75 percent of Brazil's TV sets are switched on (1.5 sets per family, on a national average).

In the first ten months of airing, just Rede Globo's GRPs (a measure of campaign weight and reach) were the equivalent of what would be used for a medium-to-heavy campaign for a national brand of cigarettes. Nearly 80 percent of target group mothers in fifteen cities had been reached. Some six million target group women each had a mean of 150 opportunities to see the campaign messages. By mid-1983, Brazil's major TV and radio networks were all running program material free. The value for just the TV time donated between August 1982 and May 1983 was something over US$700,000. The value of production and agency services (at normal market rates) was US$280,000. So nearly a million dollars worth of advertising value was bought for US$22,000, the out-of-pocket expenses that the program actually paid. Nearly a billion "opportunities to see" (OTS) were created.

Materials were created and produced for other specific tasks and target groups by the Ministry of Health and other government agencies. These included

- Booklets for education of mothers: 1.5 million copies.
- Prototype flipchart for health workers: 5,000 copies.
- Two manuals for community leaders: 70,000 copies.
- Pamphlet for doctors: 20,000 copies.
- Slide–sound set for medical students and health sector personnel.
- Set of slides with commentary script and bimonthly bulletin for mothers' groups.
- Bulletin (periodical) for pediatricians.

Three state-level photographic contests, and one at national level, were run and the award-winning photographs exhibited in public locales. Innumerable articles, features and papers ran in the press and were distributed. The program and breast-feeding as a specific topic was featured in fifteen national and international medical/health conferences in Brazil and one international congress abroad over two years.

Six hundred primary and middle-school teachers were trained in breast-feeding as a school subject. This is now an item in the school curricula of at least fifteen states.

Monitoring and Evaluation

Evaluation was built into program design. A benchmark survey was conducted before the program was launched, in two cities (Recife, in the northeast, and Sao Paulo, in the south-central region), using a sample of some 1,000 mothers and 200 health professionals. A wide range of demographic, infrastructural, information, attitude, and behavior baselines were set. The study was professionally conducted.

A matching activity was planned for a time when the program would have run two or three years. It was hoped to measure changes, if any, in breast-feeding practices and derive a better understanding of the factors at work both in breast-feeding and its premature termination. At the time of printing, the evaluation survey had indeed been conducted, but the findings had not yet been published.

But even before this formal and systematic check, straws in the wind were soon noticeable. Doctors handling postnatal and outpatient clinics reported more breast-feeding mothers and fewer feeding bottles on view, longer-duration nursing as well. The press, radio and TV originated their own material, more and more plentifully, with no prompting by immediate program action. Actresses and social personalities, once always shown with their newborn and a feeding bottle, now appear breast-feeding their babies whenever the media notice the event. Television interviewed the captain of the national women's volleyball team on her reasons for taking her baby along for a match in Buenos Aires: Breast-feeding was the main one. A leading manufacturer of lingerie asked for and got permission to feature the campaign theme in its advertising for a new brassiere adapted to the needs of nursing mothers. Brazil's vast medical assistance system modified its criteria for recognizing hospitals; rooming-in facilities now score points where they once did not. Even more numerously, government and private sector organizations are building, and seeking advice on, creches at places of work.

All this apart, a study in Sao Paulo city, using a thousand child sample, was conducted in 1984–85 by a group led by Dr. Carlos Monteiro, of the Health Department, Sao Paulo State. Results were compared with a survey of breast-feeding behavior run in 1973–74.

Increases in the duration and practice of breast-feeding were recorded in all income groups. According to the report (American Journal of Public Health, August 1987), the results serve to show that (a) urbanization, by itself, need not menace breast-feeding and (b) the declining trend in breast-feeding in the city seems to have been stayed and reversed.

The single new and major factor introduced into the researched situation was Brazil's national breast-feeding program.

SUMMARY

Brazil's breast-feeding program was an example of marketing analysis and planning in several ways. For one thing, the goal was behavioral and consumer-based. In essence, the operation began with asking what mothers should do and why they were not doing it. The answers determined the "product" offered for adoption by them (confidence in themselves and the quality of their breastmilk), after consideration of the performance cost involved. It also fixed how the product would be distributed (through the health network and professionals, community, organizations, etc.) and promoted, as well as how the competitive forces of branded products would be handled. Most important, the perspective was long term.

Before this approach was brought to bear on the problem, there had in fact been quite a lot going on. It is not as if Brazil's health authorities sat on their hands, watching their infants fall. But the efforts were characterized by the familiar faults of such action: dedicated physicians addressed mothers at clinics and hospitals, their colleagues at congresses and through professional channels; newspaper articles, TV interviews, women's groups, car stickers, and cinema slides were mobilized. But it was all fitful, unconvergent, slight, and tired too soon. Action schedules were fixed by goodwill, not by plan. Action content was concerned merely with what audiences got to know, not how this would influence target behavior among mothers. Then, of course, vastly inadequate resources were applied.

Interestingly, the pro–breast-feeding effort received greater funding and attention, only to counter the marketing effect of milk powder promotion. We might well wonder if the same resources would have been applied *to market breast-feeding*, as distinct from defending it from marketing attack.

In the end, this may be the point: Priority groups—the deprived, needy and unreached—suffer from the marketing success in their neighborhoods of fast-foods, chewing gum, and soft drinks. It would be useful to make the sweeping inroads that such products have made among people at "poverty level" and below. And yet, there is a tragic lack of technology to market among these groups such matters as better nutrition, hygiene, and health practices. In the absence of this technology, the case of these essential changes may be going by default.

Appendix

SEYMOUR H. FINE

Rutgers, The State University of New Jersey

Just as the manuscript for this book was completed, I learned that its predecessor, *The Marketing of Ideas and Social Issues* (MISI), cited occasionally in these pages, would soon be out of print. Therefore, two excerpts from MISI are included in this appendix as background material. The first is a product typology that places social products within the broader context of product offerings. The second is from MISI's chapter on social price, background for the present Chapter 9. It is hoped this appendix renders the present book more self-contained.

A BROADENED TYPOLOGY OF PRODUCTS

The broadened scope of marketing implies that product offerings could be anything considered to be of value by the parties to the transaction. What are the actual *items* that are marketed? What *"things"* do individuals exchange? Quite apart from the common characteristic shared by all commodities, that is, that they must have perceived value to the participants, how do different offerings compare, one with another? If virtually anything and everything is subject to negotiated exchange, it is useful to categorize the enlarged domain of products in some orderly arrangement. That is the undertaking of this section.

A typological model is developed and proposed as an integrative framework for the analysis of all types of offerings. (The author begs license for using the term typology rather loosely. Strictly defined, a typology must provide exhaustive and mutually exclusive categories. The model proposed here somewhat violates that definition and hence might more accurately be called a "quasi-typology.") It serves as a basis for analysis for those particular commodities highlighted in this book by pinpointing the position that concepts have within the entire gamut of products.

Even with conventional goods, a model that classifies product types is useful in framing, analyzing and comparing marketing strategy, in suggesting new venture directions and as a benchmark for assessing one's own product mix against that of the competition. However, for such a model to be useful, it must be sufficiently broad to encompass the entire set of choices—the "evoked set" facing consumers. That set of alternatives contains not only goods and services but concepts as well. Our typology permits marketers to position products against competing offerings, including those constituting exchange types different from their own.

Kotler (1973) was an early proponent of the notion of classifying nontraditional products:

> A typology of marketing activity can also be constructed on the basis of the product marketed. Under the broadened concept of marketing, the product is no longer restricted to commercial goods and services. . . . A product classification of marketing consists of goods marketing, service marketing, organization marketing, person marketing, place marketing and idea marketing. (p. 51)

The Typology. The model is based on the assumption that all goods, services and concepts (products) may be classified on two dimensions—the profit-making nature of the transaction and the degree of tangibility of the item.

Profit-making versus Nonprofit Marketing. An obvious point of departure is provided by a dichotomy of all exchange processes as being either for profit, or not for profit. This concept enjoys wide usage and denotes whether or not the seller in the marketing process intends to gain a profit over costs in the transaction. (The legal requirement is, of course, that an institution be incorporated as a nonprofit organization and/or obtain federal tax exemption status from the Internal Revenue Service.) The notion ignores consideration of profits accruing to the purchaser. Thus, a transaction in which the idea of private religion is adopted is profitable to the marketer, for example, "Reverend Ike." But here, as in all market transactions, profit in the form of psychological utility to the purchaser is usually omitted from the definition, except perhaps by implication. If the case were otherwise, that is if nonpecuniary profits entered into account, then there would be no such concept as a nonprofit transaction; all exchanges would be considered profit-making. For an exchange takes place if and only if, all parties benefit or "profit" as a result of the exchange. A blood donor profits financially if paid in cash for his or her blood; if a volunteer, the compensation takes the form of personal satisfaction, which is surely beneficial or profitable to the donor.

In the present treatment accepted usage will be followed and a transaction will be considered profit-making only if it is characterized by the seller's intent to obtain monetary profit. That actual profit might not materialize is incidental. The situation calls to mind a notice hanging on an office wall, stating: "This is a nonprofit organization; it was not intended to be, but became so due to conditions beyond our control." Although clever, the remark is nevertheless definitionally inconsistent, for a nonprofit organization is one that does not intend to earn a profit on its transactions (it might profit, for example, from investments). On the other hand, an organization is considered profit-making if such intent is evident, whether or not profit accrues, or loss (negative profit) is suffered. This affords an entirely workable distinction to determine if a transaction is profit making.

A Tangible-Abstract Product Dimension. The second dimension to be used in the model measures transactions along a tangible-abstract continuum. If a tangible good is involved, the exchange is concrete; if the "product" is an idea or a cause, the transaction is abstract. Both bicycles and birth-control information are products to be marketed; the former is a tangible good, while the latter is an abstract idea. This reasoning is not altered by the fact that birth-control information is usually associated with actual products, such as condoms, foams and so on. Even among concrete products, some are more abstract than others. A home fire alarm system is a tangible product, but it is inextricably tied to the abstract idea of safety.

For the sake of the typology, the continuous tangible-abstract spectrum is categorized into four classes, standard practice in research methodology; one converts internally scaled variables into ordinal or nominal classes to meet particular analytic needs. Here, the need is simply to create a manageably small number of categories.

The Matrix. Combination of the two-category profit dimension with the categorized tangible-abstract dimension yields the matrix shown in Table A.1, in which several dozen illustrative exchanges are listed. The list is by no means exhaustive; nor are its entries proposed as the best examples. The reader will no doubt call to mind more creative choices; the selections are merely representative and not all will be discussed in the text.

The top row lists exchanges for which no profit to the seller was intended to accrue; the bottom row lists exchanges in which profit was the principal motivation. The first column takes in tangible commodities, the second column considers services rendered, the third column covers ideas and the fourth column lists causes or social issues.

TABLE A.1 A Typology of Products

Tangible Product	Service	Idea	Issue or Cause
Nonprofit			
(1) Consumer cooperatives Girl Scout cookies Salvation Army store Blood donations Military base store Water Goods made by the disabled Pets from ASPCA CARE packages	(2) Library Post Office Chamber of Commerce Museum, Zoo Red Cross Public health care Higher education Boys Town Underwriters laboratories TVA State park Toll road Better Business Bureau Mass transit Consumer's Union YMCA, YWCA Public broadcasting	(3) Physical fitness Seat belt use Value of education Value of health Military recruiting Scouting Politics Easter seals American Cancer Society Marriage Family planning Two-dollar bill Peace Corps Fund-raising	(4) Child abuse Malnutrition Speeding Smoking Littering Pollution Civil rights Product safety Metric system Religion Voter registration Energy conservation Fair housing Population control Forest fires
Profit-making			
(5) All merchandise Blood bank (paid) Investments in real estate, securities, and commodities	(6) Country club Travel Insurance Performing arts Private health care Rental space Health spa Fashion designing Smokenders[a] Utilities Advertising agency Home improvements Spectator sports	(7) A fashion design Credit purchasing Legalized gambling Franchising Private branding Patents	(8) A fashion trend Fluoridation Smokenders[b] Recycling wastes Free enterprise Tourism Private religion, e.g., "Rev. Ike" Buy union label

Source: Fine (1981, p. 29).

[a] Service, help clients stop smoking.

[b] Cause, alleviating smoke pollution.

Examples of items appropriate to cell (1), nonprofit tangibles, include purchases made at a consumer cooperative or in stores operated by charities such as the Salvation Army. Voluntary blood contributions are nonprofit tangibles too; however if the donor is paid, the exchange is profit making and belongs in cell (5). Public goods such as those disposed of by the General Services Administration could also have been listed in cell (1).

Cell (2) depicts nonprofit services rendered by such institutions as libraries, post offices, YMCAs, chambers of commerce, museums, the Red Cross and so on. Offerings of nonprofit health care organizations also fall into this category, as do those of universities and Boys Town.

Innovative ideas affecting personal life-styles of individuals belong in cell (3), provided they originate without the profit motive. These include physical fitness, use of seat belts, boy and girl scouting, military recruiting and the value of education. The furtherance of a political campaign (party or candidate) is an idea to be adopted and hence belongs in this cell. Fund raisers market the idea that a cash contribution should be made, the amount of cash being the price for adoption of the idea.

Cell (4), nonprofit social causes, includes campaigns designed to ameliorate child abuse, speeding, malnutrition, smoking, littering, forest fires, pollution; the list is long indeed. One may add the exchange of information on civil rights, product safety, the metric system, religion, voter registration, energy conservation and so on.

Cell (5) designates profit-making exchanges of tangible products—food, clothing, automobiles and so on—probably the largest proportion of commercial transactions. A share of stock representing part ownership in a corporation is included here, as are real estate and commodity investments.

Cell (6) lists profit-making services such as those offered by travel agencies, insurance companies, purveyors of the performing arts and any items from cell (2) that bear the intent of profit: private nursing homes, day-care centers and so forth. The service of providing space for which rent is paid is also listed there.

In cell (7), one example of an idea marketed by a profit-making organization may be seen in a new fashion design, say, by Christian Dior. While this firm markets a design service to the apparel industry cell (6), at the same time it initiates styles sought by devotees of fashionable dress. These are matters that surely affect the life-styles of these people and being profit inspired, they have a place in cell (7). When adoption becomes widespread, producers of fashion apparel quickly capitalize on the popularization of such style trends cell (8) for *their* own profit. Similar cycles are followed by patents and other creative commodities.

The idea sold by Smokenders, a profit-making firm, could belong in cell (6); however it deserves a place in cell (8) as well, when one considers the current feeling that smoking is harmful not only to the smoker, but to those nearby and hence to society. Another cell (8) product is found among the various schemes for recycling waste materials. Such causes as free enterprise and tourism in America are profit motivated and also are classed as cell (8) exchanges. To find additional cell (8) illustrations one may peruse columns one and two, for suggestions of institutions that, while marketing goods and services, might also promote societal welfare in the process. As an example, a chemical firm selling fluorides to the municipal water company market, can be construed as a profit-making organization espousing the social cause of fluoridation. The same may be said for a marketer of pollution-control systems to industry.

Gray Areas in the Model. The assignment of most exchange types to the various cells is relatively straightforward, but some designations require stretching the imagination or indeed arbitrary placement. Thus, mass transit is a service rendered, yet it is an idea in the private interest that sometimes erupts as a controversial issue. When an Indian family adopted Mrs. Gandhi's vasectomy program, did such submission constitute purchase of the tangible economic incentives offered by the government? Was it the adoption of the idea of fewer children? Or were people motivated by societal benefits of population control, a public issue? A donation of one's blood without monetary remuneration, say to the Red Cross, presents an interesting type of exchange. Here, the consumer adopts a cell (3) idea marketed by an agency, that it is a good thing to donate blood. In this case the blood itself is not the product; it is the price for the idea. If unpaid, a blood donation is a barter of blood in exchange for the idea. On the other hand, if the donor is paid in cash, the exchange falls into cell (5), the sale of a tangible product, blood.

Straightforward categorization is always difficult when one tries to classify human phenomena; apologias are always in order. Hunt (1976) for example, stated that his scheme does not "imply that reasonable people cannot disagree as to which cell (in his model) is most appropriate for each issue or particular piece of research" (p. 23). One may add that disagreement itself enhances appreciation of a concept. The inevitable presence of a typology's gray areas does not detract from its overall utility.

The typology highlights the reality that consumers make choices from an extremely large assortment. Marketing strategists delude themselves if they believe their mission is just to create preferences for one brand over another. Ad designers must be aware of the great many alternative offerings vying for the consumer's time and attention, *beyond* just competing brands. To fabricate what may be a farfetched illustration, General Motors might have a stake in promoting the value of family life, because the man visiting his divorce lawyer is not able to concentrate on the question of whether to consider a Buick or a Ford. (But then some point out that divorces result in more auto sales!) In a more realistic vein, sellers of cigarettes, cell (5) are investing $5 million to combat the onslaught of the antismoking campaign (cell 4). Thus, marketers need not position products only against others in the same class; the broadened categorization scheme makes possible the positioning of products against an entire spectrum of offering in an extended "evoked set" of the consumer, that is, against other transactions for which consumers exchange money, time, effort, psyche and other scarce resources. Marketers should attempt to measure consumer attitudes not only toward their own products but also toward other offerings in the typology.

What Business Are We in? The model can assist marketers in finding answers to what is sometimes an elusive yet crucial question: What business are we in? Does one sell cars or power, medical care or freedom from pain, social work or relationship, animal shelter or responsible pet ownership? Does the employment agency sell workers or productivity? Does the politician sell self-image or security for the voter? In terms of the typology, is the Better Business Bureau a cell (2) or a cell (4) organization, that is, does it render a service or does it promote a social issue, or both? (Compare this with Townsend's well-known question asked of Avis: Are we in the car rental business, or do we provide transportation? For another example, the cosmetics producer Charles Revson is said to have remarked, "We don't sell lipstick, we sell hope.") If, as was pointed out above, Smokenders markets cell (8) as well as its cell (6) product, might this firm qualify for support from an antipollution agency?

New Markets for Ad Agencies. A number of offerings appearing in the top row, cells 1 through 4, are sometimes broadly classed as public services and fall within the aegis of the Advertising Council. What is interesting however, is that these four cells show many exchanges whose campaigns are paid for and hence are outside the Ad Council's efforts. Thus, although they are marketed by nonprofit organizations, the measuring services such as Leading National Advertisers, Inc., count their ad billings in with commercial advertising. Examples include the Salvation Army, CARE, many fund raisers, public goods of the U.S. government and labor unions.

The top row of the typology may thus suggest new areas for advertisers' interest in items for institutional ads, say for image advertising, as well as concept advertising. By a conservative estimate, top-row exchanges presently account for less than 2 percent of the nearly $50 billion of total annual advertising billings in the U.S. Does the broadened exchange typology suggest new markets for Madison Avenue? If, as it was intimated in Chapter 1, the apparent trend is away from interest in material things and toward the ideational, should the marketing of advertising similarly be redirected? Will ideas and social issues be "encores," the new product types to be sought by the advertising industry?

This section has presented a categorization scheme for all "things" that are considered products in the marketing sense, that is, things that by their very nature, may serve to satisfy needs and desires of individuals. In the most general sense, the products focused upon in this book occupy the right-hand half of our typology.

THE CONCEPT OF SOCIAL PRICE

Although ideas and issues are often spoken of as being great or weighty, they have no mass, cannot be physically delivered and are not ordinarily exchanged for cash. Yet, for a marketing transaction to take place, something must be paid out by the purchaser. This section delves into *price* as a marketing factor and calls attention to a reality of pricing sometimes overlooked by marketing planners. That reality is the concept of the price—*beyond the monetary price*—paid by an individual in purchasing a good or a service, but especially in adopting an idea or taking a side on an issue.

Many characteristics associated with a particular product offering are studied by marketers as *product attributes*, while the possibility that these very characteristics may be perceived by consumers as integral parts of the price paid in purchasing that product is overlooked. Thus the amount of time spent waiting for attention at the doctor's office may in one context be construed as an attribute of that form of health care service. However, viewed in another light, the time expended might be seen as a nonmonetary price paid in addition to the cash fee. Other nonmonetary prices include the effort expected of the habitual driver who turns to mass transit and the shame endured by the adopter of the idea of a radically unusual hairstyle.

In any given situation, whether a characteristic is likely to be perceived as a product attribute or as part of price will not always be obvious. The important concern to marketers is the determination of which viewpoint suggests more effective strategies for marketing planning. That is, if consumers do indeed perceive themselves as expending resources beyond money when they make purchases, it becomes important for purveyors to take into account these "things" given up in exchange for the product offerings.

The price vs. product attribute distinction may be restated in terms of what has been called the approach-avoidance concept. Product attributes comprise an approach vector because they attract the consumer whereas price factors repel him or her. The latter are components of an avoidance vector. The model thus has an element of pleasure/pain theory built into it. These considerations have their most obvious usefulness in the planning of promotional strategy, but they may also be important in the design of the product itself.

Price

Price is the most quantifiable, tractable and readily analyzed element in the marketing mix. It is virtually the only marketing factor addressed by economists, whether it be called admission, assessment, charge, collection, compensation, contribution, dues, fare, fine, fee, honorarium, levy, interest, penalty, premium, rent, reward, tariff, tax, toll, or tuition.

The Monetary and Social Components of Price. The price construct has two components. One is that which is most generally associated with price, the price paid in cash by the buyer to the seller. The other is a nonmonetary or intrinsic component extending beyond money, which is "paid" by the buyer in every type of exchange. It is suggested that nonfinancial prices be formally distinguished from money prices and the appellation *social price* be assigned to the former. Other terms could be used: ancillary price, supplemental price, collateral price, intangible price, intrinsic price, symbolic price, psychic price, etc. But the term social price seems most appropriate particularly since it resonates well within the domain of social marketing. The notion of social price is exemplified in such everyday remarks as "We paid dearly for . . . ," or "Freedom at any price;" one is said to "spend" time and "pay" respect and attention.

A Compensatory Formulation. The total price one pays in an exchange is comprised of the financial amount paid and the sum of various social prices, for example,

$$P = p_m + \sum_{i=1}^{n} p_i$$

where P is the total price, p_m is the monetary or financial component and p_i represents the set of social prices associated with the transaction. According to this model, a marketer can so construct a "price mix" that financial and social components might compensate one for the other. (The compensatory formulation is based on an heroic assumption of additivity which is of course, open to debate. The terms of the model are additive if and only if each term is independent of the others. On the other hand, if for example, time and life-style depend on each other, that is, if for example, more time spent causes greater change in life-style, then the model is multiplicative (interactive), and not additive with respect to those two variables. For a better known illustration, price and advertising are interactive because heavy advertising can often justify selling at a higher price and vice versa.) For example: "The parking 'problem' may be interpreted as an implicit decision to keep the money price artificially low (zero or a nickel in a meter) and supplement it with a waiting or time price" (Thompson 1968). Similarly, Lovelock and Twichell (1974) mention the sacrifice of comfort (from overcrowding in mass transit facilities) that accompanies the adoption of a low-fare program. Virtually every purchase, whether tangible or intangible, no doubt involves some admixture of both financial and social prices. In fact Adam Smith attached greater significance to the latter, holding that the real price of everything, what everything really costs to the man who wants to acquire it, is the toil and trouble of acquiring it.

The concept of social price is entirely analogous to the economic idea of *psychic income*, the psychological benefits derived by individuals, benefits considered as substitutes for money, as when one accepts a lower salary for a higher status employment position. The idea that man does not live by bread (or money) alone holds true whether one speaks of (psychic) income or outlay (social price).

Four Types of Social Price. Four categories of resources are suggested as those given up by individuals as payment (beyond money) in exchange for product offerings: time, effort, life-style and psyche. Marketers may profitably assume that target consumers are aware of these social "price tags" fastened to every form of exchange.

Time. A good many expressions synonymous with the aphorism "time is money" have achieved cliche status. What they all mean is that time expended in an activity represents benefits foregone because that time was not spent in some alternative manner, the economic notion of opportunity loss or opportunity cost. The social price tag labeled *"time"* is perceived by the consumer to inform him or her of the opportunity loss or benefits to be foregone because of the time spent in making a purchase (at least in a market society; in many societies time is not considered so valuable). It has been said that important intellectual progress occurs at a time when poetry is popular. But adopters of the idea of poetry must pay a time price to write, read and listen—a price that many harried post-industrial individuals just cannot afford to pay.

Effort. Expending one's effort in exchange for a product offering is merely bartering one's services in that exchange. This can take the form of physical action, as in the case of maintenance assistance by a parent at a cooperative nursery school, or in the travail of participating in an alcoholism program. Continual or repeated payout of effort results in fatigue that is heightened if the effort does not return satisfactory reward.

Effort is also sacrificed in giving information in an exchange; information is an important human resource. As an illustration, a wholesaler's salesman is welcomed by retailers who accept his knowledge and news of the industry in payment for their allegiance. The salesman is glad to pay this social price, even to the point of making a deliberate effort to amass a store of gossip with which to compensate his clients for their valued friendship. Another example is the exchange of a lighter prison sentence for the police informer who pays for that product with information.

Life-style. Modification of one's life-style is a price paid in many forms of exchange, as in adopting the idea of marriage, for one example. While some may thrive on diversity and change, most individuals look upon the prospect of disruption of the status quo with at least some trepidation, and this is true whether the anticipated change is for the better or for the worse. The social price of advancement to a better job could be the diminution or elimination of camaraderie with former colleagues. The prospect of having to make new friends is an awesome assignment for some people. A touching example is given by Mead (1955):

> The iron plough has sometimes been resisted as an assault upon the land. In villages of the United Provinces of India, it threatens established human relationships. A man inherits a relationship to a carpenter family whose task it is to make and repair the plough. This family is always invited to the farmer's feasts and the women are given saris. The relationship, the "pay," the gifts continue whether ploughs are made or not . . . Perhaps the farmer can be taught to repair his own plough, but it would mean personal reorientation as well as a change in the valued relationship structure. (p. 192)

One reason for the recent increase in single parent homes is that many are unwilling to pay the price of life-style change in exchange for marriage. As Levy and Zaltman (1975) expressed it, "A common complaint is that married men dislike paying the price of saying 'I love you,' and in consequence, many marital deals fall through" (p. 42).

Psyche. Part of the price of an exchange often amounts to a forfeit of self-esteem, pride, identity, self-assertion, privacy, control, freedom from fear or risk, or other such losses affecting a person's peace of mind; they are thus grouped under the heading of *psyche*. When the American Cancer Society undertook to distribute Hemocult kits for self-screening of colon-rectum cancer, two major obstacles were encountered. One was hesitancy to supply a smear of stool as part of the examination. Then too the program met with a great deal of reluctance to risk the possibility of learning the grim truth of affliction. These two psychic factors are readily seen as comprising a high social price to be paid for cancer prevention as an exchange.

Also included in this category is the contribution of one's attention to something—one "pays" attention. Bagozzi (1975) points out that "an exchange can occur between a person and a television program." The "person gives his attention, support, potential for purchase, etc." Earlier, Robertson (1971) had carried this idea still further, adding to attention the social price of loss of self-assertion:

> In attending to communication, the individual incurs *costs* and receives *rewards*—an exchange process exists. Costs incurred in attending to mass-media advertising include time and submission to "influence," since it is recognized that advertising is persuasive and one-sided. The reward involved is information, which may be meaningful to the consumer and which may be of value to him in his consumption behavior . . . It can be proposed that, basically, communication will occur up to the point at which marginal reward from an additional unit of communication equals the marginal cost attached. (p. 52)

Economic Perspectives

In all transactions some value is placed upon the commodity being exchanged and a price based on such value is determined in the open marketplace. In the case of market or economic exchange, the price is explicit in that cash or some other resource convertible into utility passes from buyer to seller. But in nonmarket or social exchanges, the value of the offerings might at first blush not appear to transfer to the seller. Does a marketer obtain utility from a buyer's relinquishment of such resources as time, effort, life-style, or psyche? If not, then nonmarket transactions are not exchanges at all, but merely unidirectional doles or gifts.

However, upon reflection, a seller's utility is often increased as a result of the consumer's payment of social price. The transit authority, by deploying fewer trains, exacts a higher social price (of all four types) in addition to the money fare charged its commuters. However, in the process, the authority surely enjoys economies in personnel salaries, fuel and so forth. In attending to and complying with an anti-littering campaign, the effort price paid by a "consumer" is passed on to the "selling" community in the form of utility of cleaner streets. Moreover, there accrues to the seller of social products, advantages of consumers' behavior changes, as well as benefits derived when the consumer passes the idea along to others, e.g., advocating non-nuclear power, opposing the ERA, continuing to car-pool and so on.

Two or more offerings (and their respective prices) are sometimes traded in a reciprocal transaction. For a social marketing illustration, Blau (1964) describes the exchange of advice among agents in a law enforcement agency: "A consultation can be considered an exchange of values: Both participants gain something and both have to pay a price. The questioning agent . . . implicitly pays his respect to the superior proficiency of his colleague. This acknowledgment of inferiority is the cost of receiving assistance. The consultant gains prestige in return for which he is willing to devote some time" (p. 108). Thus the consultant's product offering is advice, which is paid for with a forfeiture of self-esteem by the questioner. The latter's product, in turn, is prestige sold to the consultant at a price of time.

Social Price, Social Cost and Public Price. Social price as defined above might be confused with two somewhat homonymic terms, social cost and public price. In fact Zaltman and Lin (1971) mention "social cost (as) another form of expense" in the adoption of innovations by individuals, explaining that: "Social cost may come in the form of ridicule, ostracism, or even exclusion or expulsion from some relevant reference group" (p. 660). While that point is substantively consonant with the thesis of this chapter, their terminology is believed to be less than accurate. The expression "social cost" has a specific economic meaning quite different from the price of adoption as defined by Zaltman and Lin. Social costs are not expenditures by individuals, but according to Kapp (1971), refer to the costs imposed upon other members of the community when those members perceive that they suffer from the ill effects of the operation of some enterprise—smoke from generating plants, barren mounds from strip-mined areas and so on. Public prices on the other hand, are payments by people for the performance of such services as police protection and sanitation (ordinarily in tax dollars) and includes license fees for restaurants and taxicabs (Mushkin 1972, p. 5).

To illustrate the use of these three expressions assume the product is a political candidate, or more specifically, the idea(s) espoused by that candidate. Voters pay social prices in the form of time and effort to cast votes. Election expenses funded with tax monies constitute public price, and should the elected official turn out to be corrupt, society sustains a social cost of enduring the evil effects of corruption.

An obvious deficiency in this inquiry is the absence of yardsticks for measuring social prices. Monetary prices are of course, measured in terms of cash, a scarce resource. Although social price is, in general, not readily quantified, it is also measured in scarce resources. To be sure, the quantity of time available to a person is limited, and similarly, although less measurably, the amount of expendable effort is limited. How much psychological ordeal and life-style change can be tolerated without ill effects is an open question. One could attempt such measurement by self-report questions of the type: "How much more would you be willing to pay if you were assured a polite salesperson?" Resulting measures would of course just be perceptions and hence of questionable quantifiability. But value as measured by financial price is similarly the result of consumers' perceptions. When one leases an automobile, a bonus is paid over and above the cost of ownership in return for the peace of mind that accompanies freedom from repair and replacement responsibilities. The difference could be taken as the exact psychic price paid by one electing ownership in favor of leasing. Such substitute modes of consumption, based on perceptions, offer clues as to how some social prices may one day be measured as the state of the art of consumer psychology is further refined.

On the other hand measurement of the time price has not been overlooked by economists. Smolensky, Tideman and Nichols (in Mushkin 1972) give a reason for this interest: "Time prices also have intuitive appeal because time as such is more equally distributed than money" (p. 95). They point out, however, that the wealthy often substitute money for time as depicted in Figure A.1.

The consumer represented by line A, is willing to pay a relatively high cash price and a low time price for a product, and conversely for consumer B.

FIGURE A.1 Time Price versus Financial Price

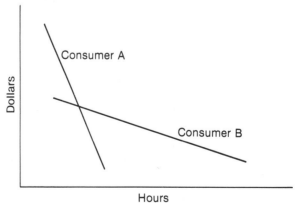

Source: Selma J. Mushkin, *Public Prices for Public Products.* Washington, D.C.: Urban Institute, 1972.

Importance of Social Price in Marketing

Price, as a controllable strategic marketing factor, is given added importance through the awareness of its nonfinancial component, P_i, in expression (1). In the same way that ordinary prices are "set," so too should social prices be employed by incorporating into the marketing mix, those considerations perceived by consumers to constitute their *total* contribution to the exchange transaction and not just the cash component. This awareness could uncover new promotional opportunities with such themes as "The time you save may be your own," and so on. The four price categories outlined above also suggest dimensions for "price positioning" a product offering against competing products, an exercise that could enhance the product planning process.

The concept has particular significance with respect to those exchanges falling within the domain of social marketing. For example, advocates of social change are virtually unanimous about the positive effects of participation in the planning process by those to be affected by the program. Yet such participation ordinarily means "payment" by target consumers of *all four* types of social price described in this appendix. It seems plausible to conclude that it is precisely because participation is so "expensive" that it is so desirable. People want to feel that they have some control in the shaping of their destiny. They are willing to invest in such control and indeed are uncomfortable if participation is not available to them for "purchase."

Implications for Further Investigation. Like their financial counterparts, social prices can be psychological prices, that is, those perceived by consumers to be surrogate measures of product quality—the higher the price paid, the higher the quality attributed to the product, and conversely. This area has been well explored in connection with monetary price and one may conjecture that conclusions ought to be quite similar with respect to social price. Are we not more suspect of the quality of the food at a restaurant if on a Sunday evening, there is no wait for a table?

Economic principles provide contexts within which social price may be further examined. One of these is the notion of consumers' surplus, the excess of price that the consumer would be willing to pay rather than go without a given product over that price actually paid. Another is indifference curve analysis. The consumer is said to be indifferent as to which of many combinations of goods are to comprise an optimum market basket subject to the constraint of a given monetary income. In a similar vein, can one speak of an optimal bundle of adoptable concepts, subject to constraints of available time, effort and so forth? It is hoped that such threads may be woven by interested consumer researchers into meaningful extensions of concepts expressed in this appendix.

NOTE

Portions of this appendix were originally published in Seymour H. Fine, *Marketing of Ideas and Social Issues* (New York: Praeger Publishers, 1981). Copyright © 1981 by Praeger Publishers. Reprinted with permission.

References

Note: Each entry ends with the chapter number(s) where it is cited; appendix items are denoted "A."

Aaker, David A. *Strategic Marketing Management*. New York: John Wiley & Sons, 1984. **19**

Achenbaum, Alvin. "Marketing That's All It Can Be (U.S. Army)." *AdWeek* 27 (May 26, 1986): 16. **7**

Achrol, Ravi S., and David L. Appel. "New Developments in Corporate Strategy Planning." In proceedings of the American Marketing Association Summer Educator's Conference, ed. Patrick E. Murphy, et al. Chicago: AMA, 1983, 305–310. **19**

Agranoff, Robert. *The Management of Election Campaigns*. Boston: Holbrook Press, 1976, 67–80. **12**

"Airwaves Used to Aid Needy." *Broadcasting* 108 (January 7, 1985): 174–176. **14**

Alexander, Clifford L., Jr. "How to Give at the Office without Writing a Check." *Electronic Perspective* (Summer 1985): 34–40. **14**

Allport, Gordon W., and Leo Postman. *The Psychology of Rumor*. New York: Holt, Rinehart and Winston, 1947. **10**

"AMA Board Approves New Marketing Definition." *Marketing News* (March 1, 1985): 1. **1**

Andreasen, Alan. "Nonprofits: Check Your Attention to Customers." *Harvard Business Review* 60 (May-June 1982): 105–110. **18, 21**

———. "A Power Potential Approach to Middlemen Strategies in Social Marketing." *European Journal of Marketing* 18, 4 (1984): 56–71. **10**

Ansoff, Igor H. "Strategies for Diversification." *Harvard Business Review* (September-October 1957): 113–124. **7, 19**

ARS/JWT. "Analysis of Test Results: Red Cross TV Commercial." Final Report, No. 81392 ARS/J. Walter Thompson Co., 1982. **8**

Bagozzi, Richard P. "Marketing as Exchange." *Journal of Marketing* (October 1975): 32–39. **4, 9, A**

Ball, Jerry. "The Big Business Telethons." *Broadcasting* (December 31, 1984): 30. **14**

Barach, Jeffrey. "Applying Marketing Principles to Social Causes." *Business Horizons* 27 (July/August 1984): 65–69. **18**

Bartos, Rena. *The Moving Target—What Every Marketer Should Know about Women*. New York: Free Press, 1982. **18**

Bearden-Mason, Michelle. "Arizona Seeks Image beyond Cactus and Cowboys." *Advertising Age* 56 (September 5, 1985): **20**

Beichman, Arnold. "The Minsk-Pinsk Story." *National Review* (September 7, 1984): 40-45. **10**

Beilenson, Anthony C. "Bring Back TVs Antismoking Ads." *New York Times* (May 20, 1987): 31. **2**

Belk, Russell W., ed., *Advances in Nonprofit Marketing*. Vols. 1, 2. Greenwich, CT: JAI Press, 1985, 1987. **4**

———. "Third World Consumer Culture." In *Marketing and Development: Toward Broader Dimensions*, ed. Erdogan Komcu and A. Fuat Firat. Greenwich, CT: JAI Press, 1988, 103–127. **22**

Belk, Russell W., and Nan Zhou. "Learning to Want Things." *Advances in Consumer Research* 14, ed. Melanie Wallendorf and Paul Anderson. Provo, UT: Association for Consumer Research, 1987, 478–481. **2**

Below, Tobe and Associates. "Views and News of Campaign Computer Service and Direct Mail." Newsletter published in Culver City, CA, and Bethesda, MD (1987). **19**

Benn, D. W. "Soviet Propaganda: The Theory and the Practice." *World Today* 41 (January 1984): 112–115. **2, 10**

Benson, Virginia O. "The Rise of the Independent Sector in Urban Development." *Growth and Change* 16 (July 1985): 25–39. **1**

Bergner, Douglas J. "The Maturing of Public Interest Groups." *Public Relations Quarterly* 31 (Fall 1986): 14–16. **2**

Berkowitz, Eric N., and William A. Flexner. "The Marketing Audit: A Tool for Health Services Organizations." *HCM Review* (Fall 1978): 51–57. **15**

Bernhardt, Kenneth J. "Consumer Research in the Federal Government." In *Government Marketing*, ed. Michael P. Mokwa and Steven E. Permut. New York: Praeger, 1981, 252–269. **8**

Bernick, Michael. "New Ventures for Antipoverty Agencies." *Harvard Business Review* 62 (November-December 1984): 44–56. **14**

Blau, Peter. *The Dynamics of Bureaucracy*. Chicago, IL: University of Chicago Press, 1964. **15, A**

Bloom, Paul N., and William Novelli. "Problems and Challenges of Social Marketing." *Journal of Marketing* 45 (Spring 1981): 79–88. **4, 9, 18, 21**

Brady, Timothy S. "Six Step Method to Long Range Planning for Non-profit Organizations." *Managerial Planning* (January-February 1984): 47–50. **1, 2, 4**

Brieger, William R., Jayashree Ramakrishna and Joshua D. Adeniyi. "Community Involvement in Social Marketing: Guineaworm Control." *International Quarterly of Community Education* 7, 1 (1986–87): 19–31. **22**

"Britain May Stamp on the Queue." *Financial Times* (June 4, 1987): 1. **12**

Brown, D. H. "4As Goes for Biggest Pubserv Campaign." *Broadcasting* 110 (May 19, 1986): 69–70. **14**

Burnham, David. "Alter the Catholic Church's Tax Status?" *New York Times* (July 29, 1988): A27. **2**

Business Week, "No Smoking Sweeps America." (July 27, 1987): 40–43, 46–49, 52. **9**

Calder, Bobby J. "Focus Groups and the Nature of Qualitative Marketing Research." *Journal of Marketing Research* 14 (1977): 353–364. **19**

Calonius, Erik, Sue Hutchison, Vicki Quade, and Brad Risinger. "There's Big Money in the Nonprofits." *Newsweek* (January 5, 1987): 38–39. **14**

Cameron, Kim. "Domains of Organizational Effectiveness in Colleges and Universities." *Academy of Management Journal* (March 1981). **4**

Canadian International Development Agency. *1984–1985 Annual Report*. Ottawa: Minister of Supply and Services, 1985. **21**

"Candidate Tells of Hiring Hooker." *Wisconsin State Journal* (May 25, 1982): 4, Sec. 4. **19**

Carlson, Robert O. *Communication and Public Opinion*. New York: Praeger, 1975. **10**

Caywood, Clarke L. "A Constitutional Jeopardy Theory: Toward a Novel Theory of Political Advertising Regulation under First Amendment and Commercial Speech Doctrines." Unpublished doctoral dissertation, University of Wisconsin-Madison, 1985. **19**

Caywood, Clarke L., and Ivan L. Preston. "The Continuing Debate on Political Advertising: Toward a Jeopardy Theory of Political Advertising as Regulated Free Speech." *Journal of Public Policy and Marketing*, in press, 1989. **19**

"Checking Out the View." *Sales and Marketing Management* 136 (April 1986): 29–30. **14**

Cho, Lee-Jay. "Averting Crisis in China?" *Bulletin of Atomic Science* 42 (April 1986): 30–33. **2**

Churchill, Gilbert A., Jr., Neil M. Ford, and Orville C. Walker. *Sales Force Management*. 7th ed. Homewood, IL: Richard D. Irwin, 1985. **19**

Clark, Peter, and Susan Evans. *Covering Campaigns: Journalism in Congressional Elections*. Stanford, CA: Stanford University Press, 1983. **19**

Collins, Robert H. "Microcomputer Systems to Handle Sales Leads: A Key to Increasing Salesforce Productivity." *Journal of Personal Selling and Sales Management* 1 (May 1985): 77–83. **19**

Crompton, John L., and Charles W. Lamb. *Marketing Government and Social Services*. New York: John Wiley & Sons, 1986. **4, 15**

Cutlip, Scott, Alan Center, and Glen Broom. *Effective Public Relations*. Englewood Cliffs, NJ: Prentice Hall, 1986. **19**

DeGeorge, Richard T. *Business Ethics*. 2d ed. New York: Macmillan, 1986. **6**

Della Bitta, Albert J., David L. London, Geoffrey G. Booth, and Richard R. Weeks. "Estimating the Economic Impact of a Short-Term Tourist Event." *Journal of Travel Research* 16 (Fall 1977): 10–15. **20**

Dholakia, Ruby Roy. "A Macromarketing Perspective on Social Marketing: The Case of Family Planning in India." *Journal of Macromarketing* 4 (Spring 1984): 53–61. **21**

Diamond, Edwin and Stephen Bates. *The Spot: The Rise of Political Advertising on Television*. Cambridge, MA: MIT Press, 1984. **19**

Dickson, Peter R. "Person-Situation Segmentation's Missing Link." *Journal of Marketing* 46 (Fall 1982): 56–64. **9**

DPA Group. *Economic Impacts of the XV Olympic Winter Games*. Edmonton: Alberta Tourism and Small Business, 1985. **20**

Drucker, Peter F. "Managing the Public Service Institution." *Public Interest* (Fall 1973): 43. **2, 4, 7**

Duhaime, Carole P., Ronald McTavish, and Christopher A. Ross. "Social Marketing: An Approach to Third-World Development." *Journal of Macromarketing* (Spring 1985): 3–12. **21**

Elle (September 1986): 56. **19**

Enis, Ben M. "Governments as Marketers: Issues of Management and Public Policy." In *Government Marketing*, ed. Michael P. Mokwa and Steven E. Permut. New York: Praeger, 1981, 343–355. **2**

Engel, James F., Martin R. Warshaw, and Thomas C. Kinnear. *Promotional Strategy*. Homewood, IL: Irwin, 1987. **19**

Fair Campaign Practices Commission. "Memorandum." In files of authors (1982). **19**

"Famine in Ethiopia Draws Generous Response." *Direct Marketing* 48 (November 1985): 44. **13**

Farley, Dixie. "FDA's Global Reach to Protect Public Health." *FDA Consumer* (November 1986). **22**

Feder, Barnaby J. "What's New at the Research Institutes." *New York Times* (April 6, 1986): 23. **2**

Feldberg, Charles. "Industry and Food Safety." Joint FAO/WHO Expert Consultation on Food Protection for Urban Consumers. Rome, December 1–5, 1986. **22**

 Fine, Seymour H. "Toward a Theory of Segmentation by Objectives in Social Marketing." *Journal of Consumer Research* 7 (June 1980): 1–13. **18**

——. *The Marketing of Ideas and Social Issues*. New York: Praeger Division, Holt, Rinehart and Winston, 1981. **1, 2, 4, 5, 7, 8, 10, 13, 19, 22**

——. "A Concept Sector Within the Economy." In *Cases and Readings for Marketing for Nonprofit Organizations*, ed. Philip Kotler, O. C. Ferrell, and Charles Lamb. Englewood Cliffs, NJ: Prentice-Hall, 1983, 343–354. **5**

——. "Social and Nonprofit Marketing: Some Trends and Issues." In *Advances in Nonprofit Marketing*, 2d ed., ed. Russell Belk. Greenwich, CT: JAI Press, 1987, 71–98. **6, 8, 10, 13**

Fine, Seymour H. and Adell P. Fine. "Distribution Channels in Marketing Social Work." *Social Casework* 67 (April 1986): 227–233. **5**

Flexner, William A., and Eric N. Berkowitz. "Marketing Research in Health Services Planning: A Model." *Public Health Reports*, 94, 6 (November/December 1979): 503–513. **8**

Forkan, James P. "Promotors Spin More Aid Extravaganzas." *Advertising Age* 57 (April 21, 1986): 102. **14**

"Four More Years: The Marketing Implications." *Marketing News* 1 (January 4, 1985): 60–62. **19**

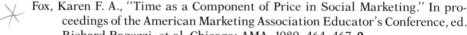 Fox, Karen F. A., "Time as a Component of Price in Social Marketing." In proceedings of the American Marketing Association Educator's Conference, ed. Richard Bagozzi, et al. Chicago: AMA, 1980, 464–467. **9**

Fox, Karen F. A., and Philip Kotler. "The Marketing of Social Causes: The First 10 Years." *Journal of Marketing* 44 (Fall 1980): 24–33. **4, 9, 21**

Gaunt, Jeremy. "Hill Campaign Spending Hits All-Time High." *Congressional Quarterly Weekly* (May 16, 1987): 991–993. **19**

Gerard, Jeremy. "For Nonprofit Theaters, A Victory over Red Ink." *New York Times* (March 10, 1987): C15. **2**

Gilbert, Nathaniel. "Campaign Strategy in the War on Hunger." *Management Review* 75 (January 1986): 49–52. **7**

Goldblatt, Joe Jeff. "Profiting from Relationships with Charities." *Public Relations Journal* 41 (December 1985): 16. **14**

Goldenberg, Edie N., and Michael W. Traugott. *Campaigning for Congress*. Washington, DC: Congressional Quarterly Press, 1984. **19**

Gould, Carole. "A Cautionary Look at Affinity Cards." *New York Times* (May 15,

1988): F9. **14**

Green, Paul, and Donald S. Tull. *Research for Marketing Decisions*. 4th ed. Englewood Cliffs, NJ: Prentice-Hall, 1978. **19**

Greene, Bob. "Heads You Lose, Tails You Lose." *Esquire* (April 1981): 12, 14. **7**

Haig, Alexander, Jr. "Haig Intends GOP Run for Presidency." *Arizona Republic* (November 11, 1986). **19**

Hanley, Kevin. "Non-Profit Learns Marketing Techniques from Ad Agencies." *Fund Raising Management* 15 (June 1984): 42–50. **14**

"Hart Campaign Debacle Prompts Media Debate about Whether a Politician's Sex Life Is News." *Wall Street Journal* (July 27, 1987): 42. **19**

Hasenfeld, Yeheskel. *Human Services Organizations*. Englewood Cliffs, NJ: Prentice Hall, 1983. **4**

Hasenfeld, Yeheskel, and Richard A. English, eds. *Human Service Organizations*. Ann Arbor: University of Michigan Press, 1975. **4**

Hatry, H. P., L. H. Blair, D. M. Fisk, J. M. Greiner, J. R. Hall, and P. S. Schaenman. *How Effective Are Your Community Services?* Washington, DC: Urban Institute, 1977. **15**

Haugen, Charles N. "Do You Have What It Takes to Be an Effective Volunteer Board Member?" *New Jersey Bell Journal* (Spring 1987): 37–46. **10**

Hawkins, Brett W. "Public Needs and Private Resources." *Society* (September/October 1986): 57–58. **14**

Hedley, B. "Strategy and the Business Portfolio." *Long Range Planning* 12 (February 1977). **19**

Henderson, Bruce D. "The Anatomy of Competition." *Journal of Marketing* 49 (Spring 1983): 7–11. **19**

Hensel, Paul J., and Alan Dubinsky. "Identification and Classification of Problems Associated with Evaluating Social Marketing Efforts." *Journal of the Academy of Marketing Science* 13 (Winter/Spring 1985): 75–90. **18**

Herzlinger, Regina, and William Krasker. "Who Profits from Nonprofits?" *Harvard Business Review* 65 (January-February 1987): 93–106. **2**

Hill, Susan. "Tournament Master." *Institutional Investor* 20 (May 1986): 23–24. **14**

Hirsch, Paul M., and Harry L. Davis. "Are Arts Administrators Really Serious about Marketing?" In *Marketing the Arts*, ed. Michael P. Mokwa, W. M. Dawson, and E. A. Prieve. New York: Praeger, 1981: 59–64. **4**

Hirschman, Elizabeth C. "People as Products, Analysis of a Complex Marketing Exchange." *Journal of Marketing* 51 (January 1987): 98–108. **18**

Hodgkinson, Virginia A., and Murray S. Weitzman. *Dimensions of the Independent Sector*, 2d ed. Washington, DC: Independent Sector, 1986. **2**

Hoffman, Kurt. "Regionalized Fundraising Campaign A Natural." *Advertising Age* 57 (March 6, 1986): 40–41. **14**

Hollon, Larry. "Selling Human Misery." *Christian Century* 26 (October 1983): 968–971. **13**

Homans, George C. *The Human Group*. New York: Harcourt, Brace & World, 1950. **7**

Honomichl, Jack. "Research Acts as Reagan's Eyes, Ears." *Advertising Age* (November 5, 1984): 1, 91. **19**

Horowitz, T. *Arts Administration*. Chicago: Review Press, 1978. **15**

Hummler, Richard. "Nonprofit Product Outpaces B'Way." *Variety* (January 11,

1984): 261–263. **2**

Hunt, Avery August. "Strategic Philanthropy." *Across The Board* 23 July/August 1986): 22–30. **14**

Hunt, Shelby D. "The Nature and Scope of Marketing." *Journal of Marketing* 40 (July 1976): 17–28. **A**

Jacobson, Gary C. "The Impact of Broadcast Campaigning on Electoral Outcomes." *Journal of Politics* 37 (1975): 769–793. **12**

Jafari, Jafar. "Understanding the Structure of Tourism—An Avant Propos to Studying Its Costs and Benefits." In Proceedings of the 32d Congress of the International Association of Scientific Experts in Tourism. St. Gall, Switzerland: Editions AIEST, 1982. **20**

"Jail-A-Thon Raises Cash." *Public Relations Journal* 41 (July 1985): 12. **14**

Jamieson, Kathleen Hall. *Packaging the Presidency: A History and Criticism of Presidential Campaigning Advertising*. New York: Oxford University Press, 1984. **19**

Kaferstein, Fritz, and Jacqueline Sims. "Food Safety." *World Health* (March 1987). **22**

Kapp, K. W. *The Social Cost of Private Enterprise*. New York: Schocken, 1971. **A**

Katz, Alfred H., and Eugene I. Bender, eds. *The Strength in Us: Self-Help Groups in the Modern World*. New York: New Viewpoints, 1976. **18**

Kelly, Orr, and Barbara Quick. "Nonprofit Groups: Are They Worth Their Tax Breaks?" *U.S. News and World Report* (January 31, 1984), 38–40. **2**

Kelley, Stanley, Jr. *Professional Public Relations and Political Power*. Baltimore: John Hopkins Press, 1956. **19**

Ketchum MacLeod and Grove. "Topline Findings of Two Focus Group Sessions Conducted to Explore Reactions to Creative Executions." Final Report. Pittsburgh: Ketchum MacLeod and Grove, Marketing and Research Department (October 24, 1980). **8**

Kotler, Philip. "A Generic Concept of Marketing." *Journal of Marketing* (October 1972): 42–49. **4, 18, A**

————. "The Elements of Social Action." In *Processes and Phenomena of Social Change*, ed. Gerald Zaltman. New York: John Wiley, 1973b, 169–190. **6**

Kotler, Philip, and Alan Andreasen. *Strategic Marketing for Nonprofit Organizations*. Englewood Cliffs, NJ: Prentice-Hall, 1987. **9, 10, 15, 21**

Kotler, Philip, and Roberta N. Clarke. *Marketing Health Care Organizations*. Englewood Cliffs, NJ: Prentice-Hall, 1987. **15**

Kotler, Philip, and Sidney Levy. "Broadening the Concept of Marketing." *Journal of Marketing* (January 1969): 10–15. **4, 21**

Kotler, Philip, and William Mindak. "Marketing and Public Relations, Should They be Partners or Rivals?" *Journal of Marketing* (October 1978): 13–20. **19**

Kotler, Philip, and Michael Murray. "Third Sector Management—The Role of Marketing." *Public Administration Review* 35 (September/October 1975): 467–472. **4**

Kotler, Philip, and Gerald Zaltman. "Social Marketing: An Approach to Planned Social Change." *Journal of Marketing* 35 (July 1971): 3–12. **4, 21**

Kozbial, Ardys J. "The Other Economy." *New England Business* (February 17, 1986): 18–24. **2**

Krentler, Kathleen. "Cause-Related Marketing." In Proceedings of the American

Marketing Association Winter Educator's Conference. Chicago: AMA, 1988, in press. **14**

Laczniak, Gene R. "Frameworks for Analyzing Marketing Ethics." *Journal of Macromarketing* 3 (Spring 1983): 7–18. **6**

Laczniak, Gene R., and Clarke L. Caywood. "The Case for and against Televised Political Advertising: Implications for Research and Public Policy." *Journal of Public Policy and Marketing* 6 (October 1987): 16–32. **19**

Laczniak, Gene R., Robert F. Lusch, and Patrick E. Murphy. "Social Marketing: Its Ethical Dimensions." *Journal of Marketing* 43 (Spring 1979): 29–38. **6**

Landy, Simon. "Condom King Reigns in Thailand." *Advertising Age* (July 29, 1985): 38–39. **13**

Lehrman, Celia K. "PSA's For Criminals." *Public Relations Journal* 42 (May 1986): 11. **12**

Levitt, Theodore. *The Third Sector: New Tactics for a Responsive Society*. New York: AMACOM, 1975. **4**

Levy, Sidney, and Gerald Zaltman. *Marketing, Society and Conflict*. Englewood Cliffs, N.J.: Prentice-Hall, 1975. **A**

Lipset, Seymour Martin. "The Sources of Public Interest Activism." *Public Relations Quarterly* 31 (Fall 1986): 9–13. **1, 2, 22**

Lipsky, M. *Street Level Bureaucracy*. New York: Russell Sage Foundation, 1980. **15**

Lovelock, Christopher H. "Classifying Services to Gain Strategic Marketing Insights." *Journal of Marketing* 47 (Summer 1983): 9–20. **18**

———. *Services Marketing*. Englewood Cliffs, NJ: Prentice-Hall, 1984. **18**

———. *Marketing for Public and Nonprofit Managers*. New York: John Wiley & Sons, 1984. **4, 21**

Lovelock, Christopher H., and John Twichell. "Low Fare Transit Plans Gain Nationwide Trails." *Metropolitan* (May-June 1974): 24–27. **A**

Lusch, Robert F., Gene R. Laczniak, and Patrick E. Murphy. "The 'Ethics of Social Ideas' Versus the 'Ethics of Marketing Social Ideas.'" *Journal of Consumer Affairs* (Summer 1980): 156–164. **6**

McCann-Erickson. "Communications/Diagnostic Research for the 'Money in the Bank' Direct Deposit Campaign." Final Report. McCann-Erickson Market Research Department, January 1984. **8**

McCarty, Dennis, Michael Poore, Kenneth C. Mills, and Sherry Morrison. "Direct Mail Techniques and the Prevention of Alcohol-Related Problems among College Students." *Journal of Studies on Alcohol* 44 (January 1987): 162–170. **12**

McCombs, Maxwell E. "Mass Communications in Political Campaigns: Information, Gratification and Persuasion." In *Current Perspectives in Mass Communications Research*, ed. E. G. Kline and P. J. Tichenor. Beverly Hills: Sage, 1972, 169–194. **19**

McDaniel, Stephen W. "Church Advertising: Views of the Clergy and General Public." *Journal of Advertising* 1 (1986): 24–29. **2**

McGill, Michael E., and LeLand Wooten. "Management in the Third Sector." *Public Administration Review* 35 (September/October 1975): 444–455. **4**

McGinnis, Joe. *The Selling of the President, 1968*. New York: Trident, 1969. **10, 19**

Machiavelli, Nicolo. *The Art of War*. Rev. ed. of the Ellis Farnesworth translation. Indianapolis, IN: Bobbs-Merrill, 1985. **19**

McIntyre, Pat. "Value Assessment and Its Relationship to Organ Donation and Advertising Appeals in Hispanic and White Subjects." Unpublished doctoral dissertation, Kansas State University, 1988. **13**

McMillan, Norman H. *Marketing Your Hospital: A Strategy for Survival.* Chicago: American Hospital Association, 1981. **1**

Manoff, Richard K. *Social Marketing.* New York: Praeger, 1987. **22, 23**

"Marketing Briefs." *Marketing News* (March 27, 1987): 1. **14**

Marsiglio, William. "Confronting the Teenage Pregnancy Issue: Social Marketing as an Interdisciplinary Approach." *Human Relations* 38 (October 1985): 983–1000. **17**

Maslow, Abraham H. *Motivation and Personality.* 2nd ed. New York: Harper & Row, 1971. **7**

Mata, Leonard. "Educational Approaches in Food Safety in Costa Rica and Guatemala: Lessons Learned." Presented to the WHO Consultation on Health Education in Food Safety, Geneva, April 27, 1987. **22**

Matthews, Leonard S. "President's Message: Political Advertising Revisited." *American Association of Advertising Agencies Newsletter* (December 1984): 3. **19**

Mauser, Gary A. *Political Marketing: An Approach to Campaign Strategy.* New York: Praeger, 1983. **19**

Mead, Margaret. *Cultural Patterns and Technical Change.* New York: Mentor Books, 1955. **A**

Merritt, Sharyne. "Negative Political Advertising: Some Empirical Findings." *Journal of Advertising* 13 (1984): 27–38. **19**

Miles, Raymond E., and Charles C. Snow. *Organizational Strategy, Structure, and Process.* New York: McGraw-Hill, 1978. **19**

Miller, Annetta, and Elisa Williams. "Peddling a Social Cause." *Newsweek* 108 (September 1, 1986): 58–59. **14**

Mindak, William, and Seymour H. Fine. "A Fifth P: Public Relations." In Proceedings of the American Marketing Association Conference on the Marketing of Services, ed. James H. Donnelly and William R. George. Chicago: AMA, 1981, 71–73. **1**

Mintzberg, H. *The Structure of Organizations: A Synthesis of the Research.* Englewood Cliffs, NJ: Prentice Hall, 1979. **5**

———. *Power in and around Organizations.* Englewood Cliffs, NJ: Prentice Hall, 1983. **5**

Mokwa, Michael P. "Marketing Control and Evaluation: A Framework for Strategic Arts Administration." In *Marketing the Arts*, ed. Michael P. Mokwa, William M. Dawson, and E. Arthur Prieve. New York: Praeger, 1980, 263–280. **2, 15**

Mokwa, Michael P., and Steven E. Permut, eds. *Government Marketing.* New York: Praeger, 1981. **4**

Morris, Michael H. "Is the Cold War a Marketing Problem?" *Business Horizons* 28 (November/December 1985): 55–59. **7**

Murphy, Patrick E. "Marketing Nonprofit Organizations: Problems and Prospects for the 1980s." In Proceedings of the American Marketing Association Conference, ed. Richard Bagozzi, et al. Chicago: AMA, 1980, 278–281. **4, 8**

Murphy, Patrick E., and Ben M. Enis. *Marketing.* Glenview, IL: Scott Foresman,

1985. **6**

Murphy, Patrick E., Gene R. Laczniak, and Robert F. Lusch. "Ethical Guidelines for Business and Social Marketing." *Journal of the Academy of Marketing Science* 6 (Summer 1978): 195–205. **6**

Mushkin, Selma J. *Public Prices for Public Products*. Washington DC: Urban Institute, 1972. **A**

"Music to a Symphony's Ears." *Personnel Journal* 64 (June 1985): 27. **14**

Napolitan, Joseph. *The Election Game and How to Win It*. Garden City, NY: Doubleday, 1972. **19**

National Center for Charitable Statistics. *National Taxonomy of Exempt Entities*. Washington, DC, 1987. **3**

Neff, David. "Admen for Heaven." *Christianity Today* (September 18, 1987). **2**

Newman, Bruce I., and Jagdish N. Sheth. "A Model of Primary Voter Behavior." *Journal of Consumer Research* 12 (September 1985): 178–187. **19**

Nichols Applied Management. *Economic Impact of the 1988 Calgary Winter Olympic Games*. Edmonton: Department of Tourism and Small Business, Government of Alberta, 1982. **20**

Nielsen, Richard P. "Strategic Piggybacking a Self-Subsidization Strategy for Nonprofit Institutions." *Sloan Management Review* 23 (Summer 1982): 65–69. **7**

Nielsen, Waldemar A. *The Third Sector: Keystone of a Caring Society*. Washington: Independent Sector, 1980. **3**

Nigro, F. A., and L. G. Nigro. *Modern Public Administration*. 5th ed. New York: Harper and Row, 1980. **15**

Noble, David. "Subsidy to Industry." Letter to *New York Times* (January 1, 1988): 16. **2**

Novelli, William D. "Developing Marketing Programs." In *Marketing Health Behavior*, ed. Lee W. Frederiksen, Laura J. Solomon, and Kathleen A. Brehony. New York: Plenum Press, 1984, 59–89. **16**

O'Connell, Brian. *Origins, Dimensions and Impact of America's Voluntary Spirit*. Washington: Independent Sector, 1984. **3**

O'Connell, Janelle K., and James H. Price. "Ethical Theories for Promoting Health through Behavioral Change." *Journal of School Health* 53 (October 1983): 476–479. **6**

(OECD) Social Studies, Social Expenditures 1960–1990: Problems of Growth and Control. Paris, 1985. **5**

Ogilvy, David. *Ogilvy on Advertising*. New York: Vantage Books, 1983. **19**

O'Leary/Kamber Report. "Presidential Politics." Issue 2 (1987): 24. **19**

O'Toole, John. *The Trouble With Advertising*. New York: Chelsea House, 1981. **19**

Pack, Janet Rothenberg. "Privatization of Public-Sector Services in Theory and Practice." *Journal of Policy Analysis and Management* 6, 4 (Summer 1987) 523–540. **2**

Palmer, Tom G. "Uncle Sam's Ever-Expanding P.R. Machine." *Wall Street Journal* (January 10, 1985): 26. **2**

Parkinson, Hank. *Winning Your Campaign—A Nuts-and-Bolts Guide to Political Victory*. Englewood Cliffs, NJ: Prentice-Hall, 1970. **19**

Patti, Charles H., and John H. Murphy. *Cases in Advertising and Promotion Management*. New York: Wiley, 1983. **13**

Patton, Michael Quinn. *Qualitative Evaluation Methods*. Beverly Hills: Sage, 1980. **19**

Pertschuk, Michael. "The Role of Public Interest Groups in Setting the Public Agenda for the '90s." *Journal of Consumer Affairs* 21, 2 (Winter 1987): 3–14. **2**

Polanyi, K., C. Arensberg, and H. Pearson. *Trade and Market in the Early Empires*. Glencoe, IL: Free Press, 1957. **10**

"Poll: Thompson's New Tactics Work." *Wisconsin State Journal* (October 9, 1986): 6, Sec. 1. **19**

"Potted Trees Exemplify Monument to Contributors." *Direct Marketing* 47 (November 1984): 98–99. **14**

Powills, Suzanne. "Hospitals Tap Business Sector for Marketers." *Hospitals* 60 (February 1986): 64. **1**

"Providing Public Television's Tools." *Broadcasting* 111 (July 7, 1986): 85. **14**

Public Affairs Branch, CIDA. *Folder A - Strategic Overview Input*. Ottawa: Canadian International Development Agency, 1984–85. Internally reproduced. **21**

Rados, David L. *Marketing for Nonprofit Organizations*. Boston, MA: Auburn House, 1981. **12**

Rados, David L., and Peter Gilmour. *Australian Marketing Cases*. St. Lucia, Queensland: University of Queensland Press, 1981: 112. **12**

Rawls, John. *A Theory of Justice*. Cambridge, MA: Harvard University Press, 1971. **6**

Reader's Digest 1987 Almanac. Pleasantville, NY: Reader's Digest Association, 1986, 966–969. **2**

Riesman, David. *The Lonely Crowd*. New Haven, CT: Yale University Press, 1950. **7**

Ritchie, J. R. Brent. "Assessing the Impact of Hallmark Events; Conceptual and Research Issues." *Journal of Travel Research* 23, 1 (Summer 1984): 2–11. **20**

Ritchie, J. R. Brent, and Catherine E. Aitken. "Assessing the Impacts of the 1988 Olympic Winter Games: The Research Program and Initial Results." *Journal of Travel Research* 22, 3 (Winter 1984): 17–25. **20**

———. "OLYMPULSE II—Evolving Resident Attitudes Towards the 1988 Olympic Winter Games." *Journal of Travel Research* 23, 3 (Winter 1985): 28–33. **20**

Ritchie, J. R. Brent, and Donald Beliveau. "Hallmark Events: An Evaluation of a Strategic Response to Seasonability in the Travel Market." *Journal of Travel Research* 14 (Fall 1974): 14–20. **20**

Ritchie, J. R. Brent, and Hu Yangzhou. "The Role and Impact of Mega-Events and Attractions on National and Regional Tourism: A Conceptual and Methodological Overview." In Proceedings of the 37th Congress of the International Association of Scientific Experts in Tourism. St. Gall, Switzerland: Editions AIEST, 1987. **20**

Ritchie, J. R. Brent, and Marcia M. Lyons. "OLYMPULSE III/IV: A Mid-Term Report on Resident Attitudes Concerning the XV Olympic Winter Games." *Journal of Travel Research* 26, 1 (Summer 1987): 18–26. **20**

Robertson, T. S. *Innovative Behavior and Communication*. New York: Holt, Rinehart and Winston, 1971. **A**

Robin, Donald P., and R. Eric Reidenbach. "Social Responsibility, Ethics, and

Marketing Strategy: Closing the Gap Between Concept and Application." *Journal of Marketing* 51 (January 1987): 44–58. **6**

Rocheleau, Bruce, and Thomas Mackesey. "Utilization-Focused Evaluation: A Case Study From the Human Services Area." In *Evaluating and Optimising Public Policy*, ed. Dennis J. Palumbo, Stephen B. Fawcett, and S. Paula Wright. Lexington, MA: D. C. Heath, 1981, 187–198. **15**

Roel, Raymond. "The Use of Sweepstakes And Other Donor Promotions." *Fund Raising Management* 16 (June 1985): 70–88. **14**

Rogers, Everett M. "New Product Adoption and Diffusion." *Journal of Consumer Research* 2 (1976): 190–201. **10**

Rogers, Everett M., and F. Floyd Shoemaker. *Communication of Innovations*. New York: The Free Press, 1981. **7**

Rosenfield, James H. "Public Service Advertising Poised For Translation into Worldwide Thrust." *Television/Radio Age* 33 (March 31, 1986): 73. **2**

Rosnow, Ralph L. "Gossip and Marketplace Psychology." *Journal of Communication* 27 (1977): 158–163. **10**

Rosnow, Ralph L., and G. A. Fine. *Rumor and Gossip: The Social Psychology of Hearsay*. New York: Elsevier, 1976. **10**

Ross, W. D. *The Right and the Good*. Oxford: Clarendon Press, 1930. **6**

Rothman, Jack, Joseph G. Teresa, Terrence L. Kay, and Gershom C. Morningstar. *Marketing Human Service Innovations*. Beverly Hills, CA: Sage, 1983. **4**

———. "Political Advertising: A Neglected Policy Issue in Marketing." *Journal of Marketing Research* 15 (1978): 58–71. **19**

Rothschild, Michael L. "Marketing Communication in Nonbusiness Situations or Why It's So Hard to Sell Brotherhood Like Soap." *Journal of Marketing* 43 (Spring 1979): 11–20. **9, 21**

———. *Marketing Communications*. Lexington, MA: D. C. Heath, 1987. **19**

Royko, Mike. "Politicians on TV: Ad Nauseam." *Chicago Tribune* (November 6, 1984). **19**

Rule, Sheila. "Tanzani, Barren of Much, Still Implants the Three R's." *New York Times* (April 21, 1987): 21. **22**

Rust, Roland T., Mukesh Baja, and George Haley. "Efficient and Inefficient Media for Political Campaign Advertising." *Journal of Advertising* 13 (November 3, 1984): 45–49. **19**

Sabato, Larry. *PAC Power: Inside the World of Political Action Committees*. New York: Basic Books, 1984. **19**

Sackett, Victoria. "Oral Roberts Bucks Eternity." *New York Times* (March 30, 1987): A 19. **13**

Sarri, Rosemary, and Yeheskel Hasenfeld. *The Management of Human Services*. New York: Columbia University Press, 1978. **4**

Savas, E. S. "Private Enterprise is Profitable Enterprise." *New York Times* (February 14, 1988): 2F. **2**

Scheirer, Mary Ann. "Program Participants' Positive Perceptions: Psychological Conflicts of Interest in Programs Evaluation." *Evaluation Quarterly* 2 (1978): 53–70. **15**

Schramm, Wilbur, and D. F. Roberts. *The Process and Effect of Mass Communication*. Chicago: University of Illinois Press, 1971. **10**

Semenik, Richard J. "State of the Art of Arts Marketing." In *Advances in Nonprofit*

Marketing, 2d ed., ed. Russell Belk. Greenwich, CT: JAI Press, 1987, 99–124. **2**

Sethi, S. Prakash. "Marketing the National Food Stamp Program: Can a Public Welfare Program Be Run like a Business?" In *Government Marketing*, ed. Michael P. Mokwa and Steven E. Permut. New York: Praeger, 1981, 96–113. **10**

Shapiro, Benson P. "Marketing in Non-Profit Organizations." *Journal of Voluntary Action Research* 3 (Fall/Winter 1974): 1–16. **4**

Sheth, Jagdish N., and Peter L. Wright, ed. *Marketing Analysis for Societal Problems*. Urbana-Champaign IL: University of Illinois Press, 1974. **4**

Skloot, Edward. "Should Not-For-Profits Go into Business?" *Harvard Business Review* 61 (January-February 1983): 20–27. **14**

Small Business Administration. "Unfair Competition by Nonprofit Organizations with Small Business: An Issue for the 1980s." 3d ed. Washington, DC: Office of Advocacy, SBA, June 1984. **2**

Solomon, Amy. "Nonprofits in Business." *Chronicle of Nonprofit Enterprise* (May 1984). **14**

Solomon, Michael R., et al. "A Role Theory Perspective on Dyadic Interactions: The Service Encounter." *Journal of Marketing* 49 (Winter 1985): 99–111. **7**

Sorenson, Theodore C. *A Different Kind of Presidency*. New York: Harper and Row, 1984. **19**

Spero, Rudolph. *The Duping of the American Voter*. New York: Lippencott and Crowell, 1980. **19**

Statistical Abstract of the United States. 107th ed. Washington, DC: U.S. Department of Commerce, Bureau of the Census, 1987. **2**

Stern, Aimee L. "Public Service Pays Off for Ad Agency." *Dun's Business Month* 3 (June 1986): 42–44. **14**

———. "Putting Faith in Madison Avenue." *New York Times* (December 27, 1987): 22. **2**

Survey of Current Business 68, 1. Washington, DC: United States Department of Commerce, January 1988, 16. **2**

Taylor, James B. "Introducing Social Innovation." *Journal of Applied Behavioral Science* 6 (1970): 69–77. **10**

Teleconference. *Sales Management Theory and Practice: A State of the Art Review*. University of Wisconsin-Madison and Oklahoma State University (March 20, 1985) videotape. **19**

Teltsch, Kathleen. "Corporate Pressures Slowing Gifts to Charity." *New York Times* (July 8, 1987): 1. **14**

"Telethon to Provide Ethiopian Aid Update." *Broadcasting* 109 (October 21, 1985): 74–76. **14**

"Tell Them Not To." *Economist* (July 16, 1988): 30. **13**

Thompson, Wilbur. "The City as a Distorted Price System." In *Marketing and Social Issues*, ed. J. R. Wish and S. H. Gamble. New York: John Wiley and Sons, 1968, 79–88. **A**

To Preserve An Independent Sector. Report of the Organizing Committee. Washington, DC: Independent Sector, 1979. **3**

Trafton, Barbara M. *Women Running—How to Run for Office*. Boston: Harvard Common Press, 1984. **19**

Tuft, Bruce L. "The Greening of the Nonprofit Executive." *Association Management* 3 (June 1986): 78. **2**

U.S., Congress, Senate, Subcommittee on Treasury, Postal Service and General Government of the Committee on Appropriations, Special Hearing on the Susan B. Anthony Coin Act of 1978, 96th Cong., 1st sess., May 3, 1979. **7**

Van Leeuwert, A. "De Status van de Marktonderzoeker." *Adformatie* (November 24, 1977): 1. **5**

Van Reekum, G., and P. Van der Velpen. "Strategische Perspectieven voor Gesubsidieerde Nonprofit Organisaties." *M & O* 4 (1985): 287–300. **5**

Varadarajan, P. Rajan, and Anil Menon. "Cause-Related Marketing: A Coalignment of Marketing Strategy and Corporate Philanthropy." *Journal of Marketing* 52 (July 1988): 58–74. **6**

Walker, Albert. "The Good That They Do." *Public Relations Quarterly* (Spring 1987): 15–20. **14**

Wassersug, Joseph D. "An Unhealthy Preoccupation with Health." *Wall Street Journal* (August 30, 1988): 18. **6**

Webb, Don R., et al. "Economic Development and the Marketing of Social Ideas." In Proceedings of the Second International Conference on Marketing and Development, ed. James E. Littlefield and Magdolna Csath. Blacksburg, Virginia: Virginia Tech University, 1988, 262–265. **22**

Weber, Nathan, ed. *Giving USA*. New York: American Association of Fund-Raising Counsel, 1988. **3, 14**

Weick, Karl. "Educational Organizations as Loosely Coupled Systems." *Administrative Science Quarterly* (March 1976). **4**

"Why the Rush to Tax Nonprofits?" *New York Times* (May 12, 1988): 22. **14**

Wiebe, G. D. "Merchandising Commodities and Citizenship on Television." *Public Opinion Quarterly* 15 (1951–52): 679–691. **21**

Williams, Oliver F., C.S.C. "Can Business Ethics Be Theological? What Athens Can Learn from Jerusalem." *Journal of Business Ethics* 5 (December 1986): 473–484. **6**

Williams, Oliver F., C.S.C., and Patrick E. Murphy. "The Ethics of Virtue: The Answer to a Misplaced Debate." Paper presented at the 13th Annual Macromarketing Conference, San Jose, CA, August 1988. **6**

Williams, Roger M. "Profit Making by Nonprofits, Part I." *Grantsmanship Center News* (January/February 1982) 15–23 and Part II (March/April 1982): 26–29. **2, 13, 14**

Wintrobe, Ronald. "Taxing Altruism." *Economic Inquiry* 21 (April 1983): 255–269. **7**

Wood, Van R., and Scott J. Vitell. "Marketing and Economic Development: Review, Synthesis and Evaluation." *Journal of Macromarketing* 6 (Spring 1986): 28–48. **21**

Wortman, Max S. "A Radical Shift from Bureaucracy to Strategic Management in Voluntary Organizations." *Journal of Voluntary Action Research* 10 (January-March 1981): 62–81. **4**

Xerox. "Professional Selling Skills III." Xerox Corporation Training Material, 1983. **19**

Yankelovich, Skelly and White. *The Charitable Behavior of Americans*. Washington, DC: Independent Sector, 1986. **3**

Yarwood, Dean L., and Ben M. Enis. "Advertising and Publicity Programs in the Executive Branch of National Government: Hustling or Helping the People." *Public Administration Review* 42 (January/February 1982): 37–44. 1

Yorke, D. A. "Marketing and Non-Profit-Making Organisations." *European Journal of Marketing* 18 2 (1984): 17–22. 2

Zaltman, Gerald, and Nan Lin. "On the Nature of Innovations." *American Behavioral Scientist* (1971): 651–671. A

Zinkhan, George M., and Ali Shermohamad. "Is Other-Directedness on the Increase? An Empirical Test of Riesman's Theory of Social Character." *Journal of Consumer Research* 13 (June 1986): 127. 7

Subject Index

Author Index